The Plot to Get Bill Gates : An Irreverent
Investigation of the World's Richest
Man... and the People Who Hate Him

Gary Rivlin

Gary Rivlin is an award winning journalist and author of *Drive-By*. He lives in Oakland, California and is the editor of the *East Bay Express*.

By the same author and published by Quartet Books

Drive—By

The Plot to Get

BILL GATES.

An Irreverent Investigation of the World's Richest Man... and the People Who Hate Him

GARY RIVLIN

 Quartet Books

First published in Great Britain by Quartet Books in 1999
A member of the Namara Group
27 Goodge Street
London W1P 2LD

A catalogue record for this book is available from the British Library

ISBN 0 7043 8129 X

Printed and bound in Great Britain by CPD (Wales) Ltd

To Kenneth L. Rivlin
(1930–1994),
my father

The things we admire in men, kindness and generosity, openness, honesty, understanding and feeling are the concomitants of a failure in our system. And those traits we detest, sharpness, greed, acquisitiveness, meanness, egotism, and self-interest are the traits of success. And while men admire the quality of the first they love the produce of the second.

–"Doc," in John Steinbeck's *Cannery Row*

CONTENTS

The Plot to Get Bill Gates

PROLOGUE:
LORD OF THE MANOR

Bill Gates loved few things more than his annual pilgrimage to a computer industry conference called Agenda. Each fall, more than four hundred of the industry's brightest stars, its moguls and its junior moguls and its moguls in waiting, descended upon the Phoenician Resort in Scottsdale, Arizona, for a weekend of golf, tennis, and two days of speeches and hobnobbing. Every week, or so it seems, brings another computer conference, each sounding vaguely like Internet Interconnectivity NetWorld Expo, but among the industry's digerati, only two annual conclaves matter: Esther Dyson's PC Forum, held each spring, and Stewart Alsop's Agenda, held each fall. There are those who will tell you that of the two, Alsop's is *the* one—in part because Gates stopped going to PC Forum around five years ago.

The Agenda crowd includes some of Wall Street's brightest stars, Silicon Valley's most heavily endowed venture capitalists, and the size 12 triple-E business reporters from whom a laudatory word in print can help launch a company. For the head of a young start-up, a moment in the limelight at Agenda is the computer world's equivalent of a young comic winning a guest appearance on Letterman; for the established CEO, an invite to address the royal court is an honor and a business opportunity but mainly a sign that he or she has arrived.

In eleven years, Gates has missed Agenda only once (he had a previous engagement with the premier of China). Agenda is a place where Gates can just *be*. He once flew to Davos, Switzerland, to deliver a speech at the World Economic Forum, anticipating having time to listen to some of the confab's more compelling speakers, but so great is the World's Richest Man's celebrity that he found he was forced to keep to his room. Away from Microsoft's campus in Redmond, Washington, Agenda is one of the few places in the world where, as one fellow Microsoft executive put it, "Bill can have a goddamned cup of coffee and schmooze." During the breaks and the cocktail hour, Gates can be found engaged in impenetrably technical conversations, arguing TCP-IP stacks and the nuances of e-mail protocols. He stands twisted like a corkscrew, one arm wrapped around his midsection as if reaching for an itch on his back he can't quite scratch, the other arm flying spastically into the air, head tilted to one side, mouth working. Meanwhile, the other sovereigns stare wide-eyed, forgetting for the moment that they are not where they usually like to be, in the center of things. For many it might be excruciatingly dull, two days of speeches and chitchat bloated with talk of JITs, GIFs, and distributed computing inside the enterprise. For Gates, though, Agenda is nerd heaven.

The Phoenician, home to Agenda since 1994, tries fiercely to convey rustic charm, but everything about it drips money. The industry's titans dress casually in short-sleeved plaid shirts and baggy khakis, but their environs expose them as royals slumming at the summer castle. A sprawling Caesar's Palace–like monument of excess, the Phoenician was financed by Charles Keating Jr., the infamous savings-and-loan felon. Set against the desert scrub of Camelback Mountain, the resort offers nine swimming pools (one inlaid with mother-of-pearl tiles), a dozen tennis courts (including a Wimbledon-style grass court), and its own private championship-caliber twenty-seven-hole golf course. Crystal chandeliers in each room. Italian linens on the beds. Italian marble in every bathroom. Rooms start at $400 a night. Agenda itself costs $3,500 a head, room and airfare not included, yet every year Alsop fights off a small herd of junior VPs pleading for the right to drop five grand so that maybe by chance they'll step on an elevator carrying Andy Grove, the chairman of Intel, or grab sixty seconds with Bill Gates in the Thirsty Camel Bar. Alsop has heard it all: "I'll lose my job." "The VCs [the venture capitalists who own a big chunk of the company] have my balls in a vice." "This one break, and we're the next Netscape." Alsop, normally a sweet-natured man with a Fred Flintstone build and a small bush of curly brown hair, fends them off as heartlessly as a bouncer working the rope at the hippest South-of-Market club in San Francisco.

Michael Dell, founder and CEO of Dell Computer, is an Agenda regular. In the fall of 1997, Dell was worth $5 billion—a mere eighth of

Gates's $40 billion holdings. Larry Ellison, CEO of Oracle, was then worth $12 billion. Intel's Andy Grove made headlines because his compensation package in 1996, including the stock options he was granted, topped $100 million—big money, but less than a month's interest if Bill Gates were simply to invest his $40 billion net worth in a money market account. One year Alsop polled his audience: Would you continue to come if Gates stopped showing up? Nearly four in ten answered no, they would not. On the grounds of the Phoenician, Gates typically saunters with his hands in his pockets and his feet slightly splayed, a blandly satisfied expression on his face, emanating the casual ease that one sees only on the faces of the rich. So relaxed does he appear that it can sometimes seem as if he's sitting while he's walking.

A few years back, Scott McNealy, cofounder and CEO of the soaringly successful Sun Microsystems, opened a talk by joking that while he was honored to be addressing the audience at Agenda, his true desire was an invite to participate in one of Alsop's fireside chats. "Please, please, oh please," the industry's class clown cajoled Alsop, to the delight of the audience. The shtick was funny, especially when delivered by an undisputedly successful man then worth more than $100 million, but like most jokes it had an edge of truth to it. Every CEO in the audience, young or old, visualizes himself or herself sitting on stage matching wits with Alsop while a packed ballroom listens and watches with hushed attention. Maybe twenty people speak at Agenda each year, but only two or three luminaries are granted the ultimate prize: an invite to fill the oversized wicker throne that serves as the fireside set piece. Andy Grove has been so blessed, as have Larry Ellison, Michael Dell, and eventually Scott McNealy. But each of these figures has been granted a fireside on the conference's first day. The session that closes the formal portion of Agenda each year, day two's fireside, is reserved for Gates.

His fellow moguls may look at Gates as a vulture, a snake, or worse, yet there's no disputing his primacy. Nothing at Agenda is as fascinating as watching the other generals around Gates. The guy who was crying into his Tanqueray the night before, chewing your ear off about what that bastard Gates had done now, clucks about him like a society matron picking up the fallen hairs of the European princess gracing her party. Agenda is Alsop's baby, but Gates is the show's main draw; he is lord of the manor, Louis XIV at Versailles. All of which makes the series of events that unspooled so publicly in the fall of 1997 at Agenda 9°, one week before Gates's forty-second birthday, all the more deliciously cruel.

Alsop had offered his introductory remarks and the first set of industry mavens had already held forth when the group took its morning break on the conference's first day. Big screens in the ballrooms and televisions set up in the hallway blinked on, and onto the screen popped Attorney General Janet Reno, standing behind a lectern at a Washington, D.C., press conference. She was talking about Microsoft.

Some people figured it was one of Stewart's little jokes: dusting off an old tape from 1993 or 1994, when the Justice Department accused Gates and Microsoft of violating this country's antitrust laws—a humorous exclamation point to the debate that had just ended. But then recognition struck: it was happening again. Two years before, also during the first break on Agenda's first day, the conferees had gathered around television monitors to watch a Los Angeles jury declare O. J. Simpson not guilty. Now, in the fall of 1997, people again stood with mouths agape. Flanked by a row of officials, her hair looking frightfully like Gates's before his mid-1990s makeover, Reno stood awkwardly at the podium, eyes magnified behind oversized glasses, dressed in a nubby red-and-blue-plaid jacket, and a plain dark skirt. She spoke in dry, bureaucratic tones stripped of anything remotely approaching excitement or righteousness. She matter-of-factly accused Microsoft of violating the consent decree it had signed with the U.S. government in 1994. Because of that, she said, Microsoft would have to pay. She announced that she was asking the court to impose a million-dollar-a-day fine until Microsoft was back in compliance with the decree—the largest civil fine in Justice Department history. Upon hearing the million-dollar-a-day threat, the halls buzzed with wonder.

In the computer industry, it's an article of faith that the government's lawyers are woefully in over their heads regarding all things relating to computers. So it's probably reading things into the timing of Reno's announcement to say that it was the government's clever way of giving the knife a nasty little twist. But whatever the cause, the timing was humiliating. It was as if federal marshals had marched into a party to slap a pair of cuffs on the guest of honor and then paraded him out for all to see.

Four hundred sets of eyes searched for Gates, but he was nowhere to be found. He was off in another room, idly picking at a bowl of nuts, patiently sitting through an interview with a reporter from *Newsweek*. *Newsweek* had a terrific scoop—except that its reporter was behind a closed door, unaware of all that was transpiring. For the remainder of the day, the dozen reporters attending Agenda circled around him like buzzards, but for the moment Gates was talking to no one outside the Microsoft family.

Sun's Scott McNealy was the fireside speaker that afternoon. The timing could not have been better. Over the years, a long list of Microsoft rivals has tried to slay the dragon. In the 1980s, the brave knights included Jim Manzi of Lotus and Philippe Kahn of Borland. In the early 1990s, it was Ray Noorda of Novell; then, when Noorda was torched, Oracle's Larry Ellison took up the lance. That was in 1995. Ellison has not given up the fight, but lately McNealy has proven himself far braver.

Kahn had an acid tongue, Manzi a street-tough fearlessness. Noorda was righteous in the style of a religious fanatic, Ellison glib and droll. A year earlier, Ellison had shown up at Agenda, overdressed in a buttery double-breasted Savile Row suit—and so late that Alsop had had to send a supplicant to fetch him from the can. When finally Ellison had taken the stage, Alsop had good-naturedly teased him about the MiG-29 he was trying to buy from the Russian government. Ellison had brought down the house when he confessed his true aim: he needed a fighting machine so he could fly fast and low over Lake Washington, to rid himself once and for all of his nettlesome rival from Redmond. Heads turned to see a stone-faced Gates surrounded by frowning courtesans.

McNealy is funny and clever, sarcastic and juvenile, and no McNealy speech is complete without a varied offering of Gates zingers. "To warm up and get it out of the way, I thought I'd do my Microsoft bashing right up front," he began a keynote address before six thousand computer developers gathered in San Francisco's Moscone Center in 1996—and once he had settled on that formula, it was as if he had no use for any other. So it went in speech after speech. There were the garden-variety Evil Empire, Gates-Is-Darth-Vader jokes, and of course cracks about the vastness of Gates's wealth ("Can you imagine being so rich you overdraw your account by four hundred million dollars—and don't even notice?"). Two weeks before Agenda, though, it wasn't McNealy's latest line that the Agenda types were buzzing about, but the breach-of-contract suit Sun had slapped on Microsoft. Even before Reno tossed her stink bomb into the party, the crowd was rubbing its hands in anticipation of McNealy's talk.

Agenda regulars know how to spot Gates—always in the back corner, always flanked by a small Microsoft mafia. Sometimes he sits with a portable computer on his lap, sifting through e-mail while presumably following the speaker on the podium. More often than not, though, he stands, the laptop cradled in his arm. That's part of the Gates legend, having a mind so supple and so powerful that he can partition his brain to "multitask"—that is, perform two or more tasks simultaneously. Gates was surrounded by his minimafia during McNealy's speech, but no computer, and he chose to stand. Elbows nudged seatmates, chins pointed Gates's way, smiles graced faces—no laptop!

Shortly before they went onstage, Alsop suggested that McNealy tone it down. Born in Washington, D.C., the son of a highly regarded political journalist, Alsop was by nature the high-tech equivalent of a policy wonk, preferring serious discussion to fireworks. "Don't Moon the Ogre," Alsop had recently warned McNealy in a column in *Fortune.* McNealy, on the other hand, was the mischievous type, a grown-up Wally Cleaver with the Beav's overbite and Eddie Haskell's devilish spirit. His speaking style called to mind a ventriloquist not particularly good at his craft. He constantly interrupted himself with side-of-mouth sarcastic comments. When Alsop asked him to tone it down, McNealy only rolled his eyes, mumbling something about mooning *him* onstage. Dressed in worn jeans and a button-down dress shirt open at the collar, his hair clipped uncharacteristically short, McNealy self-consciously settled into the fireside throne. No one knew what to expect.

McNealy didn't shy away from attacking Microsoft, but neither did he throw in his usual offering of gratuitous Gates barbs. Sure, he made passing reference to Microsoft as "the dark side" and declared the company's product line unreliable, bloated, and incompatible with other technologies. He ridiculed Windows NT, the operating system on which Microsoft was staking its future, aimed at higher-end customers but so crash prone that system managers derisively nicknamed the resulting blank monitor the Blue Screen of Death. But he aimed nothing at Gates personally.

Standing in a back corner, rocking back and forth from toe to heel, Gates nattered underneath his breath: "That's not true." "That's not true." "Yeah, like you know anything." John Markoff, a San Francisco–based technology reporter for *The New York Times,* was sitting near Gates—so close he half figured the CEO's running commentary was for his benefit. Markoff marveled at Gates's ability to bore in on McNealy with a hypnotic stare. "The news was only a few hours old, yet he completely focused in on McNealy as if nothing else was going on," Markoff said, shaking his head in wonderment at such a creature. "His whole body language was 'Let me at him.' "

Mitchell Kertzman walked away from McNealy's speech chuckling to himself. His friend had performed well, the head of Sybase told himself. He had landed jabs whenever Alsop had offered an opening, but he had stayed away from the below-the-belt personal stuff. McNealy had proved less controversial than usual, but he had been controversial. That was McNealy: you could shoot him up with a serious tranquilizer, and he'd still be more overamped than your average person on stimulants.

Kertzman was distracted from his reverie by the sound of padding feet behind him. It was Gates. Kertzman and Gates had known each other going on ten years, dating back to Kertzman's days running a software start-up in Boston that wrote software tools exclusively for Windows. The two occasionally talked at events like this one, but they were polar opposites and hardly friends. The rap on Kertzman inside the high-tech fraternity is that he's too *nice*—a playful dolphin swimming amidst the sharks and killer whales. When Kertzman took over the reins at Sybase, that put the two at odds—Sybase, once a comer in the industry, has seen its star fall in recent years in no small part because of Microsoft. But at the previous year's Agenda, Kertzman had delivered a speech chiding his fellow execs for paying too much attention to besting Gates and too little to innovation. And what is a trustworthy soul to Bill Gates if not someone once within the Windows orbit who, though he had spun free of his gravitational pull, now defended him?

"Let me ask you a question," Gates said brusquely. No hello, no exchange of pleasantries. Just a question spit out by a man anxious to get to the point. "Are all your developers and all your customers switching to Java?" Java was the Sun product that Scott McNealy had just been promoting so aggressively. It was a new programming language that promised to let any computer talk to any other.

"No."

"Then why does fucking Scott McNealy say every fucking programmer in the whole fucking world is using fucking Java?"

The two spoke for another twenty minutes. It was all business, of course. Kertzman may be the king of schmooze, but with Gates it's never anything but bits, bytes, and corporate strategy. Before that afternoon, Kertzman had never observed so much as a worry line on Gates's face in the dozen or so conversations he'd had with him over the years.

But now Gates's face was creased, his eyes small. Gates always fidgets as if he's suffering from Tourette's syndrome, but now he was practically twitching out of his clothes. Who could say how much of Gates's mood was caused by McNealy and how much by the government? But when the two parted, Kertzman shared this comforting thought with himself: even billionaires have really bad days.

Microsoft's PR staff, citing security concerns, won't say what accommodations Gates selects when he stays at the Phoenician. Perhaps it was one of the Phoenician's Villa Suites, which go for $3,000 per night, including butler service, a private Jacuzzi, a full kitchen, a fax machine, and a golf cart for getting around. To a man worth $40 billion, as Gates was in the fall of 1997, spending $9,000 for three nights' accommodations is the equivalent of 24 cents to a couple with a combined income of $100,000 a year. The fax machine beeps and chortles, spitting out page after page of legal filings; the suite's three phone lines twitch like emergency blinkers. Gates is a screamer even in ordinary times, so on this day one imagines him yelling himself hoarse. Among the decisions reached that night was that Gates should talk to the press.

The following day, it seemed that every time you caught a glimpse of Gates he was off in a corner, talking with another big-name reporter. He downplayed the significance of the federal suit, spinning it as something hatched by a set of foes who couldn't compete in the marketplace. Typical was his talk with *Business Week*'s Steve Hamm. "It's the way they play the game," he said of competitors such as Sun. "By using lawyers. Fortunately, that has no effect on the guys who come in to write software." When Gates wasn't granting an interview, he was huddled with one or another member of the Microsoft entourage.

The big show came that afternoon, when Gates and Alsop took the stage. Gates, dressed in hand-tailored khakis and a madras shirt, crossed his legs and draped an arm casually over the back of the wicker throne. But strain was etched in the muscles of his jaw, obvious in the clamped teeth of his gritted smile. Gates has been giving public talks since almost the moment he dropped out of Harvard, in 1977, but in twenty years of public speaking, his presentations have gone from laughable to merely passable. Even those at Microsoft who talk of Gates as if he were the Leonardo da Vinci of our time allow that he's not much on a stage. His voice is a high-pitched whistle that teeters on the edge of whininess, giving his talks a pleading, almost desperate sound. He speaks with a forced enthusiasm, tinny and false, and exudes no warmth, humor, or personality, despite hours of sessions with a speech coach. His one asset on stage, other than his fame, is his ample memory. He never fails to touch each of his talking points.

"I paid Janet Reno a pretty handsome sum to take that action yesterday," Alsop joked after he and Gates had eased into their seats for this year's annual chat, "so I'd really like to hear your reaction." Of course Gates didn't laugh. He began defiantly: if we decide it makes sense to integrate speech recognition software into Windows, he said, or video capabilities, or anything else we deem appropriate, we'll do that. He ridiculed the government for filing what he deemed a "very strange case"—repeating the word "strange" two more times—and blamed it on the political pressures exerted by competitors. What if you're 100 percent right, asked Alsop, but still your intransigence costs Microsoft dearly in the court of public opinion? Gates, who doesn't understand politics, flashed Alsop, who does, an uncomprehending look. "Maybe I didn't understand the question," he said. The two have known each other since 1982, and are friends after a fashion, but that's when Alsop— as he later described it—"got all caught up in my underpants." Gates stared blankly as Alsop struggled to regain his equilibrium. "It took me a while to recover, and Bill isn't exactly socially adept, so he wouldn't know how to help even if he was so inclined. That set the tone for the rest of the talk," Alsop later recalled with a sigh.*

Gates revealed none of the emotion he had shown the night before when he had run into Kertzman, but he displayed the same petulance, especially when the topic turned to Sun. He said he thought McNealy had looked "nervous" the day before. He declared Sun's products "over-priced" and dismissed the industry's fascination with Java as a "religious" thing. Inevitably, the conversation kept doubling back to the Department of Justice; each time, Gates would shrug the whole thing off. "Read the consent decree," he brusquely told one inquisitor from the audience—you'll see.

Intel's Andy Grove got more than a little angry listening to Gates. So closely linked are Microsoft and Intel, the manufacturer of the micro-processors, or chips, that run Windows software, that the two compa-

---

* That marked Alsop's final fireside with Gates. Alsop, who had recently left journalism for a job as a venture capitalist, stepped down as host of Agenda, ceding control to co-founder Bob Metcalfe. Because Metcalfe is a frequent Gates critic, that probably marked the end of Gates's participation as well.

nies are often referred to as if one: the "Wintel monopoly." Gates has helped make Grove a very wealthy man. But the relationship between the two companies has always been complex and multilayered, like a marriage between two very different people who stay together for the sake of the kids. After Gates's speech, Grove could be found sputtering in the corner. "He's acting like zis is nothing more zan another contract dispute!" he said angrily to reporter after reporter in his heavy Hungarian accent. "He doesn't see vhat it means that zis is the government."

Grove had cause for worry. The computer industry was divided into two sides. On one side were Intel, Microsoft, and two subgroups of software vendors hitching their wagons to Windows: those swimming in money and thus in love with Microsoft, and those equally flush but still resentful because success meant goose-stepping to Microsoft's orders. On the other side were the Internet browser manufacturer Netscape, Larry Ellison's Oracle, IBM, Sun Microsystems, and a host of other companies, large and small. So closely aligned were these companies, at least in people's minds, that people had started referring to them jointly as NOISE (Netscape, Oracle, IBM, Sun—and Everybody else). Suddenly "everybody else" included the U.S. government. During those two days at the Phoenician, there were high fives and knowing smiles when allies passed each other in the halls. At the Thirsty Camel, they sipped single-malt scotches and top-shelf bourbons between stinking puffs on $20 cigars, gleefully envisioning doomsday scenarios for the pencil-necked mophead from Redmond.

AS GATES FLEW HOME FROM AGENDA, the list of forces that had aligned against him was formidable. The U.S. Justice Department was only one worry among many. Two weeks before Agenda, consumer advocate Ralph Nader, a darling of the Left, had announced that he'd be hosting a two-day conference in Washington, D.C., to investigate "perhaps the most dangerous company in America today." Senator Orrin Hatch, a darling of the Right, announced he'd be holding the first of what he promised would be a series of hearings exploring Microsoft's domination of the software industry. By the time the first jumbo shrimp had been dipped in cocktail sauce at an Agenda party, at least a half-dozen state attorneys general, spotting an issue sure to draw the TV cameras, had also joined the hunt; by early 1998 their numbers would swell to more than twenty-five. The European Commission, the arm of the European Union that oversees legal disputes, announced that it was investigating Microsoft. So did the Japanese government. Even several software trade associations, which normally were cowed by Microsoft, jumped on the bandwagon.

Shortly after Reno announced she was reviving the Justice Department's case against Microsoft, a longtime Microsoft employee named Mike Murray sent an e-mail to select colleagues: What if there really was a secret plot against Microsoft? What if Microsoft's foes genuinely were in league with the government, the media, and others in a conspiracy to take down Microsoft? What if foes such as Sun and Oracle were covertly bankrolling everything from Ralph Nader's anti-Microsoft jihad to Orrin Hatch's Senate investigation? The truth was far more complicated than Murray made it out to be. From Microsoft's perspective, NOISE may seem a cabal whose actions border on the illegal, but though they meet regularly, they bicker and publicly step on one another's strategies so often that they are akin to the sectarian leftists of the 1970s. Still, that didn't stop Murray, in a second e-mail message, from fantasizing a sequel: Microsoft uncovers a smoking gun and destroys this cabal of saboteurs by prosecuting them under federal racketeering laws.

At Agenda, Gates said that the government's case boils down to a single word: Was Microsoft's inclusion of the Internet Explorer browser in Windows 95 an "innovation" (as Microsoft claimed) or the tying together of two distinct products (as the government contended)? And he was right. Such is the arcane nature of antitrust law, an expensive and complex debate over semantics that is strictly the province of full-time practitioners. Even corporate attorneys at white-shoe law firms shake their heads over its suffocating intricacies.

To read the charges the government has filed against Microsoft is to learn that the government believes Microsoft is in violation of the "essential facilities" doctrine. To look at Microsoft from the parapets of those who've faced Microsoft over the years, however, is to learn that Gates and Company are the kind who are forever bending the rules yet have memorized Robert's, Hoyle, and other arbiters of fair play so they can be the first to point an accusing finger when a foe steps slightly out of line. To spend time with those who have declared themselves Microsoft's victims (and also to watch the legal proceedings play out while lurking in anti-Microsoft chat rooms, whose participants are restrained by neither evidentiary rules nor good manners) offers a more interesting vantage point—and one far more illuminating than offered by the sundry legal filings in this case or in the broader case the federal government filed seven months later. Indeed, the government's twin cases against Microsoft are significant precisely because they shine so bright a spotlight on the complaints filed by competitors against a company that so unapologetically seeks to conquer and dominate.

The government's case against Microsoft is intriguing, but mainly as a work of political theater starring a new set of players on the national stage, wealthy and bright but politically inept. Robert Dole, Jody Powell, Judge Robert Bork, and any number of ex-congressmen, former officials, and high-powered Beltway players are all being remunerated handsomely for playing bit roles in the plot to get Bill Gates or to defend him, but influence peddlers for hire are nothing new. Far fresher are the lords of high tech, these self-made tycoons who portray themselves as driven only by the most noble impulses. There's the forty-year-old retiree, impeccably dressed in casual elegance, tan, beatific, claiming the money was never even a factor—yet not fifteen minutes later he reveals that since he was a young man he had dreamed both of retiring by age thirty and of owning a home so spectacular it would be worthy of a full spread in *Architectural Digest.* As columnist Molly Ivins has said, anyone who tells you the money's not important is worth at least a million dollars.

A twentysomething wannabe mogul parrots, without irony, sixties rhetoric about wanting to change the world. What's the product he sells that has him thinking such noble thoughts? Software that more effectively tracks visitors to a Web site.

So-and-so is a true visionary—you hear it time and again—but by "visionary" is meant not a person who sees a more just world or even someone who imagines a public park where now there is just a garbage-strewn lot; he or she is a business executive who recognizes that small pictures, not command lines, are the future of computing. Bill Gates didn't think up the icon-driven technology that allows a user to point and click on a garbage can to delete a file. The wizards at Xerox PARC in Silicon Valley invented that breakthrough. Nor was Gates the first to employ it in a mass-market product. That was Apple Computer's doing. Yet ask Gates's well-paid PR handlers and his top staffers to explain why they call him a visionary, and that's what they'll tell you: he saw before others in the industry that the future was point-and-click computing.

In August 1997, *Newsweek* foolishly hailed Gates as someone who had "achieved an unprecedented, and still growing, impact on the civilized world." On the other side of that equation, Gates has been proclaimed the most dangerous man on this planet, comparing unfavorably to Pol Pot and Saddam Hussein. In this context, the plot to get Bill Gates takes on a noble air—the forces of good banding together to rid the world of this evil. Web pages declare him the Devil incarnate and Big Brother, the CEO of a company whose goal is nothing short of global conquest. On this last point the critics are certainly onto something. In recent years, Microsoft has entered a dizzying array of new areas: cable television, publishing, banking, car sales, real estate, local entertainment listings. What difference that might make, though, is another matter. With alarm, people note that Gates is aiming to own both halves of the information flow, both the means by which information is disseminated and the information itself—what inside the computer industry everyone calls simply "content." Yet does it really matter whether the king of content is Gates, Michael Eisner of the Walt Disney Company, or Gerald Levin of Time Warner? To most people, General Electric is nothing more than a beneficent force that sells us lightbulbs and ranges, but in fact it's a perennial Top Five company on the Fortune 500 list that owns NBC and several nuclear power plants. It manufactures weapons of mass destruction and, as the country's largest mortgage lender, carries the paper on more houses in the United States than any other entity.

"You don't understand," a computer executive's wife told John Seabrook of *The New Yorker*. "We talk about Bill Gates every night at home. We think about Bill Gates all the time. It's like Bill Gates lives with us." And that was in 1994, before the World Wide Web and when Microsoft was one sixth the size of the $250 billion colossus it would become by 1998. Nowadays, it seems a conversation in Silicon Valley can't go five minutes before Gates and Microsoft are mentioned. Eyes blaze, storm clouds weigh heavily on brows, sunny moods turn stormy. Esther Dyson, host of that other must-attend computer conference, dubbed the disease "Bill Envy." "Just about every guy in this business suffers from it," Dyson says. "Bill is like the Rorschach blot of the industry. What people think of him tells you more about them than it does about him."

At some point, Gates ceased to be simply a powerful industry figure; he has infiltrated the world's dream life. "In every moment of every day," wrote the creator of the "Bill Gates Fountain of Dreams" Web

page, "somewhere on the planet someone is dreaming about Bill Gates."
The faithful have been known to make pilgrimages to the shrine, like
the thirteen-year-old who flew from Denmark to Seattle (his mother
works as a flight attendant), hoping that he'd be permitted to shake
Gates's hand (he was). There are on-line news groups such as
alt.fan.bill.gates (sample posting from this sycophantic news group:
"Bill Gates is absolutely adorable! And those glasses . . . ah, they are
sexy. Anyone know a good site that has a good pic of Bill?"), and you
could take a Gates quiz at the "Team Gates" Web site.

The Gateses, Bill and Melinda, have earnestly discussed the importance of philanthropy with Regis and Kathie Lee. Barbara Walters
bathes Bill in pathos at the same time as she strips him of any personality. Gates talks about his troubles with the government, Walters looks
on as if listening to a close friend opening up about the loss of a loved
one. Walters's eyes are watery and wide, lips tugged into a tight frown,
brow furrowed. Later, Gates gives her a long, steady, opaque look after
she has exclaimed, "You're the richest man in the world! How does it
feeeeel to have all that money?" He is a celebrity—the world's richest
man!—so when Walters's report is over and it's just her and Hugh
Downs talking in the *20/20* studio, she rushes to his defense. The government has been awfully rough on him, she says with that dewy-eyed
look. It matters not what he did, just that he's successful. He's Madonna,
he's Michael Jackson, he's Michael Jordan. The whole thing calls to
mind "Doc's" profound words in Steinbeck's *Cannery Row:* We may admire kindness and generosity, but it's greed and avarice that are the
traits of success, and we respect rich and successful people.

We invest the computer industry with so much meaning. The PC is
at the epicenter of our universe (wrote *Wired* magazine in its maiden
issue about the Digital Revolution: its "only parallel is probably the discovery of fire"); its best-known figures are hailed like Roman emperors.
Fortune gushes over His Billness like a swooning teenager ("with all due
respect to the soul man James Brown, Gates may be the hardest-
working man in big business"); *The New Yorker* chisels McNealy in
stone, casting him as David up against this Goliath in an article running
under the headline "The Sun King."

At its core, the plot to get Bill Gates is a tale of king-sized obsession
among one-dimensional workaholics who'll do practically anything to
win. At best, it is harmless hero worship, obscuring a far more interesting story residing between the lines. At worst, it's another example of a

culture so obsessed with fortune and fame that those starring in a cautionary tale are instead cast as role models. "Sometimes," sighs a woman named Nancy Stinnette, who has worked as a PR manager at both Oracle and Sun, "I feel like all of us, we're just pawns in this fight. Some very wealthy little boys are fighting each other, and the rest of us are just their minions."

**Part 01: The Great White
Whale**

MICROSOFT ADDRESSES JUSTICE DEPARTMENT ACCUSATIONS

REDMOND, Wash., Oct. 21, 1997—In direct response to accusations made by the Department of Justice, the Microsoft Corp. announced today that it will be acquiring the federal government of the United States of America for an undisclosed sum. "It's actually a logical extension of our planned growth," said Microsoft chairman Bill Gates. "It really is going to be a positive arrangement for everyone."

Microsoft representatives held a briefing in the Oval Office of the White House with U.S. President Bill Clinton, and assured members of the press that changes will be "minimal." The United States will be managed as a wholly owned division of Microsoft. An initial public offering is planned for July of next year, and the federal government is expected to be profitable by "Q4 1999 at latest," according to Microsoft president Steve Ballmer.

In a related announcement, Bill Clinton stated that he had "willingly and enthusiastically" accepted a position as a vice president with Microsoft, and will continue to manage the United States government, reporting directly to Bill Gates. When asked how it felt to give up the mantle of executive authority to Gates, Clinton smiled and referred to it as "a relief." He went on to say that Gates has a "proven track record," and that U.S. citizens should offer Gates their "full support and confidence." Clinton will reportedly be earning several times the $200,000 annually he has earned as U.S. president, in his new role at Microsoft.

Gates dismissed a suggestion that the U.S. Capitol be moved to Redmond as "silly," though he did say that he would make executive decisions for the U.S. government from his existing office at Microsoft headquarters. Gates went on to say that the House and Senate would "of course" be abolished. "Microsoft isn't a democracy," he observed, "and look how well we're doing."

When asked if the rumored attendant acquisition of Canada was proceeding, Gates said, "We don't deny that discussions are taking place." Microsoft representatives closed the conference by stating that United States citizens will be able to expect lower taxes, increases in government services and discounts on all Microsoft products.

—Anonymous e-mail, widely circulated on the Internet

CHAPTER 01

CAPTAIN AHAB'S CLUB

Back in 1993, a halcyon time when it was still possible to read through an entire magazine without coming across the name Bill Gates, Novell CEO Ray Noorda and Gates engaged in one of those public sneering matches that both antagonists might come to regret, but only later, long after the verbal stilettos had done their damage. The Utah-based Novell had devised a clever means of connecting groups of freestanding personal computers so that coworkers could share printers and computer files. This was in the early 1980s. Since that time, Novell had been drawing billions of dollars from this single product in a market that Microsoft had never quite managed to crack.

Life was torture for the Microsoft team charged with conceiving and then marketing a rival product to Novell's. First it was Microsoft Net; then, after five years of futility, it was LAN-Man (LAN for "local area network," Man for "manager"). Gates used the carrot with his minions and also the stick. Microsoft rallies were held and milestones celebrated—and then when that failed, as inevitably it did, Gates would scream. "I've never met a stupider, more inept group in my fucking life!" he'd yell in a tweedling whine. "How fucking hard can it be?" Despite everything, Microsoft could barely dent Novell's market share. By the early 1990s, Novell would rank fourth on a listing of the largest high-tech companies, behind only Microsoft, IBM, and Hewlett-Packard.

Twice Microsoft approached Noorda about buying his company; both times Gates later claimed a change of heart. Not without reason, Noorda felt taken—felt that Gates and his minions were cozying up to Novell only to learn what they could with the kimono open. Noorda could live with Gates's yearly boasts at COMDEX (*the* computer dealers' trade show) that *this* would be the year Microsoft overtook Novell.

Long ago he had made his peace with Microsoft's penchant for bad-mouthing Novell in meetings with Novell's largest customers and its practice of offering deep discounts on other Microsoft products if a big company would switch to LAN-Man. But what Noorda believed were phony merger talks proved to be too much. Noorda told anyone willing to listen—fellow computer execs, federal investigators, and eventually journalists working for the country's top business publications—that the boy wonder was really a monster in the making.

The first Noorda quote that got everyone's attention appeared in *Business Week* in 1993. "To have a heart-to-heart," he said when asked about his short-lived merger negotiations with Gates, "you have to have two hearts." In response, Gates puffed out his concave chest and charged that Noorda was growing "increasingly paranoid." Gates's number two, Steve Ballmer, a bull of a man with a megaphone voice, decried Novell as a "dirty" competitor selling a packet of "lies" to the press. And from there the fight escalated. "Bill Gates's behavior is an insult to the industry and to the world," Noorda said in another interview. He dubbed Gates "Pearly" and Ballmer "The Embalmer" and then proudly explained his little joke to anyone who asked. Gates was Pearly because he promised you heaven, while behind the scenes Ballmer prepared you for burial.

Noorda organized meetings with executives from Lotus, WordPerfect, and other companies selling software products so successfully that Gates seemed to take it personally. "We're all a bunch of sissies," Noorda declared. "Let's stand up to that little squirt!" Feature articles about Noorda, a man well into his sixties when most of his counterparts were still in their thirties, tended to use terms such as "avuncular" and "grandfatherly" to describe him, but Microsoft let it leak to the press that it tended to call old Ray the "grandfather from Hell."

Noorda has gotten so *personal*, Microsoft's executives would cluck. They'd shake their heads and talk about the toll Noorda's outbursts were taking on Gates. Poor Bill, they'd say to one another with tight frowns. Business is one thing, but saying Bill has no heart? That's just plain cruel. Ballmer is Gates's best friend, but it was Nathan Myhrvold, the company's chief technology officer and Gates's alter ego, who turned to Herman Melville's *Moby-Dick* during a high-level Microsoft staff meeting, hitting on a metaphor that allowed the group to transcend the sting of Noorda's insults.

"Sometimes I think Nathan sees his job as making everyone laugh inside our meetings," says a top chieftain who has witnessed countless episodes of the Bill-and-Nathan show. Another Microsoft employee described the relationship between the two as "an old and complicated marriage that no one outside the relationship can hope to understand." The two make an unlikely match. Whereas Gates is a furrowed-brow pessimist, Myhrvold is the cheery optimist. Myhrvold is so well rounded it's almost frightening, Gates so monomaniacal about business and technology that it makes one shudder. Every time Gates loyalists hailed his ability to discuss a wide range of topics, not just technology and business, I'd press them for examples. They would mention genetic engineering, physics, world economics, artificial intelligence, satellite technology—every example offered fell under either the hard sciences or business. Myhrvold is every bit Gates's intellectual match, but by contrast he's an accomplished chef (with a first-place finish in the worldwide barbecue cook-off held in Memphis, Tennessee), an amateur photographer, a fly fisherman, a race-car driver, and a bungee jumper.

Myhrvold can't recall precisely what prompted his flight of fancy into classic American literature, except that he's certain his motivation was Noorda and his "terrible obsession with Bill." The parallels between Noorda and Captain Ahab, the protagonist of *Moby-Dick,* were too delicious for Myhrvold to miss. Ahab loses a leg while trying to harpoon a monstrously large white whale. He could blame bad fortune and the perilous nature of the work but instead blames the fabled Moby-Dick. Was someone like Noorda any different? "These are people who took it so personally and made it a personal ego clash," Myhrvold explained. To him the CEOs distracted by Gates were like Ahab pursuing the Leviathan, with such fevered madness that only after it was too late would they realize they were about to destroy their company—and themselves. To the squealing delight of the executive committee, Myhrvold declared Noorda the charter member of what he cleverly dubbed "Captain Ahab's Club." After that, it was almost as if people inside Microsoft *hoped* that all of Gates's foes would spend their days and nights insulting their boss. Captain Ahab's Club became one of Myhrvold's leitmotifs, a running joke, sure to win yucks whenever a new member was inducted.

To talk great literature and the foibles of Microsoft's foes, I met with Myhrvold in a nondescript conference room on Microsoft's campus. He is a rotund man with blue-gray eyes that twinkle behind steel-framed glasses. His beard, a melange of browns and reds and wisps of gray, is neatly trimmed, but his head is covered by an unruly clump of curly brown hair that gives him the look of a slightly mad scientist. In 1986, he sold a start-up he had cofounded to Microsoft for $1.5 million. By 1998, *Forbes* would estimate his net worth at over $300 million.

Five years after founding Captain Ahab's Club, Myhrvold still took great delight in his invention. Reviewing its membership list, he is a thespian imitating voices, a raconteur sharing tales of obsession. Is Larry Ellison a member of the club? "A prime Captain Ahab," Myhrvold says excitedly. His credentials? "He's out there saying, 'I have ten billion dollars, but second best means losing.'" He interrupts himself with a high-pitched giggle, then continues in a higher-pitched voice. "That's so sad. I couldn't wish anything worse for him than he already has." Later, in a follow-up e-mail, Myhrvold wrote, "His shareholders better be looking for a coffin to float [him] home in." That's an indelible image from near the end of *Moby-Dick:* the lifeboat the surviving crew fashions into a coffin, to float Ahab's body home.

Scott McNealy, Philippe Kahn, Jim Manzi—Myhrvold was having a gay old time recounting the ego slips and preoccupations of these men whom he characterized as "completely obsessed over Bill . . . each fancying himself the next Bill." But then I asked Myhrvold about Gary Kildall, patient zero in any epidemiologist's tracking of the Bill Envy disease. Myhrvold could laugh at Noorda, though Noorda had practically destroyed one of the industry's great software companies, and titter like a teen at the hundreds of millions of dollars Kahn had flushed down the drain buying a dying company called Ashton-Tate. But the brightness and mirth drained from Myhrvold's face with the mention of Kildall, founder of a company called Digital Research.

"That's a terribly sad story," he said quietly, with a shake of his head. "There was a point where those guys were the Microsoft of their time. They had the standard operating system. They were very flashy—you'd go to COMDEX, and there'd be all these Digital Research limousines going up and down the street, shuttling people back and forth. They were it. And they lost it! Through incompetence.

"Later, Gary spent the rest of his life being this embittered guy."

IN 1980, the year IBM knocked on the doors of both their companies, Bill Gates was twenty-five and Gary Kildall thirty-eight. Both had grown up in Seattle, but aside from the obvious similarities—both were white males with a head for math and science—one would be hard pressed to find two more different people. Gary Kildall was first and foremost a scientist, formally trained. Bill Gates, by contrast, was a self-taught hacker, a college dropout, commercially inclined. Kildall was an original thinker, Gates a gifted imitator. After earning his doctorate in computer science from the University of Washington, Kildall taught computer science at one of the country's elite military training centers, the Naval Postgraduate School in Monterey, California. Whereas Gates prided himself on his clever software shortcuts, Kildall displayed an academic's disdain for such tricks. Kildall was charming and witty, a handsome man, tall, trim, and bearded. In contrast, the peach-fuzzed Gates was obstreperous and pushy.

Their paths had crossed years earlier, but any chance encounters between the two had only underscored how different they were. Kildall was a married father finishing his Ph.D., Gates a squirrely eighth-grader with shaggy hair and glasses and a nose too big for his face, hanging around the computer center near the University of Washington. "Like Woody Allen meets Gary Cooper," wrote Stephen Manes and Paul Andrews in their book *Gates*.

In the early days, Microsoft—Micro Soft in the company's earliest incarnation—focused on computer languages. The company took existing computer languages, written for mainframe computers the size of a room, and tailored them for what once upon a time were called microcomputers. Just as a computer is an unusable assembly of metal and plastic without an operating system, so too would it be worthless without a language written (or in this case rewritten) to its specs. Kildall's Digital Research specialized in operating systems. Its CP/M (Control Program for Microcomputers) was the Windows of its day, so dominant in the emerging PC market that the majority of programs were written to run on its platform. In 1977, Gates flew to Pacific Grove, California, to meet with Kildall. Though only twenty-one, Gates was already on the move, sniffing out a possible merger or acquisition. Kildall didn't bite, but Gates walked away with his consolation prize: a handshake agreement that Microsoft would steer clear of operating systems so long as Kildall stayed away from languages.

Gates's focus on languages was happenstance. It began when his childhood friend, Paul Allen, was walking across Harvard Square on his way to visit Gates and spotted the latest issue of *Popular Electronics* at a magazine stand. On its cover was a build-your-own microcomputer called the Altair 8080. Ed Roberts, president of the Albuquerque-based company that sold the machine, MITS, admitted it could do little more than whir and blink until someone ported a version of BASIC, the simplest computer language then on the market, to it.

"This is our chance," Allen cajoled on that wintry day in 1975, when Gates was only a sophomore at Harvard, between his first and second semesters. The pair had already founded a couple of companies together, the first while Gates was still in the eighth grade. So serious were the two about creating a third that Allen had dropped out of Washington State six months earlier to take a job in the Boston area to be nearer his friend. "We jump now," said Allen, "or we might be too late." So now they were in the computer languages business.

The pair sent a letter to Ed Roberts on official-looking stationery from one of the fanciful ventures the two had previously started. We have a version of BASIC ideally suited for the Altair, they claimed. They were bluffing, of course, and not quite thinking straight. Roberts made a phone call and reached a confused Seattle-area mother who could tell him only that her son had gone to school with a Bill Gates and a Paul Allen. When finally Roberts hooked up with them on the phone, he told them what he told everyone else who contacted him: the first one to show up in Albuquerque with a working version of BASIC wins. Over the next eight weeks, the pair practically lived at Harvard's Aiken Computation Lab, taking catnaps at the keyboard or sacking out hidden behind one of the machines. Classes were optional, meals more often than not junk from a vending machine. A Harvard freshman named Monte Davidoff would also take up residence at Aiken to work on the project, missing classes and losing sleep, but he would end up the fifth Beatle, forgotten by history.

Allen, older and more mature looking than Gates, made the trip to Albuquerque. Years after the fact, there's a sparkle to the Altair tale, a glittery moment in computer history; the world of dumb terminals connected to mainframe computers began to give way to one in which fully functioning individual computers would be small enough to sit on a desk. The reality was less magical: MITS was housed in an abandoned Chinese restaurant in a run-down section of Albuquerque overrun by strip joints and junkies and headed by a man who proved to be quite a bluffer in his own right. Just as Allen had his fingers crossed that their Altair BASIC program would work, Roberts and his engineering staff hoped that their machine would boot up. Both worked, and a deal was struck. Roberts paid Gates and Allen a flat fee of $3,000, and the pair would split $30 to $60 (depending on the version) for every copy of the program Roberts sold.

Back in Cambridge, Gates hoisted a Shirley Temple to his success, but Harvard officials weren't nearly as pleased. The director of the university computer center, Thomas Cheatham, had also been Gates's professor for several computing courses. "Obnoxious," "not a pleasant fellow to have around," "a pain in the ass"—those are the phrases Cheatham would use when Gates's fame rose and biographers began ringing his office phone. That winter, he noticed that Gates was eating up hundreds of hours of the university's computer time. Through the grapevine Cheatham learned that Gates had permitted a friend, a non-Harvard student, to work with him at the center on a strictly commercial venture. The university initiated a formal investigation, but in the end, Gates was merely admonished for permitting an outsider free reign in the computer center—a slap on the wrist. The liberties he had taken with the computers spoiled things for other students, though. Whereas once they had been permitted liberal use of the center for personal endeavors, Cheatham was henceforth much stricter because of the Gates precedent.

A month after they finished the Altair BASIC project, Paul Allen went to work for Ed Roberts as his vice president of software. Meanwhile, Gates spent another two years at Harvard, debating his future with his parents while splitting time between his class work and Albuquerque's Sand and Sage Motel. Allen finally provoked a decision late in 1976, when he left Roberts's company to go into business for himself. Two months later, in the middle of his fourth year at Harvard, Gates left Cambridge for good.* It was 1977, the year in which Gary Kildall would have his first of many business encounters with Bill Gates.

THAT GATES at the age of twenty-one would have the temerity to propose a buyout to a man older and far more accomplished than himself surprised no one who had known him back in the days when he had partnered with Ed Roberts. Roberts was a large fellow, standing six feet,

---

* Technically, Gates didn't drop out of Harvard. He asked for and was granted a leave of absence that left the door open should he want to step back onto the neatly paved road his parents had imagined for their son.

five inches tall and weighing just under three hundred pounds. An ex–military man who insisted his children and underlings call him "sir," he intimidated pretty much everyone around him except Gates. From the start of their short-lived relationship, the two of them would scream at each other in voices that carried throughout the building. The rest of the staff would quietly exchange glances: this new kid was either very brave or very stupid.

Even before he had left Harvard, Gates was making enemies in the nascent PC industry. The issue was money. Ed Roberts was making piles of money selling his machine to the hobbyist world, but Gates and Allen were earning maybe a thousand or two a month in royalties. People were paying for the hardware because they had to, but not for the software, because they could copy it free from a friend and save the $75 Roberts was charging for Altair BASIC.

These were still the pioneering days of the PC industry, when skill with a soldering gun was at least as important as the ability to write computer code and software was strictly home-brewed. Back then, virtually no one paid for software, not even big companies buying from the likes of Digital Electronics Corporation (DEC), which sold "mini" mainframes called minicomputers. The starter software on a mini came free. There was no precedent among the computer hobbyists, but at $75 a pop the answer was simple: once one member of a users' club had a copy, so did everyone else. When Gates learned the truth, he threw a fit, then penned an impassioned open letter picked up by club newsletters around the country.

The letter, written (appropriately enough) in his sophomore year, was quintessential Gates: he was right, but he went about it all wrong. He and Allen did, of course, deserve compensation for their work, but his presentation was so tactless and inflammatory it drew attention from his main point. "Most of you steal your software," he told his readers—and in case they didn't get the point, he called them all "thieves" in the next paragraph. Then there was the absurdly self-righteous and patently false claim that he and Allen had used more than $40,000 in computer time to develop the Altair BASIC. He displayed no humility about money—odd for his age and also for the time—but that would be his leg up on many if not most of his competitors to come. He lacked even a whiff of embarrassment about his desire to make as much of it as he possibly could.

The ironies and contradictions of Gates's letter weren't lost on his readers, who swapped rumors that Gates had hacked the whole thing on a Harvard computer. They'd respond by sending equally snide notes to Gates, but some could already feel a shift from the clubby nature of their world, where people wrote software that they swapped with friends. For the first couple of years, the joints had been passed around freely at the no-charge concerts in the park. But now this craven interloper was blowing the whole party. The cruelest irony would come clear only with time: the fact that there were so many pirated versions of Gates's and Allen's program out in the marketplace meant it would emerge as the de facto standard.

Gary Kildall, too, was motivated by money when, in 1973, he agreed to do some consulting work for Intel. His dreams were more modest, though, like getting braces for the kids and doing some repairs around the house. Life as a Monterey-based professor was rewarding but not exactly remunerative. He could use some extra money to provide for a family in a community whose home prices were inflated by the grandeur of the scenery.

Kildall, not Gates, was the norm, the accidental entrepreneur. When a writer named Mark Stephens, AKA Robert X. Cringely, a popular gossip columnist for *InfoWorld,* sat down to write *Accidental Empires: How the Boys of Silicon Valley Make Their Millions, Battle Foreign Competition, and Still Can't Get a Date* (later made into a two-part PBS documentary called *Triumph of the Nerds*), he'd trot out Kildall as a counterpoint to Gates. Kildall was an enthusiast who, in Cringely's words, "more or less fell into business" simply because he happened to be in the right place at the right time, not because he harbored entrepreneurial dreams of striking it rich.

Kildall's project for Intel was an interesting one, but the commute up Highway 1 was exhausting, so he scrounged up the spare parts he needed to cobble together a small computer he could work on at home.* To make it work, he needed to write a program that would allow him to create and store computer files on his crude invention, and thus was born CP/M and a company initially dubbed, in the spirit of the times, Intergalactic Digital Research. Incredibly, he wrote CP/M in only a few weeks' time.

Think of an operating system as the electrical system in a house. On

---

* This jury-rigged home computer was built using a floppy disk drive pulled from a minicomputer, a teletype keyboard terminal, and an early Intel microprocessor (the wafer-sized chip that serves as the brain of the PC).

its own, it can't do much, but without it you can't use a vacuum cleaner, a stereo, an electric clock, or a television. Think of what the technically savvy call applications (a word processing program, a spreadsheet, the hottest computer game) as the appliances one plugs into the socket. Nowadays, an OS includes everything but the kitchen sink—a calculator, a clock, a stripped-down word processor, games, a Web browser—but back in the late 1970s and early 1980s, an OS was more utilitarian. Now, as then, an operating system is what lets you magnetically store a computer file (a draft of a letter, say) on a floppy disk; it's what allows you to retrieve both the word processing program and your draft when you want to rewrite it. The OS serves as the intermediary between the keyboard and a computer screen. So many people either bought or borrowed Kildall's CP/M that it, too, was emerging as a standard that every hobbyist and would-be millionaire used to write applications. Every would-be PC manufacturer trekked to Pacific Grove to talk with Kildall about customizing, or porting, his operating system to its machine. By the time a couple of IBMers made the trip to talk about using it on IBM's top-secret new PC, Kildall had already earned millions.

Legends abound about what had transpired in Kildall's short-lived negotiations with IBM. The money men and smart guys gathered for feasts that began with a quail egg cracked over steak tartare and ended with a vintage Taylor Fladgate port. And when the conversation turned to Kildall, as often it did in the early 1980s, they would parse what had happened every which way—the mistakes, the ambivalence about a deal with IBM, the opportunity lost. Each time, they reached the same conclusion: Gary Kildall had blown it. Present at the dawn of the PC Age, possessing the crown jewels, he had refused to kiss the rings of the IBMers, maybe out of arrogance, maybe out of ignorance. The storytellers invariably shake their heads at the stupidity of it all. "If it had been me," they'd say—but of course it hadn't been.

Interestingly, it was Bill Gates who sent IBM to Kildall. By this time, Gates and Allen were safely reensconced in the Seattle area, but the surrounding scenery seemed beside the point. Gates would dress in the morning without showering, pulling a sweatshirt over his head and slipping into a pair of jeans, maybe making time to stand in his kitchen gobbling a bowl of cereal before motoring off in a brown diesel Mercedes—an old man's car. Half the time he seemed to forget to brush his teeth, or so all the jokes about his breath suggested. In 1980, he was twenty-four, but he was flying tirelessly around the world—to Europe, to Japan, to any city in the United States where there was a computer manufacturer interested in licensing a Microsoft product. When in town, he always looked tired and rumpled, his hair uncombed, his face unshaven.

For IBM, Gates donned a suit. His hair, long and shaggy in the style of the times, was plastered down—if not quite neat then at least reflecting a gallant effort to look well groomed. Still, Team IBM, dressed in dark suits and wing tips, figured this young lad ushering them in the door in the summer of 1980 must be an assistant to the man they had yet to meet, William H. Gates, President.* Yet Gates compensated for his lack of presence with smarts and eagerness. If it was possible to love a corporation, the Gates loved International Business Machines, more affectionately known as Big Blue. Long before IBM officials requested a meeting, he had read everything he could about the company. Its founder, Thomas Watson Sr., was something of a hero to him. Gates's favorite business book—maybe his favorite book, period—was Watson's *The IBM Way.*

The first order of business after the pleasantries was the introduction of IBM's notoriously noxious nondisclosure agreement. Anything we tell you, the document stated, is strictly confidential. Anything you tell us, though, you tell us at your own peril, because we will be free to do what we want with that information. Gates signed without hesitation. If IBM had demanded a human sacrifice, the only question would have been whether Big Blue minded if Gates chose one of his less productive coders.

Gates is cast as being so ruthlessly cutthroat that his word is no more permanent than the lines on a computer screen after the machine has been turned off. But the truth is more complicated. In the mid-1980s, after he raided several employees from Philippe Kahn's company and Kahn raided Microsoft, the two signed an agreement that they'd stay away from each other's staff. When, years later, Gates dangled a treasure trove in stock options in front of Kahn's chief technologist, Kahn

---

* Microsoft's first receptionist, when the company was still in Albuquerque, was hired while Gates was out of town. A short time into her tenure, she rushed into her manager's office. A ratty-looking teen had just traipsed into Mr. Gates's office; what should she do? Naturally, it was Gates himself.

phoned Gates, livid. "Read the contract!" Gates brayed. It had an expiration date. Kahn had long since forgotten the specifics of the deal; Gates had not.

IBM had wanted CP/M but not Kildall. With IBM, secrecy was everything. Xerox was entering the microprocessing game, as were AT&T, Texas Instruments, and a half-dozen other well-established players. So every set of outsiders made privy to their plans only fueled their paranoia. There was also the issue of cultures. Much has been made about the transformation of the computer industry from the button-down starched collars of the IBM company man to the pizza-stained T-shirts and long stringy hair of the Microsoft misfits. But whether its employees wore cotton or gray flannel, IBM and Microsoft weren't that different. At Microsoft they were still company men, just younger and more comfortably dressed. They didn't care what you wore, only that you were smart and laughed when Gates made jokes about how people who left their offices after twelve hours had worked only half a day.

IBM was large enough and rich enough that it had gathered intelligence on this new crop of bit players. It had taken Gates's measure and deemed him, whatever his sartorial habits, its kind of man, bound by duty and driven by ambition. It also helped that the chairman of IBM knew Gates's mother because both served on the national board of the United Way. Kildall, however, the son of a teacher, had all the wrong priorities from IBM's point of view. He let his kids play hooky and brought them to board meetings. He was like a kid himself, playing with the latest new device when he should've been cracking the whip. The world was after him to update his operating system for machines that could simultaneously process sixteen bits of information, rather than eight, but he always seemed to have other priorities. He refused to delegate, choosing to design, implement, and debug his creations on his own.

Gates demurred when IBM suggested he see about buying the rights to CP/M from Kildall. He was abiding by their gentleman's agreement to steer clear of each other's vineyards, so instead he offered to help IBM set up an appointment with Kildall in Pacific Grove. He called ahead to let Kildall know he was sending along an important customer. He didn't mention IBM, but as he saw it, he shouldn't have had to. The way he said it should have been enough, at least the way he had been brought up.

For the longest time, the official story had Kildall up in his plane doing loop-the-loops while the business proposition of a lifetime waited in his anteroom. But that only serves as further proof that it's the victors who get to write history. The source of that tale, it turns out, was Gates, who contemptuously told interviewers that Gary had been fooling around in the sky while the representatives from Big Blue seethed. The truth is that while Kildall *was* off flying that day, he was flying himself to and from a meeting scheduled long before Gates sent the mystery guests down to Pacific Grove. Besides, though Kildall headed the company, he took care of the technical side of things, much as Paul Allen did at Microsoft. The business end of things was run by Kildall's wife, Dorothy McEwen. McEwen, vice president for corporate development, was there to greet IBM that morning.

McEwen, however, couldn't get beyond the onerous nondisclosure agreement. The meeting took place in the Santa Cruz mountains, the land of unicorns, mushrooms, and magic. At Digital Research, people paused to ask themselves what kind of people would ask you to partner with them and then lay this power trip on you? Microsoft had signed without a peep, because talking with IBM was the stuff of its founder's dreams. At Digital Research, a deal with IBM meant talking about the wisdom and morality of partnering with a company that had been cleverly spoofed in Stanley Kubrick's *2001: A Space Odyssey*.* The two sides wasted hours squabbling before McEwen reluctantly signed. When IBM laid out its needs, things went from bad to worse. From where the Digital Research team sat, IBM was proposing unreasonable deadlines at the same time it was insisting on terms that might anger Digital Research's existing customers.

What happened next has been dubbed the PC industry's *Rashomon*. Jack Sams, the point person for IBM, has sworn that he never met Kildall that day. Kildall swore that not only did he meet with Sams and his team when he returned that afternoon, but they agreed that CP/M was the perfect system for IBM's needs. That night, the Kildalls headed east to start a Caribbean vacation—though the long-overdue sixteen-bit version of CP/M was still not completed. On their plane, Kildall claimed, were a couple of IBM executives with whom he spent much of the flight hashing out the potential for a deal. As the Kildalls tell it, upon his return to Pacific Grove, suddenly no one was returning his calls. Jack Sams claimed that there had never been any messages to re-

---

* HAL, the seemingly beneficent computer turned evil, had been named by subtracting one letter in the alphabet from each letter of Big Blue's acronym.

turn—and that no member of his team had been on any transcontinental flights with the Kildalls. Was an embarrassed Kildall masking the truth with fibs—or was Sams, who ended up taking a real liking to Gates, coaching and encouraging him like a son, the one telling tales? Whatever the truth, the day after his frustrating meeting at Digital Research, Sams flew back to Seattle. As Gates saw it, he had satisfied any obligation to Kildall when he made that first call, but since things had obviously not worked out, he was now free to do as he liked. So suddenly Microsoft was in the operating system business—and IBM was risking its top secret "Chess" project on the promises of twenty-four-year-old Bill Gates.

Time was everything to IBM, which was committed to getting its new PC to market in a year's time. As luck would have it, Paul Allen knew of a small company called Seattle Computer that sold what it called QDOS, for Quick and Dirty Operating System. The system was an obvious CP/M knockoff written only because its author, Tim Paterson, had grown frustrated waiting for Digital Research to update CP/M for the sixteen-bit systems that Seattle Computer sold. Paterson admitted that he had written QDOS with a CP/M manual at his side, intentionally mimicking key components to ease the task of developers accustomed to its popular predecessor (while at the same time improving on the original). The deal Microsoft hammered out with Seattle Computer gave it the right, for $25,000, to distribute QDOS to an unlimited number of users on behalf of an unspecified computer manufacturer. Microsoft dropped the Q and dubbed its new operating system DOS. Before the IBM deal, one of the few concessions Gates had made to a normal life was Sunday-night dinners with his parents. After inking the deal with Seattle Computer, however, he informed his mother that he probably wouldn't be showing up at any dinners for the next six months.

Somehow word leaked out about DOS, and suddenly computer manufacturers from around the world were phoning Microsoft headquarters. You could almost hear the *kerchung!* of the cash register going off in Gates's brain. It is said that there are two types of salesmen in the world, and they can be distinguished by their approach to selling a used car: those who would inform prospective buyers that a car had been in a serious accident and those who wouldn't. There was no doubting which kind Gates was. With all these companies interested in DOS, his goal was to buy all rights to QDOS before IBM unveiled its PC—before Seattle Computer could appreciate the full worth of all it was sitting on. Seattle Computer offered to sell Microsoft all rights to its operating system for $150,000, but Ballmer turned up his nose at what he cast as "a grab for gold." The two sides settled on $50,000. In the end, Microsoft paid a total of $75,000 for a product that would earn the company billions in revenues and serve as the foundation of the rest of its successes.

"The PC came out in 1981," Nathan Myhrvold recalled. "By 1984, Digital Research would be a footnote."

THE BLOWN DEAL with IBM wasn't the end of Digital Research, though. Kildall began making noises about suing over the similarities between CP/M and DOS, so IBM invited him onto its machine. We'll give customers a choice, they told him. (An obviously displeased Gates would tell journalists that IBM had "blackmailed" him into agreeing, but for IBM, the importance of the DOS deal wasn't the magic of Microsoft but the insurance that it would be able to offer at least one workable operating system.) But Digital Research priced CP/M at $240 a copy, whereas the list price for DOS was $40. "Gary did everything he could not to compete," Myhrvold said with a sigh.

Factors other than price also hurt Kildall. An imitator enjoys the advantage of learning from a trailblazer's mistakes, and both Seattle Computer and Microsoft had improved on Kildall's invention. There was also Microsoft's favored status. The other software IBM sold for use on its PC was DOS compatible but not CP/M compatible. You could buy CP/M if you wanted to, but not only would you pay more, you'd have no guarantee that other programs would run on the machine.

Maybe Kildall's fate boiled down to a lack of ambition, or at least the kind of one-dimensional entrepreneurial ambition that has driven much of the innovation in the computer world. This man, described by a friend as "the biggest kid I've ever known," was passionate about a range of things; his computer business was only one toy among many. Gates was willing to do virtually anything a large customer asked; Kildall, by contrast, was a scientist protecting the purity of his invention from crass commercialism. Former Digital Research employees said that Kildall had no hunger to take his thirty-employee company, housed in a charming Victorian house, and turn it into a major company that played on Wall Street. Nor did he possess the desire to hire a hard-charging CEO, for fear an outsider would spoil the family feel of

Digital Research. "This was a gentle soul we're talking about," his mother, Emma, once said. "He was very naive and quiet about everything. He had no killer instinct for business."

Clearly Bill Gates did. Gates, a mathematics major when he entered Harvard, understood game theory: with every competitor you take out, you improve your own probability of winning. When Gates heard that Kildall was about to close a deal to put CP/M onto Hewlett-Packard's new PC, he was in Palo Alto the next day pleading his case. The technical staff at HP generally preferred CP/M, but Gates persuaded HP's executives to go with DOS. James Wallace and Jim Erickson, in a Gates biography entitled *Hard Drive,* recount a 1981 conversation between Gates and a middle-level manager named Richard Leeds. The climax of the story had Gates slamming a fist into the palm of his hand and offering this admonition: "We're going to put Digital Research out of business!" Said Ed Curry, who has known Gates since his Albuquerque days, "It's part of Bill's strategy: you smash people. You either make them line up, or you smash them."

The year after the IBM-PC was released, Gates phoned Kildall about licensing Digital Research software for a new Microsoft product. The calls went unreturned. Gates finally got a chance to talk business when the two ran into each other at a computer conference. Gates gave his rival a choice between a flat-fee deal and one that paid a royalty on every CP/M-compatible product it sold. Kildall chose the flat-fee arrangement. From a financial standpoint, it was a terrible decision, eventually costing his company hundreds of thousands of dollars in lost revenue. But from Kildall's perspective, the alternative, an ongoing relationship with Gates, would have been worse.

Kildall's new dream was a product called Logo, a computer language so simple that a grade-schooler could use it. But again, he lost out to Gates. Logo's competition was Microsoft's BASIC, which had the advantage of IBM's marketing muscle behind it. "It was then that I learned that computers were built to make money, not minds," Kildall wrote. Yet it was as if Kildall hadn't learned a thing. Another Kildall passion was the possibility of multimedia on computers. He founded a company called KnowledgeSet that worked on putting an encyclopedia onto a compact disc engineered for computers: the CD-ROM. Foolishly, he told Gates that he dreamed of a conference for all those interested in CD-ROM technology. The next thing he knew, he was being invited to be the keynote speaker at a CD-ROM conference sponsored by Microsoft. Friends told him he'd only be playing into Gates's hand by accepting, but Kildall's brain didn't work that way. He delivered his keynote address, not realizing that his presence lent credibility to Microsoft's CD-ROM efforts, still in their infancy. In time, Microsoft's Encarta would become the world's best-selling encyclopedia.

Meanwhile, Gates was growing in stature. A 1981 issue of *Fortune* magazine ran a picture of Gates and Allen in a feature about the new breed of digital pioneer. Kildall was mentioned only in passing. Over the next few years, Gates rode the IBM-PC rocket ship, appearing on the covers of *Money* and then *Time* (the first of four times he would grace the newsweekly's cover). *Business Week* dubbed him a "software whiz kid." And *People* included Gates (along with Ronald Reagan and Mr. T) in its 1983 "25 Most Intriguing" list. The profiles were puff pieces, playful tousles of his unkempt hair with gentle pokes in the rib about his nerdish ways. ("A hint of Andy Hardy in his boyish grin and unruly cowlick," wrote *People* and then gushed, "Gates is to software what Edison was to the light bulb.") Perhaps most galling from where Kildall sat was that writer after writer hailed Gates for his technical acumen rather than his business prowess. What Gates and two friends had pulled off in Harvard's computer center was impressive, but it didn't compare to Kildall's achievement or those of a long list of other pioneers, including the pair of Dartmouth professors who had invented the original language on which Altair BASIC was based. But an unhygienic boy millionaire was a far more compelling story than a former academic at his whiteboard methodically sketching data structures.

The PC industry was still young then—young, male, and awash in testosterone. Gates would lord it over Kildall at every turn; when sharing a panel with him at a computer conference held in 1981 at the Playboy Resort in Lake Geneva, Wisconsin, or whenever the opportunity arose. "Of course Bill gloated," said David Bunnell, a technical writer for Ed Roberts before embarking on a long career as a computer industry publisher. "That's part of the culture." Asked if he could remember any specifics, Bunnell just laughed. That would be like asking a sports fan to remember a wide receiver dancing in the end zone after a touchdown. The receiver celebrates every time.

With time, Kildall grew to despise Gates. He told people that when he looked at DOS he saw his own brain. He claimed that Gates was having him followed, to capitalize on the next good idea he dreamed up. In the early 1990s, he began working on a book he called *Computer Chron-*

icles, a memoir aimed at dispelling the enduring myths about the early days of the industry. According to those who read this unpublished manuscript, that largely meant refuting the myth of Bill Gates. "He was rich, and he had nothing to do," said a writer who tried to help Kildall find a publisher for *Computer Chronicles.* "In a situation like that, you can sit there and obsess over stuff, and he did."

GARY KILDALL DIED IN JULY 1994 from a blow to the head suffered in a crowded Monterey bar. What exactly happened that night no one knows for certain, but Kildall, wearing a black leather vest emblazoned with the Harley-Davidson logo, apparently got into a fight. When a friend found him, he was lying on the floor, woozy and quite drunk. He died two days later from internal bleeding. The *Los Angeles Times,* one of the few publications to note his passing, ran a short notice under the headline "Gary Kildall: His Software System Lost to Rival MS-DOS." He was fifty-two years old.

A few months later, a *Wall Street Journal* reporter named Gregg Zachary wrote about Kildall's life in the trade publication *Upside.** The piece was as much an obituary for a fallen time as for Kildall. For Zachary, Kildall's life encapsulated the industry's transformation from a programmer's nirvana to big business. It was the story of Paradise Lost, as one longtime observer told Zachary, a victory of "the dark side of the computer revolution." Aesthetics lost out to profitability, community to commercialization, adolescence to the inevitable next phases of empire building. It was the fight between the nineteen-year-old Gates and the Altair hobbyists, played out on the next level.

Kildall was hardly a fallen angel who represented everything good and pure in the world. He lived, Zachary wrote, by the bumper-sticker credo "He who dies with the most toys wins." A Learjet, boats, motorcycles, three Lamborghinis, auto races in Monaco, antique cars, a home in Pebble Beach, another in Austin, Texas. Yet this man who only wanted to make a living working on computers wore his financial success like a curse, not a gift. He drank like a college freshman—or someone trying to quench an unquenchable rage. One friend described him as "lost." Another described his sudden wealth as "very disorienting for him."

---

* *Upside* is a monthly magazine for which I occasionally write and of which David Bunnell is publisher.

From the start, Gates made it plain he wanted to build a business, not just make a living. "Nothing would please me more than being able to hire ten programmers and deluge the hobby market with good software," the nineteen-year-old Gates had written in his letter upbraiding those using bootlegged copies of BASIC. And deluge he would. He wasn't just akin to an opportunist who would sell joints that had previously been handed out free at love-ins and free concerts. Figuratively speaking, he'd eventually operate a string of franchises across the country, opening hot-tub and shower concessions and subcontracting with big corporations to provide the food and drink that kept everyone at the love-in longer.

CHAPTER 02

NOWHERE, UTAH

ONE YEAR AT THE COMDEX TRADE SHOW, a Microsoft executive named Jeff Raikes stopped by the WordPerfect booth with a strange request: he wanted a family portrait from his WordPerfect counterpart, Pete Peterson. The year was 1990, and WordPerfect was the undisputed king of the word processing world, nearly a billion-dollar-a-year market dominated year after year by this runt company from Nowhere, Utah. For seven years, Microsoft had been selling a word processing program of its own, Microsoft Word. Despite the tens of millions of dollars Microsoft had thrown at what company employees were inclined to call the "Word Wars," Microsoft Word still lagged far behind WordPerfect.

Every COMDEX, Gates would tell the trade press reporters that the upcoming year would be the one when Microsoft Word would finally surpass WordPerfect. And every year, Pete Peterson, who ran WordPerfect's day-to-day operations, would take special satisfaction in the fact that it had thwarted Gates once again. Peterson was always hearing from customers phoning to say that Gates or some other top Microsoft executive had just been in to see them. The funny thing was that Gates or his minion would not sweet-talk these potential Word customers but would badger them, demanding to know why they continued to use WordPerfect when Microsoft Word was obviously so superior. Once, while chatting at an industry event, a Microsoft executive told Peterson that he was married but he and his wife were putting off starting a family until after Word had overtaken WordPerfect. Only then, he explained, would he have the spare time. It was a joke, of course—but the kind of humor that left a bad taste.

Jeff Raikes, the marketing manager overseeing Microsoft Word, was feeling the greatest pressure. Those atop the company were convinced of the superiority of their product (despite what the reviewers were saying), so naturally they blamed marketing. At a public event a few months before the 1990 COMDEX, someone asked Gates about Word-Perfect. True to character, Gates cast Microsoft as the underdog. By any measurement, Gates told the crowd, Microsoft was at a disadvantage. It had fewer programmers working on Word and a smaller Word-only marketing and sales team. The only way they could compete, Gates said, was to understand the competition as well as they knew themselves. "I want my guys waking up thinking about the competition," Gates said. "I expect this guy we've got, Jeff Raikes, to know so much about WordPerfect that he can name the kids of his counterparts and tell you their birthdays." Raikes wasn't in the audience that day, but he saw the speech mentioned in an industry gossip column. He took this throwaway line as if it were a commandment from God.

Peterson had always liked Raikes, despite the intense competition between the two companies. The industry joke about Microsoft was that the company was populated by Gates clones, know-it-alls as arrogant as they were bright. Raikes even resembled Gates, with the same doughy face, dirty-blond cowlicked hair, and big nose, but whereas his boss was prickly and acerbic, Raikes had an easy way about him. Present Gates with a point with which he disagrees, and he's likely to ask, "Are you brain-damaged?" By contrast, Raikes gently begins, "I have to disagree with you a little bit on that." Every COMDEX, Raikes would stop by the WordPerfect booth to say hello to Peterson and see what his counterparts were up to.

"Hey, you've got to help me out," Raikes began good-naturedly when he stopped by the booth in 1990. I need to learn the names and birthdays of your kids. And a picture. I need a picture of you and your family." Peterson's cohorts just rolled their eyes at this latest weirdness from the almost cultish Microsoft, but Peterson proved game. Why not? A week later, a portrait of his family was sitting on Raikes's desk. And over the next year, each of the Petersons' six kids received a birthday card from Raikes, along with joke presents bought at the Microsoft store. The gifts Peterson tossed into the garbage, but his kids got a kick out of the cards. At first he laughed along, but after a while he found the whole thing creepy. Here he was engaged in what he described as "a battle to the death with Bill Gates," and one of Gates's top people was sending best wishes cards.

When, two years later, Peterson was out of a job, feeling wounded and angry after a forced resignation, he could soothe himself with one pleasurable thought: No longer would he be living in Gates's crosshairs. "My entire life, from 1985 until early 1992, was figuring out how to stay ahead of Bill Gates," Peterson lamented. "Every night I went to bed wondering what I was going to do about him and Microsoft. Every morning I woke up thinking about it. Bill Gates was a constant factor in everything I did every day I was running WordPerfect."

ALAN ASHTON, a Brigham Young University computer science professor, had no teaching gig lined up in the summer of 1977, so, bored, he decided he'd try his hand at a word processing software program. Word processors were kludgy inventions then, with screens junked up by things like @HD@B and other gibberish code. Ashton had an idea that the screen should look like a printed page and that scrolling through a document should be as easy as flipping pages in a book. In the back of his mind, he was also thinking that his venture might mean extra cash to supplement his professor's salary.

Bruce Bastian was a student of Ashton's who loved nothing more in life than conducting the BYU marching band. Indeed, so committed was he to the music that his master's degree project was a 3-D computer program that allowed him to see his band's formations from anywhere in the stadium. Ashton was impressed, and also overwhelmed by customers knocking on his door, so when Bastian (who, after all, was still a student) lost his temporary conductorship to a more experienced hand, WordPerfect was born. By 1980, two years of working weekends and holidays while Ashton continued to teach and Bastian worked on his master's had taken its toll. Pete Peterson, who was Bastian's brother-in-law, suggested they hire a part-time office manager. This newly created part-time post paid just $5 an hour, but Peterson didn't hesitate when Bastian offered him the job. As it was, so bad was business at Julie's Draperies, the shop Peterson ran with two family members, that he was already spending his mornings bagging groceries and stocking shelves for $4 an hour at a local supermarket.

More relatives, as well as friends and neighbors, were added to the company's rolls as the demand for WordPerfect grew. Ashton generally filled any new programming openings by hiring former students. When the company decided it should advertise, Peterson drove to the local bookstore to read up on advertising. In that same fashion, Peterson taught himself branding, product life cycles, and test marketing. Still, their product was greeted with consistently rave reviews, and sales doubled year after year.

When Ashton overheard a salesman telling a customer that a new version of WordPerfect that allowed for footnotes would be ready inside three months, Ashton lectured him: A more realistic assessment is six to nine months, so that's what you'll tell the man when you phone him back. At other companies, nine months *was* "three months" in salesspeak, like the "ten minutes" you invariably hear when ordering takeout Chinese. WordPerfect would host hospitality suites at industry confabs, but though this company, run by three Mormons, eventually learned to splurge on the jumbo shrimp, they drew the line at alcohol. Their offices remained closed on Sundays. The company motto, "We teach correct principles and our employees govern themselves," was derived from the teachings of Joseph Smith Jr., founder of the Mormon Church. "Family and friends should come first," Peterson was always telling WordPerfect employees. "Don't neglect your families just to get ahead." Peterson habitually took at least a couple of his kids along on most business trips. When, in 1986, WordPerfect became the undisputed king of the word processing world, the company's founders bought everyone a trip to Hawaii.

There were hard times and downdrafts, of course. WordPerfect suffered the headaches of a thriving company based in Orem, Utah. So fast was business growing that the local printing companies couldn't spit out user manuals fast enough to keep up with the orders. Recruiting started to become a problem, as did the inexperience of those running the company. But these frustrations paled compared to concern number one, Microsoft, a company populated with overachieving computer science majors from places such as Harvard, Stanford, and Caltech who couldn't believe that a bunch of grad students from BYU—BYU!—were kicking their tails year after year.

AT THE END OF THE 1970s, Dan Bricklin, a shaggy-haired, bearded twenty-six-year-old student at the Harvard Business School who dressed like a lumberjack, wrote a computerized spreadsheet called VisiCalc, earning its inventor and his backers bucketfuls of money. So Gates, who had once envisioned Microsoft as a company that would sell computer languages and tools to fellow hackers, released a spreadsheet program called Multiplan, which Gates hoped would be a lot like Visi-Calc, only better. Released in 1981, Multiplan would be the first of many Microsoft-born programs that bombed. But Microsoft was now officially in the applications business.

Microsoft Word 1.0 hit the market in 1983, three years after WordPerfect. Word was another unmitigated disaster. It routinely crashed for no apparent reason, taking with it entire documents, even those that had been saved. A few months after the release of version 1, the company hired a well-regarded business consultant to study customer response. "The report was beyond negative," said Pam Edstrom, then the company's director of PR. "The feedback from customers was so atrocious, it was painful to read." Gates and his lieutenants debated junking the whole thing, but of course they wouldn't, not with all the money to be made. By that point there were literally hundreds of word processing programs on the market, but the growing clout of the Microsoft name meant the program sold pretty well despite its problems.

VisiCalc had opened Gates's eyes to the moneymaking potential of applications software, but it was a programmer named Charles Simonyi who showed him how lucrative a field it could be. Simonyi was thirty-one years old when he arrived at Microsoft in 1981, a seasoned programmer with an impressive résumé matched by skyscraper-sized dreams. Born in Hungary, Simonyi had escaped from behind the Iron Curtain, aided by a computer repairman. Eventually he had landed at Xerox PARC, an oasis of inventive nerds tucked away in the hills above Stanford University. Though funded by Xerox, PARC was more think tank than commercial venture. There among the redwoods were born ideas such as the icon-driven computing that, for example, would allow a user simply to click on a garbage can when deleting a file rather than typing the command line, C:\>del [filename].DOC. But Steve Jobs of Apple, not the Xerox Corporation, first cashed in on the idea, and it would be Bill Gates who would grow obscenely rich off of it.

That was the story of Xerox PARC: a long list of impressive break-throughs, many of them commercially viable yet none contributing to Xerox's bottom line. Simonyi, who eventually would buy a Learjet and spend $5 million building a house near Gates, was cut from different cloth than most of his PARC colleagues. In their first meeting, Gates spoke about his plans to control every cranny of the software industry, and Simonyi knew he had found his home. At Microsoft's first "all-hands" meeting in 1981, Simonyi laid out what in Microsoft lore would forever be known as the "Simonyi revenue bomb." Back then, any company even remotely associated with an electrical appliance (Xerox, Radio Shack, AT&T, Texas Instruments) was developing, or had developed, a personal computer. Keep writing new applications, Simonyi advised, then make sure they run on as many different hardware platforms as possible. A chart Simonyi had prepared showed this plan returning modest revenues in the short run, but so great was the demand projected over the next fifteen years that the company would have to hire every man, woman, and child living in the state of Washington to keep pace.

Though clever, Simonyi's theorem conjured up a character out of *Raiders of the Lost Ark* who stuffs his pockets with so many gold doubloons he's unable to cross back over a chasm. Microsoft's VisiCalc knockoff, Multiplan, was written for no fewer than seventy machines. It worked on virtually every machine on the market but ran well on none of them. In contrast, there was the speedy spreadsheet program created by a small Cambridge, Massachusetts–based start-up called Lotus Development. Lotus 1-2-3 ran on only one machine, the IBM-PC, but for those using an IBM machine, using 1-2-3 was the difference between wearing a tailor-made suit and one bought off the rack. Whereas VisiCalc and Multiplan were baggy in the seat and long in the leg to allow for a variety of shapes and builds, 1-2-3 was the perfect cut for the IBM-PC. Stacked against its competitors, Lotus was lightning quick, written in the native machine code rather than a generic language such as BASIC. In 1985, Microsoft grossed $140 million from all of its language products, its operating system, and the scores of Microsoft applications on the market. That same year, this one-product company logged $226 million in sales, earning it the status of the world's top software company.

Before Bill Envy there was "Kapor Envy," a disease that afflicted no one worse than Gates. Mitch Kapor was a large, sad-eyed man from Brooklyn, a former DJ turned computer programmer, a child of the sixties who was older and more worldly than Gates. Kapor, who had worked as a counselor at a mental health facility and was into transcendental meditation, named his company after the Hindu symbol for enlightenment. To Gates, enlightenment was discovering a new market where there were millions to be made and Yoga was a cool code name for a potential Lotus product killer. Computer manufacturers were begging Kapor to write a version of 1-2-3 for their machines, but Kapor kept saying no. No one could imagine Gates ever turning away a business deal, at least not one with a reasonably good chance of making money for Microsoft. The general sentiment inside the clubby software world both inhabited was that Kapor didn't much care for Gates, but Kapor, being more mellow, was never ostentatious in his distaste. The same could not be said for Gates.

"You could see it whenever the two of them got together," said a longtime industry veteran friendly with both. "Bill referred to Mitch as his friend and all that, but these were two very different people who clearly didn't care for each other."

Gates is the type who is so competitive that, for relaxation, he buys two identical jigsaw puzzles and then races his wife to see who can complete the puzzle first. Around Kapor, Gates's competitive juices practically oozed from his pores. He brashly declared at industry events that his squeaky little Multiplan would prove the death of 1-2-3. Privately, Gates sized up Kapor, who was partial to Hawaiian shirts and squishy talk about consensus building and the importance of a racially diverse workforce, as no match for his own business prowess. "You know how Bill's always doing that rocking thing when he's really engaged?" said the longtime veteran quoted above. "Around Mitch, he'd get so worked up you'd have thought he was going to attain liftoff."

Gary Kildall had declared that Digital Research wouldn't get into the applications business because it had an unfair advantage as an operating system vendor. Gates, in contrast, figured that his intimate knowledge of the prevailing operating system was his one big advantage. Microsoft both competed with Lotus on the spreadsheet front and controlled its destiny as the keeper of DOS. And if anyone believed that Microsoft was a company that would cautiously avoid even an appearance of a conflict of interest, the Multiplan group's unofficial motto cleared up that notion: "DOS ain't done till Lotus won't run." The release of DOS 2.0 didn't manage to torpedo 1-2-3, as hoped, but it did give users fits. Two investigative reporters for the *Seattle Post-Intelligencer,* James Wallace and Jim Erickson, looked into the charge that the DOS team was guilty of the software equivalent of putting rice into a gas tank. They concluded, "They managed to code a few hidden bugs into DOS 2.0 that caused Lotus 1-2-3 to break down when it was loaded."

In 1983, Gates made the back-to-the-drawing-board decision to scrap Multiplan and take a fresh approach with a new product eventually dubbed Excel. He also decided Microsoft would drop the notion of being able to run on every platform and instead do as Lotus had done and specialize on IBM and IBM-compatibles. He finally realized that people didn't care if a program ran on seventy different platforms, they just cared that it worked well on *their* platform. But then, not long after that, Kapor finally agreed to write a version of 1-2-3 for the Apple Macintosh. So suddenly Microsoft's top objective for Excel was the Mac—a decision that meant the Excel team had to throw away months of work. Maybe the problem was the fact that Kapor was proving more adept at riding the IBM wave than Gates. Maybe it was Microsoft's general lack of success in the applications world. Probably it was simply that Lotus was number one, which meant that Microsoft wasn't. But programmers at Microsoft shook their heads over the tantrums their boss threw when conversation turned to Kapor.

"I was at this party when Bill started in on 1-2-3," says Curt Monash, then a highly regarded industry analyst. The occasion was strictly social, a black-tie party held in the apartment of Gates's then girlfriend, Ann Winblad, after an art opening. Yet there was Gates past midnight, dressed in a monkey suit, rocking back and forth and chewing Monash's ear off about everything that was wrong with Kapor, Lotus, and 1-2-3. At the time, Lotus had roughly a 90 percent share of the spreadsheet market and Excel was not two years old, but Gates was already declaring it a Lotus killer. Monash was accustomed to hearing a CEO trash a rival, but he was struck by "the passion behind his nastiness and the length with which he argued his point in a social setting." Most surprising to Monash was the "combative and sneering tone" Gates adopted when Monash disagreed with him.

There were lingering bad feelings inside Microsoft because of the hasty decision to write Excel for the Mac, but at least the company was focused on two platforms, not dozens. During late-night hallway conversations, the programmers reassured themselves over cold cans of Coke that their Bill had miscalculated but righted himself. He had made the tough call, dumping Multiplan in favor of Excel. And though Microsoft Word wasn't cutting it—versions 2 and 3 were still riddled with debilitating bugs—the Word group was learning. They studied WordPerfect and the other word processing leaders. We're smart and we're committed, they told themselves. And they vowed like blood brothers that they'd know their customers so well that they could offer features so cutting edge the customers wouldn't even know to ask about them.

FOR A LONG WHILE the WordPerfect team hardly paid any attention to this clunky Microsoft-produced word processor. Sure, they knew who Bill Gates was. It would be hard *not* to know Gates. He was featured in *Business Week, Money, People, Time*—and that was just in 1983. That was the year Gates told *People*, "We want to be to software what IBM is to hardware." In 1984, he made *Esquire*'s "Best of the New Generation" list and was treated to a full-page photo in *Fortune* magazine, which described Gates as "a remarkable piece of software in his own right." The next year Gates (along with Warren Beatty, Tom Selleck, and Burt Reynolds) made *Good Housekeeping*'s list of the country's fifty most eligible bachelors. "They are all wealthy and charming, and waiting for the right woman to come along!" And he appeared on NBC's *Today* show (Jane Pauley: "You're a computer whiz. Are you a business genius, too?"). But inside WordPerfect people just laughed whenever they saw this supposed boy genius's latest offering in the word processing field. The problem boiled down to a certain artlessness—a problem Gates as much as acknowledged when, years later, he admitted that Microsoft spends so much time thinking about the plumbing, it shortchanges the toilet seat.

By 1986, though, Microsoft would be just about the only competitor WordPerfect paid much attention to. WordPerfect had a 30 percent share of the market, and Word ranked fourth with just over 10 percent, but Microsoft had the advantage as the designer of the operating system and WordPerfect feared being subjected to the same kind of monkey-wrench tactics used to hurt Lotus. No matter how good Microsoft was about sharing prereleases of DOS with outside vendors, WordPerfect's foes in the Microsoft Word group always had a leg up. They could pick up the phone and ask about some feature in the upcoming but top secret (and long-overdue) DOS 4.0 or lobby for a change that would make life easier for them. There was also the steady stream of cash that DOS generated. Every percentage point of market share captured cost millions in marketing dollars, but Microsoft, unlike smaller competitors such as WordStar, could afford it. Said Gates, matter-of-factly, laconically, and without irony, "We don't mind a war of attrition."

Another factor fueling WordPerfect's fears was Microsoft's tapeworm appetite. "As soon as they finish one meal," Pete Peterson told colleagues, "they're looking for their next one. Their appetite knew no bounds."

For Peterson, Steve Ballmer, not Gates, embodied all that he didn't like about Microsoft's piggish ways. Ballmer had been attending the Stanford Business School after two years with Procter & Gamble* when Gates, in 1980, started hounding his friend into joining them in Seattle. Much as Paul Allen had cajoled Gates to quit Harvard, Gates talked Ballmer into quitting between his first and second years at Stanford. "Come now," Gates badgered, "or it might be too late." Peterson, who holds a pair of front-row season tickets for the Utah Jazz basketball team, offered two tickets to any game to a charitable auction at Agenda.† Just Peterson's luck, the top bidder was Detroit-born Ballmer, who paid $19,000 to see the Jazz play his hometown team, the Pistons. Ballmer needed only the one seat, so he invited Peterson to join him.

"It's like it meant everything to Steve that Detroit win," Peterson says. "I mean, he was screaming and all red. This was just some nothing game in the middle of the season, but he was acting as if the season was riding on this victory. But that's Steve. The desire to win overshadows anything and everything else."

If at Microsoft the people were too overbearing, at WordPerfect they were too mild-mannered. Microsoft concocted a set of taste test–like comparisons between Word and WordPerfect and then spent a small fortune advertising the claim that nine of every ten word processor users preferred Word, even though the marketplace suggested otherwise. "This ad was statistically unsound and horribly biased," says Dan Lunt, WordPerfect's marketing director. "We asked them to cease and desist, but they dared us to try and stop them." Lunt and his cohorts talked about legal action but decided that suing a competitor was unseemly. Another time, when cofounder Bruce Bastian was demonstrating a new release of WordPerfect at COMDEX, a Softie in the audience interrupted him. "That's impossible to do," the programmer said of the demo he was watching, as if his brain couldn't quite believe what his eyes were seeing. If someone had so arrogantly interrupted Gates in a

---

* Ballmer's claim to fame at P&G: redesigning the Duncan Hines cake box.

† This auction, no longer held, was like the auctions schools used to raise money, except that these were the offerings of tycoons. Other donated prizes over the years included a ride in a CEO's Spanish fighter jet and an Apple executive's diamond earring, which Gates bought for $25,000.

similar circumstance, the Microsoft faithful would have been all over the interloper. Instead, Bastian patiently explained this new innovation to a man who had clearly identified himself as a foe.

"In retrospect, we were too darn nice," Dan Lunt said.

Emotions were running high among a group of WordPerfect execs who logged long hours over the Labor Day weekend in 1988. They were tired of Microsoft slamming their product and fed up with the arrogance of a company that believed it was its destiny to win because it was smarter than everyone else. The truth was that they were also feeling a pinch of desperation because of problems with the 5.0 release of their flagship product.

The WordPerfect group spent most of a long lunch venting about Microsoft, growing angrier and angrier. They vowed they would change so they could stay on top. "Going to war" they called it when they put their heads together like athletes huddling before a big game. Enough with the polite, gentlemanly approach to business, they agreed. They'd work harder, smarter, meaner. They'd reciprocate by bad-mouthing Word at every turn. And if stretching the rules was necessary, they'd stretch the rules. Phase one would be a "marketing boot camp," where Peterson and other executives would drill the company's sales force in the feature-by-feature superiority of WordPerfect over Microsoft Word. Next they preannounced WordPerfect 5.0, talking about next-generation features as if it were already completed. Whereas once Peterson had always been quoting either his father or the Mormon Church, now it was Darwin. "It's the law of the jungle," Peterson would say. "It's survival of the fittest. It's people chewing off each other's legs. It's a world based primarily on greed." And if you aren't willing to conform to the rules of this jungle, Peterson told his charges, you should find yourself another job.

CHAPTER 03

FIVE-CARD STUD, JACKS OR BETTER TO OPEN

HIGHWAYS 101 AND 280 run parallel through Silicon Valley, two cement spines connecting the area's baby-faced engineers and its wannabe millionaires with San Francisco to the north and San Jose to the south. Highway 101 is the road designated for the Valley's working stiffs, those who may be well-off enough to afford a home in Mountain View, where a two-bedroom box costs $600,000, but not so rich that they can splurge on the Range Rover of their dreams or a custom-made, six-speed BMW 540i sedan that must be special-ordered from Munich, Germany. The Range Rover and 540i set favors 280, a highway that gently ribbons through the coastal mountains not far from the Pacific Ocean. This road less traveled and thus gloriously free of 101's traffic woes connects bedroom communities such as Atherton, where the average home sells for double the price of a house in Beverly Hills, to the magical kingdom of Sand Hill Road, once a riding trail for the horsey set but now the preferred address for the special breed known as the venture capitalist. It's to Sand Hill Road that every entrepreneur with a brainstorm but no capital treks in hope of securing that seven-figure check she hopes will mean the difference between a wasted idea and one that puts her smiling mug on the cover of *Fortune.*

David Marquardt, a founding partner in a venture firm called August Capital, is one of the kings of this hill. After nearly twenty years in the venture business, Marquardt is undoubtedly a wealthy man, but it's mainly other people's money he plays with. Those managing insurance pools, university endowments, employee pension funds, and other large pools of capital chip in the tens of millions of dollars Marquardt and his partners invest each year; their payoff is a 25 percent share of any profits these investments generate. A work of art that sits on a table just inside August Capital's doors—a sculpture of a shopping bag collapsing from the weight of banded stacks of $100 bills—says everything you need to know about the returns even the most average venture capitalist boasts about this high-risk, high-yield game. ·

August Capital could be called the house that Gates built. Marquardt's office is decorated with the usual paraphernalia: framed family photos, favorite books, and a veritable village of the venture capitalist's favorite trinket, a Lucite-encased "tombstone" commemorating a company's debut on the stock market. Two special souvenirs, though, both sitting on a glass coffee table, help separate Marquardt from the hundreds of other venture capitalists crisscrossing the Valley, going eighty in the fast lane. One is a junky portable computer manufactured by Radio Shack in the early 1980s that Marquardt keeps around because its bundled software includes the last piece of code Bill Gates ever wrote. The other is a copy of the official paperwork Microsoft filed when it went public, selling pieces of the company as stock, in 1986. Marquardt, the only venture capitalist in on the deal, bought a 5 percent share of the company for $1 million. Assuming that he and his partners never sold a single share, that investment had returned roughly $15 billion by the start of 1999—or $1.5 million in profit for every $100 Marquardt invested.

Marquardt was a newly minted venture capitalist, just thirty-one years old with an Ivy League degree and an MBA from Stanford, when he met Bill Gates in 1980. His partners, all of them older, told him he was wasting his time foraging through this nutty new world of software. Sure, there had been wild successes such as Apple, which had gone public that year, earning one venture capitalist several million dollars on a $100,000 investment. But Apple sold something tangible, a plastic box called a personal computer, not something ephemeral such as software that was nothing but a collection of zeroes and ones. The partners at his original venture firm, Technology Venture Investors (TVI), subscribed to a saw then in vogue that software was a poor investment because the assets walked out the door every night. But Marquardt, intent on proving his mentors wrong, drew up a list of the country's most promising software firms, including Gary Kildall's Digital Research and the crew that had created VisiCalc, and proceeded to visit each in size order. The fourth name on his four-company list was Microsoft.

The way it works at this rarefied level is that, at a hot venture like Microsoft, if you don't have a connection you don't get inside the door. Marquardt's partners may not have seen the potential in software, but others did, so Steve Ballmer was playing the gatekeeper, fending off the money people clamoring to meet with his friend. That proved a lucky break for Marquardt, who had been in the class ahead of Ballmer's at Stanford. Ballmer invited him up to Washington for lunch, and Marquardt peppered Ballmer with questions about the company's product line and its long-term plans for new markets. "You're the first guy to ask the right questions," Ballmer told him. So it became imperative that Marquardt and Gates hook up.

"At this point Bill was basically working a hundred hours a week, sleeping at the office, the whole thing," Marquardt says. "So Steve tells me the only free time Bill has on his calendar over the next three weeks is this football game." Feeling pressure from his family about how scarce he was making himself, Gates had promised his mother, a University of Washington regent, that he'd join them in her private box at the game that weekend. So there Marquardt—along with Gates's parents, his two sisters, and Gammy, Mrs. Gates's mother—watched the UW Huskies play the University of Arizona Wildcats. Or, more accurately, the Huskies and Wildcats played while Marquardt spent most of three hours listening to Gates as he feverishly scribbled compiler designs on the back of a football program. Back in Silicon Valley, Marquardt gushed at the next partners' meeting, "This guy knows more about his competitors' products than his competitors do. He understands the marketplace—where he's got to be to sell this stuff—and the compromises he's got to make to get there."

Marquardt continued with the soft sell. When Ballmer phoned to ask for help with the finer points of restructuring the company, Marquardt spent hours walking him through the process, though it might have meant more time invested with no payoff. A year passed before Ballmer finally called to invite him north to talk a deal, in 1981.

Microsoft had plenty of money in the bank—so much that the company just added TVI's million dollars to its cash reserves—but Ballmer believed that a venture capital firm would impose a much-needed discipline on Microsoft. With a venture capitalist looking over company executives' shoulders, they'd have no choice but to produce financial statements and prepare regular long-range planning documents for the board of directors they would have to create. Ballmer and Gates were twenty-five years old, Marquardt barely thirty, but "somehow Steve viewed me as the adult supervision," Marquardt said.

Marquardt considers Gates a good friend. But though Gates was an usher at his wedding, he's never picked up the phone to congratulate Marquardt or his wife on an addition to the family. He's never been the type to send Christmas cards or carve out time just to hang out. There were dinners, but they'd always talk shop, more often than not at a Wendy's, sitting in a plastic booth for a couple of hours, scribbling on paper place mats at a table littered with chewed-up straws and mangled wrappings.

THE PAYOFF FOR MARQUARDT and every other part owner of Microsoft would come in the spring of 1986, when the company made its Wall Street debut. Larry Ellison's company, Oracle, went public the day before Microsoft's debut. A week earlier, Scott McNealy's company, Sun Microsystems, had celebrated its IPO. Back then, the three companies did not compete with one another, except in the sense that in the rarefied world of the national media, there was limited room onstage for more than a couple of high-tech darlings.

Sun was a hardware company that was only marginally in the software industry. In the mid-1980s, Sun was a relatively cheap way of getting a computer onto your desk that had anything resembling the power and speed of today's Intel-based machines. First there was the IBM mainframe, which cost in the millions; then there were minicomputers made by companies such as DEC (Digital, or more officially the Digital Equipment Corporation), which were impractical as personal computers because of both their price (more than $100,000) and size (imagine a refrigerator sitting next to your desk). Sun's breakthrough was the workstation, a $25,000 machine linked to other computers and small enough to fit onto a desk, yet as powerful as a minicomputer.

The Sun team was led by a hardware genius from Germany named Andy Bechtolsheim; a scruffy-faced software guru from the cauldron of Berkeley, Bill Joy; and two MBAs from Stanford, McNealy and Vinod Khosla, who as a boy in India had rented old copies of *Electronic Engineering* and dreamed of striking it rich in America. Engineers, Wall Street traders, university scientists, corporate accounting departments, government—the potential demand for these workstations seemed a market worth billions. Buying stock in Sun was more of a bet than an investment, given the competition the company faced (Hewlett-Packard was selling a copycat product, and IBM had just introduced its own workstation). But the potential payoff was huge: if the planets lined up just right, these machines might just end up on every desk in corporate America.

Sun's employees celebrated their Wall Street debut as a group, fraternity style. McNealy rented a couple of tents and ordered several barrels of beer and a truckload of six-foot heroes from ToGos. Every full-time employee, including the office help and the workers on the assembly floor, owned at least a sliver of the company, so there was no grumbling in the corners while the "haves" celebrated their good fortune.

The celebrating at Oracle was a touch classier and also involved more intrigue. Employees there drank expensive champagne from plastic cups, even cracking open some Dom Pérignon. But the latecomers to the Oracle team, especially those lower down in the pecking order, stood ruefully by, drinking the champagne, naturally, but having nothing to celebrate as they owned no Oracle stock. Even some of the newly minted millionaires felt the celebration had been spoiled by sour grapes. Nowadays, a company's founders swell with pride if the company's stock price doubles on its first day of trading. That means the shares one owns are worth that much more, at least on paper, and the buzz foreshadows an even more profitable future. But it also means the company has left a great deal of money on the table for everyone else. The company's coffers are enriched by the opening price (minus the 7 percent fee the investment bankers take), and the rest is pocketed by the wealthy insiders the investment bankers invite in at the opening price. Ellison's partner, Bob Miner, was furious at him for allowing the investment bankers to set so low a stock price when negotiating with the investment bankers. Oracle opened at $12 and closed at $15 and change, costing Oracle millions of dollars in working capital.

Gates hosted no formal celebration at Microsoft. Indeed, he was out of town on vacation the day of the initial public offering. He had hired a yacht with a crew but was otherwise by himself on a cruise to Australia's Great Barrier Reef. Microsoft stock had been priced at $21 a share but opened above $25, and closed the day at just under $28. TVI's $1 million had turned into $39 million. Ballmer was worth $48 million, at least on paper, and Paul Allen, who had left the company in 1982 when it was discovered he had Hodgkin's disease, was worth $172 million. The shares Gates had given his parents were worth more than $3 million. Gates, who still owned 45 percent of the company, was worth $350 million.

The battle to become media darling was over before the Wall Street bidding even began. Long before its initial public offering, Microsoft's PR arm had invited a writer from *Fortune* to observe the process from the inside. So, three weeks after the Microsoft IPO, there was Gates (and his net worth) again on *Fortune*'s cover, hair in a bowl cut, his bangs looking as if he had taken a pair of scissors to them himself.

Sun's four founders were rich after the company went public, but not so rich that they'd turn heads on Wall Street. Running a hardware business involved a factory, parts, and a large workforce, so that by the time of the Sun IPO, the four founders owned less than a combined 20 percent stake in their company. Several venture capitalists (including Marquardt) and Eastman Kodak owned a far larger piece of Sun than any single founder did. The Sun public offering made page 104 of *Business Week*, no picture. A couple of years would pass before readers of *Fortune* and *Forbes* would learn of this company founded by four guys meeting in hamburger shacks and cafés around the Bay Area.

Oracle sold software that helped corporations computerize huge file cabinets full of data. Ellison's story was appealing—a college dropout raised by an aunt and uncle in a working-class area of Chicago. He had beaten Big Blue at its own game, selling a cutting-edge version of a database product he had learned about by reading an IBM-generated research paper. His problem from a PR standpoint was that the press was pretty much interested only in the PC industry, not in the companies selling business-only applications hidden behind the glass. Ellison had tried selling off a piece of Oracle to raise much-needed cash in the company's earliest days, but every venture capitalist he had pitched had turned him down. He was worth roughly $100 million when Oracle went public, but it was his misfortune to strike it rich the same week that Gates would wow everyone with a net worth of $350 million. So whereas Gates received the star treatment, Ellison was ignored.

Microsoft's stock (in no small part because of all the positive publicity) tripled within the year. And when the stock price hit $91 in March 1987, Gates was officially worth more than a billion dollars. That launched a whole new round of Gates profiles, comparing him to Henry Ford, John D. Rockefeller, and Andrew Carnegie. All had built vast fortunes at a relatively young age, but Gates was declared, at thirty-one, the youngest man ever to amass that much money, even accounting for inflation. *Time,* still clinging to the notion that he was more hacker than businessman, declared him the Edison of our time; *Fortune,* a magazine whose editors ogle money like the editors at *Playboy* ogle breasts, cast this pasty white workaholic as a "ladies' man."

Yet accumulating as much wealth as Gates did in so short a period required an explanation, and the one offered more often than not was that this young mogul possessed a tenacity and ambition that, according to *Fortune,* "would make a robber baron envious." A squeaky-voiced twenty-year-old coining the motto "A computer on every desk and in every home, running Microsoft software" is precocious and clever. A billionaire who makes that same claim smacks of Manifest Destiny–like, monopolistic aspirations. He still reigned as a media darling, but the higher his profile, the more stories of his exceeding ambition crept into otherwise glowing profiles. And if his press clippings offered only hints of a backlash, the real world smacked of it. So widespread was the spreading animosity leveled at Microsoft that at a charity chili cook-off held at the 1987 COMDEX, the Microsoft team's beans were booed.

CHAPTER 04

BILL GATES FOR DUMMIES

THE TROUBLE with magazine-cover fame is that stories from people you'd rather forget are there in black and white for everyone to read. Like the college roommate from freshman year, who recalled Gates as decent enough but weird, a guy who'd sleep on a bare mattress with an electric blanket pulled over his head. And always going on about how one of his relatives used to hang out with some former governor.

You're prey for every reporter seeking a notch on his belt. There was the girl his parents fixed him up with when he was home from Harvard on a break. This was a guy, she told a pair of reporters from the *Seattle Post-Intelligencer*, who *obviously* had little in the way of experience with girls. First question out of Gates's mouth: What was your score on the SAT? The second thing was the size of *his* score. He registered a 790 on the math portion of the test but took it again because he had walked away knowing he had made a dumb mistake. Naturally, he scored a perfect 800 the second time.

Even your best friend, the intimate whom you asked to be the best man at your wedding, the man you made a billionaire, dishes a bit of good-natured dirt when a reporter from *People* phones, telling the world about this "crazy" guy everyone was buzzing about during his freshman year. "Went home for Christmas vacation with the door to his room open, the lights on, money on the desk, the windows open, and it was raining," Ballmer says. The two were the Mutt and Jeff of their dorm, Ballmer the outgoing joiner who seemed to know everyone and Gates the shy loner with few friends. No wonder: He'd sit half asleep in math class, his chin on a fist, looking bored unless he saw that the pro-

58

fessor had made a mistake. Then he'd take great joy in explaining the error. Even Gates confessed, "I was a little bit insufferable."

In college Gates had Ballmer, the computer center, and his all-night poker games, which were strictly off-limits to the scholarship kids if for no other reason than the stakes. Losses in the $1,000 to $2,000 range weren't unheard of. The game was usually High-Low, a bluffer's game. Gates's nickname in his family is "Trey," a gambler's term, but his interest in poker exceeded his abilities. At first he was just another blue blood playing in the big game: "the gravy train," one fellow player dubbed him because of his propensity to keep throwing chips after lost-cause hands. But Gates, whom Harvard roommate Andy Braiterman described as "monomaniacal" (monomania, according to *Merriam-Webster's Tenth New Collegiate Dictionary*, being "mental illness esp. when limited in expression to one idea or area of thought"), seemed as obsessed with living up to his riverboat nickname as he was with conquering the DEC PDP-10 that resided in the Aiken Computation Lab. Eventually, Gates improved his game so that he was one of the regular winners rather than a perennial loser.

"Perhaps it's silly to compare poker and Microsoft," Braiterman told the authors of *Hard Drive*, "but in each case, Bill was sort of deciding where he was going to put his energy and to hell with what anyone else thought." Braiterman may feel foolish about drawing an analogy between poker and Microsoft, but it goes a long way in explaining what drives Gates, despite his unfathomable wealth. He's still playing an all-night poker game, except he has advanced to the big boys' tournament on Wall Street.

WILLIAM HENRY GATES III was the only son born into a prominent Seattle family. His great-grandfather had founded Seattle's National City Bank. Supposedly he had been good friends with William Jennings Bryan and General John Pershing, the commander of the U.S. armed forces during World War I. Governor Robert Evans was a family friend, as was Brock Adams, who as a U.S. congressman hired the sixteen-year-old Gates to be a summer page in the Capitol. His mother, while she was alive, was the sort the local papers called a "socialite" (on the national board of the United Way, a university regent, the director of a prominent West Coast bank), his father a "pillar of the community." William H. Gates II was a past president of the state bar and a senior partner in one of those blue-chip law firms that dirties its hands with defense work only when a member of the club scuffs his white shoes. His mother was a good friend of Katharine Graham, which is how Gates III met the man he would eventually surpass as the country's richest American, Warren Buffett. The Gateses were loyal Republicans living in Seattle's best neighborhood, WASPs committed to the Protestant work ethic and a sense of noblesse oblige.

There were laps in the country club pool, tennis lessons with the court pro, hamburgers served on toast on the veranda. Legend had Gates reading the encyclopedia from A to Z when his age was still in the single digits. "Even back . . . when he was nine or ten years old, he talked like an adult and could express himself in ways none of us understood," a kid who went to sleepaway camp with Gates told one biographer. When he was eleven, he supposedly memorized the unwieldy and difficult "Sermon on the Mount." Maybe he recited the entire twenty-minute passage from the Book of Matthew, maybe he didn't, but there's no doubting that the family pastor (at a church that of course dated back to the nineteenth century) was embellishing more than a bit when he said that never in all his days had he heard so flawless and impassioned a reading from so young a lad.

That same year, Gates's parents sent him to see a psychiatrist. He was so small and shy, his father said, so fragile and in need of protection. "He's so different from the other sixth-graders," his mother would sigh. He'd sit in the back of the car, there but not there, as if a galaxy away. Mary Gates would ask her son, "What are you doing?," and he'd answer, peevishly, "I'm thinking, Mother."

"You're going to lose," the psychiatrist told his parents. "You had better adjust, because there's no use trying to beat him." * The Gateses had planned to send all three of their kids to public schools, but they made an exception for their difficult middle child. He started the seventh grade at the Lakeside Preparatory School, an all-boy prep school and the best in the region.

Open any Lakeside yearbook from 1967 through 1972, pick a random name, and it's a safe bet that person remembers this obnoxiously bright kid who practically lived in the school's computer room. "Intimidat-

---

* "He said some profound things that got me thinking a little differently," Gates would tell *Playboy* when he was the featured interviewee. "He was a cool guy. My mind was focused appropriately."

ingly smart," according to one kid; a kid lacking in social graces who snickered every time a classmate offered an obviously wrong answer, according to another. The word "arrogant" seemed to come up more than any other. Fearing what it meant that his brain seemed forever plugged into the computer, his parents ordered him off it at age fourteen, forcing him to take a nine-month hiatus. He turned to biographies—of Napoleon, FDR, and other larger-than-life historic figures—and read his father's *Business Week* the way other kids read *Playboys* pilfered from the old man. He asked his friend Paul Allen to imagine how enormous a company would have to grow to earn the top spot on the Fortune 500 list. "Can you imagine what a company that size does?" he asked Allen.

Gates was probably not the most able kid spending his afternoons at the Lakeside computer center, but he was undoubtedly the most ambitious. Virtually all the early profiles of Gates and most of the later ones would miss this point. It was his entrepreneurial spirit that distinguished him from the other misfits for whom the computer room became a refuge, not his skill punching out code. The other kids seemed content to teach the machine to play tic-tac-toe; it was Gates who said, "Let's call the real world and try to sell something." Between the eighth and eleventh grades, he started no fewer than three businesses. "We want to expand our workforce," began a Gates flyer seeking other students willing to do punch card work for $5 an hour. His partner in two of those three enterprises was Microsoft cofounder Paul Allen. "I'm easier to get along with if I'm in charge," a young Bill Gates famously told his older and larger friend.

The archetypal image of Gates from profiles appearing throughout the 1980s sets him in front of a computer, glasses clouded by greasy fingerprints and wearing a ketchup-stained T-shirt dusted with dandruff, coding from the moment he sank into his chair until he drove home in a daze well past dark. Yet this image said more about the press and about Microsoft's abilities at playing the PR game than about Gates. He hadn't done much if any coding since the earliest days of the company—and some of that hadn't been particularly good. A longtime Microsoft programmer named Marlin Eller told of the time he had asked Gates which "jerk" had written the "brain-dead piece of shit" the rest of his group was wrestling with—only to have his immediate supervisor tell him a few hours later, an Excedrin headache number 98 expression on his face, "*Bill* was the *jerk* who wrote this *brain-dead* piece of *shit.*" The last chunk of code Gates wrote was in 1982 or 1983, when he cranked out a text editor for the Radio Shack portable—the kind of project you assign the third or fourth most talented person on your team. His prowess was as a businessman, not a technologist, yet in 1990 *People* was still describing him as a "brilliant programmer" known for "writing truly elegant, bug-free computer programs," and to *U.S. News & World Report* in 1993 he was still a "mercurial computer hacker."

WITH BILL, it's never been about the money. That's what Gates defenders have been saying since the first articles reporting his net worth. "What Bill cares about is writing great software," say the Microsoft PR people. "For Bill it's all about winning; the money's incidental," say those claiming to know Gates best.

Never mind the childhood friends who recalled their classmate talking about earning his first million before his twenty-fifth birthday or the fact that he dropped out of Harvard fearing that a prime money-making opportunity was slipping away. Never mind the time he was flying home with an underling and rattled off the ownership percentages—down to the decimal point—of every software entrepreneur who might be considered his rival (and then boyishly noted that none owned a larger percentage than he did). No, his motives were pure: he was the accidental billionaire, though one who happened to have a billionaire's tastes.

Among the toys Gates bought himself after Microsoft went public were a speedboat and a sports car priced at more than $350,000. He also built for his family, as a nod to fond childhood memories, a four-house vacation compound north and west of Seattle, on Hood Canal, where Gates, his parents, and his siblings had spent idyllic summer days when he was a boy. It would be a few years before he'd unveil his plans to build a house that initially was supposed to cost $12 million but ended up costing at least $50 million and by some accounts as much as $100 million, but that's because he already had a house befitting a millionaire. He had been talking about moving into a Ramada Inn a short walk from Microsoft until his mother talked him out of it. So instead this twenty-seven-year-old bachelor who practically lived at the office bought, for $900,000, an eleven-room lakeside house with an indoor swimming pool, a boathouse, and a killer view of Mount Rainier. Years would pass before he got around to filling the living room with furniture.

He'd be accused of predatory pricing and a partnering style that one foe described as a "praying mantis business model": first Microsoft had sex with you, then it ate you. His rapaciousness would raise questions about fair play in the computer industry—but to me Gates's single most shameless act occurred while he was still at Harvard and involved his longtime friend and partner, Paul Allen.

Allen is third on the Forbes 400 list of the country's richest people, behind only Gates and Warren Buffett. He bought most of an island on Lake Washington to build an estate that includes a fully equipped health club, a regulation-size indoor basketball court, authentic Roman statues, and paintings by master French Impressionists. This rock-and-roll fanatic didn't just dream of a museum honoring Seattle native Jimi Hendrix, he built one. He owns the Seattle Seahawks football team and the Portland Trailblazers basketball team, as well as a Boeing 757. But it's like the ridiculously inflated salaries Allen must pay the young stars of his basketball team: all sense of proportion and reality have gone out the window. Sure, it's hard to feel much sympathy for a man worth as many billions as Allen. But the question remains: Why would Gates end up owning nearly twice as many Microsoft shares as Allen?

Allen was always the more personable one. He was a nerd, naturally; as a high schooler he carried a briefcase to and from his classes. But he was always down to earth and better liked than Gates. His parents were both librarians, and he lacked Gates's arrogance. It was Allen who had the moxie (and also the facial hair) to gain entry to the computer center across from the UW campus, and it was Allen who brought Gates along once he had scoped out the scene. A few years later, it was Allen who spotted the Altair on the cover of *Popular Electronics,* and it was Allen who, eight weeks later, demonstrated BASIC in Albuquerque. Gates deserved more of the credit for the initial design of BASIC, but Allen deserved more credit for the overall product. He added a host of new features to this skeletal product created in eight weeks and patched most of the bugs.

Yet Gates used those months Allen spent perfecting BASIC working against his friend. Allen had gambled his future when he dropped out of Washington State to move to the Boston area. But while he worked on BASIC he was earning a salary working for Ed Roberts. Gates, in contrast, had hedged his bets, remaining at Harvard for nearly two more years. But he had also done some work on BASIC. Where was his compensation? Always playing the angles, even when dealing with a childhood friend, he demanded a 60 percent cut of the company, and the mild-mannered Allen obliged.

Consider two of the friends who cofounded Sun Microsystems. Sun was nothing without Andy Bechtolsheim, the Stanford Ph.D. student who had invented the SUN (Stanford University Network) workstation, so the goose who laid the golden eggs was in for the biggest cut. But the dilemma confronting Vinod Khosla, the Stanford MBA who had roped the highly coveted Bechtolsheim in, was the deal he'd propose to Scott McNealy, a friend from business school. Khosla had already cofounded a successful start-up, and there was no question that he would be running Sun. He sought to sign up McNealy because McNealy had experience running an assembly-line plant. If you were looking to give McNealy an official title, you would call him chief operating officer. The protocol would be to grant McNealy something like a 10 percent share, but McNealy was a friend, and he was part of the founding team. So Khosla split his piece of the company 50–50 with McNealy.

When Gates left Harvard, he pushed for a second change in the partnership formula. He proposed a 64–36 split because, after all, he was risking a great deal by leaving Harvard—Harvard, mind you, not Washington State. And again his friend demurred rather than fight. Allen made the key contact when Microsoft was desperate to find a workable operating system it could tailor to the IBM-PC. Until he got sick with Hodgkin's disease, he ran the software development side of the company while Gates flew around the country signing up partners. Yet by early 1999, Allen's months as vice president of software for Ed Roberts would end up costing him roughly $15 billion.*

GATES WOULD EAT CHEESEBURGERS for lunch and cheeseburgers for dinner; sometimes, to mix things up, he would have a pizza or a hot dog. He was prone to temper tantrums, and when he was excited, his

---

* Gates, in an e-mail message addressed to me, was anything but defensive about his deal with Allen. He acknowledged demanding a 60 percent cut of the company because Allen was receiving a salary from Ed Roberts, yet then claimed it wasn't about the money ("Paul and I started Microsoft because of the vision we had and not because we ever thought it would become such a business success"). He acknowledged, too, the 64–36 split, but said the two reverted back to 60–40 several years before taking the company public. "It has been very important to me to emphasize how much the original vision was something we shared," he wrote in that same message, perhaps not realizing that a 60–40 split emphasized precisely the reverse.

voice would rise an octave and squeak. He would be talking with someone while walking the halls, and spontaneously he'd jump straight up, reaching for the acoustical tiles. Just as a lot of young jazz players got hooked on heroin because the great Bird used the stuff, a lot of Microsoft's earliest employees bought trampolines because jumping up and down in place, Gates once said, helped him think. That was Gates's contradiction: strip away the voice and the junior executive look, and he sounded like a grizzled mogul talking business, yet he fidgeted, twitched, and bounced like a teenager.

"Bill," said a sales rep whose tenure at the company began in 1982, "has the intellect of an octogenarian and the hormones of a teenager."

He bought cars without radios because radios are a distraction. For the same reason, he didn't own a TV until the last few years. Once, commiserating on the unwanted attention of strangers, a Microsoft manager named Bob Kruger complained about all the joking references to his brother Freddie. And Gates asked, "Who's Freddie Kruger?" Or there'd be a reference to Geraldo, and somebody would have to explain who Geraldo Rivera was. Gates once calculated that in his first six years at Microsoft, he averaged just two vacation days per year. Yet which is the more telling fact: that he took so little time off despite the grueling hours he worked or that he calculated the average and then boasted about it like a college sophomore one-upping his classmates in how little sleep he had had that week? Not surprisingly, his girlfriends were invariably industry-grown: a DEC saleswoman, a fellow software executive, a Microsoft product manager.

A lefty, he would practice writing with his right hand during meetings and other times when he wasn't employing what he calls "mind cycles." A reporter from *People* noticed a map of Africa tacked to a wall in his garage—placed so that his eyes would sweep over it as he got into and out of his car. "Your mind has a lot of bandwidth that's very unused," Gates explained. He is Mr. Spock in possession of human emotions but rigorously seeking the efficiency of a binary world. He can even *sound* like a computer, like the time he told *Time,* "Just in terms of allocation of time resources, religion is not very efficient." Reportedly he hated sunny days because it meant his less dedicated employees would be distracted by wanderlust.

Once he destroyed a $40,000 Mercedes because he neglected to replenish the engine oil. At least one biography casts him as being so consumed by work that his mother not only picked out a house for him to buy (less than a mile from the family home), she moved his belongings in and set things up while he was away in Japan. Though he lived just twenty minutes away, his mother supposedly sent him letters and cards that he kept stacked on a corner of his desk. She was constantly after him to remember to shampoo his hair and would call executives at the company to fret about her Bill: Was he taking care of himself? There were even tales that she picked out her son's clothes for him, helping him with color coordination by pinning together matching outfits—a rumor Gates confirmed in his interview with *Playboy*. You can hear the plea in his voice, the misunderstood boy suddenly sounding like a so-prano. "I'm bad at matching," he said.

He hired administrative assistants who were as much surrogate mothers as executive assistants. "I ran his life," a woman named Estelle Mathers told the authors of *Gates*. If he had an early-morning meeting on his calendar, Mathers would call him at home to make sure he was awake. She'd drive him to the airport and suggest specific outfits for a given setting. Before a big meeting or a photo shoot, she'd gently re-mind him to comb his hair. But her greatest skill was reading Gates's moods. "If you tended to interrupt him at a bad time, you could get hurt," she explained.

He possessed a phenomenal memory that allowed him to rattle off the specs of dozens of non-Microsoft products, yet he was always leav-ing things in hotel rooms: a key contract, thousands of dollars' worth of traveler's checks, a closet full of suits. So often did he forget his wallet that his assistants were practically on a first-name basis with the cus-tomer service reps at his credit card companies. On the money front, he hadn't changed much from the kid Ballmer had heard about who, freshman year, had left for Christmas break with his door open and a mess of money on his desk. Back when a few hundred dollars still actu-ally meant something to Gates, he'd leave piles of big bills lying on his work desk or send off suits to the dry cleaners with wads of bills stuffed in the pockets. He'd show up late for a date and then discover that he had no cash and he had left his credit cards on his dresser. So his com-panion, rather than the young tycoon who in 1986 took up permanent residence on the Forbes 400 list, would have to pick up the tab.

He flies coach, or at least he did until recently, because first class was something to which one grew too easily accustomed. For the same rea-son, he didn't like limousines. His office was small and modestly ap-pointed. The decorations on the wall included a poster-sized blowup of an Intel microprocessor and pictures of da Vinci, Albert Einstein, and Henry Ford. For the longest time he wouldn't accept a reserved parking spot. When he finally gave in, in the early 1990s, the official story, which made no sense, was that he relented only because too many people were harassing him for money between his car and his office. But by then Microsoft occupied its own sprawling campus, so those doing the asking would have been employees or outsiders risking security as they lurked conspicuously in the parking lot. The truth was (at least as one former employee tells it) that Microsoft PR was worried that Gates worked so late each night and arrived so late in the morning that he would start habitually parking in a handicapped parking spot rather than waste precious time. He had troubles enough without *that* staining his image.

THE ANNALS OF GAMBLING are replete with tales of desperate souls down to their last few dollars who end up walking out of a casino with pockets bulging with hundred-dollar bills. The first owner of the Pittsburgh Steelers football team, Art Rooney, once had more lint than dollar bills in his pockets, but legend has it that he parlayed a lucky streak at the racetrack into a multimillion-dollar business empire. Similarly, Wall Street can boast of any number of men of modest means who amassed vast holdings because of one great pick. Yet no bank breaker at Monte Carlo or king of Wall Street can match Bill Gates, who made the all-time greatest wager in the history of gambling.

Read the investment advisers who write for the likes of *Money,* and before too long you'll learn that investing more than one quarter of your holdings in a single stock is foolish. In Microsoft's first two years as a publicly traded company, Gates wasn't permitted to sell any shares. He was already worth $1 billion when the Security and Exchange Commission's holding period expired, but even then he sold only small lots of stock. Even as his net worth climbed—to $2.5 billion in 1990, to $6.3 billion in 1992, to $9.4 billion in 1994—he let the vast towers of chips ride. He'd occasionally buy non-Microsoft stock, but mainly he seemed to invest in other high-tech companies, such as Apple—hardly what an investment adviser would consider diversification. But had he proceeded along a more sensible path, on February 6, 1998, the day Bill Gates's Microsoft stake crossed $50 billion, he'd have been worth less than $20 billion, even assuming he had invested his remaining money in an attractive basket of blue-chip stocks. Add up the earnings of any big-time Las Vegas casino over the last ten years and then multiply that number by ten—and it still doesn't come close to matching Gates's winnings on the Wall Street crap table. The only man who might give Gates's betting record a run for its money is Warren Buffett. But worth a measly $18 billion, Buffett is a piker by comparison.

Yet the funny thing about this man is that he is a world-class worrier. One of the better-traveled parts of the Gates legend is how he can get onto a plane, pull a blanket over his head, and zonk out for the entire flight, but that's because he's an insomniac who—so his first girlfriend would tell the world—spends his nights tossing and turning in bed, fretting about every deal he has in a hopper, imagining every possible bad turn. "He could sleep instantly," she said in one interview. "He'd crawl under a desk. He'd crawl under chairs at the airport. People would lose him." *

The world around him celebrated his triumphs, but he seemed to live in the realm of potential failure. He has mellowed out some, but he has always worn his anxieties like a bad habit. His family traces his nervous rocking to the cradle and rocking horse that seemed the only means for Bill Gates the toddler to soothe himself. Maybe the best scene in the book *Gates* recounts the twenty-four hours leading up to his original deal with IBM. Surrounded by his top lieutenants, Gates spent much of the time lying on the floor ("I like to do that to brainstorm"), writhing and twitching and, between moans, imagining every bad thing that might possibly grow from this one decision. He was always the kid who complained the loudest after every test, even though he always earned an A.

Shortly after Microsoft went public, he walked around convinced the sky was falling, and in a panic he advised his father to sell every share he owned. The company, he told him, was so absurdly overpriced that disaster was just around the corner. Had his father listened, he would have lost a few million in profit for every $10,000 in stock he sold. "There were certainly lots of occasions when his attitude was 'Everything is going to hell in a handbasket,' " his father, with a chuckle, told *The Wall*

---

* She and Gates started going out after she met him at a party and demanded to know why Microsoft was avoiding a key market. His courtship with his second longtime girlfriend, a software entrepreneur named Ann Winblad, began when she disparaged Gates's best friend, Steve Ballmer, as maybe the biggest jerk she had ever met. Confrontation, it seems, was one of Gates's turn-ons.

Street Journal in 1990. His foes, of course, didn't think it was funny, this woe-is-me state of mind that always had Gates, no matter how rich and powerful he became, convinced he was the underdog.

Microsoft employees held group fretting sessions they called product review meetings, where top executives rocked as Gates rocked, falling over one another to spell out all that was wrong with a group's product plans. Describing this game of one-upmanship in the late 1980s, Ballmer made it sound like a contest to see who could draw first blood: "Everybody wants to be smart like Bill and show off. They want to say, 'Aha! I got a great idea, and you didn't think of it, or you didn't think [something] through.'" Once, a group was two minutes into a presentation when Gates abruptly stood up, looked around the room, and zeroed in on a new product manager: "Where the fuck did we hire you from?" It was an everyday part of life at Microsoft, motivation through fear-based bullying.

And of course Gates plays the Grand Inquisitor, so thorough in his prowl for mistakes and half-assed thinking he even checks the math on handouts. A group spends weeks working around the clock preparing for one of these meetings, reviving themselves when energies flag with reminders that they're meeting with Bill. With Bill! Then, no sooner are they ten minutes into their presentation than they hear "That's the stupidest thing I've ever heard." Or if they complain that a feature he wants would set them weeks behind, another favorite Bill-ism, sarcastic, short, dismissive: "You want me to do it for you over the weekend?"

He's a baseball manager long past his prime telling a young slugger that if he doesn't think he can hit the other team's flamethrower, maybe he'll put himself on the active roster to show him how it's done. Yet his supplicants seem to revel in the attention. Sure it stings, but they tell one another that Bill wouldn't challenge them like that if he didn't respect them. This mentality was spoofed hilariously in the book *microserfs*, by Douglas Coupland, a fictionalized account of the life of a small group of Microsoft employees for whom life is nothing but work on the plantation. The book opens with a "wicked flame-mail" Gates sends critiquing a block of code written by one of the serfs. "The episode was tinged with glamour and we were somewhat jealous," wrote the narrator. "Nobody on our floor had ever been flamed by Bill personally."

"Softies loved to talk about how their leader danced until the wee hours of the night," the authors of *Gates* wrote. "At company meetings, people would keep count of how many times he pushed his glasses back on his nose." On Microsoft's campus is a man-made pond everyone calls "Lake Bill." Gates's word for an undisciplined thinker is "random," so that became the ultimate put-down on campus: so-and-so's problem is that he's so random. Or "brain-damaged," another Bill-ism. When you want to get into more detail, you "drill down." When you want to reach for the ultimate compliment, you do as Bill does, using the word "super" as an all-purpose superlative—somebody is superintelligent or a product is superneat or supercool. In 1990, *Fortune* dubbed it the "Cult of Bill" (and then contributed to the same by presenting His Billness's management principles as if they were the Ten Commandments). "His adolescent-sounding techie slang creeps into nearly every conversation on the wooded Microsoft campus near Seattle," *Fortune*'s Brent Schlender wrote. "A few younger managers carry the mimicry almost to the point of caricature: When they talk, they give their vowels the same singing emphases their thirty-four-year-old chairman does." In the old days, it was "Uncle Bill," or "Mr. Bill" in homage to *Saturday Night Live,* but nowadays it's just plain Bill.

At Microsoft, the preferred hire is a young Einstein right out of a Stanford or an MIT. "Bill clones," they call these young brains, who tend to be intense, intelligent, driven, and arrogant. A friend of Mitch Kertzman, fresh from Harvard Business School, applied for a job at Microsoft, but then, just before flying out for the interview, he was offered his dream job. He had people he wanted to see in Seattle, so he went anyway, going through Microsoft's grueling serial interview process with a devil-may-care attitude. Each interviewer writes his or her impressions and sends them to the others, so that an e-mail of instantaneous feedback follows an interviewee all day. "You've made a very consistent impression with everybody," his main escort told him after his last interview. "You come across as arrogant and a know-it-all." He might have chuckled to himself about his worst set of interviews ever, but then his escort told him, "We like that," and offered him the job.

"It's eerie," said Fred Moody, who, as a staffer for the *Seattle Weekly,* has been writing about Gates and Microsoft since the 1980s. He spent several days at Microsoft when he profiled Gates for *The New York Times Magazine* ("Mr. Software"), and then spent several days a week there while working on his book *I Sing the Body Electronic.* "Gates is a presence in every meeting I've ever sat in on Microsoft's campus," Moody says. "It's like he's this ghost in the room with us. People are always talking about him or making reference to him or imagining his reaction to their idea. They're trying to please him even when he's not there." During a long leave of absence, one longtime manager realized he had enough money to never have to work another day in his life, but he returned to work because, as he said, "Microsoft's job is not finished." What young general retires from the Roman army when he still has the strength and there are still more lands to conquer in the emperor's name? "FYIFV," read a popular button seen around Microsoft for a time: Fuck You, I'm Fully Vested. Except the fully vested still came to work every day, and most still worked late into the evenings and on the weekends.

On campus, people use a favorable conversation with Gates as a cardinal might use the word of the pope. "If Bill likes your product plan, you get to *whack* other people who have been opposed to you," one middle manager explained. He fell into a sarcastic tone: " 'Well, Bill already approved this.' Or it's 'Sure, if you think that's a good idea, but Bill's already signed off on this.' " There's no more valuable ducat on campus than the Word of Bill. "Bill is a moral force," Coupland wrote in *microserfs*, "a spectral force, a force that shapes, a force that molds. A force with thick, thick glasses."

At Microsoft, you interview people while escorted by a PR rep, but I managed to slip my leash and do a few interviews on my own. One was with a man whose praise for Gates was so effusive I imagined a poster of the chairman hanging above his bed. He drives a Lexus, which is not uncommon at Microsoft. Everyone knows that Gates drives a Lexus, so the Lexus is the ultimate status car on campus (or a Porsche—Gates's previous favorite and supposedly still his sentimental one). The Lexus dealership in humdrum Bellevue, Washington, the next town over, is the "largest-volume Lexus dealership in the Northwest." This man's Lexus is blue, just like Gates's. And the frame around his license plate reads, "I'd rather be running Microsoft software."

He asked me: You know how people are always saying Bill is the smartest person they ever met? Sure. It's a staple of the many feature articles that have been written about Gates. He then asked: You know how people are always comparing Bill to Thomas Edison? It's a comment you occasionally read or hear; in, for instance, the opening of a piece in *U.S. News & World Report*. Well, he said, they don't go far enough! He was convinced you have to travel back to da Vinci to find a comparable mind.

His da Vinci comment was why he wanted to talk off the record.

("People might think I'm weird or something about the guy.") "I think Bill sees it," he said. "I mean, that's not something you can come out and say—'I look at da Vinci and see a lot of myself'—but he knows." He offers as proof Gates's comment in a magazine interview that when he first read about da Vinci in his twenties, he was blown away. Further proof is the picture of da Vinci Gates has hanging in his office and his purchase of the Leicester Codex (also known as the Hammer Codex), one of da Vinci's sketch pads, for $31 million.

"I'm always amazed by Bill," Microsoft's Bob Kruger says. Kruger, too, drives a blue Lexus; he, too, has an "I'd rather be running Microsoft software" license plate frame. "I'm always amazed at the range of things he can deal with. The breadth of things. The scope and depth. And how quickly he can learn about something, get in, and respond intelligently. I'm also amazed at his ability to drill down." More often than not, Gates's loyal charges talk about him as if he genuinely processed information in bits of zeros and ones. Other underlings make him out to be a central processing unit with "unlimited bandwidth," bestowed with a remarkable ability to "parallel-process."

Patrick Naughton, featured a couple of years back in *The New York Times Magazine* as representative of the best programmers of his generation, was the president of a Paul Allen–funded, Bellevue-based company called Starwave until it was bought by Disney in 1998. He doesn't claim to know Gates well ("It's not like we've gone golfing or anything"), but they've mixed it up at least a half-dozen times at industry events. One time they had an argument over Microsoft's e-mail protocols in a San Francisco hotel bar. "I'm being all civil, saying the e-mail protocols are giving us all fits. Bill, if there's one thing you have to fix, it's e-mail," Naughton says. "But he immediately starts in about how stupid I must be to hold this opinion. So I started giving it back to him. Meanwhile, there's this gallery of *stunned* Microsoft people, because I was *daring* to argue with Bill. He was in rare form, doing his whole physical thing. Leaning forward in his chair, doing the rocking thing, twisting and twitching, which just drives me crazy. He's getting all agitated, he's yelling at me and telling me how I'm wrong and I don't know what I'm talking about. But I kept grinding on him. And he goes, 'Okay, okay, I take that back, we fucked up on e-mail. I take that back. I fucked up on e-mail. I fucked up. It's my fault. You're right. I fucked up.' "

That Gates would cave like that impressed Naughton, but with time it would also strike him as a strange trait shared by more than a few people at Microsoft. He has plenty of friends there, but he seems to be only half joking when he describes many of them as "clones" grown in a petri dish in a "secret room on Microsoft's campus where they've popped out hundreds, if not thousands, of these little prototypical Bills.

"They're all super type A," he continues. "They're really, really smart. They're not programmers, but they understand a fairly broad spectrum of technology to a fairly deep level. And these guys talk a mile a minute. If you disagree with them, the first thing they do is insult you, tell you why you're wrong. Tell you why you're stupid. Then they talk faster and faster. I mean, they're exact clones of the Bill Gates interpersonal style."

CHAPTER 05

THE BIG ONE

BILL GATES POUNDS ON THE TABLE. You pound back. Engaged, he digs his elbows into his thighs and starts rocking furiously. Maybe it's a subconscious hero worship thing, maybe it's like when one person yawns, other people in the room yawn, too. But now you're rocking, too. "That's the stupidest goddamn thing I've ever heard!" he yells. You yell back, "You don't even understand what I'm fucking saying!" And that's before things start getting out of hand. You had been sitting in the corner of his office, Gates (as always) on his couch, you in a chair, except that now Gates is pacing, so naturally you're pacing, too. For the moment you're prizefighters measuring each other in the ring. Gates abruptly stops and stares out a window—but then the spittle spews, his face turns seven shades of red, and his hands fly into the air like bottle rockets set off into the sky.

Later, looking back on this strange ritual dance that seems an everyday part of life in the CEO's office, Jon Lazarus swells with pride. Inside Microsoft, such moments are worn like a dueling scar on the cheek of an eighteenth-century Prussian. And Lazarus is among the Softies Gates regards so highly (or at least did for a time) that their relationship might best be described as a series of screaming matches.

Since leaving Microsoft in 1996 after ten years with the company, Lazarus has worked out of a posh suite of offices on Mercer Island, a hilly oasis sometimes nicknamed "Microsoft Island" because it is home to so many of the company's multimillionaires, Lazarus included. There, this man, who used to run the Windows marketing group, sells advice to software start-ups anxious for a bit of Microsoft magic to rub off on them. Lazarus's office is a shrine to his Microsoft years. Hanging on one wall is a "Bill Gates Unplugged" poster from 1994, so blatant a rip-off of the poster advertising the Grammy Award–winning album *Eric Clapton/Unplugged* (Gates is even cradling his keyboard as if it were a guitar) that Microsoft received a "cease-and-desist" letter from Clapton's music producer. "We told them to fuck off," Lazarus said with a laugh. Lined up on a bookshelf are keepsakes of the project that probably marked the beginning of the end for Lazarus, copies of Gates's *The Road Ahead* translated into a half-dozen languages. The book was a best-seller but an enormous time drain and also a source of great embarrassment for Gates, who was technically its primary author, because the book, though published in 1995, completely failed to anticipate the Internet.

The ostensible purpose of our two-hour meeting was to talk about the companies, led by Sun, Netscape, and Oracle, that were aligned against Microsoft, but Lazarus was having none of it. "Mere pipsqueaks" he said of the current crop, "slight blips on the screen." Instead, he wanted to talk about the company that truly offended him for its Captain Ahab–ness, IBM. The fight between Microsoft and IBM over the successor operating system to DOS began shortly after Microsoft went public in 1986 and ended in the early 1990s, by which time IBM had flushed down the drain more money and market share than a Netscape might ever accumulate.

"The battle with IBM was like World War II in terms of long-term significance and casualties," Lazarus said. "All this other stuff that's come after, the fighting with Sun and Netscape and everything else, that's been like the Korean War, or, in the worst scenario from Microsoft's perspective, it's like their Vietnam, a fight that will drag on for too long. But it's still nothing compared to the fight with IBM. The fight with IBM, that was the big one."

IF IBM WERE A CITY, it would, in the second half of the 1980s, have had a population that hovered somewhere around 400,000. Back then at least, before disaster struck, IBM had more employees than Oakland, Tallahassee, or Des Moines had people. By comparison, Microsoft, in 1989, had 4,000 employees, or one employee for every hundred people working for Big Blue.

They were a strange breed, these inhabitants of the city-state of IBM in Armonk, New York. They happily conformed to the company's strict dress code and drove sensible cars. The community rebels were those who occasionally wore blue dress shirts, rather than starched white, with their gray flannel suits and wing tips. At IBM gatherings, employees would sing lustily from the company songbook, choosing from dozens of ditties set to familiar tunes.* The benevolent dictators of IBM ran the company like a welfare state. Each December, every child of an IBM employee received a perfectly wrapped, age-appropriate Christmas gift. Its Parks and Recreation Department was the envy of working stiffs the world over: the company had purchased three nearby country clubs and then opened them to its employees and their families. About the only thing the city-state of IBM lacked was an army. Even its labyrinth of standing committees served as a kind of legislative branch, offsetting the power of the company's chief executive officer.

Bill Gates's ambassador to the people of IBM was Steve Ballmer, Microsoft's undisputed number two after Allen left the company. Ballmer was a man who unquestionably had his sire's ear. Yet the officially designated diplomat to IBM was anything but diplomatic, and he managed to step on toes even as he was attempting to slap people good-naturedly on the back. He'd arrive at a meeting in IBM's Armonk headquarters accompanied by a single underling and then find himself sitting at a table with twenty dark-suited IBMers. At Microsoft, things were accomplished by getting a few smart people into a room and working until the problem was solved. At IBM, every branch of the bureaucracy had to be represented. "What are all these people *doing* here?" Ballmer would boom in a voice so loud and distracting that all other conversations ceased. Sometimes he couldn't help himself; he'd start pointing to people he didn't recognize and ask, "Why are you here? What do you do 'round here?"

There was at IBM a religious-like attachment to KLOCs (pronounced "K-locks"), an expression denoting one thousand lines of code. The IBM Way was to measure, whether in contracts or performance reviews, by the KLOC, a logical idea (like a magazine paying by the word) but a method sure to encourage flabby writing (like a magazine paying by the word). So Ballmer would mimic his host's preoccupation with KLOCs, putting on a pretend macho voice like Tim Allen in the middle of one of his routines: "This baby ought to be a 100 KLOC'er"—here he would hitch up his pants—"or a 250 KLOC'er." Then he'd laugh uproariously.

---

* Like this one sung to "Jingle Bells": "I-B-M, Happy Men, smiling all the way, Oh what fun it is to sell our products night and day."

IBM never knew what to make of Ballmer, whom *Forbes* once described as the "General Patton of software." Those accustomed to his banter would laugh along, but others brooded about this vulgar churl invited into their midst. Half the group seemed to find his energy and unguarded wit intoxicatingly liberating. The others, though, wished they could induce him to drink from a cup of hemlock.

Yet the surface differences between IBM and Microsoft were nothing compared to the differences in the self-interests of the two companies. Shortly into the life of the IBM-PC, Bill Gates was hoping his ostensible partner would fall flat on its face. The original deal between IBM and Microsoft has been likened to the sale of Manhattan Island for $24 in trinkets and beads, but that's based on the mistaken belief that IBM agreed to pay Microsoft a royalty for every copy of DOS it shipped. Actually, Microsoft could sell 10 or 10 million copies of DOS on the IBM-PC; it wouldn't make a difference to its bottom line, because IBM had paid Microsoft a flat fee of roughly $200,000. The only royalties Microsoft would earn on DOS were on machines sold by rival computer manufacturers, the so-called clone makers.

The original IBM-PC, which retailed for around $5,000, was really just a compilation of parts bought from third-party manufacturers such as Intel (the microprocessor chip) and Seagate (the disk drive), then assembled in IBM factories. Aside from the casing, about the only component actually engineered by IBM was something called the BIOS (Basic Input/Output System), an invisible but critical piece of technology that allows software (the operating system) to interact with the disk drive, the keyboard, and other pieces of hardware. That meant the only technical hurdle confronting any would-be manufacturer of IBM-compatible machines was the BIOS, which could in fact be "reverse-engineered," lawyerese for the legalized theft of intellectual property: a group of engineers was assigned the task of banging away on an IBM-PC until they'd figured out everything they could about the BIOS. Then another team, none of whom had ever used an IBM-PC, was assigned the task of writing a BIOS based on the spec list developed by the first group. With a workable BIOS, the clone manufacturers could cut deals with Intel and Microsoft, then, because they didn't have the overhead or markup of an IBM, sell their knockoff at a lower price.

Compaq Computer was the first company to strike it rich in the clone market. Created by three men from Texas Instruments meeting at a Houston-area House of Pies, Compaq sold $111 million in IBM-compatibles in its first full year. By 1985, Compaq sold $500 million worth of IBM clones; by 1990, its sales hit $3.6 billion. Dell Computer, AST, Leading Edge—these were among the computer manufacturers siphoning off billions that executives at IBM might rightfully have believed were theirs.

Microsoft collected somewhere between $20 and $50 for every copy of DOS shipped on an IBM-compatible.* The price depended on a variety of factors, including the volume a company sold and its endurance in dueling with the Microsoft bulldogs. IBM, of course, knew that Microsoft was growing rich off its misery and that Gates's people were aggressively pushing his operating system on every would-be IBM killer. And assuming they read *InfoWorld,* they knew Gates had been thinking several steps beyond IBM even before he inked the original deal. From the beginning, he told the trade publication, "We were hoping a lot of other people would come along and do compatible machines." But IBMers viewed themselves as a grand benefactor to whom a grateful Gates should be forever loyal. So when Big Blue's executives decided the solution to the clone problem was a new OS that would remain under IBM's control, they turned to Bill Gates to cowrite it. Mustering all its creative powers, IBM's marketeers named this second-generation operating system OS/2.

In retrospect, nothing about IBM's decision to rely on Microsoft again makes sense. Big Blue had a long list of gripes about Microsoft's missed deadlines and lax security; its sloppy execution was no doubt another point of contention. Company executives were still waiting impatiently for some much-needed fixes in DOS. And Microsoft was already hard at work on a second-generation operating system of its own, a new Apple-like, friendlier face for DOS called Windows. That was another sign that the two companies were working at cross-purposes. Yet in 1985, IBM executives again flew west to enlist Microsoft's help in

---

* The fact that IBM didn't balk when Gates proposed that Microsoft retain all rights to DOS is the reason so many Microsoft haters are inclined to see IBM as the Dr. Frankenstein who created a monster. In this view, Big Blue's negotiators were shockingly naive when dealing with young Bill Gates. At the time, however, IBM was embroiled in a twelve-year antitrust battle with the federal government and skittish (to say the least) about any deal that might lead to another lawsuit or more antitrust woes. Even if Gates hadn't raised the issue himself, IBM would probably have insisted that Microsoft retain ownership of DOS.

writing a successor to the deeply flawed DOS that had been quickly cobbled together and rushed to market.

Microsoft employees reacted with hosannas to the heavens—or, as Ballmer put it, "Hallelujah, right on!" Operating systems were now Microsoft's core business. If the industry's eight-hundred-pound gorilla was championing a new one, better Microsoft should own a piece of it than take on Big Blue with a Windows product that was at best only half baked. There was the magic of the IBM name and an incredible branding opportunity, which would aid its applications unit. Every time someone turned on an IBM or IBM-compatible, there would be the Microsoft name.

Yet it was as if the collective brain at IBM was not working. There were battalions of programmers in-house and so many billions of dollars in reserve the company could have bought the entire computer science departments of Carnegie Mellon, Caltech, and Purdue. IBM was the bully so oversized that the likes of Sperry Rand, Burroughs, and its other competitors in the mainframe world would be given the castrating sobriquet "the Seven Dwarfs." Yet IBM executives were so distracted by the clone makers and by Apple, which had released the Macintosh the previous year, that they didn't see the real threat. The problem wasn't the smart guys at Compaq or the marketing wizards running Apple; it was a greasy-haired kid who loved hanging out at the small museum at IBM headquarters, staring at the display cases. By the time they realized the wisest tactic was to pull the plug on the monster they had helped create, it would already be too late.

Publicly, Gates said all the right things about OS/2. He predicted that, by the end of 1989, OS/2 would "dominate" the PC world. Unveiled in early 1987, OS/2 was still a dud a year later, prompting Gates to admit that he had been overly optimistic. OS/2 would dominate, he said, but not until 1991. The press was skeptical, but Gates assured reporters that Microsoft had made a bottomless commitment to OS/2, a product he called "*the* key future technology." By 1988, his company had already spent $30 million developing and hawking OS/2, but he said he was prepared to spend millions more. "We're patient people," he told *Business Week*.

Yet the ever-cautious Gates, by that time a bi-billionaire, was hedging his bets. Microsoft had released a first version of Windows before its new deal with IBM, but the reviews had been so bad and the reception greeting its release so hostile that even the most vociferous of Microsoft haters might forgive IBM for not taking the bloated mess seriously. With great fanfare the company had announced Windows at COMDEX 1983, but it was not until mid-1985 that anyone could actually buy it in a store.* Not that anyone would want to, given the reviews. Back then, you didn't buy Windows so much as inherit it; it came preinstalled on new computers because Microsoft, which had a lot of sway as the purveyor of DOS, had convinced computer makers to bundle it at no extra cost. A second version would be released in 1987, but even then the reviewers would be only slightly less cruel. Microsoft was feverishly at work on a third version of Windows even as Gates was professing his undying belief that OS/2 would dominate computing until the millennium.

And though OS/2 might be the future, until then Gates was protecting DOS with the fierceness of a predator guarding its prey on the African plains. Digital Research, Gary Kildall's old company, developed a rival IBM-compatible operating system it called DR-DOS. Digital Research's DOS provided several much-needed fixes to Microsoft's. And because Digital wasn't Microsoft, it was gaining a growing constituency. But every time Digital Research unveiled a spiffier version that one-upped Microsoft's, Microsoft announced that it was about to offer a new release that would do the same except better. Often it was just talk, though, meant to stall defections. This was an old IBM trick dubbed "FUD," for "fear, uncertainty, and doubt": no matter what a competitor claimed to have in an upcoming release, IBM would claim it had the same feature in the pipeline. Microsoft was proving itself a gifted practitioner of the FUD game, claiming it was on the verge of releasing a new feature that wouldn't arrive for a year or more.

Microsoft also fought DR-DOS by using its sway with the computer manufacturers. According to court documents later filed by DR-DOS's owners, Microsoft twisted arms until they popped out of shoulder sockets. The emergence of the DR-DOS alternative prompted Microsoft to offer financial incentives to PC makers willing to install its DOS on *all* of its machines. Those willing to pay Microsoft a royalty for every PC shipped, whether or not DOS was loaded on that machine, were

---

* So late was Windows that the trade journalists covering the Microsoft beat coined the term "vaporware"—a long-promised software product that always seemed just a few months from release.

granted a deep discount on MS-DOS—which naturally motivated them to push MS-DOS over DR-DOS, given that they'd be paying a toll to Microsoft one way or another. (When signing a consent decree in 1994, Microsoft agreed to stop this practice, which the federal government alleged was anticompetitive and illegal.)

Not surprisingly, the computer trades were replete with rumors of a pending Microsoft-IBM divorce. But the truth was that IBM needed, or believed it needed, Microsoft to make OS/2 a reality, and Microsoft was working overtime to stay in IBM's good graces. So eager was Gates to remain on good terms with IBM that in 1986 or 1987 he offered Big Blue a 30 percent stake in Microsoft. Executives at IBM brushed aside the offer without taking it seriously—a decision that by 1998 would cost Big Blue roughly $50 billion in lost revenues.

IBM's solution to the Microsoft problem was to cut a deal with Gates and then present him with an ultimatum. OS/2 worked well only on top-of-the-line PCs upgraded with more than $1,000 worth of memory chips. So late in 1989, the two companies coauthored a press release announcing an intermediate solution. Their long-range goal was still a world dominated by OS/2, but in the meanwhile they would push OS/2 among high-end corporate users and Windows among those with smaller, less expensive systems.* The agreement also specified Microsoft would cease development of Windows by June 1990. After that, OS/2 would become the company's top priority. It was, as subsequent events amply demonstrated, pure fiction. "Riding the bear," Ballmer used to call it—holding on for dear life as long as possible before getting thrown. Wrote industry pundit Esther Dyson in *Forbes,* "Microsoft is second to none in its ability to juggle a set of conflicting relations."

ONCE THE MASKS OF GOODWILL and camaraderie fell away, the stored-up hurts and recriminations—as tends to happen in such circumstances—came tumbling out. For Gates the slights date back to the launch of the original IBM-PC. He had asked to take part in the formal

---

* According to the press release, "Nor will future releases [of Windows] contain advanced OS/2 features such as distributed processing, the 32-bit flat memory models, threads, or long file names"—all features that would be included in Windows 95. Microsoft also vowed that Windows would never be used on high-end central machines called "servers" that deliver data and software programs to PCs hooked up into networks, which is precisely what a product already in development, Windows NT, aimed to do.

festivities but had been denied. Instead he had received a form letter that began, "Dear Vendor, Thank you for your valuable contribution."

Big Blue might know everything about the mainframe and appeasing corporate customers, but it didn't know anything about the chocolates-on-the-pillow touches that apparently made so big a difference to Gates. More than a dozen Softies flew to Miami Beach for a major OS/2 event and returned to Redmond red from more than the sun. IBM had set aside seats for only two Microsoft employees, and during the main event, even though Microsoft was codeveloping and comarketing OS/2, Gates was granted the same six minutes onstage as an archrival, Jim Manzi, the CEO of Lotus. For Gates, these and other slights were ammunition, the stuff of self-righteous rages. "IBM never had a clue about dealing with Microsoft," said Jon Lazarus.

The two companies fought over everything. If it wasn't the size of the program and a long list of technical disputes, it was the marketing strategy and the target audience. Mainly, these disputes boiled down to different styles. Gates kept his teams small, providing only enough bodies to keep everyone working just at the edge of sanity. IBM threw as many bodies as it could at a problem—inside Big Blue they called this the "masses of asses" approach. At Microsoft, one owned a project until it was complete. At IBM, designers designed the software, and implementers implemented, and those riding herd on everyone were several layers below the company's top management. At Microsoft, every team leader answered directly to Gates and Ballmer.

The two companies even had different goals. At Microsoft people were thinking only about the PC, but at IBM they were thinking about the company's entire line of products. IBM insisted that OS/2 be fungible enough to work on the company's mainframe system, which generated 60 percent of the company's profits. Every time someone inside Microsoft threw up his hands in disgust, pleading with Gates and Ballmer to just walk away from the whole mess, one or the other would offer the same response: "We're smart people, we can work this out." Or Ballmer would crudely suggest a grin-and-bear-it approach. "B-O, G-U," he'd say: "Bend over, grease up."

After three years on the market, OS/2 had been adopted by only a small fraction of PC users. IBM had sold only 300,000 copies in its first three years. (By contrast, Microsoft had managed to get the deeply flawed versions 1 and 2 of Windows onto nearly 3 million machines.) IBM accused Microsoft of shortchanging the OS/2 project. Naturally,

Ballmer assured them that that wasn't true, even if it was. So maybe Microsoft no longer assigned its best people to the OS/2 project. Why should it when IBM seemed intent on screwing the project up? Besides, there was version 3 of Windows to get out the door. Eventually it came out in *InfoWorld* that Gates was intentionally dragging his feet on the OS/2 update.* The prerelease—the "beta" it shared with its best customers—of the latest version of Windows was proving to be a pleasant surprise. Some people in the company had spent seven years working on Windows. It seemed only natural, if not quite fair given Gates's promises to IBM and the developers writing applications for OS/2, that they'd want to give Windows 3.0 a chance before helping IBM kill it with OS/2.

In May 1990, three years after the release of Windows 2.0, Microsoft unveiled the newest version of Windows. Until then, even the most elaborate product release celebration was barely a cut above a kid's birthday party, with balloons and a table of refreshments in a rented room outfitted with a projector screen. But the Windows 3.0 launch was something else entirely, another sign the PC industry was exiting adolescence and entering a hard-driving adulthood. There were pre-parties for journalists and Wall Street analysts and a main event that cost more than $2 million. That day thousands gathered in fourteen cities across the globe, all hooked by satellite to New York. There was a laser light show, strobes, pounding rock and roll, and of course Gates, dressed in an ill-fitting new suit and triple-E size Clark Kent glasses, a busy tie that clashed with his striped shirt, and penny loafers. "Windows will change forever the way we use computers," Gates announced. Gushed a Smith Barney analyst to a *USA Today* reporter, "This is probably the most anticipated product in the history of the world!"

There were stories on *Good Morning America* and CNN, satellite feeds to network affiliates from Chicago to San Francisco to Phoenix to even tiny Spartanburg, South Carolina, plus a page-one preview in *The Wall Street Journal* and features in *The New York Times, USA Today,* and the *Los Angeles Times*—all in all, quite a reception for a new and improved version of a five-year-old product released by a company that only six months earlier had sent out a press release claiming that Windows was nothing but a stopgap until computer manufacturers could

---

* Gates himself posed the question this way: "What incentive does Microsoft have to get it [OS/2] out the door before Windows 3.0?"

begin to produce brawnier machines at an affordable price. An article in *Newsweek* began, "For this kind of fanfare, you'd expect software that will solve the S&L crisis *and* butter your toast in the morning."

Microsoft spent another $10 million promoting Windows in the coming weeks. It was money well spent. Over the next four months, Microsoft sold 1 million copies of Windows—a blistering pace for a new release that no company would approach until the newly minted Netscape Communications invited the world to download Netscape Navigator for free. The *Newsweek* correspondent reporting on the Windows 3.0 release asked Gates if Microsoft was trying to dominate all of computing. Gates dismissed such talk as the type of drivel one sees in "Hollywood gossip columns."

ANOTHER YEAR PASSED before the IBM-Microsoft divorce was finalized in the spring of 1991. IBM, of course, won sole custody of OS/2. Gates made the decision to end his company's partnership with IBM while away on what he calls a "think week," alone by the water in the weekend getaway he had built for his family.* But by that time the conclusion seemed foregone. Sure, Microsoft had vowed it would stick with OS/2 until it took its rightful place as the computer world's dominant operating system, but that was before the wild success of Windows. For months Microsoft employees had been asking themselves why they were tying their reputation to the clumsy failure that was OS/2.

If they needed any further proof of the popularity of Windows beyond the briskness of the sales, there were the crowds lining up to hear Gates when he delivered a speech at COMDEX in the fall of 1990. The lines snaked down a hallway, through the hotel lobby, and onto the street. The last time Gates had spoken at COMDEX, seven years earlier, he had scribbled some notes on a pad ten minutes before he was to go on and his father had run the slide projector. This time Gates read a speech written by others and rehearsed for hours with a Silicon Valley speech coach named Jerry Weisman. Dressed in a dark suit that looked as if it cost more than the combined worth of the rest of his wardrobe,

---

* A "think week" was something he did once or twice a year. He'd throw some clothes and a sack of Cup-A-Soups into the backseat of his car and drive in his usual maniacal style to the site of his fondest boyhood memories. There he'd plow through piles of reading material, walk the beach, and think big thoughts about Microsoft's future.

Gates began his spiel with a movie-quality video that cost $50,000. His big announcement was that Microsoft would be sponsoring something called the Windows World Exposition—as if Windows were an industry all its own. That January, *The Wall Street Journal* ran a page-one article reporting on the breakup of Microsoft and Big Blue. "Microsoft is now driving the industry, not IBM," the publisher of an industry newsletter told the *Journal.*

Yet those inside IBM acted as if they still believed the opposite to be true. The word came down from on high: "Thou shalt not write for Windows." They'd strangle Windows, its executives told people, by refusing to support it. Jim Cannavino, who headed IBM's PC division, made the rounds of companies such as Lotus and WordPerfect, which had bet everything on OS/2. "We're going to clip that guy's wings," Cannavino said of Gates. (Cannavino denies saying anything of the kind.) Jack Sams, who had negotiated the original deal with Microsoft, could read the handwriting on the wall. To him business was about making money, not retribution. So Sams quit.*

For years IBM had favored LAN-Man, the product Microsoft had developed to compete with Novell's networking product. But in 1991, IBM switched sides, signing a deal with Novell. Now IBM's formidable sales force would sell Novell's NetWare, not Microsoft's LAN-Man. IBM also dropped Microsoft's e-mail program in favor of one created by Lotus and cut a deal with Borland, a purveyor of computer languages and thus another Microsoft rival.

IBM became a soft touch for anyone peddling a product that could be packaged as a potential Microsoft killer. Cannavino committed $80 million to a now-dead project called Patriot Partners, the aim of which was to provide an intermediate level between an application and the operating system. That way the same version of 1-2-3 would run as easily on OS/2 as Windows or the Mac, thereby breaking the DOS-Windows stranglehold. There were two competing platforms for something called "pen computing" (using a handheld device that would require no keyboard), which was all the rage back then. One had been developed by the Silicon Valley–based GO Corporation, run by a CEO

---

* Jim Cannavino wasn't the only one. Jim Manzi took over Lotus when Mitch Kapor stepped down as CEO in 1986. "Who's going to buy Windows if we're not writing for it?" Manzi would say when people asked him about the Microsoft operating system. "We're not porting to it. WordPerfect, IBM, none of the big guys. Windows is dead without us."

named Jerry Kaplan. The other was Pen Windows by Microsoft, created after Kaplan invited Gates into his office to show him a device for which Microsoft might want to write applications. Kaplan kicked up quite a fuss, accusing Gates of ripping off GO's technology. So of course IBM partnered with GO. "We're joining forces with people who see the future the same way we do," explained an IBM vice president quoted anonymously in *Forbes* magazine.

Then there was the peace accord IBM brokered with Apple. That certainly turned heads inside the industry—and sent Microsoft's stock falling $700 million in a single day. IBM and Apple were polar opposites and fierce rivals; indeed, in the early 1980s, Steve Jobs famously flew his Macintosh development team to Armonk, New York, so they could see firsthand the "enemy" they were fighting. But the companies shared a vendetta against Gates. It was Jobs who, hoping to convince Microsoft to write applications for the Apple operating system, first showed Gates the point-and-click ease of the Macintosh and then insisted Gates visit Xerox PARC to see the magic for himself. But not long after the release of Windows 2.0 in 1988, Apple sued Microsoft, claiming that Windows violated the Macintosh copyright (a suit Apple lost). It was like that ancient proverb: "The enemy of my enemy is my friend."

IBM and Apple hammered out a series of deals, but the blockbuster—the one that would generate a front-page article in *The Wall Street Journal* and prompt the paper to declare that a "new front" had been opened in the "PC wars"—was IBM's decision to throw its weight behind a new operating system Apple had been working on for several years, a project code-named "Pink." The *Journal* likened the deal to an agreement between Ford and General Motors to share the same engine design.

"They've sold their soul!" many of the Apple faithful cried, but it was those loyal to Big Blue who should have been carrying placards of protest. Pink was woefully behind schedule and over budget, and hardly the Microsoft killer it had been touted to be. Apple executive Jean-Louis Gassée had started the Pink project in 1987. By the time he departed Apple in 1990 (one year before the IBM-Apple deal), he was convinced that this attempt to rewrite the Macintosh operating system would fail. At his farewell party, he saw Apple CEO John Scully. "There's something I need to get off my chest," a slightly tipsy Gassée began. Pink is never going to work, he said before ticking off its many problems. The original decision making had been too loose and California consensus-oriented. His development team was too fat and happy, and not hungry and driven like an underfunded start-up. Apple politics had messed things up, as had personality conflicts. "Dump Pink," Gassée told Scully. "And because I'm leaving, you can use me as your fall guy." But Gassée's suggestion, while generous, was unnecessary now that Apple had a new-found friend that throughout the previous decade it had considered its immortal foe.

THINGS TURNED OUT about as well for IBM as they did for Captain Ahab. In 1991, the company announced its first money-losing year since its inception sixty-seven years earlier. But the $2.8 billion loss was nothing compared to the $5 billion shortfall the company would register in 1992. That was the single largest loss in U.S. corporate history—a record IBM itself would shatter in 1993, when it lost another $8 billion.

During flush times, the city-state of IBM had been celebrated for its unofficial no-layoffs policy. That changed in 1990, when IBM started shedding employees at a rate of 30,000 to 40,000 a year. In 1994, the census dipped below 220,000—barely half the population of 1986. When, in early 1993, IBM's stock hit an eleven-year low, a watershed event occurred: IBM's "market cap" (market capitalization, or cumulative worth of its stock) dipped to $26.4 billion—$400 million less than Microsoft's $26.8 billion market cap. *Time,* which in 1991 had run an article on Gates under the headline "The Next 800-Lb. Gorilla," described this flip-flop of positions as a "generational shift" and harkened back to the 1920s, when "upstart" General Motors had first surpassed Ford as the nation's top carmaker. That year Microsoft held a 48 percent share of the $7 billion worldwide computer software market, *Time* reported.

"One of our big problems," said a top Microsoft executive, "is what to do with all the cash we generate."

IBM didn't give up on OS/2. The updated version the company released in 1992 won enough medals and Lucite to fill a trophy case, including *InfoWorld*'s prestigious "product of the year," an award bestowed by the magazine's software-savvy readership.* But despite the

---

* A rebellious lot, they again selected OS/2 product of the year in 1993, 1994, and then again in 1995, a not-so-subtle gesture of scorn for Windows. OS/2 would have won the award for a fifth straight year except the magazine voided the results because of online ballot stuffing.

$1 billion IBM spent developing and marketing OS/2, Windows was outselling this better-rated product by a ratio of nine to one.

"Gates has clearly won," declared Lotus founder Mitch Kapor in 1991. There was a forlorn tone to the remainder of his quote, as if he were delivering a eulogy for a bygone era: "The revolution is over, and the freewheeling innovation in the software industry has ground to a halt. For me, it's the Kingdom of the Dead."

For IBM, the twist of the knife was that Gates and Company proved to be bad winners. When a writer with *Maclean's* ("Genius at Work") made the mistake of asking Gates if he was trying to accomplish in the realm of software what IBM had done in the world of hardware, Gates's response dripped with disdain: Who would want to be like IBM? The same memo, leaked to *InfoWorld,* that had Gates admitting that his company had intentionally dragged its feet on an OS/2 update, had him boasting that IBM would be dead inside ten years, maybe seven. Microsoft seemed to suggest the same symbolically at the all-hands party it hosted in 1991. Sporting a leather jacket, Gates roared onstage riding a Harley streaming a Windows banner. The punch line was the Edsel that followed, carrying a placard that read "OS/2." Consider the logistics and expense that had gone into finding a working Edsel in the Seattle area and then getting it inside the Kingdome and onstage, just to apply salt to the wound of a former friend and ally. An IBM executive quoted anonymously at the time said, "I'd like to put an ice pick in Gates's head."

CHAPTER 06

OPENING THE KIMONO

IF EVERY PROPOSED MERGER depended on CEOs liking or even respecting each other, there'd be a lot less news to report in *The Wall Street Journal*. When someone inside an industry wants to discuss a merger, company executives owe it to the stockholders to at least feel them out. At least, that's what Ray Noorda, CEO of Novell, told himself. To him it was like a defense lawyer's obligation to tell a client about any deal the prosecution puts on the table.

Steve Ballmer, not Gates, phoned Noorda in the fall of 1989. That should have been Noorda's first clue that something was strange. The industry's top executives loved talking about it—how the phone would ring and on the other end would be a familiar whistly voice, one part Julia Child and two parts that just-hired college intern. "Hi, it's Bill Gates," he'd chirp. He'd call to try to rope them into writing software for one of his products, telling them of the millions they'd make if they shared his "vision" of the future. Sometimes he'd use a big happening inside the industry as his excuse for calling; sometimes he'd call to talk about the idiocy of some mutual competitor's strategy. He'd feel you out to see if maybe you were a useful ally, someone he could talk with occasionally to keep abreast of goings-on. Those likely to be found each fall attending Stewart Alsop's Agenda would have known: something wasn't quite right about Ballmer being on the other end of the phone.

Although by 1993 Novell was the country's second largest software company, Noorda was never part of the in crowd. He didn't attend Agenda; supposedly he didn't even have a PC in his office. He was a man well into his sixties in an industry of boys, a bottom-line guy who would talk P/E ratios and book values but rarely products. He was a World War II veteran, while his colleagues in the industry were so young that most had never even had to sweat the Vietnam draft. He was that strange beast known as a corporate "turnaround artist," a CEO who had salvaged several hardware start-ups, when, in the early 1980s, Novell's board hired him to save a small speck of a company lost at sea. He may not have had zeros and ones flowing through his veins, and he didn't have a clue as to how Novell's flagship product, NetWare, worked, but he was sharp and tireless, usually at the office by 6 A.M. He understood balance sheets, and he understood business. When Ballmer called, he was appropriately standoffish, listening but not talking, nonchalantly telling Ballmer he'd at least hear him out.

Microsoft had stood out as Novell's most nettlesome foe almost from the start of Noorda's tenure. In 1984, when Microsoft released a NetWare rival called Microsoft Net, the smart guys declared that it was only a matter of time before Novell was dead. And after Microsoft junked Microsoft Net in favor of LAN-Man, released in 1987, again the pundits put Novell on the critical list. But somehow Novell held Microsoft at bay, *gaining* market share despite everyone's prediction of doom. In 1989, Microsoft hired Mike Murray to take over as LAN-Man's new marketing manager. Murray perused the many internal reports Microsoft had written about Novell and threw up his hands. NetWare had a strong product and a loyal customer base; LAN-Man had little going for it. So he phoned Ballmer, who had been a classmate at Stanford Business School, and the two of them agreed: the solution was for Microsoft to buy Novell. Noorda was at least open to the idea, so he, Ballmer, and Murray agreed to meet at the upcoming COMDEX show.

They met for breakfast at one of the fancy hotels on the Las Vegas strip. Ballmer and Murray ate from plates heavy with eggs and meat, Noorda from a bowl of oatmeal and skim milk. Murray was there because he knew Noorda and liked him. What Noorda might have thought of Murray is something else entirely. An Apple veteran who had headed up the original Macintosh marketing team, Murray had been between jobs when he had headed to Utah to see about the top marketing job at Novell. Apparently Murray and Noorda had hit it off, because Noorda had asked if instead he'd be interested in a job as his right-hand man. Murray had been ready to take the job, but then he had gotten a call from Ballmer, and the next thing Noorda knew Murray was working in Redmond.

Ballmer, the born evangelist, delivered the hard sell. We can compete, he said, but together our two companies could own the known software universe: operating systems, applications, and the networking software that hooks everything together. Ballmer and Murray had no idea what Noorda might be thinking until a few weeks later, when a senior Novell engineer phoned Murray. Noorda had instructed a team to fly to Seattle to meet with their Microsoft counterparts. When could they come up?

A week before Christmas 1989, the two teams met near Sea-Tac Airport. They signed nondisclosure agreements, then opened the kimono. Both sides spoke with frightening frankness, sharing their strategy and long-range plans for their products. "It was total and complete disclosure on both sides," Murray said. At least a couple of Novell's engineers couldn't believe they were sharing this kind of intelligence with the likes of Microsoft, but figured that maybe that's why they were still sweating college funds for the kids while Noorda was worth roughly $400 million. Whereas Novell was talking about the strengths and weaknesses of a product with a 60 percent market share, Microsoft was revealing secrets about one with less than a 10 percent share. Noorda's strategy would be brilliant if Gates bought Novell, an incredible blunder if he didn't.

That Saturday, Noorda flew to Redmond to meet with Ballmer and Murray, though not Gates, who, he was told, was out of town and unable to make the talks. The three met at Murray's house. "I've spoken to my board," Noorda told them, "and they've given me the go-ahead." But now Ballmer and Murray had cold feet; they hadn't actually been authorized to do anything. Noorda was no doubt irked that Microsoft was still not talking specific numbers. The meeting ended abruptly because Noorda, the skinflint, had flown up from Salt Lake City on a senior citizen's coupon. The late-afternoon flight was the last plane out under this discount. Ballmer and Murray were relieved but also dumbfounded: a multibillion-dollar deal was pending and Noorda was worried about a few hundred dollars!

Gates was indeed out of town, at his Hood Canal retreat on one of his think weeks, when Ballmer called with the news. One would assume that Gates had already done a lot of thinking about a merger with Novell before sending his top lieutenant to dangle the possibility in front of Noorda, but apparently not. He knew what his friend was up to, of course, but as Ballmer and Murray tell it, Gates hadn't thought much about the idea until then. Gates phoned Microsoft board member and venture capitalist David Marquardt, who adamantly opposed the idea.

Sure, NetWare was demolishing LAN-Man, but NetWare allowed users to share only printers and files, not programs. Do Novell one better, he told them: leapfrog the technology and create an operating system that an entire office of PCs could share over a network. Several years passed before Microsoft released the product that Marquardt (among others) laid out, but Gates made up his mind then. "Sorry, guys, I can't do it," he told Ballmer and Murray. Their respective technologies were just too disparate, and Utah was a long way away from Redmond. "Bill was worried it'd end up being a mess for both companies from which neither of us might recover," Murray recalled.

Ballmer and Murray were inclined to chalk up all that happened next to a case of bad manners perpetrated by people so busy it's a wonder they could remember to brush their teeth in the morning. Only later did Murray lay out what he should have done. Courtesy dictated that at least one of them fly to Utah to meet with Noorda in person. They should have apologized for wasting his time and begged his forgiveness. They should have assured him that they wouldn't take advantage of anything they had learned during their short-lived talks. Meanwhile, the LAN-Man team should have boxed up and shipped south every technical report and scrap of paper the Novell team had shared with them. Microsoft took none of these actions. Indeed, neither Ballmer nor Murray even phoned Noorda to inform him that Gates had nixed the deal even before talking a price.

Several weeks later, an angry Noorda phoned Ballmer. This deal on the "fast track" has suddenly stalled, and he had no idea why. Ballmer, who is the sort who talks more rather than less when on the defensive, roared on about Bill not really liking acquisitions and how far away Utah seemed. "Bill likes to roam the halls at night, see what the guys are up to," Ballmer added. Murray acknowledged that Ballmer's explanation could have been "more crisp." Noorda, for his part, didn't say much. He was the reticent, keep-it-all-inside type anyway, not the kind to offer sarcastic one-liners about Novell being in Utah before they had even started talking.

"There was no power play here, but from where Ray sat, we jilted him at the altar," Murray said. "And Ray reacted like a scorned bride."

Noorda didn't hear from the Great Oz himself, but he read in the trades, shortly after his conversation with Ballmer, that Microsoft was plowing another $60 million into marketing LAN-Man. The Microsoft PR machine, wise in the ways of media manipulation, briefed the key

analysts before making its announcement—and then provided reporters with the names and phone numbers of the industry's "smartest"
analysts, by whom they meant those inclined to see things Microsoft's
way. Again the trades were predicting Novell's demise. One analyst predicted that within two years, LAN-Man would own a third of the network software market. After that, it was only a matter of time before
Microsoft would own the entire market.

TWO YEARS LATER, in 1991, it was Gates who phoned Noorda to propose a meeting. Ostensibly the agenda was again the possibility of a
merger. In the intervening two years, NetWare had gained even more
ground on LAN-Man, which was still floundering. And a few months
earlier, Noorda had grabbed the baton from Digital Research, Gary
Kildall's old company, when he had bought DR-DOS. So now Novell
and Microsoft were competing on two separate fronts. Noorda told
himself that this time he wouldn't say a word, just listen to see what he
could learn about Microsoft's strategy. Provo was still a long way from
Redmond, but Gates proposed a second round of merger talks, Murray
said, "Because business isn't black and white. And you're always looking
out, trying to hedge your bets, and second-guessing your own strategy.
And asking yourself, 'What if?' "

The two met for more than two hours at the Admirals Club at San
Francisco International. As Noorda related the story to people around
him, there were no hellos, no pleasantries, just a nod before Gates
launched his pitch. When Noorda brought up DR-DOS, Gates changed
the subject, which is when the lightbulb went off in Noorda's head. So
that's what this is about, he told himself: Gates was simply dangling the
possibility of a merger to see what he could learn about our plans for
DR-DOS. Right there, Noorda vowed that he'd teach Gates a lesson.

At first it was the kind of subtle stuff few outside the two companies
would notice. If the two met at an industry event, Noorda wouldn't
shake Gates's hand or utter so much as a hello. When Novell's engineers
started giving a cold shoulder to their Microsoft counterparts—a potentially disastrous turn of events for the hundreds of thousands of
computer users who relied on NetWare and needed it to work with Microsoft's wide offering of non-network products—Noorda wouldn't return the messages Gates left in an attempt to broker a peace.

People in Redmond ridiculed the notion that Gates would meet

Noorda in San Francisco just to learn what he could about DR-DOS. In 1991, Microsoft owned a 75 percent share of the PC operating system market (when he had been at Procter & Gamble, Ballmer said, a 40 percent share had been something to brag about). DR-DOS, in contrast, was a gnat of a product with less than a 10 percent market share. As Pam Edstrom, Microsoft's sharp-tongued and tungsten-steel tough PR maven, put it, "Right, Bill is going to go to these lengths because now he's scared Novell has DR-DOS."

But that's precisely the point. Despite Microsoft's size and success, it was still as obsessed with the world of also-rans as it was with the market leaders. Heidi Roizen, a friend of Gates, ran a small Silicon Valley software firm called T-Maker. T-Maker was a pipsqueak, Microsoft a giant, but both sold a word processor for the Macintosh. When T-Maker released a new and improved version of its word processor, Gates countered by slashing the price of the Macintosh version of Word. Even if T-Maker's product was better than Word, at least Word would cost less. "He's kind of won the world fair and square," Roizen told the authors of *Hard Drive*, "but he sure doesn't leave a lot left over for the rest of us."*

"WIN! DOZE! . . . Win! Doze! . . . Win! Doze! . . ."

Gates's problem whenever he shared the stage with Steve Ballmer was that he sounded so tinny and shrill when set against his number two. Ballmer is a backslapper who has worked sales and marketing his whole life, Gates a "capitalist brainiac" (a *Playboy* writer's term) who scores about zero on the charisma scale. So while Gates is always the headliner at Microsoft's annual employee bash, it's Ballmer who perennially steals the show.

Actually, it's more pep rally than party, these yearly gatherings of the entire clan at which the company's high priests and the pope himself

---

* When asked about Microsoft's merger dance with Novell, Gates would incorrectly remember that it was Novell that approached Microsoft, and cast his second round of merger talks as a reaction to his company's split with IBM. "We decided that maybe talking to Novell about teaming up would be a good thing," Gates wrote in an e-mail. "This had NO RELATIONSHIP to DRDOS except that we would have had to spin off DRDOS. There is NO information of any kind that would have been interesting to us relating to DRDOS. It is absurd for someone to suggest this."

spread the word among the faithful. In 1991, Microsoft rented the Seattle Kingdome, the indoor stadium where the local football team plays, to house more than eight thousand employees. Ballmer didn't deliver his speech so much as shout it. He stood on stage, punching a meaty fist into a palm, yelling "Win! Doze! Win! Doze! Win! Doze!" at the top of his lungs for so long and so hard that he ended up requiring throat surgery afterward. The snake-charmed crowd took up the chant, screaming in unison, like sports fans repeating a favorite star's first name after a game-winning home run: "Win! Doze! Win! Doze!"

Ballmer was just getting warmed up. The veins in his temples swelled like ropes, blisters of sweat formed on his bald dome. His face turned the color of tomato bisque. There's no time for gloating, he warned, not while they're still getting lunch handed to them. Lotus 1-2-3 is still kicking our asses! WordPerfect! Again he began punching his palm; people who were there that afternoon say that if anything he got even louder. "It's market share!" he shouted. "It's market share! It's market share! It's market share!" It was here that his sermon hit its crescendo. "Because if you have share, you basically leave the competitors"—he grabbed for his throat—"just gasping for oxygen." People were on their feet, fists raised in the air. Had Gates followed Ballmer onstage and ordered them to do so, some in the audience that day might just have drunk the Kool-Aid.

In 1991, with victory in the operating systems wars almost a foregone conclusion, Microsoft's obsession became applications. Mike Maples had worked at IBM for twenty-five years before Microsoft hired him away to run Microsoft's applications division. At a press briefing that same year, he was about as subtle as Ballmer had been at the Kingdome. "My job," Maples said, "is to get a fair share of the software applications market, and to me that's one hundred percent." Maybe Maples was cracking a joke, as the company's spin doctors would later claim. But to Microsoft's competitors the comment was a perfect expression of the Microsoft mind-set.

To save time, the manager overseeing the Word group shaved while driving to work. When the first version of Excel fell behind schedule, the project manager bought blinds for his office at Microsoft and moved in a beanbag chair to sleep on during the six-month push to meet the deadline. Those at Microsoft wouldn't just read a review of Word in *InfoWorld*, they'd spend an entire Saturday "dissecting it fifty-nine ways to Sunday," said former Word manager Jeff Raikes. A new expression was added to the Seattle-area lexicon, the "Microsoft widow," to describe women whose husbands might as well have passed away, so little were they around.

"We'd love to see Bill get married and have a few kids," Pete Peterson told *The Wall Street Journal* in 1990. "Then maybe he'd mellow out." Yet even here Gates seemed likely to disappoint. He no longer was the kid who preferred poker with the grown-ups to dancing with girls, but certainly the vast majority of women would find him an odd companion. He did have his romantic side (supposedly *Roman Holiday* with Audrey Hepburn is a favorite film), but a couple of burgers at a Wendy's before a movie is hardly a girl's idea of the perfect date. Even his more fanciful rendezvous were odd, to say the least. Once it was a week on a yacht off the coast of Brazil, reading his-and-her copies of a molecular biology textbook. Another time it was a trip to a California resort town, propped in bed watching tapes of Richard Feynman lecturing on theoretical physics. Well into his thirties he was still a teenage boy in angst, reciting passages from *Catcher in the Rye* to girlfriends, spooning cold SpaghettiOs from a can. And of course there was the exhaustion (stifled yawns, dead eyes, an irritable edge) from too many fourteen-hour days in a row. In 1984, *Time* magazine ran a shot of Gates with his first serious girlfriend (he was twenty-nine), who said of their relationship, "He often showed up on my doorstep dead on arrival. Girlfriends are clearly peripheral in the whole scheme of things."

By the start of the 1990s, he was no longer skipping showers, but you'd read the same quotes over and over again in the magazines: Bill Gates's idea of a good time, friends and acquaintances alike said, was talking with friends about Microsoft. Even Gates admitted as much when in 1990 he told *Fortune*, "This company is my life." Two years later he told the magazine, "Maybe ten years from now we'll be far enough along, I'll put my head up and look around." When he played, he played hard, but it was the play of his youth, a battalion or two of Microsoft employees out at Hood Canal for what he called "Microgames," where he and his parents and sisters played the judges for these good-natured competitions. One year he had six tons of sand trucked in for a sand castle competition. Usually he planned a mix of the physical (three-legged races) and the mental (brainteasers). He celebrated his thirtieth birthday by renting a roller rink for the night and inviting more than one hundred Microsoft employees over to skate. When he took up golf in the early 1990s, he told colleagues it was because he needed to get outside more. But his buddy Ballmer offered a different view when he told *Time,* "Bill got into golf the same addictive way he gets into anything else. It gets his competitive juices flowing."

AT THE END OF 1992, Stewart Alsop broke with tradition and devoted the entire program of Agenda 93 to a single theme: "How to Compete/Coexist with Microsoft." ("That's all anyone was talking about anyway, so we figured, why pretend anyone cared about anything else?" he said.) Intel's Andy Grove was hardly pleased by the choice of topics, and he arrived at Agenda 93 with a message to deliver. He was one of the industry's most powerful players, and also among its best regarded. He had at least ten years on most people in the room and had witnessed more than his share of terrible things, first as a Jew living in Nazi-occupied Hungary, then as a Hungarian living under Communist rule. Taking his fireside seat opposite Alsop, an obviously peeved Grove chastised his fellow executives for flying all that way "to engage in two days of self-pity."

There was no love lost between Microsoft and Intel—each had grown rich off the other, but both seemed intent on taking credit for the other's success—but Grove was a realist. "I'm not going to make Microsoft an angel," he said. "They are a very tough company, very tough to deal with, very hard-nosed, and I'm sure they deserve—just like we deserve—their share of criticism. But they also have to be looked at as a model of the successful business." Get over it, Grove advised. Learn to make money in a Microsoft-dominated world, or change jobs.

Yet the preceding speakers could be forgiven their wallowing. Most if not all of the CEOs and moguls in waiting sitting in the audience *did* view Microsoft as a company to be emulated—except how could they replicate Grove's success when Microsoft stood in their way? That year, Microsoft collected 44 cents of every dollar businesses and consumers spent on software for the PC and accounted for more than 50 cents of every dollar of profit generated. As an industry, the PC software firms made $1.1 billion more in revenues in 1992 than in 1991; Microsoft accounted for $975 million of those dollars. Several of the larger software companies initiated layoffs in 1992. Microsoft, by contrast, hired nearly three thousand new employees. *Upside* depicted Gates on its cover as "Super Bill," a caped crusader dressed in blue tights and a red cape. The next year he was lampooned as an old-style fat cat, top hat on head, stogie in one hand and silver-tipped cane in the other. "Gates Plays a Mean Game of Monopoly," read the headline over the accompanying article.

A next-generation word processor, a revamped spreadsheet, a sleeker operating system—all these, among other ideas, seemed pie-in-the-sky foolish. Eulogies were offered in the name of innovation, because the company now at the helm was made up of infamous imitators and hardly innovators. There were laments about Gates's strategy of spending the cash generated by Windows to methodically attack markets one after another. Who among them could withstand an attack once Gates had targeted their product? The industry was only fifteen years old, but it seemed to be suffering from advanced arthritis. In what was fast becoming a tradition, the crowd again booed the Microsoft team's beans at that year's COMDEX charity chili cook-off, when the master of ceremonies thanked Gates and Microsoft for a $30,000 donation.

"Microsoft: Is It Too Powerful?" *Business Week* posed this question on its cover in 1993. Five reporters worked on this "special report," cataloguing a long list of unflattering tales culled from scores of interviews with industry leaders.* There were the woes of the CEO of a small company manufacturing a computer mouse that had been crushed when Microsoft wouldn't renew its Windows license—because Gates had recently decided that Microsoft would enter the mouse market. There were stories of Microsoft slandering the competition, preannouncing phantom features, and bullying partners into accepting onerous terms simply because, as the keepers of the Windows franchise, it could. The magazine described these tactics as "hyperaggressiveness"—this tendency of Microsoft to "use every trick at its disposal to gain an edge, enter a new segment, or eke out one more iota of market share." Yet maybe the most revealing line in the article was one buried in the middle of the piece: "Such tactics are in the playbooks of many competitors." The difference was that Microsoft was bigger and more powerful than everyone else, so the garden-variety methods it used suddenly seemed monstrous.

---

* Among those the magazine interviewed was Rob Glaser, a trusted lieutenant of Gates until he left to start his own company in 1993. He described what he labeled the "Machiavellian poker games" he had played as Gates's designated negotiator on many a deal. "You hid things even if it would blindside people you were working with," he confessed. He respected Gates and might even have considered him a friend, but he described him as a "Darwinian . . . [who] doesn't look for win-win situations with others, but for ways to make others lose. Success is defined as flattening the competition."

Microsoft might not provide the most flattering picture of capitalism, but it provides an accurate one, and that's the point: capitalism under the glare of klieg lights conjures up the cliché that a vegetarian is a meat eater who once visited a sausage factory. Success as depicted in the mass media may be the life of the rich and famous, but there's a flip side, too. Gates acknowledged as much when he complained in an interview with *Fortune* about the new tendency to cast him as a rapacious robber baron. Why weren't there more articles about the family-run drugstores Sam Walton had put out of business as he worked his way up the Forbes 400 list? "Most success is driven that way," Gates explained. Gates had a point, but it didn't help his cause to liken his actions in the software industry to the demolition of Main Street America's mom-and-pop stores. The only difference was that superstore emporiums were old news by the early 1990s but personal computers were still a sexy topic.

The book *Computer Wars,* written by Charles Ferguson and Charles Morris and published in 1993, declared Gates "the most hated man in the computer industry." That was no doubt true, but it didn't mean Gates was without competition for the moniker. Consider Borland's Philippe Kahn. Fun-loving and well rounded but also arrogant and brash, Kahn was an ex–math teacher from France who had started his own software firm because he couldn't find a job. As with Gates, his first product had been a high-level computer language "dumbed down" for the PC—so the smart guys naturally dubbed him "the next Bill Gates," the way sportswriters are always declaring so-and-so the next Michael Jordan. His appetite for fame and market share seemed as immense as Gates's. Before it all came crashing down around him, he had built Borland into the country's third largest PC software firm, moving from computer languages to software tools and then to applications. Kahn's game was to produce software on the cheap and then undercut the competition by selling his software at a fraction of their price. "When you deal with Gates," he once said, "you feel raped." When you dealt with Kahn, others said, you felt as if you were competing against a foreign sweatshop competitor who had dumped a load of cheap knockoffs onto the market.

"Borland never did anything but lose money on its applications," said an executive with a competing firm. "All Philippe ever did was make sure the rest of us didn't make any money, either." Early in Agenda's history, Alsop rented a dunking machine and then auctioned off the right to dunk several big-name volunteers, including Kahn and Alsop. The right to dunk Alsop drew maybe $10,000, but several of Kahn's competitors (Gates included) chipped in nearly $20,000 for the right to send Kahn plunging into a vat of water.

Then there was Oracle, the eight-hundred-pound gorilla of the minicomputer software world. The company was forever telling customers it was "six months away" from projects that ended up taking several more years. One analyst dubbed it "Larry's constant"—a constant of twenty-four months because for years Ellison had been saying that Oracle on the IBM mainframe "was just two years away." When the upstart Sybase began encroaching on Oracle's business, Oracle launched its "Cut Off the Air" campaign. "At Oracle we didn't just want to beat a competitor, we wanted to destroy them," said Jerry Held, a former Oracle executive. "Even when the competitor was on the ground, you kept on stomping. And then, if they were still able to wiggle a finger, you stomped on their hand."

It was not an industry for the squeamish. By the time Alsop decided to focus all of Agenda 93 on the topic of coexisting and competing with Microsoft, there had been a separation of the real players from those for whom the business side was a necessary evil. The true geeks and idealists, people such as Mitch Kapor, who didn't have the stomach for cutthroat competition, had left the business a long time before.* By the fall of 1992, if you were still attending Agenda, you were a player or a wannabe player. And the odds were that while you might have legitimate complaints, what galled you most about Gates was that he, not you, had won.

By the end of the second day of presentations at Agenda 93, Gates was in a sour mood. "What a stupid idea for a conference!" Gates had snapped at Alsop when he learned of that year's theme. He seemed sorry he had shown up in the first place. On the conference's first day, he had drawn a big crowd in the hallway when he and Philippe Kahn had gone at it (Kahn had recently been quoted comparing Microsoft to Germany in World War II†), but mainly he had sat through the two days in stony silence. Usually people buzz about in the hallways even while people are

---

* Kapor, for instance, sold some of his more expensive props, such as his jet and his second home in Hawaii, reordering his life so that his wife and kids and his favorite cause, a group called the Electronic Frontier Foundation, took priority.

† Kahn, a Jew from France, claims that *Business Week* had misattributed this quote to him. "I would never say that; my mother was a survivor from one of the camps," Kahn

talking onstage, but when Gates finally sat for his annual fireside it was like a ghost town out there. How would he respond to all those—Lotus's Jim Manzi, Steve Jobs, Sun's Scott McNealy—who had preceded him, using their twenty minutes onstage to tee off on his head?

When reporters pressed Larry Ellison to answer for Oracle's excesses, he would respond as if his favorite business guru was Attila the Hun. Gates, by contrast, tended to sound like a devotee of Mr. Rogers. When, in 1991, the news leaked out that the Federal Trade Commission was investigating Microsoft, he told reporters that he found the whole thing mystifying. Why would the FTC even be interested in Microsoft when it simply stamped out "these little boxes, these nice little software packages"? The same *Business Week* article that carried story after story of Microsoft's cutthroat business dealings included Gates's usual depiction of life in Redmond as if the Softies were a bunch of elves from a Keebler cookie commercial. "It's not very complicated," Gates said. "Our success is based on one thing: good products." If pressed, Gates would drop the goo-goo-eyed pose and replace it with vinegary sarcasm meant to make a reporter feel like a dope for asking such airhead questions. Yeah, right, he said one time, "we're just sitting up here looking down and thinking, 'Ho, ho, ho, who shall we crush today?' "

The gee-whiz, we-just-make-great-software routine, however, wouldn't work with this crowd, made up of computer manufacturers who knew that Microsoft offered a company a great deal if it agreed to bundle only Microsoft's DOS and Windows or charged it twice as much (thereby lowering its profit margin) if it allowed consumers to choose between Microsoft and a competitor. They knew firsthand how Microsoft dealt with potential competitors such as Stac Electronics. Stac was winning rave reviews for its disk compression software, a clever way of storing twice as much information on a computer hard drive, when founder Gary Clow thought he had caught the break of a lifetime when he met Gates at a conference. Gates invited Clow to Redmond to talk about a deal to bundle his compression system in DOS 6.0, but the two sides couldn't come to terms. DOS 6.0 went on to include a disk compression product so remarkably similar to Stac's that Stac won a $120 million patent infringement verdict against Microsoft. Yet so shameless was Microsoft that the company used DOS's ability to squeeze twice as

---

says. "Half my family died then." He admitted, though, that he had been quoted accurately as saying, "Windows is like waking up and finding out that your partner has AIDS."

much data onto a disk as its main selling point. Gates himself wore a "We came, we saw, we doubled" T-shirt at the product launch.

Onstage with Alsop, Gates defended himself with sarcasm. Could he help it if he hired bright people who excelled at their jobs? "What should I tell them?" he asked, his voice rising an octave. "Don't be so smart? Take more time off?" More than 80 percent of the world's PCs were using DOS. Windows was selling at a clip of 1 million copies per month. "That's not something I'm going to apologize for," Gates harrumphed.

Some were predicting the sky would fall on Microsoft despite its successes, just as it had fallen on IBM. "The cracks are starting to show," a columnist for *PC Computing* wrote in 1992. The company had grown too large and too rich, and the flabbiness was starting to show in some of its products. Hope among those who loved to hate Microsoft came in any number of forms: the mediocre reviews that greeted most of its products; an ongoing Federal Trade Commission investigation into alleged antitrust practices. Philippe Kahn predicted that Gates's arrogance would catch up with him, as would his growing reputation as someone not to be trusted as a partner. No one will work with Microsoft anymore, Kahn told *The New York Times*. "They don't have any friends left."*

The funny thing is that for all that Gates disagreed with these assessments, he tended to sound more like the doomsayers than like the pundits declaring him lord emperor and ruler. Microsoft was ahead, sure, but what about tomorrow? he asked his fellow execs at Agenda. There were always two kids in a garage somewhere who might ace them all. And what about Novell? The wise guys had predicted that Microsoft's LAN-Man would have a 30 percent market share by 1992, but at the start of 1993, its market share was stuck at 7 percent. And what about Ray Noorda's tactics? *He's* talking unfair competition? He's out to get *me! He's* the one who violated their NDA ("nondisclosure agreement"), laying out the details of their failed merger attempt in interviews with the press. It was an unusual claim to be made by the CEO of a company

---

* The alignment of the stars and planets at the moment of Gates's birth offered another ray of hope. Catherine Duncan was a Monterey, California–based psychic who had never heard of Bill Gates when *USA Today* hired her to do an astrological reading of his fate. "Bill Gates has felt like a misfit since early childhood, always taking the unbeaten path," she wrote. "He has always had extraordinary dreams and dreams more than most people. . . . But like a torch, he burns hot and hard and could run out of gas."

that would log nearly $4 billion in sales that year, but Gates cried, "We're the total underdog!"

RAY NOORDA had never attended the right schools. Growing up in Utah, he had never met any of the right people—unlike Gates, who had. Noorda truly was a self-made man. He was an aw-shucks kind of guy partial to $100 suits who displayed none of the pomp and braggadocio that went hand in hand with success in the software industry. Whereas Gates had his megahouse and Larry Ellison his jets and a spread fit for a sixteenth-century Japanese emperor, Noorda drove a Ford pickup and lived in a house that had probably cost less than $100,000. Until 1992, he paid himself a salary of only $38,000 a year.

He was a quirky man with quirky habits who didn't care what people thought. His office was pocket-sized, with room enough for a desk, a chair, and a filing cabinet but not even a small round table and chairs. That may have been part of Noorda's charm, but it was also impractical. Customers would fly in from out of town, and he would meet them not at Novell headquarters but at their hotel. "Ray knew his own mind," sighed a disenchanted Novellite who left after realizing that he had risen so high on the organizational chart that he could no longer make much of a difference in the company. "What Ray really wanted was a bunch of lieutenants to go out and do what he told them to do." People joked about Noorda's Golden Boys of the Month: they'd move up the ranks, get a glimpse of life at the top, and then jump the first time a head-hunter smiled their way. "No one made a decision at Novell," another Golden Boy said, "without Ray's approval."

He could be a real bastard to work for. The phone would ring at six in the morning in a top manager's house, and without picking it up he would know it was Noorda. One time Duff Thompson, WordPerfect's chief counsel, joined several top Novell managers on a tropical vaca-tion. Each day began with a phone call from Noorda. There were phone calls during lunch and pink message slips waiting for them when they returned from the beach. "The poor guys, Ray struck fear into them," Thompson said.

But when the situation demanded it, he could turn on the charm. In meetings with customers and Novell partners, he was persuasive and articulate, a diplomat who so often was described in press accounts as the industry's "Mr. Nice Guy," it was as if it was an official title. Even before he launched his jihad against the Evil Empire of Microsoft, Noorda viewed himself as the Woodrow Wilson of the software industry, championing a software League of Nations dedicated to the proposition that competition didn't have to be a battle to the death. Noorda called it "co-opetition": the difficult art of cooperating with companies for the common good even as you compete against them. "This business doesn't have to be a zero-sum game," Noorda would say. "Working together, we can all win." The thorn in his side—his Third Reich—was the tirelessly grabby Gates. One year Gates's people were helping you tinker with your product so it would work with DOS, the next he was competing with you in the same business, making you feel like a fool for sharing even a shred of inside intelligence. Ecologists call it the Tragedy of the Commons. In a village with limited grazing land, a conservation plan works only if every cattle rancher signs up—because if the others see even one nonparticipating rancher wantonly feeding his herd, they realize that their own community spirit means only that no one's herd is well fed except the food hog's.

"Their job is to dominate," Noorda said of Microsoft in an interview with *U.S. News & World Report.* "It's the only way they feel safe."

After the first failed attempt at a merger with Microsoft, Noorda took to the road. He met with Manzi of Lotus in Cambridge, with the WordPerfect crew fifteen miles down the road, and with the people at Digital Research on the Monterey Peninsula. He traveled to Armonk to meet with IBM executives, he even met with industry gadfly Stewart Alsop to solicit his opinion. His goal was to form a loosely aligned anti-Microsoft confederation. With each of his counterparts, he'd begin his pitch the same way: "We're all leaders in our field, but we face this great threat . . ." Microsoft was working hard so that all its products would share the same "look and feel." So Noorda proposed that they work together so they could claim the same. He suggested coadvertising and co-marketing. And if things worked out well, they might further cut costs by sharing order fulfillment and customer support departments. Together, they could offer their own, best-of-category one-stop shopping.

The people at WordPerfect smiled politely when Noorda laid out his united-we-stand, divided-we-fall plea for cooperation. Then they sent him away empty-handed. "Ray saw clearly, more clearly than the rest of us, that Microsoft's endgame was to monopolize the entire software industry," said Duff Thompson, who sat in on Noorda's pitch to WordPerfect. "Even if we agreed, we didn't think Gates had the power to pull it off." Noorda was apparently far more persuasive in his meeting with Manzi. In April 1990, the two shocked the industry by announcing that they planned to merge their two companies. But even this effort fell short of Noorda's goal. At the eleventh hour, he proposed what turned out to be the deal breaker: a four-four split on the board of directors, rather than the four-three split in Lotus's favor that Noorda had already agreed to.* The initial deal had been hailed as a formidable challenge to Microsoft's growing dominance. After it fell apart, the consensus among the Wall Street sages was that the failed merger had strengthened Microsoft's position—a position Manzi was also inclined to take.

"We ended up wasting a lot of time and money talking with people who apparently didn't know what they wanted," a furious Manzi told *The Wall Street Journal* the day the deal blew up. By coincidence, Microsoft unveiled Windows 3.0 the next day, yet now relations between the industry's second and third largest software firms were terribly frayed. A year later, Novell bought Digital Research for $130 million, which proved to be only the start of Noorda's buying spree.

Between the failed Lotus merger and 1994, when Noorda stepped down as CEO, Novell acquired roughly twenty companies, virtually all of them, in one way or another, competitors of Microsoft. Microsoft was selling a program called Visual BASIC, a second generation of its original BASIC for the PC, so Novell bought a competing product called AppWare for $18 million. Microsoft was coming out with Windows NT (an operating system that allowed an entire office of PCs to share everything), so in 1992 Novell bought the rights to the Unix operating system, variations of which controlled one of every four of the world's computers but none of the PC market. The $350 million Novell paid AT&T for the rights to Unix ranked as one of the largest acquisitions in industry history. Yet that figure would soon seem like a drop in the bucket.

Novell's spin doctors didn't bother dressing up their motives. Unless someone slowed Gates down, they said, it would be too late. Novell would use its leverage as the purveyor of NetWare to push this alternative operating system. Off the record, Novell's PR people told reporters that a growing anti-Microsoft sentiment was its best ally. What better

* As Noorda's underlings would tell it, the more he saw of Lotus's profligate ways—its corporate jets and fancy headquarters—and the more he got to know Manzi, a Gucci-wearing marketeer who wouldn't give his counterpart his home phone number, the less enamored he became with the idea of a deal.

THE PLOT TO GET BILL GATES

way to galvanize support for Unix than by casting it as an alternative to Windows? Leading the charge was Noorda, a veritable anti-Microsoft quote machine in the months that followed the Unix purchase. Gates has no heart, he said; the company he runs lives by no moral code. It's an evil force that must be stopped. He even began floating the idea of a class action civil suit against Microsoft, claiming antitrust violations.

The more Noorda talked, the more people at Microsoft seethed. For Gates the final straw was the news that Noorda had been singing to the feds, who had started poking around in Microsoft's affairs. To sell more copies of DR-DOS, Gates told a group of financial analysts, a "paranoid" Noorda was "spreading lies about us." Ballmer went further, portraying Novell as an entrenched "monopolist" as "dirty as can be, but they play holier-than-thou."

Often inside the computer world, the foot soldiers on opposite sides continue talking to one another even as the generals fight. Jim Manzi might hate Gates, but if Lotus 1-2-3 doesn't work on the next version of Windows, customers will blame both companies. So engineers at both companies tiptoe carefully around one another, hoping they provide enough information for their counterparts to do their job but not so much that they've blabbed any vital secrets. But suddenly the Novell and Microsoft engineers cut off all communications. "It just didn't make sense," said Microsoft's Bob Kruger. "These people I had long-standing relationships with were suddenly much different people over the phone. When the mudslinging started in the press, I added up two and two. Decisions were obviously coming from the top."

OTHERS WERE ALSO SCRAMBLING to set themselves up as the alternative to Microsoft. WordPerfect was slow to port to Windows, so Lotus bought a Windows-based competitor called Ami, the third most popular word processor on the market. So now Lotus could claim it had a suite of office products, just like Microsoft. But Lotus didn't offer tools or languages, so Manzi and Philippe Kahn started talking, an amazing turn of events. Several years earlier, Lotus had sued Borland in a nasty case that had gone all the way to the Supreme Court (Lotus ultimately lost). Philippe Kahn may have disliked Gates, but he *hated* Jim Manzi. Yet in December 1992, the buzz inside the industry was a tentative merger between Lotus and Borland, leading a *Business Week* reporter to write, "These days, it seems people go to extremes to create a new industry infrastructure as long as Bill Gates isn't the chief architect."

To Ray Noorda, though, he himself was the only logical choice for ringleader. That's what he told *Business Week*, that's what he'd tell anyone else willing to listen. Who else had withstood everything Gates had thrown at him, only to *gain* market share? Gates had declared that it would be a "nightmare" if NetWare continued to whip LAN-Man, according to a 1991 Gates memo leaked to the press. Yet by the start of 1993, NetWare's share of the network market had grown to 70 percent and Novell had $500 million in the bank. That was a pittance compared to Microsoft's $2 billion war chest, but it was more than any other would-be ringleader could boast. When WordPerfect was gasping for cash, Noorda extended the company a line of credit. Novell was only one third the size of Microsoft, but by the start of 1993 it was also the industry's undisputed number two.

Noorda turned sixty-eight the year Novell bought Unix. He was a jogger and biker and kept himself fit, but he had recently had surgery to implant a pacemaker in his chest. Then there was his mind. He was forgetting the names of top aides whom he had known for years. He'd wake up in a hotel room and forget where he was or why he was there. Those close to him gently encouraged him to name a successor, but instead he only half retired. "At that point, it was like nothing mattered but Gates," said a Novell executive who at one point had taken a turn as Noorda's Golden Boy of the Month. "It was Microsoft, Microsoft, Microsoft, and Gates, Gates, Gates." By 1993, Noorda joined Gates in the billionaire boys' club,* but he seemed so . . . dissatisfied, as if nearly fifty years in the technology business would go spinning down the drain if he quit now. He was no longer interested in the around-the-clock grind of running a publicly traded company, but he also seemed incapable of handing over the reins.†

Like Captain Ahab, hobbled by a peg leg, Noorda saw it as his duty,

* To induce him to take the reins of the struggling start-up, Novell's board of directors had granted Noorda an 11 percent cut of the company's stock.

† "I had many conversations with Ray at that time, and it was very sad," Philippe Kahn said. "It'd be Gates this and Gates that. I don't blame him. I don't doubt Gates cozied up to Novell just to take a couple of looks, learn what he could about a competitor. Twice Noorda fell for it. And he was *soooo* mad. He had been naive. He was had by this much younger man. So he became very, very obsessed."

no matter what his physical condition or frame of mind, to ride the high seas in search of his prey. He had been raised a Mormon but more than forty years had passed since his two-year stint as a Mormon missionary—and now he joked with people that he had again found his cause. "I think Ray truly believed that he was on a mission of God," said Sheldon Laube, who would take over as Novell's chief technology officer after Noorda stepped down as CEO. "It was on that level with him. He truly believed his role in life was to return the balance of power to the industry. He really saw himself as the only one who could neutralize the Evil Empire. It's like that was going to be the six-hundred-foot monument his colleagues would build in his honor." Everyone jokingly referred to Microsoft as the Evil Empire, but for Noorda there was no mirth in the line. The Softies truly were the infidels in their midst. Former WordPerfect executive Dan Lunt seemed to sum up the general sentiment of the Utah software community when he said, almost as if offering a eulogy, "It was the last sad gasp out of a man who had lived until then a very full and successful life."

AT MICROSOFT people were always playing this interesting game of "What if." Gates, Ballmer, and a bunch of top managers would head off into the Cascade Mountains or somewhere else beautiful and then spend every minute indoors pulling their hair out over some brain puzzler. In early 1994 they took a trip to a stone-and-wood-beamed lodge on the coast. There small groups met from seven in the morning until eleven at night to imagine the world from the perspective of various foes. It was rigorous and institutionalized hand-wringing: imagine every bad thing that could happen to Microsoft, and then devise a strategy for averting disaster. At the end of the retreat each team presented its findings to a Gates-led team of executives.

The team assigned to Novell knew what *they* would do if they owned the NetWare franchise: keep adding to it until it had grown vital enough to act as a freestanding operating system, able to run applications and manage a computer's memory. That's what Microsoft was trying to do with Windows, only in reverse: use the real estate that first DOS and then Windows had captured on the PC and then extend it so that it would match everything NetWare or OS/2 could do. The smart guys were always preaching the power of a platform that other software companies built products for. If you have something that has emerged as an industry standard, you milk it for all it's worth.

Those assigned to the Novell group, though, thought they knew better. The buzz inside the industry was that Noorda, who was preoccupied by all the new companies he had bought, was starving his NetWare team. So when it came time to peer into the future for the benefit of the executive team, they predicted that Novell would attempt to use its leverage in the networking market to get into the applications game. The company would purchase WordPerfect, they predicted, and also Borland's Quattro Pro spreadsheet.

When the Novell team members laid out this scenario for the executive team, they immediately wished they hadn't said it out loud. Because then it was a race between Gates and Ballmer to throw at the group the pair's favorite expression: "That's the stupidest thing I've ever heard." They defended their scenario and felt foolish for doing so until two weeks later, in March 1994, when suddenly they seemed the oracles of Microsoft as another 7.0 quake hit the software world: in one fell swoop, Novell was buying both WordPerfect and Quattro Pro. Microsoft had Microsoft Office, so Novell would counter with PerfectOffice, featuring a word processor still hanging on (though barely) as the industry's number one word processor and the third-place spreadsheet.

Novell paid $1.4 billion for WordPerfect, the largest acquisition price in software history. But the Wall Street smart guys declared the price wildly excessive, especially given that WordPerfect was already "in the jaws of Microsoft," as one analyst said at the time. Novell's stock dropped so precipitously that by the time the deal was actually consummated, the Novell stock WordPerfect's owners collected was worth something closer to $900 million. Even so, $900 million was still a record. Once upon a time, the $145 million Novell paid for Quattro Pro would've been a big deal, but no longer. Not when everyone was bulking up to take on the Silicon Bully.

"We thought we were buying this huge cash cow," one former Novell executive said, "but we ended up with a big cash drain." When disaster struck, when hundreds of laid-off WordPerfect workers found themselves escorted out by Security, Novell would be blamed, but that wasn't quite fair. "The boat was already sinking, if not close to the bottom of the ocean, by the time they tried to come in and fix things," says former WordPerfect executive Pete Peterson. When Noorda's buying binge began, Paul Johnson, an analyst with Robertson Stephens, sent Noorda a copy of an academic paper that stressed the importance of a platform. After the WordPerfect purchase, Johnson again sent him the article, along with a note that read, "With all the trouble getting out NetWare 4, why are you going after Microsoft on applications???" The rumors about Novell shortchanging its core asset turned out to be accurate. The manager overseeing the NetWare development team eventually confessed that his life was a constant battle for the resources required to improve Novell's best-selling product.

Noorda stepped down as Novell's CEO soon after the WordPerfect acquisition. The Novell Office Suite was to be his crowning glory, but it would end up as the folly that would mar his name. Noorda's successor, Robert Frankenberg, complained about the "turmoil" involved in trying to integrate "twenty tribes" into his company's corporate culture. Frankenberg was Noorda's handpicked successor, but even he confessed that Bill Envy had gotten the better of his benefactor. "Ray did tend to overfocus on Microsoft, and it had gone too far by the time I got here," he said. He took another dig at his predecessor when he said, in the same interview, that customers "expect us to act like grown-ups."

Unix's 1,900 engineers remained in New Jersey even after Novell bought the company from AT&T. So Novell was trying to get two completely disparate products, NetWare and Unix, to work together, yet the two teams working on the problem were 2,500 miles apart. By contrast, when Microsoft bought a company, it sent out trucks to move everybody up to Redmond. And if during the negotiations it felt compelled to agree to allow a company to remain where it was, then at the very least there would be no discussion that the newly acquired company would henceforth be a Windows shop. Yet Novell sold an array of component parts that didn't work together, primarily because no one was knocking heads to make sure they did. "In retrospect, it's amazing what we let Unix and these other guys get away with," said a former Novell executive.

And then there were the clashes between the WordPerfect and Novell teams. The two companies were both located in the Utah Valley, south of Salt Lake City, but they viewed each other as foreigners. At the old WordPerfect, most employees had left the office promptly at five to be with their families or tend to Mormon church duties. The sales force had never toiled under quotas, and even the lowliest person at the company had been no more than five levels from the top. Under Novell's leadership, though, there were now a dozen layers between a shipping clerk and the top boss. WordPerfect managers were replaced by Novell managers, causing dissension. Departments were merged, people laid off, and key services contracted out to cut expenses. WordPerfect's sales dropped by 14 percent in 1994 and then another 9 percent in 1995. Those who could, abandoned the company—if they hadn't already.

Rather than a strong hand, Noorda left Frankenberg with a Hobson's choice: Should he sell at a cut-rate price a business going through obvious hard times or keep throwing good money after bad? When Frankenberg finally decided to sell, it was too late. A page-one article in *The Wall Street Journal* reporting on the pending sale of WordPerfect (under the headline "Acquisition of WordPerfect Hobbled Network Giant, and Microsoft Is Gaining") read more like an obituary: this company, which had laid off more than two thirds of its employees, had "lost most of its market share, virtually imploding last fall." The company lingered on the selling block, reeking more of failure with each passing month and leaving those who were left to resort to gallows humor. "Will code for food," read a block-letter sign in one window. "Software Company Cheap, Inquire Within." More than eighteen months would pass before Novell found a taker. This once proud top-of-the-line king of the word processing world was sold to Corel, a software company that was hoping to compete with Microsoft by selling its software at bargain-basement prices. Corel paid $20 million in cash and roughly $100 million in stock for a firm that had cost Novell $1.4 billion. Novell also sold Unix for $60 million, or less than 20 cents on the dollar. Novell's stock plummeted, falling 73 percent between 1994 and 1997.

And the network wars between Novell and Microsoft? After ten years of fierce fighting, after all the bile and late nights and exhortations to do better, Microsoft retired LAN-Man, folding its printing and file-sharing capabilities into Windows NT. And just like that, the network wars were over. Microsoft began to give away for free, as part of the operating system it was pitching to the corporate market, the product it had fought so fiercely to sell. Even as Novell clung to more than a 60 percent share of the market, the smart guys declared the company dead. "You can't compete with free," they told each other—and of course they were right.

With a sigh, with a whiff of bitterness but mainly relief, Pete Peterson said of Microsoft, "They're like that silly shark in *Jaws*. They keep on coming and coming and coming. You move as fast as you can, you run, you keep on running, but eventually you slip. Eventually you run out of resources." He didn't finish the thought, but he didn't have to: You run out of steam and then they're on you. And the next thing you know, every loudmouth with a column is pronouncing you dead.

THERE HAD BEEN A TIME when people inside the computer world had referred to Bill Gates as a kid, but no longer. The voice was the same, and the hair—well, if it wasn't quite well-groomed, then at least all his mother's nagging about remembering to shampoo when he bathed had paid off. The waistline was the difference. The bigger Microsoft grew, the more Gates's belly swelled. Blame it not on his voracious appetite for business but on the BurgerMaster, the greasy spoon he ordered lunch from so often that his secretary had programmed it into her speed dialer beside the phone numbers of executives from IBM, Compaq, and Dell.

The BurgerMaster order was invariably the same: a cheeseburger, fries, and a chocolate shake, gobbled while working at his desk or in a meeting with others. He didn't cook, so dinner was usually *The Economist* or *The Wall Street Journal* at McDonald's or Jack-in-the-Box. ("In terms of fast food and deep understanding of the culture of fast food," Gates told *Playboy,* "I'm your man.") And when it wasn't burgers it was pizza, beef tacos, a hot dog on the go at the airport, or something else that the Center for Science in the Public Interest would surely warn us against eating. If the body is merely an encasement for the brain and nourishment only a means of working longer hours, it was grease that served as Gates's favorite fuel.

If Nathan Myhrvold is right—if Melville provides the perfect parallel for understanding Gates's foes—the metaphor cuts two ways. If Noorda was Ahab, there was no doubting the role Gates filled. His skin was as white as a poet's from too many weekends spent sitting in front of a computer. He glowed an incandescent white, a sheen from the computer screen's ultraviolet rays and indoor fluorescent lights. Though earlier in his career he had probably weighed close to 160, by the mid-1990s he looked as if he were pushing the scales above 200. He felt the hurt of the barbs launched by his foes, so in that way he was also like Moby-Dick, who traveled the ocean with metal spears piercing his flesh. But the battle scars only seemed to make both these Leviathans tougher and meaner.

In March 1993, Microsoft sent out a press release subsequently reported on the front page of *The Wall Street Journal:* company CEO and chairman William Gates III had gotten engaged. For those hoping the right woman would slow Gates down, the news wasn't encouraging. His betrothed was a Microsoft product manager named Melinda French whom Gates had met years earlier in New York at a Microsoft media event, when Gates was thirty-two and French twenty-two. Someone outside the industry might be able to draw him into the wider world, but a homegrown product manager with an MBA would know what was Gates's first true love. French was a blue blood from Dallas who had attended the exclusive Ursuline Academy, an upper-crust all-girl prep school, before going on to Duke, where she had dated, among other prospects, William Wrigley, heir to the chewing-gum fortune. Instinctively she would understand that it was futile to compete with Microsoft.

Gates proposed to Melinda in a fashion befitting a billionaire. Microsoft's corporate PR is always making a big deal about Gates being your average Joe who just happens to be worth an ungodly sum of money, but he and Melinda were on a chartered jet after a very un-average-Joe-like weekend in Palm Springs. Melinda thought they were flying home to Seattle, but the jet was actually heading to Omaha, where Gates had arranged to meet fellow gazillionaire Warren Buffett. Buffett owned a jewelry store that he opened for the occasion so the two could pick out an engagement ring. The rock they chose was so huge that author James Wallace, in his book *Overdrive,* said French took to covering her hand when she appeared in public, out of embarrassment.

They were married on the Hawaiian island of Lanai, a secluded smaller island favored by the fabulously well-to-do and famous. So his wedding wouldn't become a media spectacle, Gates booked all the available rooms at the island's two resorts and rented every available helicopter in the vicinity.* Whoever worked the wedding first had to sign a nondisclosure agreement. Gates chartered a Boeing 737 to fly guests from Honolulu to Lanai and surprised his bride-to-be when he flew in her all-time favorite musician, Willie Nelson, to perform at a New Year's

---

* Several reporters and photographers managed to slip onto the island anyway. The authorities gave each a trespassing notice and threatened them with arrest if they returned. The *Seattle Post-Intelligencer* did manage something of a scoop by stationing a reporter armed with binoculars and a photographer with a telephoto camera on a boat several hundred yards off shore.

Eve party the night before the wedding. The two were married, Wallace wrote, on the par-three twelfth hole of a championship golf course designed by golf great Jack Nicklaus. The bride, of course, wore white (Italian silk), the groom a white dinner jacket (the Great White!) and black tuxedo pants. The 130-person affair reportedly cost Gates more than a million dollars.

Playboy interviewed Gates shortly after he was married. The interview was remarkable for its candor (Gates practically confesses to having dropped acid in his early twenties), but when asked about the predictions that married life would slow him down, Gates sounded like a computer message: "If they really think I'm going to work a lot less just because I'm married, that's an error." When interviewer David Rensin pressed the point, Gates argued that if anything, he'd have more time to spend at the office. "Married life is a simpler life. Who I spend my time with is established in advance." There would be a vacation to China and no doubt more weekends in Palm Springs (where he could still keep in touch with the home office via e-mail), but mainly he was the same man after his marriage as he was before. When the country's richest man and his wife got together with the country's second richest man (Warren Buffett) and his wife, the four of them spent nine hours playing bridge. When they got hungry, the new Mrs. Gates drove to the local McDonald's for takeout.

Part 02: Call Me Ishmael

"The most dementing of all modern sins is the inability to distinguish excellence from success."
– David Hare

CHAPTER 07

THE GREAT INTERNET LAND GRAB

Simply inventing a thing isn't enough anymore. The new rules of fame dictate that you must also grow filthy rich off your idea. Only then do you get the cover of *Newsweek* and a spot on the couch opposite Katie. Today, the science and tech world's stars are entrepreneurs, fabulously well-to-do titans honored with sweet-smelling profiles everywhere from *People* to *The New Yorker*. Nowadays, it's as if a technical breakthrough isn't a breakthrough, at least in the realm of the popular press, until someone figures out how to shrink-wrap the idea and make truckloads of money off it. The actual creators are relegated to relative backwaters such as *DBMS Magazine* and *Dr. Dobb's Journal*.

In an era less obsessed with the bottom line of accomplishments, Tim Berners-Lee, creator of the World Wide Web, might have been hailed as a visionary. Instead, any fame he might derive from his invention has been almost entirely eclipsed by the overexposed Marc Andreessen, cofounder of Netscape, whom *Newsweek* once described as the "24-year-old über-super-wunder whiz kid of cyberspace."

A nuclear physicist by training, Berners-Lee concocted the World Wide Web as a means by which he and his colleagues could share their research. They could have used the Internet, which had been around since the early 1970s. Linked via modems and telephone lines, computer users hooked into the Internet could send one another mail electronically and, if they had the right electronic address, sift through whatever a fellow user chose to post on a machine. But the Internet was static, colorless, and arcane, inhabited mainly by academics, spooks, and decidedly antientrepreneurial hackers.* The Web, unveiled in 1991, was easy to navigate—you just had to click on a related "hyperlink" to delve deeper into a topic—and lent itself to 3-D graphics and other user-friendly embellishments. It was an amazing breakthrough, but Berners-Lee's mistake, at least from the perspective of the hypercapitalistic 1990s, was that he dreamed about the Web's potential to foster a global village, not its potential to earn him a villa and a fleet of fancy cars. You'd see Berners-Lee quoted in places like *Inter@ctive Week* and pictured in the occasional sidebar in something more high profile, but he was never blow-dried and posed on the cover of a national magazine. He was just another obtuse academic working out of a sparse office on MIT's campus.

The business reporters never knew quite what to make of Berners-Lee. They could respect his brainpower, but there seemed something . . . *off* about him. He could've owned the Web, reporters told themselves, shaking their heads. Was he worth even a million dollars? Didn't he eat his insides out when he saw the billions others were making off his creation? He'd look at a reporter dumbly if one asked why he didn't cash in on his invention—as if he didn't even have a clue. The reporters would almost have preferred self-flagellation and angst to his we-are-the-world global-community spiel. Writing in *Forbes ASAP*, he bemoaned the barrage of questions about the untold riches he had allowed to slip through his fingers. Talk about preachy! He criticized society's preoccupation with his lack of wealth—a "disturbing" trend that "pervades this country." It was all so . . . *seventies.*

By contrast there was Marc Andreessen, who confessed that as a high school senior he had chosen electrical engineering as his major because one of the national magazines had published a chart showing that electrical engineers earned the highest starting salary out of college. Andreessen offered an easily packaged, red-white-and-blue tale of success, Horatio Alger without the tediousness of all those years of hard work. As a freshman at the University of Illinois, Andreessen secured a part-time programming job at the school's National Center for Supercomputing Applications. Bored working on a Web-based project of use to only a small group of academics, he daydreamed about the mass appeal

---

* By "hackers" I mean the more noble and original definition of that term, software wizards for whom solving computer-programming problems is something between pleasure and obsession.

of the Web. Eventually, he helped put together the team that wrote Mosaic, a software program that made it easier to browse the Web. Andreessen wasn't the team's sharpest programmer, nor was Mosaic the Web's first widely used browser. But the program was a good one, and Andreessen, never modest when it came time to take bows, was the first to cash in, hooking up shortly after he graduated with two of the bigger-name successes in Silicon Valley.* He was twenty-four years old the first time he appeared on the cover of a national magazine, dressed in jeans and a polo, barefoot, seated on a golden throne. Worth more than $130 million, he was emblematic of those *Time* dubbed "The Golden Geeks." ("They invent. They start companies. And the stock market has made them INSTANTAIRES.")

Andreessen was the perfect Web poster boy, impossibly young to be so rich yet still, in Gatesian fashion, inclined toward burgers and malts at the local dive. He was dubbed "the next Bill Gates" by *Forbes* and no doubt others, and his company, Netscape Communications, served as the yeast that allowed the Web hype to rise. Of course: the Internet remained a well-kept secret until producing its first cyberstar, this oversized Baby Huey with an astronomically oversized brokerage account. Andreessen would be profiled in *The New York Times, Newsweek, U.S. News & World Report, GQ,* all the big business magazines, and *Rolling Stone.*

Netscape went public in 1995—the same year that the government, after two decades of concessions to the free market, relinquished all control of the Internet. Perhaps it's just coincidence that the year the Internet was privatized was also the year it became a story you couldn't escape. In its special year-end double issue, *Newsweek* dubbed 1995 "The Year of the Internet." It was an indisputable appellation if the sheer volume of words were the criterion. Though 1995 was also the year America was captivated by the so-called Trial of the Century, there was no contest when the topics were set side by side. Three quarters of the way through 1995, industry analyst Richard Shaffer ran a Lexis-Nexis news search and found that articles about the Internet were outpacing dispatches from the O.J. trial by more than two to one. "Was there ever a

---

* The head of the University of Illinois's National Center for Supercomputing Applications asked Andreessen to stay on at the center after graduating, but Andreessen left because a precondition for a full-time job there was that he leave the browser project, then called Mosaic. "Some forty people had a role in creating Mosaic," the center's head told Andreessen. "Don't you think it's time to give someone else a chance to share the glory?"

time," *Newsweek's* highly regarded contributing editor Steven Levy asked, "when surfing was performed in a bathing suit, outdoors?"

How significant was the Internet? The editors at *Newsweek* imagined the Web changing the way we communicate, shop, and read, but that was nothing compared to what the cyberpundits were prognosticating. George Gilder, one of Reagan's supply-side gurus before reinventing himself as a techno-Utopian, imagined the Web bringing about an egalitarian society worthy of a *Star Trek* episode. "The most deprived ghetto child," he wrote in *Forbes*, "in the most benighted project will gain educational opportunities exceeding those of today's suburban preppie." Gilder also predicted that the Web would mean the death of television and the end of the U.S. Postal Service. Not to be outdone, MIT's Nicholas Negroponte, another high priest in the cyberchurch, saw the Web as a key to world peace. John Perry Barlow, the Grateful Dead lyricist turned Web freedom fighter, believed that only by traveling back to the time of the caveman could we understand all that was happening around us. "We are in the middle of the most transforming technological event since the capture of fire," Barlow wrote.

IN SILICON VALLEY, people tended to view themselves as the greatest assemblage of brainpower and creativity since Florence under the Medicis. Yet 1993 and 1994 had been the Dark Ages, when virtually every software shop in the Valley had found itself in a rut. Programmers and their bosses cried into their pale ales, longingly recalling the earlier days of the wide-open plains. Where were the great inventions? What could reignite their creative spark? The big thing then was Interactive TV, the killer app "video on demand"—any movie, anytime, at a click of a button. But hundreds of millions of dollars later, Interactive TV was proving to be a colossal failure. More noble pursuits such as artificial intelligence were turning out to be similarly colossal busts.

Somehow it all seemed like Bill Gates's fault—the tediousness of it all, the stifled innovation. He and his invasion force were like so many spaceships hovering above the planet, sucking the life and creativity out of them. Even the most highly regarded software houses were cranking out "bloatware," obese versions of old products stuffed with ever more features. The term on everyone's lips in the early 1990s was "Wintel": PCs running the Windows operating system and powered by Intel chips. By 1994, Wintel machines accounted for four of every five PCs sold in the United States. Microsoft was a grim shadow over the industry, so dark and oppressive one could barely dream.

The World Wide Web, then, was received like a gift from the gods of technology. Microsoft may have won the PC wars, but there was now an entirely new and pristine field on which everyone could compete. One of the Valley's own, Jim Clark, the entrepreneur behind Netscape, led the way. Clark was a former Stanford professor who in the early 1980s had founded Silicon Graphics, makers of the machines that breathed life into the dinosaurs populating Steven Spielberg's *Jurassic Park.* Tired of the squabbling inside the company he had founded, Clark quit, figuring he'd get into Interactive TV. He had never heard of Andreessen or Mosaic and didn't know much if anything about the Web, but that was the amazing thing about these wizards inventing the future: they were a bunch of Columbuses, getting the credit for discovering America even though they'd actually been looking for spices in the Far East. Some people Clark knew told him about a sharp and ambitious twenty-two-year-old named Marc Andreessen. Clark sent him an e-mail, and, a few rides on Clark's yacht later, they were partners in a company they called Mosaic. Clark dangled a lot of cash to lure Andreessen's former mates from the University of Illinois's supercomputer center and dropped Mosaic in favor of Netscape only after the university threatened to sue. Clark invested $4 million of his own money in the company, founded in the spring of 1994. By the end of 1995, he would be worth more than a billion dollars.

Netscape Navigator was a simple-to-use piece of code that let users cruise the Web in sparkling Technicolor. It was one potential Microsoft killer; Sun's Java programming language, unveiled in May 1995, was another. The promise of Java was that any program, if written in Java, could run on any computer anywhere, no matter what the operating system. Java, George Gilder wrote in *Forbes ASAP,* represented "a fundamental break in the history of technology" that loomed as "a menace [to] Microsoft's software supremacy." The parking lots of the Valley's most successful firms were suddenly filled again, even on weekends. And every unoccupied patch of real estate—every failed Chinese restaurant from San Jose to Santa Clara, every abandoned furniture showroom from Palo Alto to Burlingame—became the birthplace of yet another start-up with the term "net" or "web" in its name. The entire Valley was in the throes of a revival.

Smart money. Dumb money. Cheap money. Early money. Money in a hurry. Nervous money. Money of every kind rained down on the Valley. There were high-tech companies that wanted to buy their way into the game and companies linked in one way or another to communications (media conglomerates, long-distance companies, cable TV concerns), so frightened they might miss the future that they took the next red-eye west with checkbook in hand. We're protecting our brand, executives told themselves. We're investing in the future. But mainly they were doing it because the next guy was.

AMONG THE VENTURE CAPITALIST SET, 1995 will forever be known affectionately as the year of the Great Internet Land Grab. Venture capitalists—or "VCs," in Valleyspeak—are professional money managers who invest on behalf of wealthy clients and institutional funds such as university endowments and employee pensions, trading cash for an ownership stake in fledgling companies. The basic game remained the same: invest a million or two in a tiny, anonymous company in return for a major equity stake, and then cross your fingers that this would be The One that exploded into the next Microsoft. But the frantic, stampedelike quality of 1995 meant that normal safeguards such as due diligence proved to be a nuisance.* The most successful venture capitalists tended to be those who poked a stake into the ground as quickly as they could so that the next guy coming around the bend wouldn't claim that patch as his own.

"I saw one of the traditionally conservative firms make an offer to an entrepreneur at the end of a first meeting," said John Fisher, a partner in a Silicon Valley–based venture capital firm that specialized in the rawest of start-ups. "No follow-up calls, no checking of references—just an offer of one million dollars for a piece of their company. I've never witnessed a feeding frenzy like that in my life." Among the worst culprits? He and his partners at Draper Fisher Jurvetson. "We were slapping down bets as fast as we could," Fisher said.

They would make some lollapalooza-sized mistakes, costing investors such as Yale and Duke millions of dollars. But what were a few million down the drain here and there (amounts Fisher described as "blips") when one day you might hit the big strike that would pay out in the hundreds of millions? Besides, sitting on the sidelines was a far

---

* Due diligence is when you poke around under the hood to make sure you're buying a car that has a working engine.

greater mistake than losing a few million dollars. Who among Valley insiders wasn't buzzing about New Enterprise Associates (NEA), one of the Valley's most successful venture firms, which had turned Jim Clark away when he was in their offices hungry for cash? The venture capital firm of Kleiner Perkins Caufield & Byers bought an 11 percent share of Netscape for $5 million in 1994. By the end of 1995, its stake in Netscape would be worth more than $400 million.

The established venture capital firms represented the smart money. They were the professional money managers with connections and a track record. Jostling at the trough of the VC's rejects were the unlucky entrepreneurs, including trust-fund brats playing with Daddy's money and young MBAs looking for investment opportunities on behalf of the old money set. The Valley's old hands had seen it before. In the early 1980s, it had been the disk drive craze. Something like a dozen disk drive companies had gone public within a two-year period, each projecting a 30 percent market share. Five years later, only a few had been left. There was the Videotext craze, which sucked up hundreds of millions from a Who's Who of big media companies, and handheld computers, which sucked up hundreds of millions more. Had you invested in Compaq or Dell years ago, you'd be a very wealthy person today. But how do you know which company will grow to be a Dell and which will end up a Kaypro?

Netscape went public in August 1995. Conventional wisdom dictates that summer is the worst time to take a company public, but Netscape executives spotted a chance to eclipse Microsoft's launch of Windows 95, scheduled for later that month. The company initially planned to sell its stock at $14 a share, but the demand was so great that Netscape and its Wall Street underwriters doubled the price to $28 just before the opening bell on the appointed day.

Even a doubling in the offering price didn't scare people away. An hour after the market opened, stock in this company, which had never shown a profit, was trading at $71 a share. Netscape was just sixteen months old, and its main product was something it gave away free. But by day's end, the company was worth as much as or more than such Wall Street stalwarts as Boise Cascade, Bethlehem Steel, and Owens-Corning. Netscape was projecting a relatively miniscule $13 million in sales in 1996. But by the end of 1995, its market capitalization would exceed those of United Airlines, Apple Computer, Marriott International, and Tyson Foods.

The Internet was the perfect Wall Street deal, creating instant net worth out of thin air. The Wall Street smart guys even coined a term to describe these companies suddenly worth hundreds of millions, if not billions, though they had yet to earn a penny: "concept buys." Stock pickers likened an investment in Netscape to an investment in RCA before the phonograph took off. Suddenly every entrepreneur with an Internet-related idea was dreaming of an IPO: If Netscape is worth $6 billion, why can't my company be worth a billion? Or if not a billion, then at least a few hundred million? Netscape was hemorrhaging money, but somehow it simultaneously legitimized the Internet as a commercial medium. "The Net changes everything"—it was every entrepreneur's mantra, at once an off-the-rack response to those suggesting that Microsoft had already won and a license to pass off anything as the New Truth.

"The Net changes everything"—it became the stock answer to every unanswerable question, the all-purpose explanation for why someone might just fork over $1.5 million to a quartet of odd ducks "uhm"-ing and "you know"-ing their way through their pitch. The Internet was an industry without revenues, so the newest paradigm held that "mindshare" counted more than money. "Mindshare"—a fancy way of saying "brand recognition"—was inevitably part of the answer when you asked a young CEO how he planned on making money when his company gave away its product for nothing. And if, despite all his talk of revolutionary change and the future, the conversation flagged, he dangled dollar signs in front of everyone's eyes. It was never "Invest a few million dollars, and I'll earn you a nice return on your money." It was always "Give me a few million dollars, and in exchange I'll allow you to own a piece of the future. Invest in our company, and it'll be a license to print money."

No matter what the costume or the demeanor, the pitch was always more or less the same. There'd be the same hyperbole about the Internet (All of human knowledge at the click of a mouse! It'll dwarf the PC revolution!). Entrepreneurs repeated the same clichés ("Eat lunch—and you'll be lunch"; "We need to rethink our rethinking"), cited the same statistics (television advertising was a $58 million business in 1949, in 1995 it was a $38 billion business), and quoted the same gurus. Venture capitalist John Doerr's declaration that the Internet "represents the single greatest legal creation of wealth in history" has been repeated so many times, the quip might as well be chiseled in stone. The more gifted practitioners passed themselves off not so much as competent executives than as visionaries. That way people were investing not just in one idea, but in a particular person and his future ability to ride out radical changes in the landscape ("The only thing certain is uncertainty"). And, of course, every pitch ended in more or less the same fashion, evoking everyone's Netscape-like dreams of glory, despite a lack of profits in the foreseeable future. "We see," an entrepreneur would inevitably say with a confident smile, "an initial public offering in the neighborhood of three hundred million dollars sometime in the next eighteen months."

In 1994, Michael Wolff ran a modest four-person company that published hard-copy hipster guides to the Internet. His break, a feature in *The Wall Street Journal* that drew the attention of a former college classmate, Robert Machinist, who was rich—estate-in-Greenwich-Connecticut, uniformed-servants rich—also proved his downfall. "A hundred thousand dollars was my dream," Wolff wrote in a wonderfully entertaining account about the grand failure of Wolff New Media, "a hundred million was his." As Wolff described it in *Burn Rate,* Machinist was money in a hurry, but also money striving for the big strike. Machinist assured Wolff that he could get him $5 or $10 million for his company, but why? Anything south of $15 million, what's the point? He confided that his true goal was a public offering somewhere north of $200 million.

The dumb money in Wolff New Media was $5 million from a twenty-eight-year-old ripe for the plucking. He was a rich swell with family money and—Machinist tells Wolff—an "incredible hard-on" to be a player. At least in Wolff's telling, Wolff New Media was only one of two fabulous flameouts in which this foolish young pup had invested Daddy's money.

Wolff's book, a tell-all that is funny and insightful in turn, would gain notice for its withering sketches of some of the industry's better-known figures. But his most unflattering portrait turns out to be of himself. From the outside, it might have seemed that Wolff had reached the top. He had become the founder and CEO of a seventy-person company, invited to speak at conferences around the country and hailed as a cutting-edge visionary in flattering media profiles. But on the printed page he strips himself of all that plumage. On paper he might have been worth more than $5 million, but his credit cards were maxed out and he couldn't afford to pay his own salary.

He lied to stall a confrontation with his dumb-money investor, inflicting on his father-in-law a pretend open-heart surgery. He was particularly adept, he wrote, at fleecing those who "had no real experience [with the Web] to get in the way of their enthusiasm." One of the better scenes in *Burn Rate* was also one of the more disturbing. In great detail, he described the exhilaration and guilt he and his wife (who served as both his lawyer and his conscience) experienced while meeting with a computer magazine company so anxious to cash in on the Internet that it paid $5 million for a database of information worth virtually nothing.

In his grander moments, Wolff pictured himself as the new medium's Edward R. Murrow or Henry Luce. But mainly he pictured himself filthy rich. His prime motivation, he confessed, "was the prospect of making millions quick. Of making more money than you ever dreamed of. Of making the kind of money that would allow you to do all the things you ever dreamed of doing without the bastards getting you down. Fuck-you money. The sweetest lucre." He usually omitted this little speech from his pitch.

"The Internet is the single most important development in communications this century," he said during a speech he delivered in early 1995. "It not only combines radio, television, and telephone but dwarfs them and has begun the process of making them obsolete." Remarkably, he later wrote, people didn't challenge him when he offered these sweepingly absurd statements because they wanted to believe them. He was among those claiming that "as many as 40 million people" were using the Web in 1995. "The real number of people who could access the Web was probably no greater than one million, and perhaps half that," Wolff wrote.

Netscape would emerge as the most enduring symbol of the Great Internet Land Grab. Yet Wolff New Media seemed more emblematic of the times. Some would grow rich off the Web, and many legitimate businesses would emerge. But far more companies failed than succeeded. And most, like Wolff New Media, represented an all-or-nothing roll of the dice. A company might someday be worth a billion dollars, unless someone else beat it to market, in which case it would end up auctioning off the computers and desks for ten cents on the dollar. That was Wolff New Media: worth $300 million—until it failed, and then it was worth next to nothing.

Even a giddy Panglossian like Gilder poked fun at the lunacy of it all. Add "on the Internet" to your pitch, Gilder wrote in *Forbes ASAP* at the start of 1996, and "even the analysts will nod, and the market will bow." Up in Redmond, Microsoft's chief technologist, Nathan Myhrvold, was thinking the same thing. "The thing I find amazing . . . is that somehow the phrase 'on the Internet' seems to remove critical analysis of anything else in the sentence," he wrote in a 1995 memo addressed to Gates and other top Microsoft executives. "The Internet . . . has generated plenty of fear, loathing, excitement and above all—hype. But most of what you hear about the Internet is, in my opinion, quite misguided."

Myhrvold went on to tsk-tsk the crassness of what he dubbed "Internet mania." One can imagine his nose wrinkled and upper lip raised in a slight sneer as he dismissed the entire episode as rooted distastefully in greed. Myhrvold had recently returned from a weekend in Paris, where he had attended a restaurant equipment show, on the prowl for cutting-edge gadgets for a home kitchen on a par with that of a three-star Parisian restaurant. A few days away from the office had given him some perspective. "The lure of easy gold," he wrote, "makes people go crazy with speculative fever."

CHATTING IT UP on *Good Morning America, Larry King Live,* the *Today* show, *Letterman.* Riding high with a book atop *The New York Times'* best-seller list. Ascending from richest man in the United States to richest man in the world. Packing hordes into computer stores kept open past midnight for a product upgrade. Sipping San Pellegrino with the beautiful people in Hollywood. Mulling the future over single-malt scotch with media moguls and billion-dollar deal makers at Herb Allen's hunting lodge in Sun Valley, Idaho. Shooting a round of golf with the president. Yet 1995 turned out to be a lousy year for Bill Gates.

It wasn't supposed to be that way. In fact, 1995 was supposed to be a year of great triumph for Gates. After a vexing series of delays, Microsoft's flagship product, Windows, would again lumber to center stage. Code-named "Chicago," this fourth-version Windows upgrade had first been projected for release in the spring of 1994. But the date had kept on slipping. The press had been merciless, just as it had been brutal about the slippage in the publication date of Gates's book. That was another big monkey off Gates's back that year: the publication, finally, of *The Road Ahead.*

Standing-room-only crowds greeted him wherever he traveled to hawk his book, which lasted thirteen weeks on the *Times'* best-seller list.

In its second week, Gates knocked Howard Stern off the top spot on the *Times'* list (but of course Gates had to ask, "Who?"). And had there ever been a product release (of a mere upgrade, no less!) as amazingly great as the Windows 95 launch? There were cover stories in *Newsweek, Time,* and *U.S. News & World Report* and several long features in *USA Today.* The company bought the entire run of a day's worth of *The Times* of London, so it could give away 1.5 million copies, all of which had a front-page banner ad that read, "Windows 95. So Good Even the Times Is Complimentary."* Matthew Perry and Jennifer Aniston, stars of the TV show *Friends,* were hired to narrate a Windows 95 training video, and Jay Leno was hired to play MC at the actual launch (Leno's best line: "Bill Gates is so rich, ladies and gentlemen, his chauffeur is Ross Perot"). Gates even ad-libbed a joke. Leno was hemming and hawing about taking his turn at the mouse, and Gates cracked, "I think we paid you enough. You should do the demo." (Bill made Jay laugh!) "The coolest thing I've ever been part of," Gates told anyone who'd listen.

Maybe the problem in 1995 was that book.

The book was a mistake from the start. He admitted as much early on in *The Road Ahead,* when he confessed that if he had known how hard it would be to write it, he wouldn't have taken on the project in the first place. (Bill arrogant? See, he can admit when he's wrong.) We're passionate, we're exhilarated, editors would tell Gates's representatives when they shopped it to New York's biggest publishing houses. The hitch would be that the publishers felt they needed to meet Bill in person. "Mr. Big feels a need to hear the basic idea in Bill's own voice," they'd say, but those inside Microsoft knew the execs were just schoolboys who wanted to meet this man worth billions. That should've provided Gates with his first clue right there.

Gates went with Viking (at $2.5 million the highest bidder), but then, how could he find time to write? The second half of 1993 and most of 1994 turned out to be a terrible time for sitting quietly with his thoughts. First there was his move. His $50 million techno-Utopia house was terribly behind schedule, so, in July 1993, Gates plunked down $8 million to buy a four-bedroom house until his new one was ready. There was also his new status as a groom-to-be. First it was three

---

* The plan in Poland was to hold a press conference in a submarine, so the participants could imagine a "world without windows," but that ended up being one of the launch's few glitches.

weeks riding Land Rovers with his betrothed on safari through Africa. For Gates, who was thirty-eight at the time, three weeks away from work broke his own personal record by two weeks. Then it was a wedding on the fast track because his mother was seriously ill with breast cancer. They had chosen as their wedding date January 1, 1994 (who conducts business that week anyway?), but for Gates that meant missing one of his quiet weeks out at Hood Canal, not to mention the interminable distractions involved in arranging a million-dollar wedding. Then there was the postwedding hoopla, including a honeymoon on a private island in the South Pacific accessible only via private jet and a big bash when they returned home (limousines shuttled hundreds of guests to and from a secret location). And the dust was no sooner settling when Gates's mother took a turn for the worse, reentering the hospital. *You* try writing a book with all that going on.

Gates was always close to his mother. The two spoke as often as three times a day, at least in the early days of Microsoft; reporter James Wallace reports that occasionally he took her along on company business trips, and he felt guilty if he went a week without a face-to-face visit. At Christmas 1992, she said to her son, "Why don't you give Melinda a ring?" Ten weeks later, Gates's engagement was front-page news around the world. His mother died in June 1994, at the age of sixty-four.

Meanwhile, there was the week-in, week-out grind of the modern-day mogul in an age of media convergence. The industry scuttlebutt had him buying a minority stake in NBC from General Electric, but instead Microsoft put up half a billion dollars for a half stake in a new cable network called MSNBC. Then there were meetings with Michael Ovitz at Creative Artists, Gerald Levin at Time Warner, and John Malone at TCI. Another distraction was Microsoft Network (MSN), Microsoft's answer to AOL (America Online) and CompuServe. Plus there were the everyday headaches of product review meetings so he could stay atop the dizzying array of products Microsoft was now selling.

So of course the book was late. (But do you think people cut him even an inch of slack?) Myhrvold and a local writer named Peter Rinearson, along with a small platoon of Softies, had a hand in the book. But writing a book, it seemed, was just like cranking out software; the more people who got involved, the longer and more complicated everything became. After he handed the thing in, the news hit the trades that Viking was demanding "draconian" revisions. So in the mid-

dle of everything else he had on his plate, he was out at Hood Canal trying to "humanize" the book. "Show your softer side, Bill," the Viking
people counseled—but all they would get was blank looks. By the time
he got the manuscript out the door, he was ready to hang Jon Lazarus,
the Microsoft executive who had talked him into writing the thing in
the first place.

And that was before the press and his critics took turns skewering
him once the book hit the stores. In every review, it was "Gates missed
the Internet."* Establishment figures such as David Gergen on *The
NewsHour with Jim Lehrer* took him seriously, but inside the industry
he was a laughingstock. Gates was only stating the obvious when he
confided to Lotus founder Mitch Kapor that the Internet had blind-
sided him. This was during Gates's attempt at a rapprochement with
the man who had accused him of bringing about a software "Kingdom
of the Dead." Kapor ended up telling the world about this confidential
confession when reviewing the book for *USA Today*.

So what if he was late to the Internet? It had been around since the
1970s, so it seemed to him that *everyone* was late to that party. Tim
Berners-Lee had invited people to share in his creation in 1991. So where
had Jim Clark and John Doerr and the rest of them been in 1992 and
1993, when he'd been busy winning the word processing and spreadsheet wars? So what if he was a few months late to the Internet—he'd
had a few other things on his mind, running Microsoft. Jim Clark's first
company, Silicon Graphics, and Microsoft had both gone public in the
same year. If you had bought shares in Microsoft then, you'd have
earned something like forty times your investment. During the same
time, shares in Silicon Graphics had gone up by about a factor of ten. So
who was the true visionary?

Yet it was time to tee off on Gates's head. Joseph Nocera, writing in
The New York Times, called the book "bland and tepid"; James Fallows,
writing in *The New York Review of Books*, offered that Annie Leibovitz's
cover photo was terrific but the rest of the book was downhill from
there. A reviewer for *Barron's* (!) criticized Gates for whitewashing his

---

* Gates added some twenty-twenty hindsight prognostication by way of changes to
the paperback edition. Gone is the talk of the Information Highway; in its place are the Internet and World Wide Web. The chapter entitled "Race for the Gold" was renamed "The
Internet Gold Rush," and "Implications for Business" became "Business on the Internet."

past, when everyone knew "billion-dollar Bill clawed his way to the top through sheer competitive lust." Even the accompanying CD-ROM proved sport for the critics. It was riddled with typos and, even when running on Windows 95, proved to be crash prone.

After a public appearance in New York to promote the book, a reporter started yelling at him, "Bill, Bill, what do you think of Java?" Did the guy even know what an API was or what it meant that Java helped programmers deal with multithreading and memory leakage? Did he even know that Java was a programming language? "That's a very technical question," Gates said sarcastically before ducking out of the hall. Wherever he went, the questions were about not Microsoft but either Sun or Netscape. The fickle media had a new billionaire to hail, and in Marc Andreessen they had a new boy wonder.

Then there was Gates's appearance on *Late Night with David Letterman.* Whose bright idea was that? He had never seen the show, so before going on he watched it a few times but still didn't get it. It was part of the book tour and no doubt helped sales (so it wasn't a *complete* waste of time), but the whole thing was so—*random.* Someone put a hard hat on his head (the new house he was constructing—get it?), he didn't know what he was supposed to do once he got out there, and Letterman (who *is* this guy?) couldn't manage a single sensible question. The scene, the *Barron's* reviewer wrote, reminded him of the 1988 presidential campaign, when a helmeted Michael Dukakis had taken a ride in an army tank and ended up looking like a little kid playing soldier. Gates had that same bewildered look as Dukakis. Bill Gates, neon-lit in 1995, was a flop.

PEOPLE IN SILICON VALLEY celebrated Gates's misery as if they had just learned the tyrant running their small island had contracted a fatal disease. "Why Bill Gates Wants to Be the Next Marc Andreessen," blared the cover of the San Francisco–based *Wired.* The big news that December was Microsoft's licensing of Java from Sun (high five!). Anyone who was anyone in the Valley had at one time or another heard some snot-nosed, cocky Microsoft product manager boast, "We don't license software from other companies, we set our own standards." Or "We could do that in-house in a week." Microsoft had a competing technology in the works, but it paid Sun $14 million for the right to use Java. "A remarkable capitulation," reported the Associated Press.

Proof that Microsoft had missed the Internet could be found in places other than the pages of a vanity book. Gates sent his top staff a memo he titled "Sea Change Brings Opportunity." Except he failed to list the Internet as an element of this sea change, though by that time Netscape was already going full throttle. The Internet protocols in Windows 95 were all wrong, prompting a reviewer for one of the computer trades to write, "Anyone who's worked with Internet stacks would have known better."

Age no doubt played a part—Gates turned forty years old in October 1995—but mainly the problem boiled down to profit margins. Microsoft was a company populated by devout capitalists who couldn't get beyond the fact that this free medium showed no apparent prospect for producing a steady revenue stream. To Gates, investing in the Internet must have made as much sense as buying up communes in the sixties. Had he been younger, he might have seen the parallels with the start of the PC, when he had persevered despite the prevailing view that software wasn't something anyone bought. He would have joined the commune, taken over, and then built condos.

The media, always into a good fight, feasted on Microsoft's hardship. Gilder labeled Microsoft "fat and middle-aged." The *Los Angeles Times* (repeating a hopeful notion dancing through the minds of many) suggested a parallel between Microsoft and IBM: just as Big Blue had grown mighty during wave one of the computer revolution only to be crushed by wave two (the PC), the king of PC software might just be pounded by the Internet tidal wave. *Business Week,* in a special issue on the Web, ran a sidebar handicapping the probable winners and losers. Microsoft was the first company named in the losers' box.

The pièce de résistance came when Goldman Sachs analyst Rick Sherlund removed Microsoft from its list of recommended stocks. "The company is late [to the Internet], and competitors are benefiting from time-to-market advantages," Sherlund wrote. Because of Netscape (potentially "the Achilles' heel of Microsoft") and because of Sun (Java helps "shift the center of gravity of PC computing"), "we are simply not as enthusiastic a buyer of [Microsoft] shares." The ultimate insult came when Sherlund recommended that in place of Microsoft, the firm's clients purchase stock in Netscape.

Goldman Sachs wasn't just any investment house, and Rick Sherlund wasn't just any analyst. Goldman Sachs, which ranked at or near the top of any listing of Wall Street's most elite firms, was the investment bank that had taken Microsoft public in 1986. Its reports were faithfully read by virtually every top money manager in the country: those running portfolios for university endowments, insurance companies, pension funds, and mutual funds. Sherlund had worked on the Microsoft initial public offering, and he had been on a first-name basis with Gates ever since. It was never let's-have-you-and-the-wife-out-to-Connecticut-next-time-you're-in-New-York, but since the start Sherlund had been pushing Microsoft's stock as hard as anyone. Sherlund had several times been named Wall Street's top technology analyst, in no small part because he had championed Microsoft stock among his firm's blue-chip list of clients.

The day of Sherlund's report, the price of a share of Microsoft stock fell by more than 10 percent. "Gates Loses Two Billion Dollars in Single Day," headlines blared. Over the next few weeks, Gates lost nearly $4 billion. Shortly thereafter, when asked about Sherlund, Gates cracked, "He's your man, he's great—if you want to run a spreadsheet."

It was amazing, really. Only a few weeks before, Microsoft had released its latest quarterly figures: sales up 63 percent, profits up 53 percent. It had more than $4 billion squirreled away in the bank, a stash that was growing at a rate of $100 million a month. That was plenty of rainy-day money, except that the smart guys were declaring that Netscape had an invincible lead in the suddenly essential browser business.

Around the Valley, phones were ringing, e-mail was sent, fists were thrust into the air: We've got him now. We've got that mophead on the ropes. In early December, on Pearl Harbor Day it turned out (an accident—the date kept slipping because of delays), hundreds of analysts and reporters descended on the Seattle Convention Center to hear Gates declare Microsoft an Internet company. He blah-blah-blahed about all the exciting Internet-related products Microsoft had in the works, and Softies were on hand to demonstrate works in progress, but the reporters were so underwhelmed that many led their stories not with Gates's speech but with the news that Microsoft had paid Sun to license Java. The whole event had been slapdashed together (anyone doubting it only had to read the behind-the-scenes accounts published by *Business Week* and *Time*). After a night of screaming the night before, Gates was so exhausted (and perhaps also sick to his stomach: he later told *Time* that it had been an "eight-cheeseburger night"), he sat slumped on the floor despite the presence of the reporters. The years seemed to be taking their toll. He was on the wrong side of forty but still trying to maintain the pace he had when he was twenty-five. He was carrying an extra thirty or so pounds, and his wife was at home, five months pregnant. Maybe he was finally slowing down.

CHAPTER 08

BILL ENVY

On a foggy winter morning in February 1997, I parked a dusty pickup between a pair of BMW sedans in the parking lot of the venture capital firm Kleiner Perkins Caufield & Byers, the most envied and sought-after venture capitalists in the Valley. I had an appointment to spend the day shadowing the firm's youngest partner, an intensely energetic man six years my junior named Ted Schlein. Schlein was new, but the firm had been around long enough to have racked up an incredible string of greatest hits, including Sun, Netscape, America Online, and Lotus. Over the next twelve months, two more Kleiner-backed Internet start-ups in the company's portfolio would go public: @Home and Amazon.com.

Housed in a brown-shingled A-frame that evokes a ski chalet, surrounded by redwoods, Kleiner Perkins's headquarters sit perched in the foothills that loom above the Valley. That morning, the Zoghlins, burly and beefy in Chicago fashion, had arrived at the Kleiner offices in search of $6 million to $12 million to transform their two-year-old, Internet-related consulting firm into a global powerhouse. Three months into the job, Schlein had yet to ink a deal, but he was feeling hopeful about this father-son team.

When people try explaining Silicon Valley's extraordinary success, they usually start with Stanford, but that naturally leads to the question of why Silicon Valley rather than the environs surrounding Harvard, Duke, or Yale? The inevitable next answer is venture capital. The San Francisco Bay area accounts for roughly 3 percent of the country's population, but more than 30 percent of the venture capital invested in recent years had been invested here. It's home to nearly half the country's six hundred or so venture capital firms, and at any given time there are

a couple of thousand VCs scouring for the next "opportunity." Six billion dollars in venture capital in 1995, $10 billion in 1996, $11.6 billion in
1997—"There's so much money out here," one of the Valley's better-
known pundits, Paul Saffo, told me, "the venture capitalists are finding
there's not enough rat holes to put it down." Ask some of the Valley's
more intrepid souls how they plan to take Gates down at least a peg or
two, and they'll respond that their "secret weapon" is the venture capitalist.

If you are looking for the locus of anti-Microsoft sentiments and
money, Kleiner Perkins is that place. People inside Kleiner subscribe
naturally to a philosophy that investments are nothing but a means to
an end, a way of making as much money as they can on behalf of their
investors and (given the 30 percent cut they take from the top)* themselves. But Kleiner funded Netscape and Sun (Netscape and Sun "shift
the center of gravity of PC computing," Rick Sherlund wrote) and then,
in the summer of 1996, unveiled its Java Fund, a $100 million invest-
ment pool created to quicken the spread of Java by investing in Java-
related start-ups. The firm's usual array of investors (mainly university
endowments) threw money into the Java Fund pot, but so, too, did a
veritable who's who in the anti-Microsoft cause, including Sun,
Netscape, Oracle, and IBM.

At Kleiner, people go to great lengths to place a distance between
themselves and those who snort fire when the topic turns to Bill Gates.
Kleiner's top star, John Doerr, even approached Gates about investing
in the Java Fund, though—according to one Gates aide—the invite was
so last minute (two or three days before the Java Fund was unveiled)
and the dollar amount so relatively insignificant (less than a million
dollars) that the whole thing smacked of superficial symbolism. But because those at Kleiner dream Microsoft-scale dreams, they must invariably confront Microsoft. Whether or not they liked the appellation,
Kleiner was ground zero in the fight against Microsoft.

Schlein, thirty-two years old at the start of 1997, ran the recently
minted Java Fund. The typical VC has an MBA from Harvard unless he
has one from Stanford, but Schlein had a different kind of pedigree: a
father who sat on Apple's board of directors and a brother-in-law who's
partner in one of the Valley's other top venture capital firms. Schlein
had ten years' experience with a local software firm when, after a set of

---

* The industry standard is 20 or 25 percent.

tennis, a Kleiner partner broached the idea of his heading a new fund the firm had in the works. As Schlein described it, the offer was pure Silicon Valley: six months of nothing happening, followed by a mad dash to finalize a deal that just *had* to close over the next few days.

Venture capitalists call it "auditioning the future": partners gather around a conference table where, like Hollywood casting directors, they listen to the spiel of entrepreneurs whose written plans sounded impressive enough to gain them an hour or so of the firm's time. Maybe one in every five entrepreneurs sending Kleiner a business plan is invited to pitch the partners, but even this elite group stands a long way away from receiving funding. Kleiner receives hundreds of business plans a month but invests in maybe twenty-five companies a year.

To ask for their millions that first morning, the Zoghlins arrived ten minutes late and dressed as if they intended to spend the day sauntering through Fisherman's Wharf. Several of Schlein's partners were already in the room when the senior Zoghlin boasted that his son's company was already large and profitable, despite no outside venture capital. "Now you can say we're thinking about sleeping with the enemy," he added. Schlein's eyes bulged in alarm, and his face turned red. "Be nice," he said good-naturedly, trying to laugh off the insult.

The junior Zoghlin—it was his show—worked hard at projecting a nonchalant demeanor, but this twentysomething overachiever came off as smarmy and unschooled in the subtler points of seeking money. The half-dozen Kleiner partners attending the meeting didn't bother hiding their impatience as the junior Zoghlin slowly made his way through his pitch like a telemarketer unable to divert from a prerehearsed script. Only when he turned to the bottom-line potential did the partners perk up.

After father and son left, Schlein and his partners allowed me to listen as they pulled apart the pros and cons of buying a piece of the Zoghlin's company. I sat in on more pitches followed by more debriefing sessions that day and in subsequent visits to Kleiner. I joined Schlein during strategy sessions with his portfolio companies and as he met with cohorts from places such as Netscape and IBM. I took to the road with him, and then with one of his partners, as they "kicked the tires" at companies in which Kleiner had already invested. It was always a rush, fascinating days that I took to ending by sipping a pricey bourbon (I drew the line, however, at cigars), but after a time what struck me most was the preoccupation with Bill Gates and Microsoft, Gates especially.

Not a single conversation passed without at least a passing reference to the man—and more often than not, it was far more than simply a passing reference.

When the junior Zoghlin had the stage, his laptop froze, requiring him to restart his computer. "Thank you, Bill Gates," he said, as we stared dumbly at the projection screen. To fill the time, he mumbled more derogatory remarks about Windows, though the problem turned out to be with a network connection. In the debriefing that followed the pitch, Will Hearst—more formally, William Randolph Hearst III, who joined the partnership in 1995 after stepping down as publisher of the *San Francisco Examiner*—was the one partner in favor of exploring a deal with the Zoghlins. He ticked off a couple of reasons he was bullish and then offered this kicker: this was one area in which they wouldn't be competing with Microsoft.

"Not yet, at least," Schlein joked.

On tap that afternoon was a young CEO seeking a second round of funding: $3.5 million, some of which had already been committed by the VC who had put up the first round. He offered a much crisper presentation than his predecessor, but no sooner was he done with his pitch (for a start-up that lets you easily mix-and-match software programs) than the topic turned to Microsoft. Question one: "If this is successful, isn't Microsoft going to have to buy you or kill you?" And then: "If this is as good as you say, why hasn't Microsoft tried this yet?" Later that day, while I was interviewing Schlein, he told me he likes to drill entrepreneurs in the art of the "elevator pitch." I asked him what he meant, and he explained it this way: "You're on an elevator, and Bill Gates gets on at the fifth floor. You have to the ground floor to get him interested in your company. Go."

Tagging along with Schlein meant forever jogging to keep pace and then, once in his car, nervously clutching a car door strap as he threw his BMW into sixth gear while simultaneously punching numbers into a cellular phone. But it also meant a constant stream of reminders that in Silicon Valley people saw themselves as living in the Age of Gates. Over lunch, while chitchatting in hallways, over the phone, when discussing strategy, Bill Gates and Microsoft were the leitmotif. Our second day together began with a meeting with an IBM executive. This conversation was off the record, but suffice it to say that Microsoft came up a lot. Afterward, Schlein returned a message from an old colleague whom he hadn't talked with since becoming a venture capitalist. I could hear only Schlein's end of the conversation, but it was obvious they were talking about the Java Fund. "We don't see it as anti-Microsoft," he said, adding, "We even invited Bill in." It was a line I'd hear Schlein deliver no fewer than a dozen times over the coming weeks. That afternoon, talking with the founder of another Java Fund company, Rob Shostack, Schlein asked, "What if I could get us a deal with Microsoft?" Shostack hemmed and hawed until Schlein named a price: "What if we could get you two hundred million?" It was a number Schlein pulled from the air, but it was enticing enough. "Sold," Shostack said.

Near the end of my first day at Kleiner, I had hovered near the firm's grand fishbowl conference room, where, around an oak table so oversized it had had to be delivered by helicopter, partner Russ Siegelman was meeting with a group of young men more appropriately attired for a grunge concert than for such stylish surroundings. After the meeting, the group made a beeline for Kleiner's Sub-Zero, which is perpetually crammed with leftovers from the firm's daily catered lunch, raided it, and then piled into a late-model Lexus with a Garfield the Cat suction-cupped to the back window. This was the monthly board meeting of Clickover,* which Schlein had described as the Java Fund's "rawest" start-up. I decided on the spot that I needed to convince Russ Siegelman to invite me to the next Clickover board meeting.

At Clickover, Bill Gates loomed more as inspiration than as a dreaded foe or a potential angel with deep pockets, in part because Siegelman had been a top Microsoft executive before becoming a partner at Kleiner, and also because Clickover President Tom Churchill falls squarely into that category of people who worships Gates the way a previous generation of twentysomethings revered Che Guevara. He told me he drove a Porsche—and added, in case I didn't know, that a Porsche had been "Bill's" preferred car before the Lexus. Microsoft seemed his point of reference for all things great: Clickover was attempting to accomplish in its field (advertising management) "what Microsoft has done everywhere else." He dreamed the same Napoleonic dreams of domination and talked about "killing" and "destroying" the competition. In time, I discovered that most young high-tech entrepreneurs spoke that way. Churchill's goal, like the goal of most every wannabe high-tech mogul with a business plan, was "ubiquity," a eu-

---

* Clickover has since merged with another start-up. The new company is called Ad-Knowledge.

phemism for his company owning a Microsoft-like share of a given market. Yet despite his cutthroat dreams, his vocabulary was surprisingly boyish—another Gatesian trait, though this one no doubt rooted in their common trait of being highly intelligent people with a limited linguistic range and spending too much time immersed in a world of bits and bytes. People were "supersmart" or "massively wrong," products were "ultragreat" or "hypermisdirected" or just "crummy," things were "cool" or "supercool" or "neat."

The company's next board meeting was held not at Kleiner but at Clickover's headquarters, a converted furniture showroom that had been sponge-painted orange and decorated with flickering Christmas lights. Held in a back room across from the bathroom and next to a set of recycling bins, the term "board meeting" might be overstating things. Five of the firm's nine employees sat around a castoff table to meet with Siegelman, the company's moneyman. The meeting wasn't called to order; it simply began when people started talking, fifteen minutes before Churchill wheeled up on a mountain bike. No one recorded minutes, and the meeting ended abruptly when Siegelman suddenly remembered he had a barber appointment.

Siegelman played the role of the father who says he's there strictly in an advisory role but then can't help himself. It's your company, he told them, it's your show—but he seated himself at the head of the table and it was his agenda they followed. It was as if Siegelman were back in Redmond, displeased with the progress of one of the teams under his charge. He chided them for not selling customers on a nonexistent feature and yelled at them for not hiring a kid whose work they liked simply because he was still in school. "Any way you can do it, convince him to drop out," Siegelman ordered them.

What did the boys of Clickover think of Siegelman's advice? Several days later, I sat down with two of the company's marketing guys, both in their midtwenties. They confessed to some uneasiness, especially with Siegelman's suggestion that they pass off a screen shot as if it were already a completed product, but they generally accepted his advice as pearls from a wise sage. "You know," one said, eyes wide like a little boy telling me about an important person he knows, "Russ was a direct report to Bill." My reaction apparently wasn't on a par with the information being conveyed, because his cohort felt compelled to add, "We don't just mean he'd sometimes be in the same meeting with Gates. I mean, if you looked at the organizational chart, he reported directly to him."

．　　　．　　　．

AFTER A FEW DAYS OF THIS, I started counting: twenty-seven consecutive interviews, and one way or another, with no prompting, the subject eventually (if not immediately) turned to Bill Gates. And it wasn't just because for the moment I was spending too much time at Kleiner Perkins, either. At his Agenda conference, Stewart Alsop complained that Gates was all anyone seemed to talk about anymore. The audience were like Kremlin watchers reading meaning into wisps of evidence, investing significance in every facial tic. What do you think it meant that he sighed or laughed or looked away bored? Those lucky enough to have engaged him in conversation dropped his name ("I was talking to Bill, and he said . . ."), and later, drinking in the Phoenician's Thirsty Camel Bar, people engaged in their favorite pastime, dumping on Gates—about his power, his greed, his methods.

That was what the grand irony in the fascination with Silicon Valley was. While the world collectively fixed its gaze on stars such as Sun's Scott McNealy and the team that created Netscape, the latter had their eyes locked on Redmond. It didn't matter if you were talking with the Valley's top guns or its rawest would-be star, the connective tissue binding the area together was the preoccupation with Gates. They might have hated him, resented him, envied him, or maybe even respected him, but they certainly didn't ignore him; so deep were their feelings that it sometimes seemed as if they could talk about no one else. He cut an enormous figure in the industry, yet they only made him bigger.

Bashing Microsoft seemed a garden-variety way of blowing off steam, like cursing the humidity during a hot spell. In Silicon Valley, Michael Lewis wrote in *The New York Times Magazine*, Microsoft jokes were "the equivalent of German jokes in France." *The New Republic* ran an article exploring this brave new world in which you could type out "Microsoft sucks" and, using a search engine, discover Web sites that depicted Gates being poked in the face, shot like a duck in a shooting gallery, and morphing into Satan. "I literally have conversations about Microsoft with everybody, every day, all the time," San Francisco–based novelist Po Bronson told *The New Republic*. "It is omnipresent." At the end of his second novel, *The First $20 Million Is Always the Hardest,* Bronson began an author's note, "When I told people in Silicon Valley I was writing a novel about their industry, so many of them asked me, 'Is it about Bill Gates?' that for a while I considered titling the novel 'Not Gates.' "

There was a "Bill Gates Bought Our Balls" Web page that included a picture of Gates excusing himself, fingers delicately to his lips, looking bloated. It seems that as of mid-1997, Gates owned a full three fifths of the male population's testicles, with plans for picking off the remaining two fifths by the year 2000. There were a "MicroPap" Web page ("We own you, your mother, and your dog"), a "Microsuck" page, and a "Microsnot" page, which won my personal award for the funniest bit of 1997 with a mock press release about the company's expansion into the nation-state market: "Microsnot is pleased to announce the acquisition of England, a leading country. . . ." There was an "Evil Empire Page" (hosted by a Michigan-based custodian) and one called "Yet Another Anti-Microsoft Page," whose author wrote, "I created this page to show why I think Microsoft is trying to take over the world."

There is an "alt.destroy.microsoft" newsgroup and one called "alt.os.windows95.crash.crash.crash." One of the Web's better-traveled jokes was a Letterman-style top ten list, "If Microsoft Built Cars." Consequence number three: "We'd all have to switch to Microsoft Gas™." And consequence number seven: "New seats will force everyone to have the same size ass."*

And then there were the sycophantic: one Web site let you view work-in-progress photos of Gates's home, and any number of them gave you (via software tied to a Wall Street ticker) an almost up-to-the-moment worth of his portfolio. Or you could log on and play the "Bill Factor" game: plug in the name of any star, and see the degrees of separation. For instance, if you typed in "Nicole Kidman," the separation would be three degrees: Kidman is married to Tom Cruise, Cruise starred with Kevin Bacon in the movie *A Few Good Men,* and Gates had met Bacon at a party a year or two earlier.

At the start of 1997, Gates appeared on the cover of *Time* for a third consecutive year—marking the 114th issue of *Time* in which Gates's name had appeared, according to the accompanying editor's note. The article ("In Search of the REAL Bill Gates") was several times the length

---

* Someone inside Microsoft retaliated by imagining the conversation between a customer and the Microsoft Auto help line, underscoring Microsoft's frustration with the typical computer user's inflated expectations:

Customer: "I have to return this car. It stopped working."

Response: "Look, you've just run out of gas."

Customer: "You mean I just paid $17,000 for this car and now you want me to go buy something else?"

of the usual *Time* cover story and written by no less a figure than the magazine's managing editor. And why not? The magazine had named Gates the country's second most powerful man, behind only Bill Clinton (and don't think there weren't some in high tech who weren't so sure which Bill truly deserved to be listed first). At the start of 1997, Gates was worth more than $24 billion, or $11 billion more than he had been worth twelve months earlier. That meant that in 1996 he had earned $30 million per day, or $3 million an hour (assuming a seventy-hour week), or $22,000 for every minute he breathed.

It seemed as if you couldn't pick up a business magazine that didn't have at least one article about Microsoft. The bigger and more complex the computer world was getting, the more the media and everyone else seemed to demand a human face that made it manageably human. By puffing up Gates so that he was Bullwinkle-in-the-Macy's-Thanksgiving-Day-parade big, somehow it made the computer universe more manageable and easy to understand.

Fortune's coverage could be downright pornographic, like its fan magazine–like photo essay "of the man in action" in May 1997. There was one double-page spread of Gates tying his tie, another of him gazing into the distance on a plaza in Bombay, a third of him talking to reporters in New Delhi. "If he wasn't flogging Windows software so zealously, you'd swear Gates was a presidential candidate," read the accompanying essay. Given the magazine's coverage, you certainly *would* think he was running for office. There was a series of shots of Gates in flight—first tapping away on his laptop, then snuggled in a plaid blanket, and finally asleep with that same blanket draped over his head. There was another full-page shot of him reading his e-mail. Some of the photos were beautiful, gel-print black and whites, but that, and a cover shot that took you so deep into Gates's face that you could see the saliva in his mouth and tiny sprouts of stubble where his razor had missed, only fueled the notion that the spread was corporate eroticism.

You could detect a bit of blush in the weekly note *Fortune's* managing editor ran at the front of the magazine. "There he is *again*, Bill Gates on the cover of our magazine," he began. But as every publisher knows, short of Princess Di and a few others, there is no easier way to spike sales than finding an excuse to put Gates's picture on the cover.

By the time I had gone to something called the Internet Expo in San Jose in the winter of 1997, my antennae were already tuned in to the Gates watch. I walked the floor and then eavesdropped at a nearby bar after the conference was over for the day, snooping for anything Gates-related. I wasn't disappointed. Everywhere, there were people engaged in serious talks about Microsoft's "hegemony"—a political science term for one nation's undue influence over all others, which I had quickly learned was every journalist's favorite metaphor for Microsoft's power. I even caught someone boasting that he had been on the same commercial flight as Gates (the same plane, I tell you!), but there was no need for supersleuthing, The Expo opened with a keynote by Sun's number two, Ed Zander. Zander began with a boast: he'd be using no Microsoft software that day (applause). No PowerPoint to power his slide show (more applause), no Windows to crash his demo in midpresentation (appreciative laughs). Finally, he said, here was a chance to glimpse a "world without windows."

Zanders next spoke of the various "paradigm" shifts within the industry. It seems that in the computer industry, paradigms shift more often than some of us shift gears in a car. But this part of his talk ended up being anything but a dull recitation of the many shifts of thinking in the world of technology. He flashed on the screen several slides offering "famous last words." One showed Bill Gates declaring, in the early 1980s, "Sixty-four kilobytes ought to be enough for anybody" (nowadays, sixty-four kilobytes of memory—not even one tenth of a megabyte—probably wouldn't be enough to power a game of computer solitaire). Another slide had Gates saying, "The Internet is a fad," and a third had him dismissing Java as nothing but hype. Eventually Zander even spoke about Sun's product offerings.

A month later I attended a Sun-sponsored convention called JavaOne. A row of booths on the convention floor suffered a power outage—and immediately there were cracks about the devious hand of Bill Gates and his gremlins. A few weeks later, Gates showed up to speak at a Web-related conference in Santa Clara—the heart of Silicon Valley and therefore enemy territory. There, one of the industry's cyberstars, Michael Dertouzos, while taking his turn at the podium, placed a firm hand on Gates's shoulder. Another industry titan, Bob Metcalfe, inventor of the Ethernet and cofounder of a company called 3Com, cracked later that day, "If you had the chance that Mike did to touch Bill Gates—wouldn't you have used both hands?" Then there were the golf balls a Valley executive gave away as gifts. The balls were stamped with a photo of Gates and the gag line "Take a whack."

What was happening in Silicon Valley? Everything seemed merely an asterisk to Microsoft. There were countless articles about software firms of all sizes in the Valley, but try finding one that didn't eventually have a transitional paragraph that began something like this: "And then there's the lurking Microsoft question." Gates was the yardstick by which every other CEO would be measured. How able was a young CEO? Well, how well did she dance with Microsoft? The ones who did it well were amazingly adroit, not unlike those in Greek mythology who survived the treacherous waters guarded by Scylla and Charybdis: you were the boat, Gates was the river. Get too close to the churning waters to your left—share too much during a negotiating session with one of his minions—and you'd find yourself so deep in a whirlpool your technology was suddenly part of the river. But cautiously swing too far to the right—if to avoid the whirlpool altogether, you decided not to cooperate with Microsoft at all, thereby snubbing Gates—you might find yourself devoured by the snakes lurking in the trees.

In California's pioneer days, a certain kind of man, to prove his machismo, would take to the mountains to kill a grizzly bear. (Back when California was still home to any grizzlies, that is—this practice killed off the state's grizzly population shortly into the twentieth century.) Now, it seemed, the state's new pioneers proved their mettle by poking at the beast while continuing to share the same patch of forest. Netscape cofounder Jim Clark called Microsoft "evil," fellow cofounder Marc Andreessen was partial to Mafia-related comparisons. Sun's Scott McNealy referred to Gates as "Butt-head," and liked to joke that Microsoft Office was a giant "hairball" that was the real reason for a fall in the Japanese yen. During one speech, McNealy declared, "To kill Microsoft—that's the top priority for us." Customers, profits, product improvement—all seemed as if they should be higher priorities than "killing Microsoft."

During one of my earlier excursions to Silicon Valley, everyone had been abuzz about Microsoft's purchase, for $425 million, of WebTV, a homegrown company started in a former BMW dealership in Palo Alto. The general sentiment was generally one of betrayal, at least within the narrow borders of the Java Fund universe. Never mind that the aim of any striving entrepreneur is to make a mint and that $425 million was an absurdly inflated sum for a company that had few customers and was less than two years old. Never mind, either, that Microsoft had bought the company using stock rather than cash, and, since it had gone public in 1986, its stock had gone up by an average of 60 percent a year (try getting that kind of return if someone hands *you* $425 million cash). WebTV CEO Steve Perlman was an ex–Apple executive; didn't that mean he should stand for *something*? As one person told me at the time, a storm of that magnitude hadn't descended on the Valley since the local papers had announced that Stanford would be breaking ground on a new William Gates Computer Science Building.

CHAPTER 09

ANIMAL HOUSE

A DIFFERENT KIND OF CEO would have sat judiciously on his anger. Sure, he might have ranted and cursed and complained about a perceived slight by an important business periodical. He might even have acted as if he intended to pick up the phone and chew out the offending reporter. But he would have reined in his anger because the matter was a trivial one and this was *The Wall Street Journal.* Sun Microsystems' Scott McNealy, however, was hardly your typical CEO. He decided to call the dipshit from the *Journal* despite the protests of the PR aide sitting at his side and give him a piece of his mind.

The year was 1994, and that morning's *Journal* had run a seemingly insignificant item reporting on Microsoft's sales figures for Windows NT, the company's new entrant in the high-end operating system business. The article was buried deep inside section 2—hardly a prominent spot. The reporter who wrote the piece hadn't even intended for it to appear in the paper, but he was new and had sent to the wrong queue a dashed-off write-up of a quickie Gates interview meant to appear on the Dow Jones news wire. What really riled McNealy were the generic "We are pleased with the progress" quotes from Gates. Like every other corporation in America, Sun routinely sent around no-news press releases, putting similar happy-talk claims into McNealy's mouth, but you'd never have known it from reading *The Wall Street Journal.* But when Gates said he was pleased with the sales figures of a new product, his words were received even by the business world's most sacred text as if he were God himself handing the stone tablets to Moses.

"Little Billy Big Bucks." That was how McNealy referred to Gates when he reached the *Journal* reporter who had written the story. "Little Billy Big Bucks says something, and you automatically put it in the paper," he complained. "Little Billy Big Bucks says things are going great with NT, so then it's stop the presses."

The reporter was speechless. He remembers McNealy repeating the phrase at least three or four times, each in the same taunting, nyah-nyah-nyah-nyah tone: *Little Billy Big Bucks.* He had been reporting on the computer business for going on ten years. He felt embarrassed for McNealy. And he thought, "Grow up, Scott."

From McNealy's perspective, though, the inequity was too stark to ignore. To get to the top, his company had mowed down a veritable murderer's row of competitors, including IBM, Hewlett-Packard, and DEC. What Microsoft had accomplished was impressive, but whom had Gates had to beat? The likes of Novell, WordPerfect, Lotus, and Digital Research? *Fortune* had declared Sun the country's fastest-growing company in the second half of the 1980s, and though the company had stumbled at the end of the decade, Sun's performance through the first few years of the 1990s had been almost as impressive. Yet at the time of McNealy's phone call, do you think the editors at *Forbes* or *Fortune* had seen fit to put his face on its cover even once? McNealy had gotten engaged at around the same time Gates had. Gates's announcement had made page one of the *Journal*, while McNealy had been lucky if he were treated to a squib in the local press.

McNealy finally broke his shutout with an appearance, in 1997, on *Fortune*'s cover—thirteen years after taking the reins of the high-flying company he had cofounded and only after Gates had graced that magazine's cover no fewer than five times. But this small victory may not have tasted as sweet as McNealy had imagined. For one thing, there was the cover shot. A few months earlier, while in New York on business, McNealy had stopped by the offices of *Fortune.* His company was hot, riding the hype generated by its creation of Java, a new computer language ideally suited to the Internet. McNealy talked about Java running on everything, from huge mainframes to cellular phones and even on a "Java ring," which he imagined people wearing rather than carrying keys. At *Fortune,* after he ranted for a while about the magazine's propensity for puffing up Gates, he cut to the chase. "What do I have to do to get on the cover?" he asked. Someone said, "If you wear a cape and the Java ring, we'll put you on the cover." As McNealy told it, he didn't hesitate. "Done." So there he was on the magazine's cover, wearing a red satin cape, a Java-ringed fist raised in the air, flashing a broad goofy grin: "JAVAMAN."

McNealy might have had no qualms about posing as Javaman, but he couldn't have been too pleased with the spread inside. If the magazine genuinely saw him as a caped crusader, he was the haunted variety, driven by dark demons. The art accompanying the article was a series of cartoon-strip panels, including one that showed McNealy reading an issue of *Time* with Gates on the cover. He was frowning and obviously irate, the new Ray Noorda now that Noorda had retired. And there was the article itself. The same *Fortune* staffer who had treated Little Billy Big Bucks to a puff piece six months earlier described McNealy as a "shoot-from-the-lip CEO" and a "trash-talking two-dimensional comic book figure."

Bummer.

MCNEALY WAS A MAN easy to underestimate. He had a boyish face and bucktoothed smile and, even past forty, possessed a young person's pride in a night of heavy drinking and carousing. His self-image—the image he took great efforts to project publicly—was that of a beer-swilling regular Joe still partial to jeans and sweats even if he happened to be worth hundreds of millions of dollars. Ask this CEO of a $20 billion company about his years at Harvard, and he'd tell you he had majored in beer and golf. He'd be roped into a white-linen meal at a fancy French restaurant and ask for a Bud, just to yank Frenchy's chain. He preferred a greasy grilled cheese sandwich while playing pool with the guys at the Dutch Goose, a down-and-dirty Menlo Park student hangout, or a burger and fries at McDonald's. Indeed, it was over Big Macs that McNealy and Sun cofounder Vinod Khosla had celebrated their first $150,000 from a venture capitalist.

The joke in Silicon Valley was that McNealy wasn't the chairman and CEO of a publicly traded Fortune 500 company but president of a fraternity that happened to manufacture high-speed computers. A man could walk into McNealy's office and instantly feel transported back to his teen days. On one wall was a jersey autographed by members of the local hockey team; scattered elsewhere were sports-related mementos of all kinds. Invariably a few hockey sticks were stacked in a corner, along with McNealy's pads and other hockey equipment. "Bummer" was his usual way of expressing disappointment, "go for it" his preferred means of informing subordinates that he approved of their plans. He was a clever, quick-witted man who was always playing the cutup. At Sun, the high five was the unofficial handshake, "Kick butt and have fun" was quite literally McNealy's corporate motto. And in case anyone missed the message, McNealy starred in a company video entitled "Never Grow Up."

There were regular beer blowouts, companywide water pistol fights, and elaborate April Fool's Day jokes, like the time a group of engineers tore out a wall and cleared the furniture so they could transform McNealy's office into a par-three golf hole that included a fresh-sod fairway, a pair of sand traps, and a putting green.* So fiercely does the testosterone pump inside Sun that a woman reporter for one of the big business magazines commented that whenever she spent any time there, she walked away thinking everyone was perpetually on the verge of snapping one another with wet towels.

"Basically," says Sun's John Gage, one of the company's earliest employees, "if you don't like Scott, you don't work here."

At some companies, the CEO might occasionally wear jeans to the office but keeps a decent set of clothes in the closet just in case a big customer or the press happens by. McNealy, however, would defensively apologize if a reporter caught him wearing a sport jacket and tie. In 1995, he took to the skies in the Sun corporate jet for a fourteen-day, seven-country business trip that included visits with top government officials. As a fashion statement, he refused to pack a necktie. So to meet with the president of Turkey, McNealy wore a dark blazer over a white Sun polo shirt, a pair of tan khakis, a pair of loafers, and—only after considerable badgering by his staff—a borrowed tie. *Forbes ASAP* had sent a writer and a photographer along to document the trip. McNealy

---

* The pranks weren't always so harmless, however. Once, the company rented out a Newark, New Jersey, hotel ballroom to host a celebratory dinner for its national sales force. The drinking had been heavy by the time someone threw a roll at the boss, presumably because he was talking too long. Maybe the speaker's mistake was to throw it back, because soon the place was embroiled in a major-league, John Belushi-in-*Animal-House*-style food fight. One participant recalls a woman running past him, chocolate mousse in her hair dripping down onto a silk suit. In a tone falling somewhere between amusement and shame, another recalled first the waiters and busboys running around, grabbing for every breakable they could get their hands on, and then the arrival of a squadron of Newark cops. No one was arrested right then, but others were later arrested for trashing rooms.

"There was no discussion afterwards that we had done anything wrong," said one participant. "We were banned from this hotel forever, but that just added to the cool of it."

first feigned wiping his nose with the tie. Then, while knotting it, he mugged a sneer as the photographer squeezed off a shot. He seemed a new man, *ASAP* reported, after hitting Moscow. His staff had finally scouted out a set of golden arches.

In 1988, Sun paid the comedian Pat Paulsen to entertain the troops at the company's annual all-hands meeting. "What's the difference between Sun and the Boy Scouts?" Paulsen asked. "The Boy Scouts have adult supervision." And there stood McNealy, roaring in delight, wearing his jeans and high-tops, So then Paulsen asked, "Who's running this place anyway, Beaver Cleaver?"

This man, whom cartoonists would lampoon by putting a veritable skyscraper of teeth in his mouth, had the Beav's overbite but Wally Cleaver's good manners and Eddie Haskell's mischievous spirit. And though he was Sun's chief prankster, he was also the perfect son. After his parents divorced, his mother, Marmalee—"Marm" to his friends and workmates—moved into a house less than a mile from her son's. If you knew Scott, one friend said, you knew Marm; they were that close. She cheered her son on when he was playing in one of his league hockey games, and she joined him when he was traveling on business. If McNealy made it to that year's Agenda, you'd see Marm sitting poolside at the Phoenician, and she'd be there schmoozing with whoever happened along during the social hours. She was also a fixture at Sun's annual shareholders' meetings. One ex-girlfriend, who had dated McNealy while she worked at Sun, described his home as "a boy's locker room" with hockey sticks and more sports paraphernalia everywhere and little in the fridge beyond beer, condiments, and maybe some eggs. "But the furniture was nice and the place was generally clean because Marm took care all of that," she said.

He would ask out women in the company, but that was standard for single guys up and down Silicon Valley—a continuation of college, where you asked out girls in your class because where else did you meet people except on campus? The word, though, was that the boss might be quite a catch but he was a crummy date, always droopy-eyed and drained. Between yawns he'd complain about having no life outside his company. With his hockey buddies the grueling hours came out like a boast or maybe as an explanation for all his huffing and puffing out on the ice. He would always talk about how many cities he had been in and the hours he worked and all the partying despite how little sleep he got—as if he were squeezing just a little more out of life than the next guy. He'd offer with a boastful smile, "I have a sleep deficit that'll never be repaid."

When finally McNealy settled down—well, how he met his wife, Susan, says it all. A bunch of his old prep school buddies were in town for a wedding in the early 1990s. Bleary-eyed the day after the bachelor party, they were hanging out in the student union at Stanford when they decided they'd play one last joke on old Alan before he tied the knot—and one guess whose idea the whole thing was. The plan was to convince the prettiest coed they could find to act the seductress with the groom-to-be—like Cybill Shepherd in *The Heartbreak Kid,* except they'd meet *before* he was married rather than on the honeymoon. They jumped when the perfect candidate walked by—and she was cool about it, almost purring, as if she really wanted the guy. After the joke was over, the groom's little brother got her phone number, but he was in the navy and shipping out right after the wedding. The way McNealy's buddies tell it, McNealy then grabbed the number with some clever line about Junior sailing into the sunset on his boat. For their first date, McNealy bought a six-pack and called her from his car phone, inviting himself up to drink some beer. Not long afterward, the friend of a big-time business reporter mentioned that he had seen someone he thought was Scott McNealy at a raucous sushi restaurant with a woman eighteen years his junior, really knocking back the saki and howling with the crowd. When the reporter asked McNealy if that was true, he said matter-of-factly, "Sure, that was my first date with my wife."

HE WAS A CEO as likely to make an audience groan as laugh. There was the time when his dog, Network, the company mascot, joined his master on stage as McNealy addressed a large auditorium of programmers and partners gathered in San Francisco to celebrate Java. Onstage were several cardboard fire hydrants labeled with the names of Sun rivals, including Microsoft. The punch line came when McNealy walked his pooch to the various hydrants and ordered him to lift his leg. "Network, evidently more tactful than his master, declined," wrote one reporter.

Yet there was another side to McNealy, the sharp hands-on manager who seemed to know the details of every facet of Sun's operation. A new employee traveled with McNealy to a meeting of financial analysts and walked away thinking his boss had been "Kennedy-esque": youthful, hair brushed back, completely in control and at ease as he called each analyst by his or her first name. "He'd get a question, take a breath, and then deliver with just the right pitch," this employee said. Inside Sun, he was the head coach slapping his players on the back, barking out orders from a clipboard and slamming it to the ground when things were not going right.

He was strikingly smart but decidedly anti-intellectual: He couldn't recall the last time he had cracked a book, let alone read a novel for pleasure. Once, when he was asked his favorite book, he answered, *How to Putt like the Pros.* It took him three tries to get into Stanford Business School—and then he boasted that he had gotten by with a minimum of effort. He may not have had the highest GPA among his Stanford classmates, he liked to say, but he had the best GPA for the hours invested, making him the most "effective" student on campus. When once the head of Sun human resources proposed that the company buy artwork to dress up the lobby, McNealy practically blew a gasket. "You want me to spend money on a bunch of paintings?" he sputtered. The company instead hung pictures of the products it sold.

He saw himself as a business maverick, and the character Tom Cruise played in the movie *Top Gun* was an all-time favorite, so he saddled his firstborn with the name Maverick. (He and his wife named their second son Dakota.) The family dog was Network, because Sun's motto was "The network is the computer." Whenever he stepped into the public eye or posed for a picture, he seemed dressed in company paraphernalia: a polo with the Sun logo stamped over the heart, a Sun baseball cap, a Java bomber jacket.

He was forever driving his Sun subordinates crazy, dumbing himself down when they needed him to appear smart and sharp. Sun's earliest customers were university researchers, pharmaceutical companies, and design shops inside behemoths such as Boeing, General Motors, and Lockheed, because PCs couldn't run computer-aided design programs or calculate complex mathematical formulas, and waiting in line for shared time on a mainframe or a mini was too frustrating. The next frontier after the country's scientists and engineers was the bond traders and money managers on Wall Street and in the country's biggest banks, where fluctuating exchange rates and complex products such as derivatives cried out for a Sun workstation. McNealy was always game for a trip east to close the deal (you'd just have to call him and he'd say,

"I'm there"), but no matter how they pleaded, Sun's New York–based sales team couldn't convince the boss to don a suit. When at the end of 1995 *USA Today* asked a range of people, including McNealy, to share their thoughts for the upcoming year, McNealy vowed "to have my only suit dry-cleaned" (other vows for 1996 included "beat[ing] Bill Gates to the Internet party" and a shot at *Late Show with David Letterman*—as Gates had had the previous month).

"It's like sometimes he was trying to come off as superficial," said an ex-employee who figured he'd sat in on a dozen-plus meetings with McNealy and prospective customers in his seven years at Sun. "He'd make himself less substantive than he was. He seemed to enjoy project-ing this image that he was just this regular guy out of Detroit." The truth was that he was the son of a rich auto executive, a reverse snob who wanted to be viewed as anything but what he was. As a teen, he had occasionally golfed in a foursome with Lee Iacocca, and his Stanford applications included a recommendation letter from the CEO of the Ford Motor Company.

"McNealy is obviously in a different league than most of the people I've ever come across," the ex–Sun employee continued. "He's incredibly smart and obviously successful. But I'll tell you, he could come across as a real blockhead."

McNealy was a born CEO, yet there was a time when he had told anyone willing to listen that the top spot in a big company was the last thing he wanted. Sun's first CEO, Vinod Khosla, remembers a dinner at a Benihana early in the life of the company. "He vowed he'd never work as hard as his father," Khosla says. "He wanted to run a small factory, a machine shop maybe, raise a few kids, retire early." McNealy had seen the toll his father's busy life had taken on his mother and of course him-self. He thought of all the hockey games his father had missed, though McNealy's prep school team had reached the state's semifinals, and of all his no-shows at all his tennis matches at the club. The younger McNealy dreamed instead of filling his weekends playing golf and host-ing barbecues for friends, a sauce-splattered "World's Best Griller" apron tied around his waist, a spatula in one hand, a beer in the other, 2.3 kids running underfoot. Vacation homes so he could hobnob with the swells? A yacht? A small fleet of Ferraris? This son of Detroit dreamed of owning a wide-bodied Cadillac (liked to say he drove "good ole Dee-troit iron") and a big-screen TV to watch sports on, but that was about as wild as he let his dreams go. He was worth more than $50 million when, in 1991, he told *Forbes,* "I mean, how many hockey sticks can one person buy?"

Yet he was his father's son, a hopeless workaholic, loyal to those with whom he worked and more ambitious than maybe even he realized. From the start, Sun's four founders worked long hours seven days a week; the idea wasn't to build a modest-sized company that would allow them to live comfortably but to make the big strike that would render them all rich beyond imagining. Weekly staff meetings were held on Saturdays, Thanksgiving and Christmas were half days, and New Year's Day meant sleeping in before heading to the office. Bill Joy, the company's software guru, lived in Berkeley, forty-five minutes away, so several days a week he slept in his car rather than make the commute or splurge on a hotel room. McNealy, who ran the workstation assembly plant, played the role of good-time Charlie, slapping backs and cracking jokes, the king of the one-liners.

McNealy seemed completely in his element, but then, two years into his tenure as plant manager, his cofounders proposed a palace coup. The company's outside investors had lost faith in Khosla's ability to run Sun. The faster the company grew, the louder and more frequent were the complaints. McNealy stuck loyally by his friend, who had brought him into the company (and with whom he was also living), but Sun's board eventually forced Khosla out. (Officially, he "retired," though he was only twenty-nine years old.) The company contemplated hiring the sailing buddy of Tom Perkins (the Perkins of Kleiner Perkins, one of the two principal venture capital firms behind Sun), but the other venture capitalist on the board, David Marquardt, deemed the man a light-weight, and a fight ensued. McNealy, then twenty-nine years old, was named interim CEO, a position no one, least of all those who had placed him there, expected him to hold for very long.

"I knew Scott as a sports nut, a drinker, and a total fuck-off," says Marquardt, who was in the class before McNealy's at Stanford. "From where I sat, Vinod had recruited his drinking buddy from school, which wasn't exactly a ringing endorsement for CEO."

Kleiner's John Doerr, the other venture capitalist on the board, was similarly inclined to view McNealy as a temporary solution. "I'm worried, Scott," Doerr confided in McNealy after his promotion. Doerr allowed that he might have the world's worst memory, but he'll never forget McNealy's response: "He looks at me and gets this really serious look on his face. His eyes got really small and he says, 'You just watch.'"

· · ·

THERE MAY EVEN HAVE BEEN A TIME when Scott McNealy and Bill Gates genuinely liked each other. Back in the 1980s, they were both man-child CEOs from strikingly similar backgrounds. Whereas Gates had grown up in Seattle's most exclusive neighborhood and gone to Seattle's top private school, McNealy had grown up in tony Bloomfield Hills and attended the exclusive Cranbrook School, the Detroit area's best. Both were old men before their time. Whereas Gates pored over his father's business magazines, McNealy poked through his father's attaché case, devoting hours to making sense of the reports and spreadsheets that occupied so much of his old man's time. Their grade point averages were one difference between the two—whereas Gates was an A student, McNealy was a B, but McNealy had scored high on the SAT and his father was a Harvard alumnus.* McNealy showed up in Cambridge, Massachusetts, in 1972; Gates arrived in 1973.

"I didn't drop out," McNealy cracked at a Harvard conference on the Internet years later. "And I'm still trying to make up for his two-and-a-half-year head start."†

Sun and Microsoft reached an important milestone two weeks apart when both companies went public in the spring of 1986. Back then, if the two companies competed, it was strictly on the fringes of their respective businesses. Sun was a hardware company that manufactured workstation computers that started at $20,000; Microsoft wrote software for mass-market PCs that cost in the low thousands. Sun did sell a competing operating system, but just as Microsoft had flirted only briefly with a version of Windows written for higher-end workstations, Sun's brief foray into the world of PCs never amounted to much.

The same adjectives used to describe Gates were applied to McNealy: hardworking, intensely smart, incredibly competitive. Both surrounded themselves with bright, aggressive people rather than yes-men. The two also shared the same management-by-bullying style. Like Gates, McNealy would immediately challenge a new employee, pushing hard to see if he or she would push back. George Paolini, for example, began

---

* Once, when asked about his less-than-stellar grade point average, McNealy responded, "They called me the illiterate genius: I could think real good, but I couldn't talk real good."

† Actually, Gates had about a half-dozen years on McNealy, if this race could be said to have started when Gates joined Paul Allen in Albuquerque to turn his full-time attention to Microsoft.

his tenure at Sun as a speechwriter for McNealy. His first face-to-face meeting with his new boss was in Jakarta, at the start of a two-week swing through Asia. Paolini's assignment was to write a travel journal that would then appear under the boss's byline in *The New York Times'* business section. Paolini watched as McNealy made a show of chewing out some vice president. Then, instead of introducing himself, McNealy turned to him and barked, "So what's your story?" Paolini reminded him of the assignment. "So why aren't you taking notes?" McNealy sarcastically asked. Now that Paolini has spent years observing McNealy, he doesn't doubt that his response, equally barbed, was the perfect one: "Because you haven't done anything worth writing down yet."

Gates and McNealy didn't run in the same circles, but when their paths crossed, they were obviously drawn to each other. Both were ushers at the wedding of David Marquardt, the venture capitalist who had financed both companies in their early years. What people recall about either from the reception that followed was the two of them off in a corner. The band played, couples danced, and people mingled, but—as Stephen Manes and Paul Andrews, coauthors of *Gates,* tell it—the two were "very obviously hammering out some high-powered deal." Why not? They were both ambitious men in their early thirties for whom work was life and life was work. Why waste a sunny Napa Valley, California, day when there might be money to be made?

"I consider Gates to be a very dangerous competitor," McNealy told *ComputerWorld* in 1992. "There's nothing nicer I can say about someone than that."

These two warrior chieftains were bound to collide. They may have been friends after a fashion, but they represented dueling philosophies within the world of computing. Gates was part of the crowd that saw the PC as the *über*-machine. These were the people who gathered at Stewart Alsop's Agenda and Esther Dyson's PC Forum each year and believed, as they believed the sun rose and set each day, that with each passing year the PC would steadily move up the user food chain, growing stronger and more powerful, performing tasks once the sole province of a more expensive class of machines. By contrast, McNealy boasted that he had never owned a PC and never would. McNealy hadn't written a line of code in his life—early in Sun's history he took a basic electronics course just so he could understand what his cofounders were saying—but he was firmly aligned with the gearheads who tended to view the PC as an amusing plaything good for games and typing but inadequate for accomplishing real work. To the typical Sun engineer, comparing a Wintel machine to one of theirs was like comparing a walkie-talkie set used by twelve-year-olds to those employed by the police in life-and-death situations.

Among the PC crowd Windows may have seemed inevitable, but to this latter group, the world was obviously going the way of Unix, the pocket protector crowd's operating system of choice. Developed by a pair of scientists at AT&T's Bell Laboratories, Unix was industrial strength enough for government agencies needing to bounce top secret messages off satellites and stockbrokers trading large blocks of equities. So why couldn't it handle routine tasks such as loading a word processor and saving a spreadsheet? Unix hooked computers together in ways that Novell and Microsoft could only dream of doing: with Unix you could share and swap programs and not worry that the whole system would tip over because you pushed it too far. By contrast, Windows was a crash-prone, mass-produced toy, held together by the electronic equivalent of baling wire and duct tape.

Yet beneath their attitude of superiority lurked envy.* By the start of the 1990s, it may have been cool to be a nerd, but only if you were in the PC camp. The lack of uniformity within the Unix world was another issue that no doubt made more than a few engineers jealous when they contemplated the Windows world. Windows was Windows, but there were Berkeley Unix, AT&T Unix, Sun Unix (called Solaris), and so on. Each was fundamentally the same but different enough that they were not interchangeable. Imagine English as it's spoken in each English-speaking country—a Londoner in Lubbock, Texas, would get by, but picture a lorry driver looking for a bobby or a place to buy petrol and a container of take-away. There were periodic attempts to unify around a single version of Unix, but all those in the Unix world believed in the superiority of their own particular dialect as fiercely as they believed in Unix itself. Microsoft's PC dictatorship had its advantages.

Microsoft's first serious run at Sun came in 1993, when Microsoft released Windows NT (the NT stands for "new technology"). Microsoft advertised this latest version of Windows as powerful enough to handle tasks formerly the province of workstations and also to run the power-

---

* Indeed, the engineers at Sun suffered so serious a case of PC envy that for a time the company had on its drawing board a PC that would run on Sun's "Sparc" chip—the "Sparc'ntosh."

ful back-office "servers" that connect a small department of PCs (in time, these servers would become the host machines for countless Web sites). At that point, Microsoft's claims were only wishful thinking, according to everyone from the slide rule set to the big-name Wall Street technology analysts, but peering into the future, one could imagine improved versions of NT siphoning off an ever-greater share of Sun's business. "It's a great opportunity to just grab, grab, grab something new," Ballmer explained in an interview with *Business Week*.

Those at Sun, however, dismissed the first release of NT with the arrogance of people convinced of their own superiority. Microsoft had lured away from DEC a bona fide big-name star to head up its NT team, but despite this, Sun's technologists were inclined to dismiss NT as the usual PC hack. They'd read about all its bugs and glitches and smirk; over lunch, they'd shake their heads about a so-called networking product that didn't even include the basics that allowed users to communicate over the Internet. "NT is cutting edge," went the joke inside Sun, "if this were 1987." Those arguing that Microsoft was, if nothing else, persistent were first accused of having been brainwashed by the trade press and then told that Solaris and its Unix cousins were so far ahead of NT that Microsoft would always be years behind.

Yet looking down at NT from this lofty perch meant missing the many things wrong with their operating system of choice. Unix was still strictly command-line computing without the friendly point-and-click icons offered by Apple's and Microsoft's operating systems. Those who weren't familiar with Unix were usually out of luck. "RTFM," which stood for "Read the fucking manual," seemed every Unix vet's favorite acronym. But it's not as if there were a thick guide sitting on a shelf somewhere. Reading the manual meant knowing that you had to type ">man" and hit CTRL U or CTRL D to navigate up or down. Even inside Sun periodic wars broke out between the managers and secretaries, who pleaded for easy-to-use Apple or Wintel machines. The Sun machines they had been issued didn't have the standard features of the rest of the PC world, such as a spell checker or a basic calendar program that allowed an executive to share her schedule with her assistant. The secretaries, however, always lost.

That's the way it always was in this company, populated by true believers, most of whom had at least a master's in computer science, if not a Ph.D. They viewed Unix not from the consumer's perspective but from that of an engineer—and given that Unix was so obviously superior to Windows, why would anyone be drawn to the latter? It would be like choosing a Chevette over a Porsche, they liked to say, but the analogy was more apt than they may have realized. Most people can't afford a Porsche, and most of those who can prefer automatic transmission to the Porsche's famously hard-to-use stick shift.

Friend and foe alike said it all the time: Sun is a religious company populated by zealots who can't comprehend people worshiping another god. They were the smartest kids in their class, unaccustomed to thinking they might be wrong. If a competitor's product sold better than theirs, there was something wrong with the wider world. "At Sun," one former programmer said, "I worked with some of the smartest people I've ever met. But collectively they could be dumb like a mob." That was never clearer than after he announced he was leaving Sun—to go work at Microsoft, of all places. He tried to explain that Microsoft was doing something cutting-edge in his chosen area, but it didn't matter.

"It's like this brotherhood feel there, 'We all work at Sun, we'd never work anywhere else,' " he said. "I noticed it when other people left, there'd be this big swell of emotion followed by confusion. Like, why would anyone leave Sun for someplace else?" Leading the way would be the head zealot, Scott McNealy. "He takes someone leaving very personally," said one former manager, who compared his exit interview with McNealy to a sermon from a cult leader berating one of his flock for losing the faith.

His sermons weren't just for the Sun tribe, either. In the late 1980s, several muck-a-mucks from Lehman Bros., the big Wall Street brokerage house, flew west to meet with McNealy and other Sun executives. The issue was two competing technologies, one being championed by Sun, another that had been embraced by a wide coalition of Sun competitors, including DEC and Hewlett-Packard. Sun's system supported only its own technology because the company believed it to be superior. The people from Lehman Bros. didn't care which side won, only that they could use Sun systems to handle either. As a company, it was spending between $10 million and $15 million a year on Sun hardware and software, making it one of Sun's largest customers. Yet the executives couldn't convince Sun's technologists to rewrite a portion of its operating system. They figured a sit-down with the top man would solve their problems. Instead, McNealy delivered a twenty-minute speech selling Sun's technology over that being pushed by DEC, HP, and other Unix vendors.

"While Scott's talking, I'm looking around the room," said one former Sun employee. "People weren't too happy, to say the least. Here was an important customer here to have the CEO's ear for an hour, but he's not listening, he's just up on his soapbox giving a speech about everything that's wrong with DEC and HP."

It was something to admire in a CEO, this fierce belief in the superiority and the integrity of the products created by his people, but it also revealed a fundamental character flaw: McNealy possessed almost a preternatural need to see himself as the underdog fighting the good fight against larger and darker forces. In its earliest days, Sun's top foe had been a rival workstation maker named Apollo. By the time Sun incorporated, Apollo was already a publicly traded company many times the size of Sun. But Apollo sold a proprietary, or closed, system: its machines worked only with Apollo software and Apollo accessories. Sun adopted the opposite strategy, selling so-called open systems that allowed users to buy mix-and-match off-the-shelf components from different companies. In reality, a Sun user would be locked into buying Sun add-ons and Sun-specific software, but it was a smart selling point, and in at least the short run it saved a user a lot of money. McNealy viewed the competition as a battle between democracy and freedom on one side and the tyranny of a Soviet bloc dictatorship on the other. "Open system for open minds," went the Sun advertising campaign.

"Scott's always been very much into having enemies," says an ex–Sun executive. "I think one of his proudest moments was when he convinced the man who ran marketing at Apollo, Ed Zander, to come to work for Sun [Zander is now Sun's chief operating officer]. It was like he had the head of a vanquished king on a post." After Apollo, the enemies were IBM and DEC, when both companies entered the workstation market, and even the venerable Hewlett-Packard, after Sun's Palo Alto–based neighbor bought Apollo.

"Other companies have competition, Sun Microsystems has enemies," industry pundit Richard Shaffer wrote at the start of this decade. After McNealy delivered a speech at the Churchill Club, a Valley-based public affairs organization, someone asked him, "Scott, what could stop you?" And he shot back, "Kryptonite." In feature after feature, it was the "brash" Sun and its "cocky" or "arrogant" CEO. Sun at its worst was the deal it cut, in 1987, with AT&T to write a merged version of the Sun and AT&T operating systems. "Our attitude was 'Goddamn, we own Unix now, we're going to shove it down your throats whether you like it or not, HP, SGI [Silicon Graphics], IBM,' " confesses a former top Sun officer. " 'You're going to do it our way now. We're friends with AT&T now, so fuck you if you don't like it.' We ended up being such bastards about it that we gave everyone else in the Unix world a reason to band together. We were so arrogant, they decided to teach us a lesson."

Sun competitors formed a group called the Open Software Foundation (prompting McNealy to joke that the group's acronym really stood for "Oppose Sun Forever"), but then McNealy only upped the ante. In a sit-down with *Business Week,* he wrote the name of his larger foes on a whiteboard. He X'd out each one as he laid out his long-range plans. "It's unstoppable," he said, prompting the magazine to describe him as a "zealot . . . taking every opportunity to thumb his nose at the industry's old guard." As promised, McNealy bested his counterparts at DEC, HP, and IBM, leading Sun to the top spot in the workstation field. But at the same time, Sun and AT&T's attempts to unify the Unix world only splintered it further. "We played right into Microsoft's hand," said the former Sun officer.

Yet whatever the reason, McNealy needs an enemy—the bigger the better—against which to rally his troops. He's like a hockey player who picks the biggest player on the other team, slamming him against the glass just to prove he's not intimidated. Whether Sun liked it or not, it had a new, large foe in Microsoft, which meant that McNealy had a new enemy. All he needed was a weapon.

CHAPTER 10

JAVA HIGH

YOU CAN TELL A LOT about a person by watching him play ice hockey. Scott McNealy would be the first to admit he's not the most graceful or talented guy on the ice, but he gets the job done. He's the one digging the puck out of the corners or checking the other team's bully against the glass. He's not particularly fast on skates, but he'll score the ugly goals, muscling his way through two defenders and then putting in the rebound. And there's his ebullient spirit: he's always the first to slap a teammate on the back after a good play.

League games were every Tuesday, Saturday, and Sunday night. No matter how savage his schedule, if McNealy was in town and had no pressing work commitment, he'd suit up on game nights. He'd curse his rubber legs, his work schedule, and the hours he spent cramped into airplane seats, but when his line was on the ice he'd be there, even if that meant he looked as if he were about to suffer a coronary. By game's end, he'd be the guy covered with the most ice shavings, hockey's equivalent of the baseball player with the dirtiest uniform.

"Scott's a guy who makes up what he lacks in talent with hustle," says Patrick Naughton, an ex–Sun employee who for several years played on the same line with McNealy. "No one hates losing on the ice more than Scott. And no one will hustle more when totally gassed. He's a big-time team player, generous with the puck, and he never gets down on people."

The two played together for a couple of years without McNealy once asking Naughton about his work at Sun. There would be Buds and grub at the Dutch Goose after games, and there'd be the occasional barbecues at McNealy's house in the coastal mountains with Marm and the rest of the guys. McNealy had no doubt asked around about Naughton, and presumably he knew he was a ringleader among a small group of Young Turk programmers hot to change things inside Sun. But it was only in 1990, while the two of them were watching NHL highlights on ESPN and Naughton told McNealy he wanted to leave Sun, that the two had their first serious talk about Naughton's career. Naughton, young and ambitious, was fed up fighting what he called the "corporate anti-bodies" inside Sun screwing with his and his colleagues' software, so he had accepted a job offer from Steve Jobs to work at his post-Apple venture called NeXT. Right away McNealy was all over him about leaving, promising the twenty-five-year-old Naughton that Sun could change. Naughton stuck to his guns, so McNealy changed tack: Before you go, he said, help me learn from this experience. "Do me a favor," he said. "Write me an e-mail laying out what you'd do if you were God."

Naughton poured every ounce of righteousness into a missive that one colleague described as "one long primal scream." He raged about all that was supposedly wrong with Sun before laying out his ideas for the project he had been working on for most of his two and a half years at Sun. The response was vintage McNealy; he responded to Naughton's diatribe with a single line: "Hang in there, I'm all over this." A few days later, a McNealy lieutenant offered Naughton a pay raise and a generous options package. He also offered him a key role in a new group whose mandate was so fuzzy that it wasn't clear whether it would be a hardware or software project. Jobs was furious when the two spoke that weekend, first screaming at him, then switching to sweet talk, then reverting back to anger when Naughton wouldn't budge. McNealy had offered him an opportunity he couldn't walk away from. Magically, Naughton was now charged with putting together a team to figure out how Sun might cash in on the world of computer-chip-driven small devices (for instance, cell phones and handheld computer games), in which no single company's architecture as yet dominated.

Only a few years earlier, Naughton had been an engineering student at a tiny New York school, Clarkson University, better known for the occasional player it sent to the National Hockey League than the software engineers it produced. He applied to Microsoft, but Microsoft, which tended to hire from only a select set of schools, sent him a form-letter rejection. Clarkson had a couple of workstations from Sun, so he sent a résumé there, winning an interview with James Gosling, an engineer who would later be described, in the pages of *Newsweek,* as the "world's greatest programmer." Gosling was a Buddha-like presence, balding and bearded with blond hair that bushed into rings of curls that cascaded past his collar. Gosling took an immediate liking to the cocky but talented Naughton, who, after finishing the last of his final exams, headed west and was surprised when he discovered that Silicon Valley was so far away from Los Angeles.

Naughton had played on his high school soccer team, and in college had become quite a whiz with a hockey stick. Both skills stood him in good stead at Sun, which was like sleep-away camp: the better the athlete you were, the more popular you were likely to be in the corporate hierarchy. As luck would have it, Naughton was assigned the office next to Gosling's, which played a big part in his ascendancy at Sun. When Sun cofounder Bill Joy, one of the gods of the Unix world, stopped by to check on the progress of Gosling and his group, Gosling asked Naughton, then twenty-three, to give the demo. In his earliest days at Sun, Naughton was so innocent that he figured Joy was yet another middle-level manager poking his nose into their business until noticing Joy's employee badge number: Sun employee number six.

In time, though, Naughton learned. He played the business game just as he played hockey, head up, always in the middle of things, the first guy to throw his gloves in a fight. He could debate business strategies for hours; he was audaciously eager to mix it up with the powers that be if that's what it took to champion a pet project. That was fine with Gosling, who, when he was invited to take a seat on an upper-echelon software architecture committee at Sun, sent Naughton in his stead. By all accounts Gosling was a brilliant computer scientist but a puppy in the hurly-burly world of Sun corporate politics. At least back then, Gosling regarded Naughton as a blessing, a sharp technologist who actually enjoyed the business side of things. The two were again paired on this new top-level project, which pleased both the mentor and his politically savvy disciple.

A couple of the older hands at Sun convinced Naughton and Gosling that their only hope was to house the project off-site under the cover of secrecy. Only by creating what engineers call a "skunk works" would their team have the time and freedom to figure out exactly what they were doing. That was how Steve Jobs had created the Macintosh, and that's how Bill Joy and his colleagues had designed the network-based file-swapping system that stood as Sun's single greatest software achievement. "A skunk-works project," explained Bill Joy, "means not having to waste all this time in meetings explaining again and again what you're up to." Several years earlier, Joy had moved to Aspen, Colorado, to set up something he called SmallWorks, a small lab intentionally set up an airplane ride away from corporate headquarters.

McNealy had proposed that they code-name the operation "Project Stealth," but Naughton, Gosling, and others chose "Green," fearing that anything but a bland name would only call attention to their work. They kept the group intentionally small ("small enough to hold strategy sessions around a single table at my favorite Chinese restaurant," Naughton said), and every member was sworn to secrecy. For several months, Naughton, Gosling, and a few others met with Joy and fellow Sun cofounder Andy Bechtolsheim at Joy's Aspen home, hoping, as Gosling put it, "to catch the next wave, except first we had to figure out what the next wave would be." After that, however, they were pretty much on their own.

In April 1991, unbeknownst to anyone apart from McNealy and a few other top people at Sun, a group of four engineers rented a small office several miles from the company headquarters, where they plotted a Sun victory in the Windows-less world of small consumer devices. Joy would serve as their taskmaster and liaison with the senior management group, but he lived a thousand miles away.

Thus was born the project that eventually produced a new programming language called Java, giving Scott McNealy the secret weapon he coveted in his battle with Bill Gates. Expectations were raised still further when the Green project, two years after its birth, moved into the very same Palo Alto offices that had housed the DEC- and IBM-led coalition that had been created expressly to thwart Sun's attempt, in cahoots with AT&T, to take over the Unix world. Sun would spend tens of millions of dollars before producing a product somebody proved willing to pay for. Suddenly McNealy, a notorious tightwad who proudly hung a "Cheap Operating Officer" sign in his office, was anxious to talk shop with Naughton after the games.

"How's it going?" McNealy would ask.

"Real well," Naughton always said in response.

"Okay, I trust you on this."

"I know, I appreciate that."

"You're not going to fuck me, are you?" McNealy would ask his young charge.

. . .

THE SKUNK-WORKS OPERATION meant that Green was like any Silicon Valley start-up. So imagine low-rent furniture in a nondescript office populated by barefoot people wearing shorts. Empty pizza boxes were stacked in one corner; in another sat so many cases of Coke you'd think these six were survivalists preparing for Armageddon. The ripped-out innards of handheld computer devices of all makes and sizes were scattered everywhere, and occasionally the place reeked from the burning of solder and the sparks from hammered-together hardware.

There were the usual start-up flourishes. They bought ice-cream bars by the case and charged them to the company, because they told themselves they were worth it. Some of the Nintendo-variety computer game devices they bought from the company coffers, they never quite got around to ripping apart. One critical decision was reached while soaking in a Lake Tahoe spa (at a Sun executive retreat Naughton had to crash because he didn't rank high enough on the Sun organizational chart); others were thrashed out while staring at the face of a soaring Rockies peak in Aspen. There were also the usual offerings of near-death experiences to lend their tale an air of excitement, and of course there were the make-or-break demos that seemed doomed until just moments before the appointed hour, like a bomb defused at the end of a Hollywood movie only a few ticks away from exploding.

The typical feature article, whether about Sun, Netscape, or any of dozens of Silicon Valley successes, romanticized these wizards at work, but in that regard these accounts were about as realistic and believable as the typical summer blockbuster. Reality, while offering an enticing tale, was never quite so satisfying. At Netscape, there were office chair football games, the occasional beer blowout, and the obligatory weirdo who shrouded himself beneath a blanket as he worked. Andreessen roared around the Valley in a candy red Mustang (before buying a top-of-the-line white Mercedes equipped with a $3,000 stereo system) littered with pizza rinds and empty Oreo packages. Yet for all the endless words spilled over the excitement at Netscape while banging out the world's first commercial browser, the company's software engineers seemed to offer a far more honest appraisal of their lives when they named all the conference rooms in their building after famous prisons.

In the Green project, there were synergistic moments when talking internal architectures with a colleague felt like a Vulcan mind meld, but the truth was more mundane. It was shoulders that ached from too many hours at a computer, neck muscles that spasmed, and eyes infected by rubbing them with dirty fingers. Marriages frayed, relationships ended. The birth of Java is a fascinating story, not so much because it's a gee-whiz triumph of the nerds but because it's a tale of missteps, near-fatal detours, and corporate infighting. It includes its share of thrilling, inventing-the-future moments, but those tended to be punctuation marks at the end of very, very long sentences.

Project members worked seven days a week, averaging twelve to fourteen hours a day, for the better part of two years. Naughton hurt his knee playing hockey—and the next day he was in the recovery room tapping away on his laptop. Gosling smashed his elbow during his maiden voyage on in-line skates: he, too, coded while recuperating. That Gosling was working eighty to a hundred hours a week didn't help his first marriage, which ended in what he described as a "rather messy divorce." A third member of the team, perpetually on the verge of cracking, talked incessantly about fleeing to a thatched hut in Costa Rica. Naughton developed several facial tics. Sometimes he'd just stare at his pinkie and wonder if it would ever stop twitching.

They started off as four and quickly grew to six and then maybe a dozen as they came closer to producing a finished product. What they had in common, other than talent, was that each counted himself among Sun's walking wounded, disaffected veterans who had experienced their share of disappointments watching the fruits of their labor die on the vine for reasons having nothing to do with the quality of their work. One of their funnier creations was the No Balls Club. NBC nominees, if they passed muster, would be inducted through a formal ceremony. "These were people who'd look at their career, look at their stock options, look at their salaries, look around their big corner office—and go, 'That's okay, I won't step up for this one,'" Naughton says. They turned this same cynicism on themselves. "Our problem," Naughton says, "was probably that we had too many balls and not enough brains, politically."

When they weren't complaining about the powers that be, they complained about one another. Their self-imposed deadline came and went, and for the next nine months they grew increasingly surly and defensive. Naughton seemed to capture the mood of the times well with this line about his relationship with Ed Frank, the group's hardware expert: "I would yell at Ed about hardware problems for no good reason, and he would trash me back more viciously." The relationship between Gosling and Naughton was particularly tense. They met every Friday, but after a time they wondered why they bothered when meeting only served to institutionalize Gosling and Naughton's weekly screaming match.

Programmers call it a "death march." In the summer leading up to a demo the team planned to show Bill Joy and a couple of others at the top of Sun, they practically lived at the office, going home every few days to shower and grab some clean clothes. By that time, Naughton was up to eight Cokes a day—the equivalent of polishing off an entire sixty-four-ounce jug of Coke and then emptying half of another.

The attempted coup came after they had produced a working prototype. Each team member was paid a handsome salary; each had been granted Sun stock options. But at least a couple of the group members asked why they were working so hard for Sun when they could be working just as hard for themselves. If this were their own company, they reasoned, at least they might get rich from the slavish hours they toiled. A small rump group arranged a lunch with Joy and Bechtolsheim, who were inclined to view the gambit as a theft of Sun's intellectual property. "I'm sorry, but dat's not ze vay it verks," Andy Bechtolsheim, born and raised in a small town in southern Germany, kept explaining. One teammate quit shortly after this lunch, understandably righteous about all the hours he was working but oblivious to the greed inherent in his power play. The rest of the group was inclined to milk the incident for laughs. "I'm sorry, but dat's not ze vay it verks"—for months it seemed the punch line to every other joke someone cracked.

Having produced a working prototype, the group expanded and moved into larger digs. The project was renamed "FirstPerson," but it remained a black op that people learned about strictly on a need-to-know basis. The plan was to sell Sun computer chips to consumer electronics companies such as Sony and Toshiba at $50 apiece, but the Japanese and other manufacturers explained that the economics of consumer devices didn't work for any chip costing above $5. The software the Green team hoped to sell with each chip was equally doomed. By PC standards, Java required a relatively modest four megabytes of memory, but that was still far more obese than anything the cheap chips in phones and VCRs could handle.

FIRSTPERSON WAS NO LONGER a complete secret inside Sun. Anyone with an ear to the ground knew about this hush-hush off-site operation involving Bill Joy, James Gosling, and some of the company's more talented engineers. But that's about all anyone knew, which only added to the mystique. The unwritten rule at Sun was that you didn't steal personnel from other groups, but FirstPerson had been granted carte blanche to hire anyone it wanted. It seemed as if half the engineers were hoping they'd be next, even if they had no idea what was going on. Meanwhile, almost everyone who was part of FirstPerson wanted out. Plan A had proven a total bust, and the group had no Plan B.

In the spring of 1993, Patrick Naughton learned that Time Warner's cable division was offering a huge bounty for a software system sturdy enough to serve as the backbone of its Interactive TV system. So now FirstPerson, two and a half years after McNealy had challenged Naughton to pretend he was God, was among the herd joining the Interactive TV stampede. FirstPerson went on a huge hiring binge. But in the end that only meant that more people, around fifty in all, were disappointed when Time Warner chose Sun rival Silicon Graphics.

Wayne Rosing was Sun's chief technology officer when, several months prior to the collapse of the Time Warner deal, he demoted himself to run FirstPerson. Every Friday, Rosing would address his staff in the company break room. There was never anything concrete to report, so instead he spoke about all the big strike plans the company had in the works. There was always an impending blockbuster deal with an equally blockbuster company. After Time Warner, it was supposedly with Sprint, TCI, Disney, 3DO, even a plan that had Sun stamping out cable set-top boxes itself. And if it wasn't some big deal, it was some big event: an upcoming cable show or a writer from *Wired* who had heard of some big-deal skunk works inside Sun. "With Wayne it was always 'next week,'" said Arthur van Hoff, a Gosling recruit who joined First-Person in 1993. "Except next week never came." Rosing's Friday talks were incessantly interrupted by the robotic voice of a "Terminator" pinball machine set up in a corner of the cafeteria. "*Hasta la vista,* baby," it would taunt.

People coped in different ways. A programmer named Jonathan Payne, who had joined Green during the project's death march, pretty much spent his days hanging around the company cafeteria. "I was so pissed off that all I really did for a couple of months was play pinball," Payne said. Another programmer, Tim Lindholm, spent so much time on the Terminator machine that he gave himself permanent nerve

damage in one hand. Others spent hours on their computers playing
Doom or sat with their feet propped on their desks, reading technical
journals. "Everyone was completely depressed," Payne said. "People
would show up at eleven and then leave at four. They would go on
three-hour bike rides in the middle of the day. It's like we spent most of
1993 sitting around hoping something would happen." People also busied themselves updating their résumés and feeling out friends for jobs
at other companies.

Even Gosling was looking around for a new job, though leaving
would mean abandoning, after three years of toil, a once-in-a-lifetime
project. Early on, the original Green team recognized that it needed a
simple programming language that would be able to chop large software programs into small pieces that could then run on a wide assortment of devices. These included handheld computers and home
appliances, such as a telephone or television set. But they discovered
that no such language existed, and Gosling volunteered to create one.
All his life he had been hacking on-the-fly solutions, and he relished
this new challenge.

At twelve, rooting around his grandfather's junkyard, he built an
electronic tic-tac-toe machine from spare parts salvaged from a phone
and a television set. He lived in a farming community just outside Calgary, Canada. Neighbors were always phoning the Gosling home to see
if young James might stop by: the engine on the combine wasn't working again. He was fourteen when a class trip took him to the University
of Calgary computer center. He memorized the codes university personnel punched in so that he could subsequently gain access to the
computer room. Days he should have been in class he spent reading
computer manuals and teaching himself how to program the center's minicomputers. A year later, the astronomy department gave the
fifteen-year-old a part-time job writing a program that would allow it
to analyze data transmitted by satellites.

His first job after earning a computer science Ph.D. was at IBM.
There, in the early 1980s, he helped design Big Blue's first-generation
workstation. Only after many bleary-eyed nights did it dawn on
Gosling that the powers that be at IBM had no intention of properly
marketing a machine that, if successful, would undercut its lucrative
mainframe business. His first project after jumping to Sun was equally
doomed. He headed the team that created a product for all Unix users

called NeWS, but it was released while Sun and AT&T were at war with the other Unix vendors. NeWS may have won rave reviews in the programming community, but Gosling looked on in frustration as this product he had spent five years creating was torpedoed by industry politics. And now there was Green/FirstPerson, its prospects for success seemingly just as bleak. Feeling what he described as "cynical, depressed, and very, very angry," he wanted out. He phoned someone he knew at Microsoft.

"I look at them as just a bunch of dumpster divers," Gosling said. In other words, they were imitators who created by copying the work of others. "But Microsoft was also a company that had both the will and might to push products they believed in. The thought that went through my mind was 'Well, I might be working on inferior stuff, but at least it would see the light of day.' "

Microsoft offered Gosling a job, but moving to Redmond would have meant taking a 30 percent pay cut and walking away from stock options potentially worth hundreds of thousands of dollars. The Microsoft human resources office didn't seem to care about his credentials or status as one of the Unix world's more creative talents. "It's common when recruiting a top person to offer a counterbalancing exchange on options," Gosling said, but the Microsoft's human resources official told him the company's policy was to value other company's stock at zero. And he thought, what a perfect expression of the Microsoft master plan—to assume that the value of the stock of every other high-tech company would eventually be zero. "It was," Gosling said, "easily the most deeply offensive interview experience of my life."*

IN THE FALL OF 1993, Scott McNealy gave Wayne Rosing an ultimatum: Devise a new plan, or I'm pulling the plug. In one of his Friday talks, Rosing promised the troops he would deliver a new plan by year's end, but that vow only further undermined his credibility. Some wiseass

---

* Gosling confessed this early in 1998, several years into a protracted Sun-Microsoft fight. A few weeks earlier, before a packed auditorium at San Francisco's Moscone Convention Center, Gosling had thrust a pie into the face of a Gates look-alike appearing on stage. He described his boss as "downright belligerent" in his opposition to Microsoft. So who can say how much all that had happened in the intervening five years colored his view of his day visiting Microsoft's offices in Redmond.

hung a daily countdown: 29 days to Wayne's business plan, 28 days. "The due date came and went without so much as a mention from Wayne," Naughton says.

Rosing was a scientist by training, not a manager. As some of his colleagues tell it, he seemed to lose interest as soon as FirstPerson's plan for selling chips and software to the Japanese failed. His underlings complained that he was always off hobnobbing with industry luminaries. He seemed to be everywhere in the world—Hawaii, the Galapagos Islands, Europe—everywhere, that is, except in his office, running FirstPerson. "He was like this apparition," said one member of the First-Person team. "You'd see him in the cafeteria once a week but never anywhere else."

Responsibility for the FirstPerson business plan fell to Naughton and Kim Polese, a young marketing employee not yet thirty years old who had been assigned to the team less than two months earlier. "You could say I got a lot more than I bargained for when I signed on," Polese says.

The pair proposed a radical plan: FirstPerson should walk away from the millions the company had already dumped into Interactive TV and focus instead on selling to America Online and the other nascent online services. That meant moving into the realm of the PCs and Macs. Rosing initially got behind this new plan but was then bombarded by skeptics; this after all was Sun, where a technology geared to the PC was tantamount to heresy. So Rosing called a special non-Friday meeting in which he ended up announcing that he had changed his mind: they would stick with Interactive TV. Naughton was in the Yucatán talking up FirstPerson with a group of Panglossians led by MIT's Nicholas Negroponte, so it fell to Polese to defend their plan. She felt so sandbagged, she walked out in midmeeting. "Wayne was a great scientist and a great engineer," Polese said, "but CEO was probably not his strong point."

Things went from bad to worse when Rosing tried to fire Naughton. But Naughton fought back, running around FirstPerson with a personnel employee at his side, documenting his case against Rosing. So then Rosing left. By that point, so had most everyone else. The group had peaked at maybe seventy employees but had shrunk to twenty. Polese was reassigned to another unit, but she stayed on the project because she believed in Gosling's language and recognized that to let the group disintegrate was to see his work die. "At that point, nearly everyone was in a near-suicidal funk," Gosling says.

. . .

BILL JOY tells the story of the first time Patrick Naughton showed up at his house to talk strategy. Naughton sat there so quiet and wide-eyed that Joy wondered why he was even there. "I don't think Patrick said a single word the whole night," Joy said. "I guess this was the young Patrick, before he became so self-confident." Joy delivered this line in a tone meant to convey irony, as one might tell a story about a young Bill Clinton shy around girls. A couple of years after leaving Sun, Naughton wrote an essay for *Forbes ASAP*. He began by sharing with his readers his feelings about being so famous. You can plug my name into the Alta Vista search engine, he told them, and it will return no fewer than four thousand hits. People ask him about leaving Sun, but though he has his regrets, "Given that I'm the president of a company that has five of the top ten Internet properties on the planet, it's okay."

Ask James Gosling about his fame in the computer world and he'll turn crimson. Pay him a compliment, and he'll mumble a barely heard thank-you. In contrast, Patrick Naughton flashes a hockey player's mouth full of capped teeth and says, "I know" when you compliment him on a product he helped create. "When I first met Patrick, I really liked him," Gosling said. "But his ego got away from him as his career progressed. He became difficult to talk to."

Naughton took credit as the brain behind FirstPerson's other key product, a Web browser written in Java and eventually dubbed Hot-Java." It's true that Naughton pushed the group to write HotJava (he called his presentation "Why Mosaic Sucks"), but it was Jonathan Payne who banged out the first draft of HotJava.* From the perspective of his colleagues, another of Naughton's sins was that in interviews and on the speaker's circuit, he gave himself sole credit as the group soothsayer who had spotted the commercial potential of the Internet. To Gosling, migration to the Web was one of those group decisions for which no one and everyone deserved credit. "Everyone remembers the lightbulb going off inside their head, so they felt the idea was original to them," Gosling said. "But that lightbulb went off because of the swirl of activity around them. In retrospect, the Web was a natural."

That FirstPerson reinvented itself as an Internet company shortly

---

* Payne and Naughton worked together on a revision of HotJava. Naughton, though, would show off HotJava to the vice presidents at a meeting to which Payne wasn't invited.

into 1994 was the grand and final irony of Gosling's hacked language. It had been written as if he had had the on-line world in mind all along. A programming language that could chop big packets of data into small pieces that would then be reassembled on a user's machine was ideally suited to a world constricted by the bottlenecks of telephone wires and modems. This language, written to communicate with a wide array of small devices, was also perfect for a network created to connect a wide array of computers and operating systems. Java was the Esperanto of the digital world, a network-friendly language that could be understood, regardless of the operating system or chip, no matter where it landed.

THE GENERAL CONSENSUS inside Sun throughout 1994 and into 1995 was that the company had hit a wall. The workstation, the company's bread-and-butter product, was facing the prospect of PCs that grew exponentially faster and more powerful with each year. The scientist or designer who had once had no choice but to spend $20,000 on a workstation was at least considering a PC outfitted with a souped-up Intel Pentium processor costing roughly one tenth the price. There was also the encroachment of Windows NT. The analysts placed Sun, like every other Unix-based company, on the endangered species list. G. Christian Hill, *The Wall Street Journal*'s San Francisco bureau chief, likened Sun to the survivors in *The Poseidon Adventure:* you can keep heading for higher levels as a ship sinks, he said, but eventually you hit the top compartment. Then you have no place to go.

Sun was no longer even the hot story inside the workstation world. Rival Silicon Graphics had invented the workstations that Steven Spielberg's magicians used in *Jurassic Park* to create the illusion of an island populated by dinosaurs; it was those same machines that were used to create a molten-metal evil android in *Terminator II*. McNealy first saw the cover of *Business Week* declaring Silicon Graphics "The Gee-Whiz Company" right before a meeting with Sun PR executive George Paolini. "You see this fucking thing?" McNealy asked Paolini. After blasting a string of expletives, McNealy then phoned the reporter who had written the piece. "At that point he just started cursing some more," Paolini said.

At the end of 1994, during the dead week between Christmas and

New Year's, Paolini and Eric Schmidt, who had taken Rosing's place as the company's chief technology officer, were engaged in one of the woe-is-us conversations endemic in the Valley at that time. Everything that was to be discovered had already been discovered. Microsoft owned everything. They were a couple of guys in their late thirties already reminiscing about the good old days.

As the company's chief technologist, Schmidt knew all about First-Person. Paolini was still in the dark, however, knowing only that it was some hush-hush project that no one could talk about. Schmidt showed his colleague the HotJava browser. Paolini remembered uttering a few "holy smokes" as Schmidt gave a quick demo, but he also remembered that Schmidt didn't make a big deal of it. A former newspaperman relatively new to the world of high tech, Paolini told himself that what he was looking at probably wasn't as cutting-edge as he figured.

Those working on FirstPerson weren't necessarily any more optimistic. Rosing and Naughton were gone, as was most everyone else, so the captainless ship just listed along. Though he hated the scene, Gosling traveled the trade show circuit, showing off HotJava and hoping someone would bite. "I had no great illusions of success," Gosling said. "I just thought by getting it out into the light of day, I might give it life." Ironically, FirstPerson was still technically a secret project, so though Gosling was showing off HotJava on overhead screens around the country, most people at Sun didn't even know it existed.

For Gosling, the turning point was a conference everybody called TED, held in Monterey in the winter of 1995. Gosling had no intention of attending this meeting, more officially known as the Technology, Education, and Design Conference; he was keeping strictly to the geek circuit, whereas TED was executives only, the kind of event people attended to rub shoulders with the titans running Sony, AT&T, and other so-called convergence conglomerates. But TED organizers had asked a Sun executive named John Gage to deliver a talk on the Web, and Gage figured he'd show off HotJava. When Gosling learned of Gage's plan, he tried to talk him out of it. He feared that a failed demo in front of such a high-powered group would cinch Java's death. But TED was the next day, and Gage already had a tape of HotJava in hand, so Gosling decided he had no choice: he would run the demo as Gage spoke. For Gosling the moment of truth came when he downloaded from a Web site hundreds of miles away a seemingly static picture of a molecule, projected onto a big screen. The image came to 3-D life as he passed the mouse over it. "The whole audience lets out this collective sound, like everyone trying to catch their breath at once," Gosling said.

For Kim Polese, FirstPerson's young marketing manager, the breakthrough was an article appearing in the *San Jose Mercury News*. She had approached the *Merc* at great peril to her career at Sun. Eric Schmidt was ready to wring her neck for agreeing to an outside interview, with the *Merc* of all places, a newspaper that everyone from McNealy on down was convinced had it in for Sun. Polese had never even spoken with a reporter outside the computer trades. She woke up early the morning the article was scheduled to appear and then felt crushed by disappointment when she saw no article after paging through the business section. So anxious was she to see what the reporter had written that she failed to notice that it had been bumped to the front page. With time, she would become CEO of one of the Valley's hottest start-ups. She would be featured in publications ranging from *The Wall Street Journal* to *Time*, but years later she remembered the exact date of the *Merc* article and could recite verbatim its headline, "Why Sun Thinks HotJava Will Give You a Lift." Even Schmidt admitted that the gambit had worked. That weekend he had attended a party where people had buzzed about little else.

"My phone started ringing the day that article appeared and never stopped," Polese said. "I'd put down the receiver, and two seconds later it would ring again." On the other end of the line were reporters, analysts, computer jockeys looking for something to enliven their Web sites, even people from inside Sun. "That one article," she said, "changed everything." With Java, you could add animation (a spinning logo, a bouncing ball, a mascot that could wave hello) or turn a dull game into an addictive interactive experience. You could scroll a stock ticker across the bottom of a screen or dedicate a corner to automatically updated sports scores. Polese had chosen the *Merc* because she figured it was the one daily newspaper that every business reporter assigned the Silicon Valley beat was certain to read. By year's end, Java would be featured in more than a hundred newspapers and magazines, including *Time*, *Newsweek*, *The New York Times*, *The Wall Street Journal*, and *The Economist*.

Most of the feature stories spotlighted Gosling, but few even alluded to the Sisyphean nature of his accomplishment. Gosling's picture appeared in *Newsweek* and *Forbes*, but he was never accorded Andreessen-sized celebrity status. For one thing, he wasn't worth anywhere near

$100 million (though McNealy did grant him a "president's award" of 10,000 shares of Sun stock that would be worth more than $4 million by the start of 1999); for another, whereas Andreessen wore his fame as if it were something to which he was entitled, Gosling looked on it all with one eyebrow raised and a bemused smile on his face. One moment he'd be wrestling with fractal algorithms; the next he'd be putting on a nice shirt because a photographer was coming. In time, he would describe himself as a "performing dog" who spent far more time talking about coding than actually doing any. In mid-1996, he'd stand before thousands of people chanting "Ja-va, Ja-va, Ja-va." Not knowing how to respond, he would joke, "I feel as if I ought to be giving a benediction or something."

NETSCAPE WAS THE FIRST company to license Java. Some in FirstPerson thought it shortsighted for the company even to consider a deal with Netscape when it had HotJava. Bill Joy, who negotiated most of the Java deals in tandem with Eric Schmidt, also believed that HotJava was better than Netscape Navigator, but he also realized it was irrelevant when there were already tens of millions of copies of Navigator on the market. "What you want to do is attach yourself to a rocket ship," Joy explained. "And Netscape was a rocket ship."* After a time, though, it was no longer clear which company was fueling the ride. Late in 1995, Netscape changed the name of one of its developer tools from Live-Script to JavaScript. LiveScript didn't include a single line of Java code, but that wasn't the point. This single announcement generated 110 news articles.

Programmers embraced Java because it represented a vast improvement over the language most of them used, C++. Java used the same syntax as C++, so it was familiar, but it solved some of the language's inherent problems. Java was simple, compact, and more security-conscious than C++, an important feature when people were swapping programs over a public network. Yet Java would have remained a story

---

* Sun had tried to hire Andreessen shortly after he graduated from the University of Illinois, but by then he was already talking with Netscape cofounder Jim Clark. As Bill Joy told it, Andreessen politely told him thanks but no thanks: "I think his exact words were 'Sorry, but I'm going to work with Jim Clark and make a hundred million dollars.' "

confined to places such as *PC Week* and *InfoWorld* had the FirstPerson team not pitched it as a tool for adding zip and life to the Internet.

Schmidt and Joy debated approaching Microsoft about a licensing deal, but they agreed it was too early. They still had no idea how much they should charge for their creation, and Legal was still fiddling with the appropriate contract language. They figured they'd get the kinks out during negotiations with other companies. Joy didn't really know Oracle's Larry Ellison, but he cold-called him and left a message, and a few minutes later Ellison called him back. "I said, 'We have this Java thing and we want you to do this, that and the other,' " Joy said. "And he said, 'Okay, I've kind of heard about that. Let's do it.' " More deals followed, including contracts with longtime rivals IBM and Silicon Graphics.

That summer, *Forbes ASAP* ran a lengthy essay written by technology pundit George Gilder and titled "The Coming Software Shift." As he is inclined to do, Gilder opened the article with breathless hyperbole, calling to mind a character from Greek mythology who runs from town to town, at a near-death pace, just ahead of advancing troops. Java, he wrote, marks "a fundamental break in the history of technology" that "menaces Microsoft's software supremacy." The article appeared just after Microsoft had unveiled Windows 95, yet Gilder was predicting that the operating system would be rendered irrelevant in this brave new world of Java. McNealy faxed the article to his top execs with a two-word directive: "Read this!"

Later, when people would try to diagnose the transformation of Java from programming language into religion, they'd point to this article. "That piece changed everything," Schmidt told *The Wall Street Journal.* "I date Java the religion from that article." Before Gilder, Polese said, Sun had been thinking of Java as something it would pitch to programmers. Post-Gilder, company executives respun their story: Java was the world's new Microsoft beater, a technology that would break the world of its reliance on the Microsoft platform. If a program could land on any operating system, one of Microsoft's most convincing arguments—that the computer world would be a more user-friendly place if everyone just adopted Windows—would be rendered moot. "We knew the Web was a big threat to Microsoft, and it suggested they were vulnerable, but we didn't see a way to position Java to help in that fight," Paolini said. "Until Gilder. After the Gilder piece came out, we rethought everything we were doing with Java: our positioning, our message, our R and D, everything." *

The Gilder piece had its biggest impact on McNealy. "The moment he could map Java to his problem—namely, how to harness the Internet to stop Microsoft from swallowing us all—he became its biggest supporter," Eric Schmidt said. "Gilder gave him the big picture: that there was this alternative, and Sun had it." McNealy had already spun First-Person back into Sun and put Schmidt in charge of the division, eventually dubbed JavaSoft. After Gilder, though, he was constantly on Schmidt to push Java harder and faster. Shortly after the article appeared, McNealy called Schmidt into his office to chew him out. Schmidt had taken the reins at JavaSoft only a few weeks earlier, but apparently he was already falling short of McNealy's mandate to "push this puppy hard."

"You're not spending enough money," McNealy told him.

"I'm spending it as fast as I can."

"It's not fast enough."

"It's still early; I'm just getting my team together," Schmidt explained.

"I'm increasing your budget by five million dollars this quarter. Spend it."

Initially, Sun people had been careful not to overpromise when talking about Java. Let's not get so far out there, they told themselves, that we disappoint people. But the more the outside world validated their work, the more confident they became. And then, as if to make up for lost time, they took Gilder's implicit advice to overhype Java as a solution to most of the world's ills. There would be Java T-shirts, Java hats, and denim shirts emblazoned with Java's steaming-coffee-cup logo. Sun's top executives wore Java leather bomber jackets when addressing audiences of programmers, and Sun employees ate lunch at the Java Java Café. Java Java Java: local user groups formed, devotees met on-line to discuss its finer points; even a Java lobby formed to promote its use. "Silicon Valley has never seen anything like it," *The Wall Street Journal* reported. "A world-wide cult dedicated to a computer-programming language."

---

* Actually, Sun's PR staff had been jittery when Gilder began sniffing around the company earlier in the summer. He had spent hours at a café pressing Gosling for the nerdy details of his creation, and Paolini had found Gilder "so cryptic and obtuse" that he had no idea if *Forbes* was about to trash Java or declare it the real deal. The one thing he didn't suspect, he said, is that "Gilder would declare us the Second Coming."

. . .

NEGOTIATIONS BETWEEN MICROSOFT and Sun began in mid-October. The opening parry came when Schmidt met with Microsoft's Nathan Myhrvold at a conference held in Princeton, New Jersey. They were both Princeton alumni, and when Schmidt noticed that they were both speaking at this event, he suggested they meet for a drink. The computer industry was incomprehensibly vast unless one occupied its top echelon, in which case you could say, as Schmidt did, "This is a small industry. Everyone knows everybody else." The two weren't exactly friends, but they had been chatting with each other at industry events for about ten years.

"Have you guys thought about Java?" Schmidt asked. Schmidt remembered Myhrvold mumbling something about being so busy he had barely given the question a thought, but Myhrvold later admitted that that had been a reflexive ploy. Over the next hour he peppered Schmidt with detailed questions that indicated that he had actually devoted a great deal of time to thinking about Java.

Schmidt and Myhrvold met on a Saturday. That night Myhrvold sent a lengthy e-mail to the appropriate Microsoft executive. He said he was dubious about Java but resigned to its status as the industry's latest cause. From his lofty perch as Microsoft's chief technologist, he had witnessed the release of any number of new, heralded computer languages. The only difference this time was that the Internet was amplifying the usual mania "so that it was far stronger, deeper, and more irrational than the others." But like everyone else at Microsoft, he was a devout capitalist who understood that if customers wanted Java, Microsoft should provide it. Even if the whole thing were nuts, Microsoft would be crazier still if it didn't ride the wave.

First thing that Monday, Schmidt heard from a Microsoft senior vice president. "I want to send a team down to talk," he said. "I want you to send a team up here. I want to see your terms." After hanging up, Schmidt stared dumbly at the phone for a few moments before choosing the single word that summed up his feelings: "Wow!"

The Microsoft technical team dealt with Schmidt and Bill Joy, patched in via speakerphone. Joy despised Microsoft and hated Gates. In his Java piece, Gilder would describe Joy as "Microsoft's most persistent critic." For Joy, who had planned on a life in academia until drawn to Sun, the Holy Grail was a world of clean, elegantly written code. He was an uncompromising perfectionist who would become visibly angry when describing the perverse popularity of Microsoft's sloppy, bloated code. He was Updike to Gates's Grisham, a true practitioner of his craft yet somehow far less popular than the hit maker who cranked out easy reads. Yet Joy was among those standing firmly on the affirmative side during the endless internal debates about a deal with Microsoft. "The Netscape deal means Java could succeed," Joy kept saying. "A deal with Microsoft means it can't fail."

Still, years of pent-up bile seemed to find a release when Joy patched in to join the Sun-Microsoft negotiations. Schmidt and several Microsoft counterparts would be kicking around the broad outlines of their potential relationship, and the speakerphone would suddenly crackle with expletives. It would be Joy, saying something like "Fuck Microsoft. I don't even know why we're fucking talking to you. And fuck Bill Gates. No one here can stand him. Why are we doing anything to help this fucking guy grab even more business?" Or Team Microsoft would be drilling for some detail about Java, and again a vituperative disembodied voice would fill the room: "Why doesn't Bill take his fucking chips and go to his fucking home and leave the rest of us the fuck alone?" Alone, the people from Microsoft joked that Joy was so worked up, they could hear pellets of spittle bouncing off his phone.

Microsoft employees were accustomed to the snide remarks. They'd be asking Company X about the particulars of its technology, and then someone would interrupt, "With all due respect, why should we trust you with this information?" Or there might be a stray comment about the widely held belief that at Microsoft a partner was an expedient, a short-term necessity until self-interest dictated it assign a team of high-priced lawyers the job of finding a loophole through which to escape. But Joy's performance that day, said one participant, "was absolutely extraordinary. This was an ad hominem attack for an hour and a half about my boss. I've heard my share of nasty things about Microsoft, but this was unparalleled." Ironically, he had been eagerly awaiting a chance to talk with the great Bill Joy. "He belongs in anyone's pantheon of computer developers," said this Microsoft negotiator. "In my book he's top ten, unquestionably."

More than a month passed before the two companies got around to talking dollars and cents. "We were proceeding with incredible caution," said Microsoft's Bob Muglia, who helped negotiate the Java deal. "We were aware every moment that we were dealing not just with a competitor but one whose core plans had them using this technology competitively against us." The two sides negotiated day and night in the days leading up to Gates's "We are an Internet company" Pearl Harbor Day speech. The two companies signed a letter of intent just nine hours before Gates officially announced the deal during a speech attended by hundreds of reporters and analysts.

Gates spoke for two hours, but then he mentioned the Java deal and it was as if a bomb had gone off. The press started exiting en masse, rushing for the press room phones or a quiet place to talk on a cellular. "Capitulation!" screamed a page-one headline in *ComputerWorld*. That would be the word that defined Microsoft's decision to sign the Java deal. "Microsoft's capitulation stands as a defining moment for Sun and its 41-year-old CEO," *Business Week* would report a few weeks later in a cover-story profile of McNealy. "Even the mighty William H. Gates III—whose software dominates the huge PC market—concedes that McNealy's Sun has the right stuff."

Actually, the two companies had only signed a letter setting out the rough outline of a deal. Many more grueling rounds of negotiations lay ahead. Microsoft set as its deadline a San Francisco conference for more than five thousand Windows programmers held each March. There, the company would either announce it was using Sun's version of Java in the next release of its Internet Explorer browser or explain that negotiations with Sun had fallen through and therefore it would use its own Java-compatible product. The final deal was signed just before 5 A.M. and announced at the start of the conference three hours later. For the rights to Java, Microsoft agreed to pay $14 million over four years.

Suddenly everything was breaking Sun's way. Sun in the spotlight meant the company sold more Sun machines. By the end of 1995, more than one out of every three "servers" hosting a Web site were Sun computers running Sun software. Sun even managed to steal a little of Silicon Graphic's Hollywood pizzazz by getting credit for providing some of the machines used to make the movie *Toy Story*. *Business Week* put McNealy on its cover. The company's stock nearly tripled in 1995.

"We're all having a blast," McNealy told *Business Week* at the start of 1996. "I just wish I didn't have to sleep." He did add, though, that he had at least one concern. "I'm a little worried about Windows," he said. "I hope they survive. We need the competition."

CHAPTER 11

THE BORG

IN SILICON VALLEY, people never lacked for unflattering nicknames for Microsoft but "Evil Empire" seemed the favorite. It was a muscular, dramatic analogy, and suitably bellicose. Most important, it allowed the Valley to wear the white hats. "There are two camps," Scott McNealy told *Newsweek* late in 1996. "Those in Redmond, who live on the Death Star, and the rest of us, the rebel forces." And if Gates were indeed "Darth Gates," as McNealy was always saying, that meant McNealy was Luke Skywalker, leading his ragtag bunch into battle.

McNealy's cohort, Eric Schmidt, was also inclined to view Microsoft as a foreign invader, though he at least limited his comparison to this planet. "They're like the Chinese Army," Schmidt said of Microsoft in his set talk delivered hundreds of times in 1996. "They send wave after wave of soldiers at you, all of them expendable." Microsoft would squeeze hundred-hour weeks out of its employees until there was nothing left, but an unlimited supply of fresh troops was available from the fifteen thousand résumés the company received each year. "It's impossible to beat Microsoft in a war of attrition," Schmidt would say.

Microsoft as the Borg, a recurring enemy in the *Star Trek* series, was another favorite analogy, in part because *Star Trek* is so popular among the digerati set and in part because the comparison seemed so apt. The Borg was a mythical civilization of interchangeable beings, indefatigable, acting as one, receiving orders from a central brain via hardware embedded in their own brains. The Borg traveled the universe in a forbiddingly huge mass of impenetrable metal, indiscriminately devouring whatever lay in its path. "We are the Borg," it announced when coming upon the humans piloting the Starship *Enterprise* in the movie *First Contact*. "Lower your shields. Surrender your ship. We will add your biological and technological distinctiveness to our own. Your culture will adopt to service us. Resistance is futile." Once subsumed, free will would be replaced by devotion to the ship's central brain. The drones might act slow-witted in the fashion of an automaton, but the Borg was a particularly formidable foe because its anthropomorphic brain could learn and adjust, thwarting every new trick the humans threw at it.

Those in Redmond may have chafed at such analogies, but the Microsoft faithful were no less inclined to borrow military terms to describe the competitive landscape. When on December 7, 1995, Gates declared Microsoft an Internet company, he cast Microsoft as the United States and Netscape as Japan when, on the fifty-fourth anniversary of the bombing of Pearl Harbor, he paraphrased Admiral Yamamoto: "I fear we have awakened a sleeping giant." Back at Microsoft's headquarters, the troops were working too hard to watch, via closed-circuit TV, this six-hour marathon staged for the press and the Wall Street analysts. But the message was delivered with machinelike efficiency to the company's twenty thousand employees. Gates's speech was e-mailed to every employee, who then received a videotape of Gates via interoffice mail.

"Sometimes people are inclined to see Microsoft as this huge supertanker, but that's not right," said Thomas Reardon, who makes anyone's list of Microsoft employees playing a critical role in the company's transition to the Internet. "We're a bunch of speedboats—a bunch of PT boats—not always going in the same direction. So when Bill got up there and said that the Internet is our top priority, that ended all the noise and debate. The significance of that speech, at least internally, is that it righted all the boats, it set all the PT boats in the right direction."

At other companies, people would take sides. They'd grumble in impromptu hallway gatherings, they'd debate the wisdom of this edict from on high. At Microsoft, however, when the generalissimo stepped out onto the balcony to lay down the law, the disciples loyally followed. Microsoft was now an Internet company, and the Internet would pervade every aspect of the company's business. The Great Brain had declared it, so now everyone was saying, in unison, that cashing in on the Internet was Microsoft's top priority.

A JOURNALIST VISITING MICROSOFT to interview a Microsoft employee—to probe any member of the Borg society when he or she is plugged into the central brain—is never left alone. A full day's worth of interviews means that ten minutes before the first meeting, someone who will be that journalist's constant companion meets him or her at a security desk and bids him or her farewell at the car after the final appointment. Typically, the escort is one of the four-hundred-plus employees who work for Waggener Edstrom, the Microsoft PR agency—"Wagg-Ed" to those in the know. The Wagg-Ed representative carries in her hands a file folder with the journalist's name on it that includes articles he or she has written and assorted impressions of him or her contained in memos written to the file (I peeked one day while my escort was in the bathroom). The escort informs the journalist that she is there to help, to facilitate and close loops that need closing, but the deeper truth is that she is there to monitor every bit of data being shared with the media about Microsoft and, in emergencies, to stomp on the brakes. If follow-up phone calls are necessary, your Wagg-Ed escort listens in.

I drew Pam Edstrom, the "Ed" in Wagg-Ed. Edstrom has spearheaded Microsoft's PR efforts since 1982, first as a full-time employee and then as a partner in her own agency. Prior works have described the cat-eyed Edstrom as a "spitfire" or "dynamo," but that's because she's a small woman, energetic and also pushy when she needs to be. Her daughter, in an unflattering kiss-and-tell book (*Barbarians Led by Bill Gates*) cowritten with a longtime Microsoft programmer, described her mother as "one of the most aggressive, calculating, successful public-relations executives in the country." She probably meant it as a compliment, but it sounded like something Joan Crawford's daughter might have written.*

I wanted to talk with Thomas Reardon, but Edstrom wasn't keen on the idea. Reardon wasn't exactly a Wagg-Ed favorite. I found out why after I sent him an e-mail proposing a backdoor meeting. He'd go only through Wagg-Ed, he responded, because "I've gotten in trouble too many times for going around them." The problem, it seemed, was his disloyal propensity to disconnect from the pod. But I pushed, and if people at Microsoft understand nothing else, they understand aggressiveness. Edstrom placed him on my schedule.

---

* I'd imagine she also didn't make her mother very happy when she and her cowriter, Marlin Eller, referred to Gates as "the company mascot—a sort of high-technology Colonel Sanders."

People refer not to Microsoft's offices but to its "campus." It's a sprawl of two- and three-story look-alike buildings of brushed cement and tinted glass, the new science building stripped of personality. Set on twenty-three acres, there are soccer fields and basketball courts scattered about, even a wooded trail.* A former Microsoft programmer once wrote that the architecture reminded him of a minimum-security prison, but he was mixing the look of the place with its feel. There's something hermetically sealed about Microsoft—what novelist Douglas Coupland described as a "Biosphere-2-like atmosphere." It felt more Las Vegas than student union, with no clocks on the walls and free drinks nearby so workers have one less excuse for wandering off. The kitchens have no tables or chairs, discouraging watercooler chitchat. Most of the buildings have a ground-floor cafeteria; some Softies believe they were intentionally kept small, thereby discouraging long, lingering lunches.

Reardon's Microsoft office was something to behold. The door was open but he wasn't there when Edstrom and I arrived a few minutes after the appointed hour. There was nothing in the way of decorations on the wall or tchotchkes on the shelves. There wasn't even a computer anywhere in sight. We both figured that Edstrom had jotted down the wrong office number, but then Reardon's next-door neighbor set us right. "You've never met Thomas?" he asked in a way that put one in a frame of mind to expect anything. When he finally showed up, Reardon explained that he suffers a bad case of Microsoft paranoia: he has a single computer (rather than the standard-issue two), a laptop that he takes with him whenever he leaves the office. The still-packed boxes dated back more than two months. "It's been a super-busy time," Reardon explained.

Unlike many other young Softies who unconsciously emulate the Boss, Reardon doesn't rock back and forth like Gates, but he possesses the same inability to sit still. He's Uriah Heep in Dickens's *David Copperfield*, a rubber-limbed contortionist, wrapping his arms around himself, entwining his legs as if intending to rope them around his chair, fiddling with his fingers as if trying to tie them into knots. Reputedly, he's a Gates favorite, if for no other reason than his comportment over the years at what insiders call the "BEC" (Bill and the EC—the executive committee): the product review meetings where Gates and his top peo-

* The day I walked it, I didn't see another living soul.

ple grill the project managers. These meetings have proven treacherous for all but the strongest-willed individuals, yet Reardon is that rare breed who seems to thrive in this environment.

Reardon was a founding member of Microsoft's browser team. Back in 1994, he was part of a small group, Gates included, that was debating whether to create a browser internally or—as the company had done with DOS—buy one on the open market, which would save time but invite the scorn of those code warriors who believe that real programmers write their own. Microsoft was so far behind Netscape and other companies that logic demanded that it buy or license. Then, during negotiations, the company pummeled first one company, then another, threatening to build one itself if it wasn't given a better price. More often than not it was Reardon, Microsoft's main negotiator, who did the pounding.

Reardon and two teammates flew to Mountain View in the fall of 1994 to suss out the possibility of a deal with Netscape. As Reardon remembered it, the vice president of marketing with whom they met wasn't even polite about it: We have no interest in a deal with Microsoft, he said. "They were very antagonistic," Reardon said. "Very black-and-white on the issue.* Eventually, the company inked a deal with Spyglass, the company that had bought the browser code Marc Andreessen had helped write at the University of Illinois.

The Microsoft way is to offer an absurdly low figure and then make the adversary claw for every additional dollar. Its deal with Spyglass was typical. Microsoft opened the negotiations by offering a onetime flat fee of $100,000 for the worldwide rights, even though the company was proposing to sell it as a companion product to tens of millions of its Windows users. That was more money than Spyglass had in the bank, but its negotiators held out for agonizing weeks. Finally, the two sides agreed on $2 million.† The product would be dubbed Internet Explorer—"IE" to the computer-savvy.

---

* In time, Netscape executives would have their own tale to tell of a later meeting with Microsoft. Andreessen charged that Gates's minions visited Netscape in June 1995 to propose that the two companies divvy up the browser market: let us have the Windows users and we won't write IE for non-Windows machines. The government would make it a central point in its case against Microsoft—at which point Microsoft would vehemently deny the charges.

† Just as Microsoft was about to seal the deal with Spyglass, Netscape's Jim Clark contacted Gates: "You know, before you do this Spyglass thing, you ought to come talk with us." For more than a week Gates was officially out of the office and unable to sign the Spy-

Early in 1996, Microsoft leaked a Gates memo in which he had likened the Internet to a great "tidal wave." Dated in the late spring of 1995, it was released to prove that Gates hadn't been a complete lunkhead about the Web. Yet it was written in the style of someone covering his tracks ("Perhaps you have already seen memos from me or others here about the importance of the Internet"), and somehow its message never got through. Despite this memo, people inside Microsoft still argued with Reardon and his cohorts when they pushed for a long list of Internet-related tasks. But then Gates laid out his December 7 strategy of "embracing" the Internet (rather than creating a unique set of Microsoft protocols for communicating via the Internet, as was being discussed internally) and "extending" it to create all sorts of proprietary footholds, making it only logical for a company to use Microsoft's set of Internet solutions. Only after that speech did Reardon notice that no one argued anymore whenever he or one of his cohorts pleaded for more Internet-related staffing.

For Reardon, life before Gates's December 7, 1995, call to action had been intense, but afterward it was as if nothing existed outside the Internet bubble. "We were absolutely obsessed with this seven days a week," Reardon said. Wider events such as the 1996 presidential election and a summer of natural disasters were faint echoes. Seeing friends—at least those not also part of his work life—were luxuries for which he rarely made time. Yet whereas an outsider might see only the dull ache and droning emptiness of such an existence, Reardon recalled the time as maybe the most fantastic year of his life. "Everyone felt bound together by a mission," he said.

Sacred cows were killed, long-term projects entirely retooled. The company needed to get busy figuring out ways to cash in on Java, so the head of the tools division called together one of his groups to inform them that they were now part of his Java team. "Clear the source code off your machine," he told them, "and start working on Java. Today." For those for whom Gates's directive meant walking away from an unfinished project, killed after maybe two and a half years of toil, one imag-

---

glass contract while Microsoft explored a last-minute deal with Netscape. "That was absolutely at their invitation," Reardon says. "The deal with Spyglass was pretty well done by the time J. [Allard] and I flew down to the Valley for a last-ditch, 'maybe we should take a closer look at this' talk." The two sides talked for two days, never reaching any kind of deal.

ines a consolation dinner before they return to the office for the 10 P.M. primer on the intricacies of Java's new threading technique.

Per Gates's orders, every product manager and every programmer rethought whatever it was they were working on. How might a product be rejiggered to exploit the Internet? If you were working on children's games in the consumer products division, the interest was no longer in what could be done on CD-ROM but what could be done over the Internet. The software tools division was now the Internet tools division, and the browser group, which a year earlier had employed only six people, had grown from thirty people before December 7 to several hundred shortly into 1996. In three months' time, the company had created a newly christened 2,500-employee Internet division—what Reardon, unintentionally parroting Eric Schmidt, described as a "human wave assault." Roughly eight hundred of them would weave into Windows what the tech crowd called "Internet functionality"—the tools required to create a quickie Web page or to send an Excel spreadsheet over the Internet to a fellow Excel user.

Following AOL's lead, Microsoft had created Microsoft Network (MSN), a world of chat rooms and other services reached by modem but walled off from the rest of the Internet. But despite the tens of millions of dollars the company had spent on MSN, and despite thirty months of work, MSN was reinvented after December 7, reborn as an Internet access service that served as a gateway to whatever the Internet offered. The company's highly touted Blackbird technology, a tool that had allowed vendors to create "storefronts" on the old MSN, was dropped, as were the hundreds of vendors Microsoft had lined up to set up shop in what initially was to be a proprietary mall. AOL, once a despised competitor, was now aggressively courted as a valued friend because Microsoft wanted its own browser bundled on the tens of millions of unsolicited software CDs AOL was raining down on U.S. consumers.

At Netscape, CEO Jim Barksdale encouraged every employee to take a three-day weekend each month. That spring he shut down the building for an impromptu Netscape Escape Day. That was hardly the mentality that Gates encouraged inside Microsoft. Six months into its rebirth, a *Business Week* reporter toured the company's tools division. It was well past quitting time on an inviting Friday evening in May, but nearly half the offices were still occupied. "Empty cups of espresso and the sleeping bags hooked to the backs of doors speak volumes about the night ahead," *Business Week*'s Kathy Rebello wrote. "And the next night and the next. And probably the next year.

"Microsoft, already the ultimate hardcore company, is entering a new dimension."

An e-mail making the rounds inside the Microsoft system made this point through humor, comparing the conventional advice one would get from a touchy-feely human resources director to the Microsoft credo. The conventional wisdom might dictate, "Listen to the wisdom of your body," but the Microsoft way was "Work until the physical pain forces you into unconsciousness."

"Always attempt to do everything," the e-mail counseled. "You ARE responsible for it all." Learning to say no only "shows weakness, and lowers the stock price. . . . If you find yourself relaxed and with your mind wandering, you are probably having a detrimental effect on the stock price."

A potential Microsoft partner would log on to read his e-mail in the morning and notice the three messages he had received from a Softie since leaving the office late the night before, all time-stamped past midnight except the last one, which showed that the Softie had already been back at his desk early the next morning. Gates said at an early 1996 press conference that he awakens each morning thinking about browser share. So the Microsoft faithful joked that they had a new priority: working late so Bill could get a good night's sleep.

IN THE OLD DAYS, Bill Gates, locked in debate about something product-related, would be the last to leave after a meeting or a social gathering. He'd be animated and engaged, no matter what the hour. By the mid-1990s, though, he might still be among the last to leave, but often he looked exhausted, strained, put upon. Even if he couldn't quite formulate the words, his body language would scream, Can't we talk about this another time?

Yet he hardly slowed down despite all those billions. On the road he still liked to boast of all that he had crammed into one of his habitual sixteen-hour days: three photo ops, a pair of speeches, seven customer meetings, not counting the two hours he had set aside to see a city's new Microsoft office. When in town he no longer lived at the office on weekends, but he still spent a lot of his time on Saturdays and Sundays in front of his computer, catching up on e-mail, working on a speech, sifting through reports. In April 1996, Melinda Gates gave birth to the couple's first child, Jennifer Katharine. Microsoft grants new fathers four weeks of paid leave, but Gates was back at work three days after Jennifer was born. There was the Internet to conquer. He was the leader, the man with his finger on the mouse, pointing the way to the future.

Yet if the calamity of the moment had not been the Internet, it would have been something else. Despite all that Microsoft had accomplished, Gates still ran Microsoft as if it were constantly at the precipice of doom. At most publicly traded companies, the annual briefing of Wall Street analysts is a time to boast of all it will accomplish over the next year. At Microsoft, though, it was the same year after year: first company executives would report the dazzling numbers the company had again turned in, but they would lay out everything that could go wrong in the coming twelve months. Sounding like a mutual fund prospectus, droning on about past performance not being a guarantee of future success, Gates always spoke as if this would be the year, no doubt about it, that the stock would go south.

"I don't think you'd be interviewing me . . . if we were any less nimble," Gates told *Time* at the end of 1996. "You'd be writing our epitaph." It was pure Gates, revealing the healthy paranoia of an aggressive CEO but so hyperbolic as to be absurd. By 1996, the Windows franchise was generating roughly $4 billion annually, and the company's Office suite was outpacing even Windows in terms of profits generated. Also contributing to the bottom line were the company's consumer division, its tools and computer languages business, and any number of other profit centers. Yet here Gates was imagining financial ruin if Microsoft took anything but first place in the race to cash in on the Internet. *Time* bought that line: "An epic battle is taking place between Microsoft and Netscape," the magazine exclaimed in a subheadline. "The victor could earn untold billions; the loser could die."

At the end of 1996, Microsoft had $9 billion in the bank and Netscape $203 million. Somehow, though, Gates made Microsoft out to be the underdog up against an entrenched foe. Microsoft ranked thirty-ninth in profits on the 1996 Fortune 500 list of the country's largest publicly traded corporations and ninth in the category the magazine calls "market value" (the cumulative worth of all its stock, synonymous with market capitalization), at $61 billion. This company supposedly facing ruin was worth more than Exxon, Chevron, Procter & Gamble, Citicorp, or General Motors. Even the company seemingly fueling

Gates's paranoia, IBM, was hardly the failure he and others made it out to be. At the start of 1996, IBM was again worth more than Microsoft, with a market value exceeding $68 billion. This "has-been" logged $72 billion in revenues in 1995 (sixth overall on the *Fortune* revenue chart) and ranked fifth in profitability. Sure, its stock had languished in the late 1980s and early 1990s, but, even if an investor had bought shares in IBM at its 1987 high, she would still have more than doubled her money by early 1999.

So what did the Internet threaten? For one thing, the God-given right people at Microsoft felt they had to collect at least 50 cents on every dollar generated by the PC software market. For another, missing this golden opportunity would mean the company's stock would suffer. The company's market cap exceeded that of General Motors not because Microsoft brought in more money each year—GM ranked first in revenues at $169 billion, Microsoft 219th at $6 billion—but because year after year the company consistently posted profit margins exceeding 25 percent a year. That ranked Microsoft sixth on the 1996 *Fortune* list in terms of profit rate. GM, in contrast, earned 4 cents on every dollar of revenue, ranking the auto giant 281st.

Microsoft's problem was one of expectations. The stock price continued to grow at a phenomenal rate, greater than 60 percent per year between 1986 and 1995, only because it maintained both its enviable profit rate and its reputation on Wall Street as a perennial winner. A 10 percent profit rate (which would still have ranked Microsoft among the country's hundred most profitable publicly traded companies) wouldn't cut it—not for the man that *Business Week*, without even bothering to attribute the words to someone else, called "high tech's most ruthless competitor."

Reardon and his colleagues, of course, embraced Gates's challenge when he announced that the Internet was nothing short of a life-and-death struggle for survival. At Microsoft, the only thing people enjoy more than the prospects of all-out war ("We're the PT boats") is watching the stock continue to soar. Barksdale had banned stock tickers from the premises at Netscape and discouraged talk of the stock price, but at Microsoft the typical employee had the company stock price scrolling by all day, every day in a ticker at the bottom of his or her computer screen. Microsoft's stock had split in 1990, 1991, 1992, and again in 1994, but "Mr. Softie"—as the company was affectionately known among Wall Street traders—would remain the Street's darling only if the company conquered the Internet as it had done in the world of operating systems and applications. Only then would the stock options that every programmer was counting on for his or her retirement offer the jackpotlike returns that had enriched so many Microsoft millionaires before them.*

The starting pay for a programmer right out of school was in the midforties. A twenty-two-year-old who earned $45,000 was paid far more than the average American worker, but it was still no cause for celebration given the hours and the pay at many of Microsoft's less profitable competitors. Repressed wages (as well as a lousy vacation package—two weeks a year through the first five years) was one way the company maintained such a high profit rate. Most of an employee's compensation was generated through the company's generous stock option plan, which didn't cut into the bottom line.† New employees were granted options when they were hired (typically, in the 500- to 700-share region for those right out of school, more if they had previous programming experience) and accumulated additional options if a manager felt their skills and drive showed future promise. An employee could also set aside 10 percent of his or her salary to buy Microsoft shares at a 15 percent discount.

Ask a Softie why he works so hard, and you'll hear a lot about pride ("I was intent on proving that even a company as big as Microsoft could do really cool things," Reardon told me), but that answer obscures the fact that the stock price is the accepted benchmark of the company's success. "They want to take away your kids' college education," some middle manager was always saying about Netscape (or Sun or whatever the enemy du jour). "They want to destroy your retirement." Work as if the company's life depended on it, Gates had said. But the fact was that the company's survival wasn't at stake so much as the future worth of the stock. Assuming the stock grew at the same rate in

* It's impossible to say how many so-called Microsoft millionaires roam the earth because those granted stock options, once those options are fully vested (after 4½ years), have no obligation to hold on to those options. In the early 1990s, though, several Wall Street analysts took a stab at a reasonable guess, including Credit Suisse First Boston's Michael Kwatinetz, who in 1992 guesstimated that at least 3,400 of the company's 11,000 employees were working millionaires.

† A stock option is the right to buy a stock at the price on the day it is granted: if an employee is granted options on 1,000 shares of stock when it is trading at $40 a share and twelve months later the stock is trading at $90 a share, that employee would be $50 a share (or $50,000) richer.

the second half of the 1990s as it did in the first half, an employee with a total of 3,000 options would be worth $1.5 million. At the beginning of 1996, Gates owned roughly one fourth of the stock in the company, or 550 million shares. That would mean the top dog's net worth might just crack $100 billion in the year 2000. Think of it: Bill worth more than $100 billion. Cool!

THE DAY OF Gates's Pearl Harbor Day speech, reporters asked Netscape's James Barksdale for a comment. His mistake was to crack a clever joke. "We're brave," he said. "We're well financed. And God is on our side." Nothing related to Internet Explorer was funny at Microsoft. So wherever you turned in the Internet Explorer group, you'd be reminded of Barksdale's words. They were memorialized on computer-generated banners hanging on walls; they scrolled repetitiously across people's monitors when their computer was in screen-saver mode.

Microsoft was a formidable company that needed no external incentives, yet Netscape executives were providing plenty of them. People in the Valley called it "breathing your own fumes"—believing your own hype. "No horse head in the bed yet," Andreessen had cracked when asked about Microsoft—and up in Redmond people got all indignant about a joke likening them to the Mafia. Then there was Andreessen's line, brash and cocky, about Microsoft never catching up, given his company's insurmountable lead. "We're gonna smoke 'em," he said—and of course that quote, too, was repeated in the fashion of a football coach trying to pound the maximum effort out of his team. Not a day passed in the Internet Explorer group, Reardon said, without at least one horse-head-in-the-bed joke.

"Predators," Netscape founder Jim Clark said of Microsoft in an *Upside* interview.

"Arrogant assholes," people in Redmond said of Netscape.

Andreessen was sending e-mail to everyone, even people he barely knew, matter-of-factly referring to Microsoft as Godzilla, the Evil Empire, or just "those idiots up in Redmond." The Valley's older hands could only shake their heads. Said one well-regarded Valley CEO, "When you met with them, their attitude was, 'Fuck Windows. It's aging, it's ugly, it's fat, it's Byzantine.' I'd just sit and listen, but the whole time I'm thinking, Why do you want to irritate Gates? Why do you want to wave the red flag in front of the bull?"

For public consumption Microsoft's goal was trumping Netscape feature for feature. Privately, the aim of the Internet Explorer group was to teach Netscape a lesson. Netscape's stock fell 18 percent, or $28.75 per share, on the day of Gates's Pearl Harbor Day speech. But Microsoft employees vowed they wouldn't be satisfied until the price of Netscape's stock had fallen by at least two thirds.* Microsoft had less than a 5 percent share of the browser market in the spring of 1996, but that only motivated people to work harder. Microsoft employees did what they do best: chase taillights, 20,000 nerds with their feet to the pedal twenty-four hours a day, seven days a week, eyes glazed, popping No-Doz, never stopping for a decent meal or much of a break. Netscape Navigator could play sound, so the Explorer would also play sound— CD-quality sound. It was a poorly kept secret that Netscape was working on software that allowed a computer user to talk over the Internet via telephone, so Microsoft was working on software it called NetMeeting that would allow conference calling.

"Oh, our eyes have seen the glory of the coming of the Net, we are ramping up our market share, objectives will be met," began a ditty dubbed the "Battle Hymn of the Reorg" published in the *MicroNews*, an in-house newsletter. Went another stanza:

> *Our competitors were laughing, said our network was a fake,*
> *Saw the Internet economy as simply theirs to take.*
> *They'll regret that fateful day*
> *The sleeping giant did awake.*
> *We embrace and we extend!*

THE SOFTIES WON because they were dedicated, experienced, and smart. They won because everyone, from the top man down to the new programmer hired right out of school, had the technical know-how. They paid what Thomas Reardon called "rabid attention to customers," and even the shaggiest-haired programmer possessed an unapologetic

---

* "During the lunch break," James Wallace wrote of December 7, 1995, in his book *Overdrive*, "Microsoft treasurer Greg Maffei, a cell phone up to his ear, had walked up to a Microsoft vice president named Paul Maritz and told him, 'Netscape's down $30.' 'Good,' replied Maritz, a smile spreading across his face. A few seats away, another Microsoft executive overheard Maffei murmur, 'That's not good enough.' "

devotion to the dollars-and-cents implications of every decision. Size was another obvious advantage. Netscape employees were ecstatic because the company earned $346 million in fiscal year 1996, but Microsoft earned more than twice that amount just from the interest on its cash on hand.

Yet Microsoft also won because it was the global power in possession of nuclear weapons that wasn't afraid to drop the bomb if necessary. Long before Gates's Pearl Harbor Day speech, Compaq had been selling machines preloaded with Netscape Navigator. When Microsoft came out with IE later that year, Compaq stuck to its deal with Netscape. Microsoft packaged IE with Windows, so IE came preloaded on every Compaq machine, but it wasn't featured on the opening screen as Microsoft intended. So Microsoft threatened its longtime partner with a "Notice of Intent to Terminate License Agreement." You're free to feature whatever browser you choose, Microsoft informed Compaq, but if you choose Netscape Navigator over IE you'll lose the right to sell Windows on any of your machines.

Federal antitrust laws forbid a company that monopolizes one market from gaining a monopoly in a second by requiring that people buy the second product in order to gain access to the first. Except that Microsoft refused to acknowledge that Windows was a monopoly, though the rule of thumb among antitrust lawyers is that anything above a 70 percent market share constitutes a monopoly, and by that time Windows enjoyed a 90 percent market share. And though the company marketed IE as a freestanding product separate from Windows 95 (you didn't have to be a Windows user to use IE), it claimed that Windows 95 and IE *were* a single product. Microsoft's contract with computer makers strictly prohibited them from customizing Windows 95, even if the change entailed nothing more than a rearrangement of icons. Compaq was huge, the world's leading supplier of PCs, but it knuckled under with barely a fight. It dropped Netscape altogether.* Gateway 2000 and Micron Electronics, two more large computer makers, also told government investigators that Microsoft had twisted their arms when they

---

* Another Microsoft tactic, according to antitrust lawyer Gary Reback, was price breaks for manufacturers agreeing to preinstall IE. He claimed that at least one of his clients had been told it would have to pay $3 *more* per system for Windows 95 if it didn't bundle IE with the machines it sold. Microsoft, however, refuses to comment on the contracts it signs with its partners.

considered selling machines featuring Netscape's browser. Then each, bowing in fear, frantically spread the word that they had spoken with the feds only because the law had compelled them to do so.

"We are going to cut off their air supply," Microsoft's Paul Maritz said of Netscape at a gathering of industry executives in 1996. "Everything they're selling, we're going to give away for free." Steve Ballmer said pretty much the same thing in an interview with *Forbes:* "We're giving away a pretty good browser as part of the operating system. How long can they survive selling it?" And Gates, who was inclined to view his company's assault on Netscape's market share as a war of attrition, told the *Financial Times,* "We are still selling operating systems. What does Netscape's business model look like [if that happens]? Not very good."

In early 1996, company officials sent around a strategy memo calling for a six-month attack on Netscape. The company's managers were instructed to obtain exclusive agreements with the country's five largest Internet access companies: AOL, CompuServe (since purchased by AOL), AT&T WorldNet, Netcom, and MCI. "You should be able to break most of Netscape's licensing deals and return them to our advantage because our browsers are free," according to this memo, which surfaced during the Justice Department's probe of Microsoft. The big prize was the top service provider, AOL, which by the spring of 1996 had more than 6 million users. Netscape was so confident it had a deal with AOL that the company sent out a press release crowing about this rejection of Microsoft's technology. But the next day AOL announced it had signed a deal with Microsoft—an ironic change of mind given what would take place two years later. AOL's chief executive officer acknowledged that Netscape had the superior browser and that it was clearly the leader in its field, but Microsoft could offer AOL a small patch of priceless real estate, an icon on the Windows start screen. By the end of 1996, Microsoft had accomplished its sweep: the country's top five Internet access companies had abandoned Netscape Navigator in favor of Microsoft's browser.

The Internet access companies were one front in the browser wars, the Web's more popular sites another. The big news that fall was that Microsoft was *paying* Web publishers that charged an entrance fee, such as *The Wall Street Journal* and Investors Edge, to offer several months of free service to anyone visiting their sites using the Internet Explorer. A third front was the so-called market influencers—worldwide consulting outfits such as KPMG Peat Marwick, which recommend products to hundreds of big businesses. Netscape believed it had a rock-solid deal with KPMG when a Microsoft vice president talked his way into a breakfast meeting with Roger Sobini, the KPMG executive on whose shoulders a decision fell. Netscape CEO Jim Barksdale was scheduled to give the keynote at KPMG's annual meeting; Netscape software was already being installed on KPMG machines. A contract had already been signed, and money had exchanged hands. But over the next several weeks, Microsoft kept piling on the incentives. First it was early access to Microsoft's software; then it was deep discounts on other Microsoft software products. Finally, Microsoft offered $10 million to offset implementation costs. Eventually Sobini relented. "The company has such deep pockets and so many ways to tie a simple software sale to broader business opportunities," *The Wall Street Journal*'s David Bank wrote, "that it can, in effect, pay customers like KPMG to use its product."

"We understand why Microsoft is what Microsoft is," Sobini told the *Journal.* "They're smart. They're tough. They're relentless." At Microsoft, people had acted insulted when Andreessen's "horse head" comment implied the company was like the Mafia, but what was the KPMG deal if not an offer the accounting giant couldn't refuse?

AT SOME POINT, Netscape retained the legal services of Gary Reback, a top lawyer at Wilson Sonsini Goodrich & Rosati, a 375-lawyer firm headquartered in the heart of Silicon Valley. In August, nine months after Gates's speech, Reback sent a letter formally complaining on Netscape's behalf to the Justice Department's Antitrust Division. The letter, wrote *Time*'s David Jackson, charged Microsoft with "every anticompetitive behavior short of kidnapping programmers." Reback accused the company of embedding secret hooks inside Windows to allow its browser to run faster than Netscape's and alleged that Microsoft paid Internet service providers up to $400,000 if they agreed to fiddle with their software so it would disable Navigator. The letter cited a customer who said he preferred Netscape but Microsoft had offered him $18,000 in free software, so he had gone with Internet Explorer. That was money, Reback said, "directly from Microsoft's monopoly over operating systems." The company even accused Microsoft of offering "international telecommunications customers $5 for every installed Netscape Navigator that they removed from their corporation and installed with Internet Explorer."

Officially, Microsoft dismissed this passel of charges as "bizarre" falsehoods fabricated as part of its David-versus-Goliath marketing campaign. In an interview with *The New York Times,* Nathan Myhrvold likened Netscape's actions to "Nixon-era dirty tricks." Internally, people sniffed about a company so insecure about its flagship product that it cried to the government for help. To the old-timers it was Ray Noorda and Novell all over again.

In time, Justice Department officials would accuse Microsoft of illegally using its Windows monopoly to muscle its way into the Internet market. Yet by the time the government acted, virtually every technology analyst in the business had already counted Netscape out. "The fact is, they came in two years late to help Netscape," Gary Reback said. "It's like they called 911 and the police don't show up for two years." Meanwhile, Netscape was left to fend for itself.

"You can't fight a bigger army with inferior weapons or even with equal weapons," said a well-known Silicon Valley CEO who requested anonymity. "Military history shows that in a face-to-face battle, the team with the superior manpower wins. But here Netscape was facing Gates with bows and arrows, and Gates had nuclear weapons. Netscape shot their arrows for a while, and they did some harm. And they did it with panache and bravery. At the end of the day, though, the winner was obvious."

The usual product cycle for a hot application is a new version once every twelve to eighteen months. But Microsoft released Internet Explorer 2.0 only four months after its initial release, and IE 3.0 was available just a year after version 1.0. The release of IE 3.0 in August 1996 doomed Netscape, even though it released an updated version of its own product that same month. Some reviewers still preferred Netscape's browser, but others (including Walter Mossberg, *The Wall Street Journal*'s influential "Personal Technology" columnist) gave the nod to Microsoft, especially given that Navigator cost $49 and IE was free. There were an estimated 38 million copies of Netscape Navigator in use, and the company still enjoyed an 83 percent market share compared to IE's anemic 8 percent, but it didn't bode well for Netscape that people with no stake in the so-called browser wars now saw little difference between the two. Within three weeks of the new release of IE, Netscape's stock shed half its value.

Within a month, Netscape waved the white flag. For the past year, the company's marketing pros had been hammering the "browser wars" angle because it was an entrée into the big magazines without spending a dime on advertising. But now that the top-dog business reporters and big-foot analysts were falling all over themselves crowning Microsoft the winner, Netscape's saber rattling had outlived its usefulness. Barksdale complained that the whole Netscape-versus-Microsoft commotion was nothing but the "current blood sport" dreamed up by the news organizations. The real battle wasn't over the browser, he said, but over the race to sell Internet software to corporate America. "You'd have to be crazy to be a start-up with a business plan with the primary objective of beating Microsoft," the company's marketing chief told *Fortune*. "It's an honor to be characterized that way, but that's not what we're trying to do."

When, nine months later, Microsoft released a fourth version of IE, the company celebrated in San Francisco. After the party, a crew of tipsy programmers hired a truck to drop an oversized lowercase "e"—the Internet Explorer's logo—at Netscape headquarters, under Barksdale's window. The team attached a greeting card to their gift, a picture of a crying baby with a note inside. "It's just not fair. Good people shouldn't have to feel bad. Best wishes, the IE team."

Barksdale put up a brave front. He harkened back to his days as a top executive with a start-up calling itself Federal Express. "UPS had more money than God," Barksdale said. "Certainly more money than Microsoft. When they got into our business, we were scared to death. Well, today FedEx is a $10 billion company." There'd be more news flurries, more headlines. But Netscape was now just another software company competing against the likes of Microsoft and IBM. The Borg had sucked the life out of it. The momentum—and the magic—were gone.

CHAPTER 12

"BILL GATES IS SATAN"

STEWART ALSOP, the host of Agenda, wrote in *Fortune* in September 1996 that he was already contemplating Netscape's funeral. Microsoft's Internet Explorer had barely been on the market for a year, and its market share was at maybe 10 percent. But to Alsop that only meant it would take another year or two before his prediction came true.

"Chairman Bill Gates turned the software behemoth on a dime," *Newsweek* wrote in its year-end issue. Turning on a dime—that was the preferred cliché inside the industry. And if it wasn't a dime on which Gates turned, then he reversed field like a star running back or changed direction in midair like Michael Jordan. "Gates has done what few executives have dared," said Jeffrey Katzenberg, capturing the conventional wisdom in an interview with *Business Week*. Katzenberg was a Dream-Works cofounder, which made him a peripheral partner of Gates. "He has taken a thriving, $8 billion, 20,000-employee company and done a massive about-face."

Actually, it took Gates about eighteen months to turn on that dime. And he didn't turn on a dime on December 7 so much as set into high gear efforts that had already been moseying along at Microsoft. At the start of 1997, Microsoft was still a company that made virtually all of its money from operating systems and office applications (or what the Microsoft faithful call "productivity applications"), but the press wrote with wonder about his skill as if he had taken a moribund buggy whip–manufacturing plant and retooled it to take advantage of the coming market for leather automobile seats. He could turn straw into gold, he could turn water into oil. He was Merlin the Magician. George Gilder declared him unquestionably the top CEO of his time.

EVERY AGE, it is said, gets the icons it deserves. The wide-open Wild West of the nineteenth century gave us the robber barons. The go-go greed of the overconsuming 1980s gave us the rapacious Michael Milken and Ivan Boesky. The money-drenched, harried 1990s, then, demanded a workaholic, unrepentant overachiever worth in the tens of billions of dollars. Ours is a time ruled by mutual fund mania: we may have been chastened by the worst excesses of the 1980s, but as long as a company is not dumping oil in a harbor and it actually *makes* something, what's there not to love? Microsoft is a company we can embrace, a tobacco-free, environmentally friendly company that gives America a competitive edge. So what if Gates is the Genghis Kahn of capitalism— if occasionally a story spotlights the brutish, or at least boorish, ways of this slope-shouldered bully and his junkyard dog sidekick, Steve Ballmer? Money is the story of the 1990s, and its most able practitioners are our impresarios. Who at one point or another hasn't thought how easy the rest of life might be if only, ten years ago, she had bought a piece of this man's "vision"?

It's an era of oversized monoliths and also-rans; according to a trio of stock pickers who wrote a book called *The Gorilla Game,* it's the gorillas and the chimps. And of course on page 1 of their book, Microsoft serves as example number one, the mightiest gorilla of them all: by 1997 a 22,000-person company with a market cap bigger than that of General Motors, Ford, and Chrysler *combined* (though the Big Three combined bring in thirty times the revenue). Ours is an era of monolithic brands—Starbucks, Home Depot, Blockbuster Video, and all those Ross Dress for Lesses and Victoria's Secrets that make America seem one continuous mall. Yet what brand dominates its market more than Microsoft dominates software? "CEOs have emerged as a kind of royalty," Gregg Zachary wrote in *The Wall Street Journal.* And who lords it over more territory more mightily than Gates? In 1996, *Time* concluded that seven of the ten "most powerful Americans" were CEOs, Gates top among them.

In 1993, a clever writer for *Fortune* figured out that Gates was rich enough to buy back all the products his ninety-nine nearest competitors had sold in the previous year, burn them, and still be worth more than either Rupert Murdoch or Ted Turner. And that was when he was worth a mere $7 billion, still flip-flopping places with his friend Warren Buffett on the Forbes 400 list of richest Americans. By the end of 1996, Gates owned $20.7 billion in Microsoft stock. By October 1997, he was worth more than $40 billion, and the competition for the mantle of richest American would cease to be a race. By that point, he could buy Netscape whole, shutter its doors so that the stock was worth nothing, and still his holdings would exceed the *combined* net worth of the second (Buffett at $21 billion) and third (his old partner Paul Allen, worth $17 billion) richest Americans. Ballmer was sixth on the richest-Americans list, with a Microsoft portfolio worth $8.3 billion. The richest, third richest, and sixth richest people in the country, all from one company. That meant the net worth of the three top stakeholders in Microsoft had rocketed by more than $34 billion in the previous twelve months.

Gates represented a new breed of CEO, but how different was he from the Milkens and Boeskys of the 1980s and the robber barons of yore? In 1996, Microsoft employed a new chief operating officer named Bob Herbold, a gray-haired eminence hired away from the longtime Wall Street darling Procter & Gamble. Soon Microsoft began "outsourcing" functions formerly handled in-house. First it was the company copy center, then the mail room. Next came the sixty-three people who worked the front desks in Microsoft's various buildings. "The Real Estate and Facilities group this week announced that the receptionist function at the Corporate Campus in Redmond is being outsourced, effective April 3 [1996]," began an article in the company newsletter, the *MicroNews*. In other words, the receptionists would no longer be company employees, and thus Microsoft would no longer bear the cost of their 401(k) plans, their health insurance, or other employee benefits. "We seek to focus on our core competencies," a Microsoft official explained. Besides, a receptionist had no hope for advancement if he or she remained at Microsoft, whereas an outside group specializing in "reception services" offered a more promising career path.

Yet no matter how gentle a spin Microsoft put on these layoffs, these were all reasons invented after the fact, reasons to offer other than the truth, which is that the company sought to add a few more pennies to its bottom line. The up-front costs of the transition (severance pay and such) meant the company would see only "slight savings" in the short run, a Microsoft bean counter told the *MicroNews,* but he was confident of greater savings over time. At that point, Microsoft's cash on hand was growing at a rate of $200 million per month. The company's profit margin ranked it second on that year's Fortune 500 list. Outsourcing these sixty-three receptionists might actually have raised it from 25.2 percent of revenues to just a hair under 25.3.

While AT&T and IBM reigned as Wall Street's darlings, everyone from the CEO's office down to the typing pools and mail rooms enjoyed those companies' retirement benefits. The CEO stood to gain a much larger slice of the pie, of course, but the kitchen help, custodians, and night security guards at least got *something*. At Microsoft, in contrast, food services, custodial services, and security are handled by outside vendors. At the beginning of 1996 there weren't many blue-collar jobs at Microsoft, but at least there were the 600 or so employees who worked at the company packaging plant, where diskettes and CD-ROMs were duplicated, boxed, and shrink-wrapped. But then Microsoft outsourced that function as well.

At the beginning of 1998, Microsoft had roughly 5,000 temporary employees on its payroll—nearly a quarter of its workforce. Microsoft was hardly alone in the oxymoronic practice of employing long-term temps, but a *New York Times* investigation of this new trend declared Microsoft "perhaps the leading practitioner." Temporary employees, of course, get no benefits. Microsoft matches fifty cents on every dollar that a permanent employee contributes to a 401(k), up to 6 percent of his or her salary, but these temp workers, like the outsourced receptionists and mail-room clerks, work for a different company. In the example the *Times* offered, a full-time employee paid $57,000 a year would cost Microsoft as much as $94,000 a year, assuming he or she took full advantage of the benefits offered. Using these calculations, Microsoft saves roughly $37 million for every 1,000 temps. In 1996, that added more than $100 million to the Microsoft bottom line—or roughly what Bill Gates earned in two days that year. The company was swimming in billions but still pinching pennies.

Yet greed in the face of such spectacular riches was hardly something Silicon Valley could lord over Microsoft. Hewlett-Packard was held up as the Valley's model citizen, but the *Times* also singled out HP and Intel for using semipermanent temp workers to retard costs. Ten years ago, HP's janitors were full-time employees paid a livable wage of $12 or $13 an hour, according to Marc Cooper, writing in *The Nation*. But the company fired its janitors, switching to a company that pays its employees around $5 an hour. After five years on the job, a janitor earns $6.20 an hour, or $13,000 a year, assuming he or she is never sick and works holidays.

If the janitors are the Valley's serfs, the programmers are its lords and princes. Too busy to make time to see the dentist? At Netscape, the dentists arrive twice a week in a suitably equipped Winnebago that parks in the company lot. 3Com offers on-site film development, Oracle a grocery store. Any number of companies offer dry-cleaning pickup and delivery, and a start-up called PointCast has kept its engineers at work longer by outfitting its offices with a washer-dryer. At Excite, housed in a huge warehouse, you can get around via the big red slide, one of six pink bikes, or a Hippity Hop rubber ball. The company has an in-house masseuse, an on-site yoga class, and free pizza once a week. At Oracle, the seared ahi isn't free, but it's subsidized, as is the company sushi bar—and there's no charge to use the company health club, a beautifully appointed 36,000-square-foot facility. City planners in Redmond require that new buildings offer fewer parking slots than there are employees, thereby encouraging carpooling and use of public transportation. But how can Microsoft's royalty be expected to waste valuable time on a public bus or remain slaves to a coworker's schedule? So at its newer buildings Microsoft offers valet parking.

Vans shuttle employees among the thirty-odd buildings at Microsoft. Once, alone on a shuttle, I asked the driver if he worked for Microsoft. "Yeah, right," he snorted. This man, who described himself as being on "the wrong side of fifty," told me he had nothing set aside for retirement, yet every day he seems to read another article in the local papers about the Microsoft miracle and wishes he owned even a hundred shares.*

In 1997, Microsoft sent around a press release declaring itself corporate America's most generous giver to charity. Shortly thereafter, its claim that it had donated $73.2 million in "cash and software" that year was debunked on page one of *The Wall Street Journal.* For one thing, all but 15 percent of that figure was software, which one foundation head dubbed the "junk bonds of philanthropy." For another, Microsoft had valued the donated software using retail prices, so that a copy of Microsoft Office that cost a dollar or two to stamp and box was listed as a $599 donation. Using that measurement, IBM had actually given $20 million more than Microsoft—except that IBM didn't value its charitable contributions using retail prices. There was also the argument that

* A full 60 percent of the U.S. adult population owns no stock at all—no mutual fund shares, no pension, no 401(k).

Microsoft's donating software to a school or a library is hardly an act of charity.

"Giving away software is a sound marketing strategy," Tom McNichol wrote in *Salon,* probably the most thoughtful of the Web-based magazines. "But it's not philanthropy, any more than it would be if the Ford Foundation gave away millions of dollars' worth of free transmission parts that only fit Ford cars."

In 1997, Gates personally donated $20 million to Cambridge University for a new computer science building that would bear his name. The previous year he had given $15 million to Harvard (for the same purpose) and $12 million to the University of Washington. The philanthropic world, however, looked no more kindly on Gates than it did on his company. The informal rule of giving among the fabulously well-to-do is 1 percent of their net worth each year. In the ten years leading up to 1997, Gates had given away a total of $70 million, or one third of 1 percent of his total net worth up to that point. He spent nearly half that much buying a single bauble for himself, one of Leonardo da Vinci's sketchbooks. Gates is so rich he outbid the Italian government, buying this sketchbook, which he keeps locked under glass in a beautiful domed library inside his house, for $31 million.

"It doesn't matter how much you've got, you want more," fellow mogul Ted Turner told Larry King after Turner promised $1 billion to the United Nations. "Look at the ballplayers, look at Bill Gates. I mean, he feels like he can't get by." In the previous nine months, Turner's net worth had jumped from $2.2 billion to $3.2 billion. His donation to the United Nations, he said, was "not that big a deal." By contrast, Gates's net worth had jumped by $20 billion during roughly that same period.*

To stem his growing image as a philanthropic skinflint, Gates announced that he and his wife were setting up the $200 million Gates Library Foundation. But this was another of these gifts that blurred the lines between charitable giving and corporate positioning. Microsoft would donate $200 million (retail) worth of free software, and the foundation would spend most of its money training library personnel in the intricacies of using Windows-based PCs and the company's Internet Explorer. This was another gift that not incidentally would advance the Microsoft cause. It was also a pittance to a man worth $40

---

* A 1998 survey conducted by the U.S. Trust Corp. of California found that on average the richest 1 percent of the population gave 8 percent of their after-tax income to charity.

billion. By the start of 1998, Gates had donated a total of $270 million, amounting to much less than 1 percent of his net worth.* Later that year, he and his wife announced they would donate $100 million more to help pay for the vaccination of Third World children—less than one half of one hundredth of his capital gains that year.

For years Gates has said he will give away most of his money, but not until he's ready to slow down. "I don't have time to figure out what charities make sense," he has said, perhaps not realizing that no one, especially those of us who actually sweat our bills every month, quite has the time to properly pursue such endeavors. This man renowned for his boundless energy, who with macho pride talks of fitting eight, ten, twelve meetings into a day, claimed he didn't have the time. Somehow, though, he has found time for any number of side businesses. Several years back, he and fellow Seattle-area billionaire Craig McCaw went partners on Teledesic, a satellite company. Gates also created a company called Corbis, which owns the digital rights to *La Giaconda* (the "Mona Lisa") and countless other famous paintings, as well as the Bettman Archive, reputedly the most comprehensive collection of photographs in the world. Why not? It was a potentially valuable property, given the demand among Internet publishers for popular images.

Gates's lack-of-time excuse is a line one hears all the time from young cybermoguls when asked about their lack of philanthropic giving. Gary Reback's law firm, Wilson Sonsini Goodrich & Rosati, ranked second, at $565,000 per partner in 1997, when the *San Francisco Chronicle* featured a list of the Bay Area's ten most profitable law firms that year. But the firm ranked dead last with a reported seventeen hours of pro bono service per lawyer *per year.* Who has the time to pay attention to anything but the job at hand when they're doing their part to invent the future?

Instead, these young tycoons have invested in themselves. Thirty-two-year-old Brian Pinkerton paid $600,000 for a house in the Valley among the horsey set of Atherton (the country's sixth richest town, according to *Worth* magazine), only to destroy the home as soon as he took title, meaning he paid $600,000, plus the wrecking and removal fees, for a houseless lot. "It was definitely livable," Pinkerton explained

---

* Gates, however, had *Slate,* the Microsoft on-line magazine that lured editor Michael Kinsley to the Northwest. *Slate* praised Gates for his corporate giving, despite his growing number of critics, ranking him and his wife third on its list of the country's most generous philanthropists, behind only Ted Turner and George Soros, whose $500 million in contributions were also in cash rather than in kind.

in an interview with *The Wall Street Journal*. "I just wanted something bigger." Buying homes that the new owner would reduce to rubble was becoming so common that the local realtors gave the practice a name: "scraper" deals. The *Times*'s Patricia Leigh Brown labeled the trend "conspicuous construction." There were the Proulxs, also of Atherton, rich from Tom Proulx's luck as a cofounder of Intuit.* The Proulxs loved their home, but wouldn't it be great if the backyard was a nine-hole golf course? So they purchased three neighboring lots so they could build a course and then hosted a party outside a house they'd be tearing down. "The first thing we did," Barbara Proulx told *The New York Times*, "was hit golf balls through the picture windows." One can just hear the squeals of delight after each crash of glass.

Michael Dell, the richest man in Texas and sixteenth on the 1997 Forbes 400 list (worth $5.5 billion), wrangled with the county appraiser over the worth of his sixty-acre, 22,000-square-foot home. The county said his home was worth $22.5 million and thus Dell owed $600,000 a year in property taxes, but Dell claimed it was worth only $6 million, which would mean a tax bill of $160,000. The problem was finding an appropriate comparison in Austin, Texas, where Dell's is the only eight-bedroom, twenty-one bathroom home with a conference room and the now-obligatory home gym. When Mike Markkula, one of the brains behind Apple, tried to build a home in another enchanted neighborhood in the hills above Silicon Valley, the town opposed his proposed house as too oversized even for this neighborhood of oversized homes. Markkula argued that he should be granted a waiver because he was expanding the community's affordable housing base. What was the "substantial public benefit" that would have earned him a variance? A cottage he would be building for the new home's caretaker.

High tech wasn't any worse than a lot of industries, but the point was that it wasn't any better, either, despite the new breed of leaders and their mountains of cash. It was a predominantly white, male world—and the odds were that if someone wasn't white, then he was either Asian-American or foreign-born. In 1997, Microsoft could be criticized for having a workforce run by men and less than 5 percent black or

---

* As an engineering student at Stanford, he happened to be standing near the department bulletin board when Scott Cook posted a flyer calling for a programmer willing to work in exchange for an equity stake in a company he was founding. By 1995, when he retired at age 32, Proulx's stake in Intuit was worth more than $40 million.

Latino—but Sun, Oracle, and Netscape were hardly in a position to criticize. In the early 1990s, the feds slapped a fine on Oracle for rejecting minority applicants despite a workforce that was .02 percent black and .03 percent Latino—and cited the company for paying some women and minority workers less than their white male counterparts. In 1996, Nicola Miner, the daughter of Oracle cofounder Bob Miner, showed up at the annual shareholders' meeting to confront Larry Ellison: What is your company doing about the woeful lack of women in its top echelons? she asked. And why doesn't a single woman serve on the Oracle board of directors? Sun was cited by the federal government in the early 1990s for failing to recruit minorities, though companies above a certain size are required by law to do so if they do business with the federal government. In 1996, regulators cited Netscape for missing its deadline to set up a diversification program—again as required under federal law.

Microsoft provides health insurance to the partners of its gay and lesbian employees. Its maternity-leave policy is as progressive as they come. But the company was just under ten years old when it hired its first female executive, Ida Cole, to take over as the head of business applications. Cole left that job in less than a year. It wasn't that Gates and his lieutenants were overtly sexist so much as overtly male. With Gates and Ballmer, it was always "the guys" this and "the guys" that—and it showed. Cole's first mistake—according to the book *Hard Drive*—was a warm and fuzzy speech shortly into her tenure, thanking everyone for working so long and hard. Her second mistake was granting a male employee two weeks off after the birth of his third child so that he could care for his two small children while his wife recuperated, a decision Gates told her was "unwise." The final straw came when Cole returned from a three-week absence after surgery to remove a benign mass that the doctors had initially feared was ovarian cancer. She had delayed the surgery because her group was promoting a new version of Excel. She had shortened her recuperation to meet another deadline. But upon her return Gates screamed at her for not knowing a ship date had slipped while she was gone. She demoted herself to a job in the company's international division, far away from this boys'-club atmosphere.

Microsoft's workforce was one-third female, but there was still a tendency among some male programmers, as late as the early 1990s, to design screen savers that depicted nude women, so that a female programmer visiting a male colleague to talk code would find herself distracted by the computer equivalent of a machine-shop girlie calendar. A group of women complained to a top Microsoft manager, but for their effort all they got was a company memo discouraging the practice. That should have been no surprise, given the Microsoft hierarchy. None of the company's top fourteen officers is a woman, though 11 percent of the Fortune 500's corporate officers are women, according to the group Catalyst. And of the fifty vice presidents listed in Microsoft's 1997 annual report, only three (6 percent) are women.

For Evan Marcus, a systems engineer from Fair Lawn, New Jersey, the motivation was the imponderable vastness of Gates's wealth. That's why Marcus, in 1996, despite two young children and a full-time job, posted a "Bill Gates Net Worth Page." How rich was Gates? At $40 billion, he could buy every major-league team in the four major sports—football, basketball, baseball, and hockey—yet still hold enough Microsoft stock to retain his number one ranking on *Forbes*'s list of richest Americans. If his wealth were rendered in dollar bills laid end to end, they would stretch to the moon and back more than eight times. If rendered in $100 bills, the accumulated cash would weigh more than four hundred tons. Gates could send $6.50 to every man, woman, and child on the planet and still have a billion and a half in the bank to handle what Marcus calls "incidentals."*

Once you've reached the end of Marcus's Bill Gates page, you can connect to any number of Gates-related Web pages, including Brad Templeton's "Bill Gates Wealth Index" site and the "Make Me Richer Than Bill Gates" page that Jim Denison hosts. Denison, of Richardson, Texas, offers many options to those who might contribute to his fund. You can send him the whole amount (contributions at the $40 billion level qualify you as Denison's "Friend for Life"), or forty people can send him $1 billion each ("you become my new best friend"). "This document is a parody," Denison writes, "and not to be taken seriously:

---

* At the start of 1999, Gates was worth more than $70 billion. By that point, his wealth, if rendered in dollar bills, would stretch to and from the moon fourteen times. If rendered in $100 bills, it would weigh 690 tons. He had enough to give the planet's 6 billion inhabitants just under $12 apiece.

unless you intend to contribute to the 'Make Me Richer than Bill Gates Fund,' in which case I will take you seriously, even if nobody else will."

In 1993, Brad Templeton was talking to Gates at an industry conference. One thought kept running through his mind: "$31 per second, $31 per second." That's how much Templeton had calculated that Gates had earned since founding Microsoft, assuming he worked seventy hours a week, except holidays.

Templeton now hosts a page called the "Bill Gates Wealth Index." He is a founder of *ClariNet*, the Internet's largest newspaper, but his "too-small-a-bill-for-Bill" index might be his real claim to fame. Years earlier, he figured that if Gates came across a $20 bill on the ground, it wouldn't be worth the four seconds it would take to bend down and pocket it. By mid-1997, when Gates's worth exceeded $40 billion, Templeton calculated it wouldn't be worth Gates's time "if, on his way into the office, should he see or drop a $500 bill. . . . He makes more just heading on to work." By that point, he was accumulating money at the rate of $150 per second. That's $500,000 an hour over the previous twenty-two years, or $35 million a week.

Visiting Templeton's Web page allows you to stack your wealth up against Gates's. Let's say your net worth is $100,000. At $40 billion, Gates's net worth is 400,000 times larger. So if you paid $400,000 for a house, that would be $1 in what Templeton dubbed "Gates dollars." A top-of-the-line notebook computer? Less than 2 cents in Gates dollars. That $10,000 dream trip to Europe? Three cents. "You might buy a plane ticket on a Boeing 747 for $1,200 at full-fare coach," Templeton writes. "In Bill-bills, Mr. Gates could buy three 747s: one for him, one for Melinda, and one for young Jennifer Katharine."

Richard Petersen's motivation wasn't the magnitude of Gates's money so much as the potential good Gates could do if he was so inclined. "Initially I just put out a question on my site: 'What could Bill Gates do with all his money?' " Petersen said. "But I ended up taking it off because mainly what people said was he should give some to them. There were a lot of gold diggers, too—women who wanted to marry him, that kind of thing."

Petersen is emblematic of the new creature known as a Web publisher. In early 1996, he created Z Publishing, a one-room company based in San Francisco and outfitted with a couple of expensive-looking PCs set atop garage-sale furniture. He had no idea how he'd ever make any money as a Web publisher, but then he didn't really have to. Petersen wasn't blow-up-a-house rich, but he had socked away some cash from his days as a software entrepreneur, and he was well off enough to indulge in time-wasting hobbies such as hosting what he eventually dubbed "The Unofficial Bill Gates Page."

Petersen's first Web venture was a Bill Clinton page. Gates was his third endeavor, after a page about the pope. As of mid-1998, more people had visited Petersen's Gates page than the Clinton and pope pages combined. There wasn't much to Petersen's Gates page—a few paragraphs of background and bio, a few interesting observations (for instance, that Gates, as the head of Microsoft, has sold far more CDs than even Michael Jackson), and links to other Gates-related stuff: pictures of the Gates mansion under construction, articles appearing in the popular press, entries from a book called *The Secret Diary of Bill Gates, Aged 40¼*. But Petersen had chosen the perfect name for his site and there was the winning graphic that graced its top corner, a head shot of Gates spliced onto the buffed body of a weight lifter in pose. It didn't mean any money in Petersen's pocket, but soon his page was drawing thousands of visitors each month.

Petersen's Web site has not only a public "guest book" but also a private one that lets you send e-mail directly to Gates (click here for "Bill's e-mail address"!). This private corner of the page is off-limits unless you know the code, but that isn't too difficult to decipher: Bill666. Some of the people sending Gates mail just want to tell him he's swell; others just want to tell him he's a louse. But, as Petersen warned, the majority write to Gates because they covet his money.

There was the sadly naive, like Donna of Gainesville, Florida, who wanted nothing more in life than to stay at home raising her two girls. But her husband, as wonderful as he might be, didn't earn much money. "I'm sorry to ask," Donna wrote in closing, "but I hope that you see it in your heart to help us. Please." A recent Vietnamese immigrant had been accepted into a dental school, but she had no idea how she was going to swing the $40,000 tuition—maybe Gates could pay part? Early in her post, Jennifer of New Jersey admitted that she had been "floating through the years trying to figure out what the hell I'm going to do for the rest of my life." But she was back in school and sure she would be a great asset to Microsoft—if only Gates would send her enough money to finish school, pay the rent, and get herself out of Visa debt. "You would write it off for tax purposes," she counseled—and, besides, it'd be "real cool" to hear from you.*

THERE'S A WEB-BASED Microsoft Evil Empire Network and another Web-based group calling itself SPOGGE (rhymes with rogue)—the Society for Prevention of Gates Getting Everything. There's also a Society Against Internet Explorer, and at the Web site www.enemy.org you can join the anti-M$ mailing list, whose members sometimes refer to Gates as the Evil One and the company's flagship product as something like "Windoze," "Winblows," "Winblah," or "Winshit." There's a "Boycott Microsoft" site, an "Official Microsoft Hate Page," and a site called "Why I hate Bill #1 . . . 19" (reason #19: "Microsoft Money says it all"). Early in 1997, a "Stop Gates" page initiated its green-ribbon campaign. After that, there were computer-generated green ribbons pinned to most of the more popular anti-Microsoft Web pages.

There were sites depicting Gates as a Nazi, others that revealed Gates as Satan, and still others where Gates's face served as a communal punching bag. You can repeatedly whack at an image of the world's richest man at the "Punch Bill Gates" page (alternatively, you can bop John Tesh, Martha Stewart, or Michael Jackson), or you can spend your day playing a game passed around over the Internet called "Billy Killer," which allows a player to shoot at images of Gates that pass like ducks in an arcade. The more times you hit the target, the more points you accumulate. David Shenk, author of *Data Smog,* did a Web search: the term "kill Bill Gates" appears twice as often as "kill Bill Clinton."

Plugging into this world proved easy enough. I typed in "www.microsuck.com" and discovered the Web page for a company called "MicroSuck," whose motto is "Who do you want to copy today?" (Microsoft's actual slogan is "Where do you want to go today?"). The page's statement of purpose, if one could call it that, is postcard thin: "Our basic point: Life is too short to settle for a sucky OS like Windoze95." From the MicroSuck site it was like six degrees of separation: I was never more than a few clicks away from scores of anti-Microsoft

---

* When *The New Yorker* included Gates's e-mail address in an article called "E-Mail from Bill," Gates received roughly five thousand messages more than normal over the next few weeks. The mail ranged from book suggestions to the woman who wrote to say she was traveling to Seattle soon, did he have a restaurant recommendation?

sites. You can fritter away plenty of time hating AOL or Intel over the
Internet at sites such as Nester's "AOL Sucks" page or the "Intel Secrets
Home Page." But only the world's richest man and the computer
world's mightiest mogul inspire so much animosity that it would take
weeks to sift through it all. There are even several pages that "prove,"
through numerology, that Gates is the Antichrist because the letters of
his name add up to 666, the biblical sign of the beast. The only problem
is that the letters in Gates's name add up to 666 only if you fudge the
numbers.*

"What do you do if you want to get attention nowadays?" asks Microsoft spokeswoman Mich Mathews. "You say to yourself, 'Why don't I
criticize Microsoft? Maybe that'll get me some press.'" Yet reality isn't
that simple. For Mitch Stone, the motivation was a Microsoft advertisement in the *Los Angeles Times* in August 1996 announcing that the company would be giving away its browser free. Stone was a Mac user who
had never much cared for Microsoft, but this transcended his personal
preference for one product over the other. To him it was a case of a
ruthless corporation using its deep pockets to try to crush a smaller foe.
That weekend he wrote an essay calling for a boycott of Microsoft. He
sent it to a few friends, who passed it along to others, and the "Boycott
Microsoft" site was born.

Stone, who began his campaign at the age of forty-two, was the most
unlikely of anti-Microsoft crusaders, a self-employed historic preserva-
tionist whose only connection to a computer was that he used one to
run his business. But when he trolled the Web in search of anti-
Microsoft sites, what he found only seemed to offend him. "I saw a lot
of 'kill Bill' stuff and a lot of profanity," he said. "Little of what I saw
struck me as very thoughtful." Within months, he was getting as many
as 1,000 hits a day.

Unlike most of his comrades in the anti-Microsoft cause, Stone is a
true Web publisher. Whereas the author of the typical anti-Microsoft
Web site spouts off for a few paragraphs before linking you to articles
about Microsoft, Stone has published a long list of feature articles written specifically for his site. Over the years Stone has written many,

---

* To a computer an A isn't an A but a binary figure represented by 65, the letter B 66.
Adding up the numerical value of each letter in Gates's given name, William Henry Gates
III, adds up to well over 666, and the letters in Bill Gates fall three digits short. But by dub-
bing him Bill Gates III you reach 666.

though certainly not all, of these pieces—ten other bylines are listed in the table of contents. In a six-page document Stone calls his "manifesto," he explains that he has taken on the task of publisher and editor because the business press is too busy "regurgitating corporate press releases to take their investigative responsibilities seriously."

Fully navigating Stone's site takes hours. Beyond the manifesto, there's an archive of Stone's monthly "keynote" addresses, and newcomers are encouraged to read his fifteen-page "Case Against Microsoft." There are the site's "Not Invented Here" room, its "Dirty Tricks" list, and a lengthy compilation of the dozens of companies and technologies Microsoft has bought over the years because the company wanted to move into a new market or simply because it wanted a competing product off the shelf. There's a "Monopolist's Cookbook" (the master recipe includes Microsoft's propensity to enter negotiations with a company just to get a gander at a competitor's product) and also a "Monopoly clock," fashioned after the nuclear "Doomsday clock." Like the latter, the former is usually just minutes away from midnight.

How thorough is Stone's site? There's an entire set of rooms dedicated solely to the topic of Windows NT, where you can read about NT's security flaws, its bugs, its high-profile failures, and the hyperbole Microsoft has employed to oversell this operating system that, despite new releases, has never quite lived up to the company's promises.

Stone seems particularly offended by Microsoft's propensity for shamelessly appropriating the innovations of others and repackaging them under the Microsoft name. He's a loyal Apple devotee who has never forgiven what he views as Microsoft's rip-off of the Mac interface. "This penchant for stealing the ideas of its more inventive competitors might be laughable, were it not for Microsoft's amazing talent (through the magic of virtually unlimited marketing budgets) for making the plainly ludicrous appear as verity." Unlike most of his Web-based anti-Microsoft cohorts, Stone doesn't fantasize about destroying Microsoft; he seeks only to bring to bear whatever pressure he can to get the company to change its ways. "The message of the boycott is simple," he writes. "If Microsoft does not wish to be seen as a corporate pariah, they must revise their attitude toward the marketplace."

D. J. WALETZKY created the "Bill Gates Is Satan" page as a tenth-grader attending the Bronx High School of Science. Several months before creating the page, Waletzky had convinced his parents to buy a top-of-the-line PC running Windows NT. NT had blown him away in the store, but he learned the hard way that what had impressed him wasn't the operating system itself but the power of the machine needed to run it. Via the Internet, he learned that Microsoft had shipped NT fully aware that it was riddled with bugs (though it's never "bugs" when Microsoft talks to the general public; its help desk and PR people, like those at many other software companies, are careful to use the term "known issues"). It crashed constantly and gave him all sorts of fits, which is how he came to read the fine print on the box indicating that Microsoft would charge him every time he phoned them for help.

"When I learned that tech support cost $95 per incident call, something just snapped," Waletzky said. "To write buggy software was bad enough, but to charge $95 to help people having to deal with these bugs struck me as the act of a guy intent on screwing everyone over." In the fall of 1996, a class assignment required that he create his own Web page. Waletzky had been thinking about an "I Hate Newt Gingrich" Web page, but then he started reading about Gates: how PC software had been free before Gates and how Microsoft had bought for a song the operating system that would earn the company billions. And then one day, while hanging out with friends and bemoaning his NT headaches, the words just sort of popped out of his mouth: "Bill Gates is Satan."

Now, when Waletzky calls Gates Satan, he isn't saying he believes him to be a fiery red biblical figure with a pointy tail. If you ask him, Waletzky will tell you he's a socialist who doesn't believe in God, nor in the Devil for that matter. "Royal asshole" is closer to the spirit in which Waletzky uses the term. The guy who smashes your car window to swipe your tape player is Satan. That jerk at work who's always laying claim to other people's ideas: he's Satan, too. Or a guy who has so much money it would stretch from here to the moon eight times, yet squeezes another $95 out of you every time you need help and not incidentally makes you look like a dope in front of the 'rents—that's a man who truly reigns as the Prince of Darkness.

The promise of the Web was the sense of community it would foster, cozy virtual villages that would counteract the alienation of the flesh-and-blood world. Waletzky was something of a minicelebrity in the world of Bill haters, but it's not as though he felt anything he'd remotely call "community." His e-mail correspondences with his fellow travelers were little more than short bursts of excitement about "cool" new sites they had discovered or sympathy expressed for a site such as the "Official Microsoft Hate Page," booted off machine after machine until finally finding a home on a host computer in France. He subscribed to what he calls the "hating Microsoft" mailing list (anti-ms@enemy.org) but admits to finding the usual back-and-forth numbingly dull. At times the volume of e-mails he receives is overwhelming. But he doesn't remove his name, he said, "because you can learn stuff you can't find out from reading *PC Week*."

Waletzky's page is set against a bloodred background and features appropriately Gothic lettering, with contrasting photos of Gates and Satan. He asks people to notice the resemblance, though of course there isn't any. He's no doubt preaching to the choir in the few paragraphs of explanation he posts at the top of the page under the banner "Why you and everyone you know should hate Bill Gates if you don't already"— and he's playing to his audience when he writes, "Even Adam-Smith-loving, scum sucking, materialistic money-grubbing capitalists should hate Gates for his destruction of the concept known as competition— Bill Gates didn't work half as hard at programming as he did with behind-the-scenes deals with major firms (like IBM) and shameless and aggressive promotion, not to mention dirty tricks." He offers a list of suggestions for those sharing his viewpoint, including autodial campaigns to clog the company's toll-free numbers and fake magazine subscriptions sent to Gates. And if you happen to pass Gates on the street? By all means, "spit at him with the utmost contempt."

In less than a year's time, Waletzky's page had been seen by viewers numbering in the tens of thousands. "You fucking rule!!!!!!" a guy going by the screen name Trip Dailey wrote in his guest book. Darien wrote to say that Gates wasn't Satan but actually Adolf Hitler. But Gates had his defenders even in this hostile territory—people like Alex, who accused Waletzky of being bitter " 'cause Bill is a sex idol and you aren't." The most unexpected piece of feedback, however, came from a group of avowed Satanists. They embraced Gates as one of their leading lights. Their only regret? "Unfortunately, Bill is not one of our personal comrades. We'd be richer for his friendship/exploitation."

CHAPTER 13

WHAT ABOUT ME?

ZACH NELSON was running corporate marketing at Sun Microsystems when a headhunter phoned. Would he be interested in the top marketing job at Oracle? Nelson's the affable kind who will good-naturedly hear out anybody, but what he was thinking as the headhunter talked was this: "No way." Oracle was the last place in the Valley he would want to work.

Like a great many of his colleagues, Nelson could quickly catalogue Larry Ellison's faults. He had never met the man and barely paid attention to his company, but a negative view of Oracle's flamboyant CEO was something people working in Silicon Valley picked up by osmosis. Ellison's clownishly outsized ego. His notoriety as a womanizer. A capricious management style that had him going through senior executives more often than George Steinbrenner went through baseball managers. One day you were one of Larry's pets, vacationing with him in Hawaii or Japan; the next day you were out. By all accounts he was charismatic, driven, shrewd, and maybe even brilliant, but he seemed more caricature than real.

Nelson had no reason to think any better of Oracle. At one time, he might even have been impressed with this hot-engine company that had doubled its revenues for eight consecutive years (sales at Microsoft, by contrast, have grown by less than 50 percent a year since it went public), but then, in 1990, the truth was revealed: Ellison admitted his company had been "mistakenly" logging sales before products had been shipped. He also confessed that his company was so poorly managed that its top managers couldn't tell him how much money the company was truly bringing in or how much product it was actually shipping out. Oracle's stock price fell by more than 75 percent, and the press feasted on the company's misery, shining a harsh light on its every mis-step. There were reasons why the top marketing job at Oracle, despite a six-figure salary and a generous stock option package, had remained va-cant for nine months before Nelson filled the post.

Why did Nelson even agree to meet with Ellison? "That's the ques-tion I asked myself when I walked into Oracle to meet him," he said. The money was one factor, boredom with his job at Sun another. Oracle seemed the ultimate challenge. "I expected Larry to be this total jerk, but he turns out to be this really good guy," he said. "We're sitting there talking about sports and regular stuff. He's totally likable and incredibly articulate. Just a normal guy. And he spoke frankly about his past mis-takes and how he had changed. And I'm like, 'What's wrong with this picture?' " On the spot Nelson deemed Oracle an unwritten book, and he declared himself just the man to write it.

Sun, Nelson's old company, was only a few miles down the freeway, but the two cultures couldn't have been more different. For Nelson the move was like graduating from the jeans-and-running-shoes life of business school to the suit-and-tie reality of the working MBA. At Sun, the CEO dressed like a grad student, so everyone else did. At Oracle, the CEO favored custom-made suits from London's Savile Row and Hermès ties, so at Oracle you dressed well if you saw career advancement in your future. Whereas at Sun you worried that a prankish McNealy, if he caught you wearing a tie, might snip it with a pair of scissors, at Oracle an Hermès tie served as the ultimate status symbol. "You could read the Hermès logo only if you spread out the underneath flaps," Nelson says. "So you'd be in meetings at Oracle and there'd be people sitting there with their ties flapped open, so that everyone knew it was the real thing."

The aesthetic feel of the two companies was another difference. Sun's corporate offices were attractive but functional, designed with both eyes on the bottom line. By contrast, Oracle's executive office tower was something to behold. Expensive art hung on the walls, *House Beauti-ful*–type urns sat on pedestals, and plush carpets graced the floors. Whereas the lobby furniture at Sun was a cut above Office Depot qual-ity, at Oracle the chairs were designed by the renowned turn-of-the-century architect Charles Rennie Mackintosh.

Nelson hadn't been on the job two months when *Fortune* published a special issue heralding the titans and pioneers who had created the country's software industry. Men not nearly as rich as Ellison, running companies not nearly as large or as powerful as Oracle, were featured, yet Ellison was relegated to footnote status. The main reason for the oversight was that Oracle's database software, designed to manage vast filing cabinets of information, ran on minicomputers and mainframes, and even the more sophisticated business journals gave short shrift to any company not focused on the PC. But Ellison was the sort who tended to read the personal into everything, and he viewed the oversight as a personal repudiation. In a voice that alternated between anger and hurt, he asked his new marketing director what there was about him that caused the business press to shun him. Did they not like him? Did they not respect him?

The trade press treated Ellison like a star, but the only time the big-book business publications had paid him any attention was in 1990, when they had arrived to write his obituary. But that should only have added to the legend: less than three years later, Oracle's stock was worth more than twice what it had been before its crash, and Ellison's net worth exceeded $2 billion. Bill Gates was the standard against which everyone else in the industry was measured, so of course Ellison stated his displeasure by drawing an analogy to Gates. "If Bill Gates had pulled off what I pulled off"—a statement he didn't need to finish. Nelson phoned a *Fortune* editor he knew and yelled into his ear for a while, calming down only when he was offered the consolation prize he sought: his first cover story in a national magazine, sixteen years after Ellison had cofounded Oracle with two partners.

When you work PR for someone like Ellison, you don't manage him so much as keep your fingers crossed. He's like a Hollywood starlet who draws the spotlight to herself by doing something so outrageous she's certain to gain notice. Ellison was a master of the ill-conceived remark, like the time he told a reporter with *The New York Times* that he signed his name only in green ink because green was the color of money. His cronies, who knew it wasn't true, asked him why he had said it when it made him sound Howard Hughes weird. Ellison just laughed. Partway through the interview he had grown bored, so to enliven the moment he had started creating tall tales about himself. Could he help it if the fool believed him? But of course that green ink indelibly stained almost every feature that followed. After Ellison bought himself an Italian fighter jet, Nelson told him, "Whatever you do, don't let anyone take a picture of you sitting in the cockpit." So of course whenever Ellison met a photographer, practically the first thing he would do was offer to pose in his Marchetti.

The *Fortune* piece was every bit the cozy profile that Nelson had been wishing for. "He's tall, thin, and urbane," staffer Alan Deutschman wrote. Later in the piece, Deutschman described Ellison as "disarmingly funny" and "quick-witted." Nelson flinched when he learned that Ellison had agreed to pose for *Fortune* wearing a kimono (Ellison fancies himself a modern-day samurai), but even that fostered Ellison's image as an industry titan. "In his Japanese-style garden, Ellison ponders his plan to change the ways knowledge is amassed and stored," read the photo's caption.

Yet Nelson's boss was anything but pleased. As promised, the magazine had put Ellison on its cover, and the photo was a flattering one. The problem was the headline: "Software's Other Billionaire." Ellison read the words and no doubt flinched. Even in his belated debut as a national cover boy, he was being defined as *not* Bill Gates. He was the lesser of the industry's self-made billionaires. The story of his life.

HE WAS BORN near the end of World War II to a single mother who abandoned him at the age of nine months. His adoptive father—his mother's uncle—was a Russian immigrant who had created his American surname from Ellis Island. Whereas Gates was born with a platinum spoon in his mouth and raised in the reassuring womb of a loving family, Ellison was a working-class kid from Chicago who didn't meet his birth mother until he was well into his forties. He was close to his stepmother, but his stepfather was a harsh-edged man whose disapproval was a daily part of Ellison's life. Yet apparently that wasn't enough, for Ellison invented even deeper hardships for himself. "Every time I read about my adopted brother," his older sister joked, "the old neighborhood seemed to drop another notch on the socioeconomic scale."

He told *Fortune*, in 1993, that he had been raised in a "tenement" on Chicago's South Side. Two years later, in *USA Today*, he had grown up "poor" in a rough part of town. Oracle's public relations arm was even bolder, writing press releases casting Ellison as a product of an "impoverished, crime-ridden neighborhood," as if he were a dead-end ghetto kid who, despite the long odds, had somehow overcome the projects. In *Forbes ASAP* he was from a "rough" neighborhood, in *Investor's Business Daily* the neighborhood was "notoriously rough," in the *San Francisco Chronicle* it was a "ghetto." The truth, however, was that he had grown up in a tidy community, home to its share of judges, doctors, and university professors. His stepfather had known failure, but by the time his nephew came along, the senior Ellison was working respectably if dully as a bean counter for the local public housing agency. Their two-bedroom apartment was small and money may have been tight, but it was hardly the rough-and-tumble world that Ellison conjured up later in life.

According to Oracle's PR department, Ellison had degrees from both the University of Illinois and the University of Chicago. *The New York Times* was among the publications reporting that Ellison had earned a master's in physics from the University of Chicago. *Business Week*'s Richard Brandt bothered to check and discovered that Ellison didn't have a bachelor's degree, let alone a master's. He had logged only two years at the University of Illinois before transferring to continue his undergraduate studies at the University of Chicago. The new story, this time straight from Ellison's mouth, was that he had all but earned his undergrad degree from the University of Chicago, except that he had refused to take a French proficiency test. It was a fun tale that would have revealed a swashbuckling, devil-may-care side of Ellison—had it been true. Ellison attended the University of Chicago for a single semester before buying a turquoise Thunderbird convertible that he drove west to Berkeley in 1966, lured by the flowing freedom of the times. Unlike our president, he told *Business Week,* "I did inhale."

Ellison, however, was hardly a bubble-blowing hippie eschewing the material life. He'd keep his hair neatly clipped and was married at age twenty-three. (The two divorced after seven years of marriage.) From the start, he was dreaming big, even as he worked a string of low-rung computer-related jobs at companies such as Wells Fargo and the Fireman's Fund. He was still in his twenties when he purchased his first house. He bought a $1,000 racing bike and an expensive car, and was already making payments on one sailboat when he borrowed money to buy a bigger one. When he wanted a nose job, he didn't go to just any plastic surgeon, he flew to Beverly Hills. "He had champagne tastes on a beer budget," his first wife told Mike Wilson, author of the book *The Difference Between God and Larry Ellison* (*God Doesn't Think He's Larry Ellison).*

"Oracle" was the code name of a database project Ellison worked on for the Central Intelligence Agency in the early 1970s. After finishing, he convinced his boss and a second programmer that the three should quit their jobs to write a better database product. They did and eventually

THE PLOT TO GET BILL GATES

sold it to the CIA. The air force was the second customer of this company, founded in 1977 and eventually named Oracle. Ellison talked incessantly about striking it rich—and he lived as if he had already attained that aim. He was already residing in an expensive house in the upscale community of Woodside and building another when the bank initiated (but never carried through on) foreclosure proceedings on both. His company was starved for cash in its first half-dozen years, forever a check or two away from missing payroll, yet he moved the company into an office on Menlo Park's Sand Hill Road, maybe the toniest address in all Silicon Valley.

"Larry had no sense of money," said John Luongo, employee number 34. "He'd spend money on things he couldn't afford because he didn't know better."

Ellison also lacked, as if he didn't know any better, the proper fear of much larger foes. At Oracle in the early 1980s, people worked in shifts because the company couldn't afford a larger office. But even then, Ellison tended to view publicly traded companies in the same field as mere speed bumps on the road to the top. "There was the company called Cullinet that was forty or fifty times as big as we were," Luongo said. "Larry would talk about passing Cullinet inside of five years, and we'd all just laugh. But none of us were laughing when five years and three months later we did it." Ellison celebrated his triumph with an advertisement that depicted Oracle as a fighter jet that had just shot Cullinet (and other Oracle competitors) out of the sky. A disclaimer at the bottom of the ad read, "Our use of Cullinet, Information Builders, etc. trademarks in this advertisement is the least of their problems."

There was a lot of laughing and joking in the early days of Oracle. More often than not, the instigator was Ellison. He would say something so vainglorious or outrageous that people could only laugh and say, with a shake of the head, "That's Larry." He tended to be at his funniest when spoofing his own thirst for blood. "Larry was always riffing about what we'd have to do to our foes before he'd be happy," said an ex-employee who worked at Oracle in the early 1980s. "Once he got started, it's like he wouldn't stop until he had us all in stitches." One time it was a pep talk about defeating a larger company named Ingres. "He said it wasn't enough that we beat Ingres on a sale, Ingres had to go out of business," this ex-employee said. " 'I want them on their knees. Begging for mercy. Pleading for their life. Confessing their every sin.' Everyone was laughing, so he'd start leading us in a chant: 'Kill, kill, kill.' "

When the company went public in 1986 and its coffers were suddenly bulging, Ellison came up with the idea of throwing money at the most promising graduates from the country's top schools. The idea was that this transfusion of young blood would stimulate the energy level of an already overstimulated environment. When the first class arrived at Oracle, Ellison took the stage at a meeting for the new hires and paraphrased Genghis Khan: "It's not enough that we win, everyone else must lose." It was quintessential Ellison, bombastic and over the top, like a radio shock jock looking to get a rise out of his listeners. His loyalists giggled, but later at least a couple pulled him aside after several of the newcomers, unaccustomed to Ellison's wit, had threatened to quit. One told him, "Larry, lose the Genghis Khan thing, you're scaring the kids." But Ellison liked the sound of the line, enjoyed the way it rolled off his tongue. It was the joke of an educated man, clever and urbane, the perfect expression of his self-image as a modern-day samurai warrior. So he added it to his repertoire, repeating it until it made its way into an Ellison profile appearing in the *Times'* business section. The comment generated hate mail. "Oracle," said one of the big-foot technology beat reporters, "is run by a really bright sociopath."

HE WAS A PREENING DANDY constantly tugging at a sleeve or smoothing down his suit jacket, his face puckered as if he were aware of himself every moment he was in the public eye. Picture Richard Gere in the movie *Pretty Woman*—except that the heart of this thrice-divorced man never seemed to soften. A few hours before he was to wed his third bride, he handed her an eleven-page prenuptial agreement: sign it or the wedding is off. Less than three months after the birth of their second child, he left her.

He was a man of many poses and a multitude of facades. Every mannerism seemed practiced and refined: every twist of the lip, every sniff of the nose. When sailing his yacht, he stands perfectly at the wheel as if in a movie; when glad-handing a room of analysts or investment bankers, he throws his head back in manufactured chuckles while self-consciously trading bons mots. He delivers his cleverest lines with a haughty look on his face, his eyebrows drawn up and his tongue quite literally poking his cheek. The pride he exudes at such moments seems genuine. His charcoal eyes, beneath invisible eyebrows, seem warm only when he chooses to be charming. When assuming his more familiar samurai pose, his eyes go icy. Even in repose his mouth seems slightly curled into a permanent sneer.

Convicted junk-bond king Michael Milken was a trusted business partner ("one of the most humane, most gifted human beings I've ever met in this lifetime," Ellison said of this man, who used to sponsor an annual Predators' Ball). Rupert Murdoch was a sailing buddy. His best friend was Steve Jobs—from the technology press's point of view, maybe the most unpleasant of the computer bunch. After a time, Jobs's joke became Ellison's: They were each other's best friend because they were each other's *only* friend. "In his view," said one longtime business associate, "he was just rising to the top of the food chain in the same way that a lion doesn't think too much about the antelope it takes in the bush for dinner."

Ellison was an industry anomaly, at once more personable and refined than the usual technology entrepreneur but also more aloof and crass. Even in Oracle's earliest days, he was never a twelve-hours-a-day, seven-days-a-week kind of guy. Even then, there were daily tennis matches, long walks, and impromptu days off whenever he needed them. "Sometimes he'd just abdicate without warning," said an employee who worked for Oracle in the early 1980s. "He'd totally disappear for a few days at a time."

At Intel, Andy Grove worked in a cubicle with no door. At Microsoft, Gates has granted himself a modest second-floor office precisely twice the size of the lowliest programmer's. Ellison has a private office the size of a small auditorium, yet more often than not he works at home. He's tan, trim, and muscular, a health nut among this weisswurst-skinned set oozing French-fry grease. He makes time for two-hour workouts under the watchful eye of a personal trainer (the same as Joe Montana's, he'll tell you), and, unlike your typical high-tech CEO, he possesses innumerable interests outside work and the sciences. He tries to make it to Japan every year for the blooming of the cherry blossoms. He's an avid cyclist, races yachts, and owns a small fleet of jets. He fancies himself an A-list playboy whose social calendar is always crammed with dates.

The corporation as an extension of the Great Man at the top is one of the enduring cliches of business-periodical puff pieces. More often than not the assertion is absurd in this era of stitched-together conglomerates, but Oracle and Microsoft are two notable exceptions. Both men run companies they created; both tend to hire in their own image. And, just as people sometimes speak about "Microsoft" and "Bill Gates" as if they were one and the same, people use "Oracle" and "Larry Ellison" as if they were synonymous. For years Ellison wrote every Oracle ad himself. He personally signed off on every promotion and raise, and for years no one was hired at Oracle until he or she had met Ellison.

The same scenario played itself out over and again. Ellison would be at least an hour late for the appointment. But then a prospective employee's expected thirty minutes with the chairman would end up as a two- or three-hour chat about any topic under the sun. With Luongo it was their mutual interest in Japan, with an engineer named Andy Laursen it was physics, with Zach Nelson it was pro sports. A prospective employee might think he or she had caught Ellison in an expansive mood, but the conversations were a test. If you backed down when Ellison disagreed with you about something, he'd go for the kill. If you stood up to him, he'd respect you. That's when you'd get his unique version of the "welcome to the company" speech.

At Sun, McNealy or one of his minions welcomed you to a hardworking family where everyone was expected to pull his or her weight. At Microsoft, you were congratulated for joining a "great" company that hired only the "superbright" and told that if you worked hard and proved yourself committed to the cause, you'd have no problem there. At Oracle, Ellison explained the rules for surviving the Oracle jungle.

For David Yachnin, the speech came after an hour or two talking about downhill skiing. "He says to me, 'I'm going to build a huge company. I need people who can run really, really fast to help me do that,'" said Yachnin, an ex–Oracle salesman. "'I'll pay you a fortune, but if you miss your numbers, you're out of here. We're carnivores here. If you're the kind who needs hand-holding, if you're looking for a long-term thing, go work for DEC or H-P.'"

Yachnin was twenty-six years old in 1986, the year he started at Oracle. His base salary started at $80,000, plus another $10,000 annually as a car allowance. He was granted stock options that eventually would be worth hundreds of thousands of dollars. If he exceeded his quota, he earned his target income, which was in the $200,000 range. He hit his quota his first three years with Oracle, moving up from an account executive to a regional manager. But when his region missed its sales quota in his fourth year, Yachnin was fired.

"Picture 27-year-olds making $300,000 a year and willing to promise *anything* to close a sale," wrote *Fortune* shortly after Oracle's stumble at the turn of the decade. To conjure up the Oracle sales force, imagine the shady hucksters in the movie *Tin Men*—except at Oracle they drove silver Jags and lived in double-lot homes bought after an impatient few hours of house hunting. They would sell a $325,000 package to a customer but neglect to mention, at least until the check had cleared, that the client would need to spend tens of thousands more upgrading the system before it would be usable. Or they'd ship a blank tape or a tape filled with gibberish, then play innocent when the customer called to complain. They'd promise to straighten things out as quickly as they could and then, after hanging up, congratulate themselves for buying an extra week's time. They would boast about new features in an upcoming version of a product, even though the features were years away from completion. Oracle Europe cut a deal that promised a Turkish-language version of a product even though there was no Turkish version in the works nor plans for one. Not surprisingly, a study by one well-regarded consulting outfit found that Oracle's customers tended to look on the company as a bunch of "thieves, crooks, and bandits."

Periodically an order came down from up high, usually just before the close of a quarter: the company expects another half million, or million, or two million dollars in sales from your office. "They didn't care how we pulled it off," Yachnin said. "Just so long as we got the million." So near the end of the quarter, the sales force would cut deals with regular customers: Give us $500,000 now, and we'll give you a 50 percent discount on anything you buy with that money. Then they'd fax a contract into the main office to make it appear as if the customer had spent the money on an actual product. Salespeople were caught forging signatures or fudging contract dates. The motto in the sales offices was "G.T.M., G.T.F.M.": Get the money, get the fucking money.

In the prison system, the maximum-security penitentiaries reserved for the toughest young cons are nicknamed "gladiator schools." That was Oracle. At Oracle you watched your back and maybe even wore protective gear around your midsection to avoid shankings. If you didn't openly covet your boss's job, people would raise an eyebrow. Did you lack the requisite ambition? David Yachnin told of a colleague who had spent months landing a $500,000 sale only to lose out to another salesman from the same office, who closed the deal for $400,000. "The head of sales not only allowed it, he admired that kind of initiative," Yachnin said. If five salespeople were competing for the same account, according to a joke making the rounds of the Oracle sales force, the odds were good that three were from Oracle. Occasionally the company initiated mass firings when a sales region came in below its number. "Sorry, gang, we've hired the wrong people, you're all out of here," they'd be told.

At most Silicon Valley companies, managers had overlapping responsibilities because technologists, rather than MBAs, were in charge. At Oracle, overlapping duties was a strategy meant to foster internal competition. Employees learned never to ask others how their weekend had gone because that meant they were lightweights who pulled out of the fast lane for a weekly two-day rest. Underlings brashly disagreed with bosses, wasting no time with the finer points of diplomacy. A supervisor would be called a moron or a fool even if the person across the table were two or three rungs below in the corporate hierarchy.

Those whom people dubbed "Larry's boys"—Oracle's untouchables—were the worst. They'd intentionally miss a meeting with a supervisor they didn't particularly respect and get away with it. Or if a woman complained that one of Larry's boys was sexually harassing her, she was told to do a better job avoiding him. "I know Larry, he'll never fire me," one of the boys would tell a superior or a superior's superior—and of course he was right. Back in the 1980s Ellison drove a red Ferrari, so they drove Ferraris. Ellison would say whatever popped into his head, without passing it through a filter, and so would they. Ellison dated whomever he wanted to in the company—when he was sued for sexual harassment in the early 1990s, it came out that he was simultaneously dating three Oracle employees—so no one could be surprised that inappropriate sexual conduct was rampant inside the company. One ex-Oracleite, a woman, described the company as a world populated by "a gang of rampaging cowboys"—and Ellison was their ringleader.

"Oracle was like this place without any parents around to set down the rules, so the kids ran around loose all the time," said Nancy Stinnette. She was a director in the company's marketing department, responsible for a staff of about thirty employees. She would receive her marching orders and flinch. "Larry wants us to shove this up their ass," she would be told. "Larry wants us to really kick them in the balls." She quit barely a year into her tenure because to her Oracle was a "horrible place" and because she was "tired of being resented as the heavy playing the role of parent, laying down commonsense rules."

A crash seemed inevitable. Ellison, who by the end of the 1980s was worth roughly a billion dollars, was spending less of his time on work and more time traveling and playing with his expensive toys. He'd go

Hollywood with *Buzz,* a Los Angeles–based magazine he helped finance. The company's bean counters came to him to complain that the books were filled with time bombs, but Ellison treated them like narrow-minded bureaucrats who spoke a language he didn't quite understand. From where he sat, they were throttling Oracle's growth, acting like cops and riling some of his best people. Unlike the sales force and the company's programmers, those working in the company's finance group were not granted stock options. The man Ellison chose to serve as the company's chief financial officer was a novice in the realm of finance and also the head of one of the company's product divisions, meaning that the more sales his group booked, the bigger his bonus.

The company missed its numbers in the first quarter of 1990 when the company was forced to disallow $15 million in unrealized deals. The next day Oracle's stock fell by 31 percent. Ellison reacted to this bad news by upping the ante: Oracle would not only match its ambitious estimates for the next quarter, he declared, it would sell enough software to make up for the previous quarter's shortfall. The company then initiated the "Go for the Gold" program. It would pay commissions and bonuses in sacks of gold rather than by check. The opportunity to grab fistfuls of gold, it was thought, would provide the extra incentive employees needed.

The "Go for the Gold" initiative forestalled disaster, but only for a few months. Ellison's overaggressiveness, and the overaggressiveness of his sales force, had finally caught up with Oracle. Internal audits exposed scores of questionable deals and contracts adding up to tens of millions of dollars. Consultants were caught billing customers for hours they didn't work. One salesman was caught booking a sale to a nonexistent company he had conjured up to collect a commission. Oracle not only fell short of its estimated revenues, it showed a $36 million loss for the quarter. The company's stock fell from a high of more than $28 a share to a low of less than $5. In six months' time, Ellison's stake in Oracle fell from $954 million to $164 million, a loss of $790 million.*

Ellison claimed he had gone for a long run the day the roof fell in on

* After a lengthy investigation, the Securities and Exchange Commission filed a long complaint against Oracle. "Oracle double-billed customers for products, double-billed customers for technical support services, invoiced customers for work that was never performed, failed to credit customers for product returns, booked revenues that were contingent . . ." Oracle eventually settled the case out of court, paying a $100,000 fine without admitting liability.

his company. He told an elaborate story of gazing at the waves lapping at the shore and the cliffs looming over him as he ran along the Pacific, scenarios racing through his head. But even this tale of angst proved to be another fabrication. "I wasn't capable of taking a walk over a hundred yards," he eventually confessed in an interview with *Vanity Fair.* "I stayed in the house. I watched the stock ticker all day, watched it drop and drop and drop." Then, when he finally returned to the office, he began firing people, dismissing literally half the company officers.

For the moment Ellison seemed humbler, chastened. You could hear it in his voice, you could read the fear in his actions. Ellison hadn't sold any stock since taking Oracle public four years earlier, though he owned roughly one quarter of the company. But following the company's great tumble, he started selling blocks of stock regularly. He taught himself the basics of high finance. He hired a seasoned pro from Booz•Allen & Hamilton to serve as his number two and joked that finally Oracle had an adult in charge. "We were an adolescent company," he said in an interview with *Forbes ASAP.* "I thought only about getting to the next quarter."

Yet there would be no come-to-Jesus confession, no reemergence as a chastened fighter suddenly swearing off kidney punches in the clinch or shots below the belt. He had been humbled but hardly transformed; if anything, his comeuppance only sharpened his competitive zeal. In the early 1990s, Oracle initiated its "Cut Off the Air" campaign against Sybase, an all-out assault on a smaller foe that included (at least according to *Fortune*) bogus performance numbers in its "Gentlemen, Start Your Snails" anti-Sybase ad campaign.

Over lunch with a friend, Ellison expressed incredulity that Ingres, then the company's largest competitor, hadn't gutted Oracle when it had its chance. Right after Oracle's fall, Ingres received hundreds of résumés from Oracle employees wanting to abandon the sinking ship, but though there was Oracle blood in the water, the company didn't pounce. Instead, it threw away the résumés. "Larry told this story with utter scorn on his face," this friend said. "Like, 'Don't they know this is war? Don't they know what you do to your competition when given the chance?'"

When in 1997 a scrappy Oracle competitor called Informix took a hit not unlike Oracle's 1990 dive, Ellison showed how it was done. "We all dropped everything to work on Informix for the next few weeks," said an employee working in the company's marketing department. A crew that *ComputerWorld* dubbed Oracle's "marketing barracudas" worked the phones, calling every beat reporter and analyst covering the database field. Another team put together an ad campaign offering a one-third discount to any Informix user willing to jump ship to Oracle. The company's sales force visited every known Informix customer, armed with reams of data spelling out the company's woes. Explained one former manager who carried out some of the seamier elements of the Cut Off the Air campaign, "At Oracle, the idea is that you do whatever you have to do to keep a foot on the neck of the competition. And then, when you're tired of listening to their pleas for mercy, you stomp down hard enough to crush their windpipe."

Maybe it made perfect sense, then, when in late 1995 Ellison emerged as a potential savior in the anti-Microsoft cause. This man inclined to jokes depicting Gates as the Darth Vader of the computer world must have recognized that he was the perfect embodiment of the Star Wars credo "To defeat you I must become you."

"CAN LARRY BEAT BILL?" *Business Week* asked in the spring of 1995. At that point Ellison was worth more than $3 billion, a figure that ranked him among the country's two dozen richest people. In Silicon Valley, where one's stock portfolio is the means of keeping score, Ellison was lord and master. Back then, Intel cofounder Gordon Moore was worth more than Ellison, but Moore had long ago handed over the reins to Andy Grove; he was the semiretired chairman and no longer a player (in 1997 he became chairman emeritus). The only one who looked as if he might give Ellison a run for his money was Netscape's Jim Clark, but as of 1995, you could have added Steve Jobs's and Andy Grove's net worth to Clark's, and Ellison would still have enjoyed more than a billion-dollar advantage. At that point in his life, Ellison could have invested every dollar in a money market account and lived off $150 million a year in interest. But though Ellison turned fifty-one that year, none of that much mattered. Bill Gates was a household name; Ellison was that other billionaire whose name no one outside the industry seemed to know. Gates's every pronouncement was received like Moses presenting the Ten Commandments. When Ellison spoke, his words usually fell on deaf ears.

"On any other mountain," *Business Week*'s Richard Brandt wrote, "Lawrence J. Ellison would be king." The funny thing was that Ellison, by any definition but his own and maybe the media's, *did* reside on a different mountain. Oracle sells complex software systems and consulting services to large companies needing to navigate vast stores of data. Its product tracks parts for Ford Motor and reservations for United Airlines, and lets those atop McDonald's figure out where its Happy Meals are a hit and where they're a bust. AT&T, Xerox, Sony, General Electric, and the New York Stock Exchange are among the companies using Oracle software. Microsoft does sell a set of database products, but it pitches them to individuals and small businesses—hardly customers with the money to hire the consultants or staff required to run an Oracle database product. Whereas at Microsoft a top-of-the-line software product might set a consumer back $600, Oracle sold systems that *began* at around $50,000. In the early 1990s, the two companies competed in the dash to cash in on the Interactive TV competition, but in retrospect that seemed more a cause to commiserate about than to lock horns over.

In 1995, Oracle was one of the thirty most profitable publicly traded companies in the country. It ranked among the top fifty in terms of market cap. But when that category was broadened to include all software companies, Oracle ranked second in terms of size and profitability. Microsoft, of course, was first. Those who knew Ellison knew that secretly he harbored a dream of topping the list of richest Americans. He also saw high-profile greatness in Oracle's future. His ultimate goal, he said in an interview with a magazine called *Icon*, was "to make Oracle the most important company in the world." That meant passing Microsoft.

How preoccupied was Ellison with Gates even then? In 1994, Ellison sat down for a Q and A with *Upside*. "The first thing I want to talk to you about is the information highway," the interviewer began, but before he could actually pose a question, Ellison interrupted: "Speaking of which, Bill [Gates] just ran a demo on the information highway and it was a disaster. . . . Everything blew up on him repeatedly." Later, during the same interview, apropos of nothing, he sarcastically said, "I'll go back and quote my dear friend Bill Gates." He invited a *San Francisco Examiner* reporter to drive around town with him, and when she asked him about his money, he'd joke, What's another billion? "There's nothing I couldn't buy—except maybe Microsoft." During an interview with Charlie Rose, in early 1995, he sniffed that he didn't mind "Microsoft's monopoly," only "the mediocrity of their technology."

Ellison had ten years on Gates, but there were uncanny parallels between the two men and their companies. Gates and Paul Allen officially codified their partnership in 1977, the same year Oracle was created; both took their respective companies public in the spring of 1986, just one day apart. (Ellison would probably want it mentioned that Oracle went first.) But from the start Gates was the bigger mogul. After these back-to-back public offerings, Gates had a paper fortune worth more than $300 million, while Ellison's was only $93 million. Ellison was trailing Gates by more than a three-to-one margin before the race had really begun.

The two might even have liked each other if not for their dueling bank accounts. Both were best known for their hardball business practices, but both fancied themselves first-rate technologists who just happened to be good at business. They were both screamers with a propensity to ridicule underlings when they made a mistake. Both were envied and feared by some and hated and resented by others. In many regards, they were kindred spirits in the rarified world of high-tech CEOs.

Maybe Gates was thinking the same thing when, in the late 1980s, he called Ellison to propose a get-together. Gates had no specific deal to propose, but Microsoft was just starting to get into the low-end database field, so probably this was one of his infamous information-gathering missions. If Ellison was worried, he didn't show it. He sent one of his lieutenants to the airport to pick Gates up and bring him to Ellison's home. Ellison then shuttled him back to the airport in his red Ferrari Testarossa, a car that then cost roughly $300,000.

Ellison's assistant of thirteen years, Jenny Overstreet, spoke with her boss right after his meeting with Gates. As she related the tale to Ellison biographer Mike Wilson, Gates certainly got the better of the first encounter. "Larry is such a stream of consciousness communicator that he was just going and going and going," Overstreet told Wilson. "Finally he just stopped himself. He realized Bill wasn't saying anything. He was just listening with his head tilted to the side." For a time the two spoke regularly by phone, but that was before the two companies started competing head-to-head over Interactive TV. Gates would profess to liking Ellison personally, but in an interview with *Business Week*, the Microsoft chief dismissed Ellison's claims about Interactive TV with this quote: "Larry's hype had expanded to fill his ego."

Ellison's anti-Microsoft jihad began in earnest right after the launch of Windows 95. *USA Today* declared Windows 95 "the most talked-about product launch since New Coke's introduction in 1985." It was, Lee Gomes wrote in the *San Jose Mercury News,* "how the Ten Commandments would have been launched, if only God had Bill Gates's money." Ellison loved nothing more than a splashy big-noise launch, but that was when all the fuss was over an Oracle product. Ellison seemed to take Windows 95 personally, like a prissy media critic who couldn't stomach corporate-driven hype.

Ellison began at least one meeting not by addressing the chosen topic but by ranting about the attention the media paid to an *operating system,* of all things. Or someone would walk into his office carrying a trade magazine with something about Windows emblazoned across the cover. He'd shake his head and cluck that an operating system didn't really *do* anything. "It's a freakin' *upgrade,*" he would say—and not even a particularly good one at that, if the big reviewers were to be believed.* What about the issues that really mattered? What about Bosnia? "I just couldn't deal with it [the Windows 95 hype] anymore," Ellison told writer Bryan Burrough. In a couple of weeks, he and Gates would both be in Paris, scheduled to speak at the same computer conclave. By then, Ellison had had his fill of Windows 95, as well as Java and Netscape. It was time to change the subject.

In Paris, Ellison unveiled what he alternately called an "Internet appliance," an "Internet terminal," and a "network computer." "Network computer," or NC, was the moniker that would stick, but, ironically, it was uttered after a slip of the tongue. He was starting to call his invention a "multimedia personal computer," but he stopped midsentence to correct himself. "It's not a personal computer, it's a *network* computer," he said. That about summed it up, this half-baked product presented to the world before it even had a name. Even Oracle's number two, Oracle USA President Ray Lane, confessed that the NC was rooted in Ellison's desire to trump Gates. "It was just a speech Larry was trying to stick to Bill, not a strategy," Lane told *PC Week* several months later.

The network computer was a stripped-down PC without a hard disk

---

* *The New York Times'* Stephen Manes described Windows as "an edifice built of baling wire, chewing gum, and prayer," and Walt Mossberg wrote in his *Wall Street Journal* column that the company still had a long way to go before it could call Windows 95 userfriendly. "Windows 95 is pretty bad," Stewart Alsop wrote in *Fortune.*

or CD-ROM. Users' files and computer programs would be stored on host computers that would be accessed as one accesses Web pages. With time, the NC would be repositioned as a possible Microsoft killer, but Oracle's original motivation was to salvage the tens of millions of dollars the company had spent on Interactive TV. It had invented a cable set-top box for Interactive TV, which had gotten Ellison and some of his lieutenants thinking about a no-frills computer. Why couldn't a computer be more like a television? they asked themselves—or more like a phone? Just plug the thing in, and it works. All the complicated switching equipment would reside in centrally located sites, under the watchful eyes of experts. The price would be a consumer-friendly $500.

At most companies, this germ of an idea would be lovingly nurtured inside the company's labs, to be unveiled to the world only once the company had conquered some of the product's more nettlesome challenges. Oracle, however, wasn't most companies. Its marketing director, Zach Nelson, had no idea Ellison would be announcing the NC that day in Paris. Neither did Andy Laursen, the designer wrestling with an NC prototype, nor Farzad Dibachi, the executive who just a few days earlier had helped Ellison draft his Paris speech. Even Ray Lane would confess that he had had no idea what Ellison had up his sleeve. Sighed Andy Laursen, "At Oracle, you get used to things being in the press before they're realized as full product concepts."

Ellison's presentation began straightforwardly enough: Just as the center of gravity had moved from the mainframe to the PC, the Internet would mean a shift from the PC to cheap devices that derived their power from the network. With the Internet, a user's software and files could reside on the network rather than on one's own machine. Businesses might be interested in the NC because a single systems manager could update every user's software centrally, thus reducing a corporation's annual operating costs. (Studies popular at the time showed that the average corporation spent between $8,000 and $12,000 per PC per year.) Instead of paying $600 for Microsoft Office, a home user could "rent" a word processing program if and when he or she needed it. Ellison didn't take the next logical step, but there was no need to, given his well-publicized anti-Microsoft stance: Windows, an 11-million-line operating system, would be incompatible with a diskless computer.

Had he stopped there, Ellison would have been quoted by the usual trade rags before fading into the mist. His speech was typical for these kinds of events, a computer executive pontificating on the future of computing. But then, during the Q-and-A session that followed, Ellison declared, "The PC is a ridiculous device," an expensive and overly complicated beast costing corporate America thousands of dollars per machine per year. With the king of PC software sitting in the audience, Ellison declared that as soon as the network computer arrived, the PC would "no longer be the center of the universe." And when might that be? "As early as next year," Ellison answered. His comments won him headlines around the world.

Two weeks after his Paris speech, Ellison, along with a half-dozen or so other high-tech CEOs, met with President Clinton for what the White House called "Net Day." The idea behind the event was to throw Clinton's weight behind a project aimed at wiring California's schools*—and, not coincidentally, impress the wealthy of Silicon Valley with the president's appreciation for technology one year before he was to stand for reelection. Ellison's company sold expensive software systems to Fortune 1000 companies. He seemed an odd choice to attend a small meeting about wiring the PCs and Macs residing in America's public schools, but he had been one of the Democratic Party's top donors in 1992, and therefore his presence was mandatory. For Ellison this was his chance to shine in front of "William Jefferson Clinton, the President of the United States," as he grandly described him in an *Upside* interview. "Larry's a contrarian," Zach Nelson said. "So I'm sure when he was sitting there with Clinton among all these PC guys, he wanted to drop a bomb in the conversation and end up the dominant dog in the meeting."

The meeting wasn't many minutes old when Ellison proposed his $500 computer. Then, like a fire alarm salesman who lobbies for mandatory smoke detectors, he suggested that the president embrace a goal of a computer on every student's desk by a given year. "It would be like John Kennedy saying we're going to put a man on the moon by a certain time," he suggested. It was hard to tell if he was playing an amateur George Stephanopolous or hitting the president with the hard sell.

Clinton invited Ellison to ride with him to his next event. Maybe he was impressed by Ellison's brilliance, but more likely he wanted to flat-

---

* "Everyone was saying how hard it would be to get the schools networked, so I put together a document showing that it wouldn't be terribly difficult if the money was there," Sun's John Gage said. "Well, the White House got a copy of it and the next thing I know, I get this call saying the president and vice president were coming out in eight days to support my project. And I said, 'What project?' "

ter Ellison so that he would write the president another multi-zero check. "The limo I arrived in is bigger than this one," Ellison boasted. Clinton shot back, "That might be the case, but mine's safer."

Still high on the fumes of Paris and the president, Ellison was only getting warmed up. At an analysts' meeting held in Philadelphia that September, he promised that he'd be demonstrating a fully working NC by the end of 1996. He flew to Alsop's Agenda to tweak the PC crowd, declaring their beloved machine was "old hat," and then returned to Europe for a Geneva trade show, where he pitched the NC as a "Windowless machine" that would challenge Microsoft's might. "No longer will there be Microsoft to control what you can and cannot do on the desktop," he declared. This time he promised a working prototype by the next February, with NCs in full production by the end of the year. A month later he was promising production of the NC "in quantity" by the summer.

Ellison's next big stop was COMDEX. For years Ellison had shunned this convention pitched to PC devotees and gadget buffs. He'd had no plans to attend the 1995 show, but then, a week before the event was to begin, he realized it would serve as the perfect venue for a PC-versus-NC debate. Every square foot of meeting space was taken, but Ellison phoned hotel impresario and fellow gazillionaire Stephen Wynn, who offered him one of the dining rooms in his hotel so they could host a panel discussion that would feature Ellison and Ray Smith, the head of Bell Atlantic.

At that point, according to *Upside* magazine, the company had only one engineer banging away on the NC (though they had several PR people assigned to the project). The company still had no prototype, nor even preliminary sketches showing what it might look like. "We were playing in this high-stakes poker game with all the cards turned down," Andy Laursen said. "We were bluffing like mad." Yet for Zach Nelson, that only heightened the pleasure of their PR victory. "We had no booth," he said. "A week before the thing starts, we had no hotel reservation. We didn't even pay to register. But every news story out of COMDEX that year was about the NC."

At COMDEX, Stewart Alsop challenged Ellison's claim that he could sell the NC for less than $500. Alsop started firing questions: How much would the microprocessor cost? Wouldn't the memory alone eat up a couple of hundred dollars? A modem means another hundred—and what about a screen, the cheapest of which costs around $300? "Of course he couldn't answer my questions," Alsop said. "But Larry being Larry, he just starts making up answers on the spot." Some in the audience started hissing. The entire concept struck Alsop and others as patently absurd. Ellison was the CEO of the world's most successful database company, yet he was now talking about entering the consumer electronics business, a field in which the company had no experience. "And his sole motivation seemed to be that he had come up with an idea that would mean people didn't have to use Windows," Alsop said.

When, in the coming weeks, skeptical reporters and Wall Street analysts phoned Ellison for details, Oracle PR diverted them to Andy Laursen. "That was definitely the most unpleasant experience of my life," Laursen said. "People weren't just skeptical, they'd get very angry. They'd yell at me, 'There's no way this is going to work. Are you nuts?' " The pundits drew parallels to one of the industry's biggest busts, the Apple Newton, a handheld computer based on a handwriting program that couldn't decipher most people's handwriting. Wise guys in the press dubbed the NC "Larry's magic box" or, worse, his "dumb box." Oracle called the device the "$500 computer," but even that ended up a point of ridicule. When finally it hit the market, it was a $500 box that actually retailed for $699, or well over $1,000 if you wanted the computer monitor and memory needed to make the thing work.

But who cared? Ellison appeared on the NBC evening news the week of COMDEX, and also on CBS's *Coast to Coast*. A big article in *The New York Times* declared the NC "the buzz of the COMDEX trade show." Sure, the article went on to call the NC a "fantasy" computer—but the *Times*! Charlie Rose paid homage in the spring of 1996, and Ellison's picture appeared in *USA Today*. *Newsweek* photographed him sitting in front of a weight machine wearing a tank top; *Time* arrived shortly after that to photograph him for *its* NC-related profile. Eventually, Ellison would be treated to a long profile in *Vanity Fair* and appear as a guest on *Oprah Winfrey*. Do you think Gates ever got thirteen pages in *Vanity Fair*? Or Oprah? "I'm gonna find me a school, and I'm gonna give some computers, too," Winfrey said as the hour was coming to a close. "I'm inspired by you, Larry. That's a brilliant idea." Oprah!

CHAPTER 14

THE SILVER MEDALIST

LARRY ELLISON was at his health club, working out on the StairMaster, when an acquaintance walked over to talk with him about yacht racing. A new class of boat called "maxis" would soon be permitted to enter world-class races. Maybe Ellison would be interested in having one built. Ellison had pretty much given up the sport years earlier, but he was intrigued. If nothing else, it meant another shiny new toy.

Lawrence J. Ellison doesn't do things halfway. The seventy-eight-foot championship-caliber maxi he had had built was the finest that money could buy. He made sure of that in the months he spent wooing a man he described as "the world's best designer." Once the boat was ready, he commissioned a crew of sailors with America's Cup experience. Even his new yacht's name underscored how serious he was about winning: the *Sayonara*, a name that would taunt the competition once Ellison and crew left them bobbing in their wake.

Ellison entered the *Sayonara* in the 1994 TransPac (Trans-Pacific), a 2,600-mile race from Los Angeles to Hawaii. He had spent millions of dollars building and then staffing it, but he placed second.* A different kind of man might have derived pleasure from so strong a performance in a competitive sport, but Ellison seemed to embrace as his life credo that awful Nike slogan from the 1996 Olympics: The silver medal means not taking first. What kind of man settles for the silver when it's the gold that everyone truly covets? That was his answer when he was asked

---

* "He was scary," one crew member said of his captain's earliest days behind the wheel in an interview with the *San Francisco Chronicle*. He's not too bad now, he added, but that's after a couple of years of coaching from a "John Madden type who did a fair amount of shouting." As in "Larry, what the #*! are you doing?"

about the *Sayonara,* and that was his answer whenever someone asked him about Microsoft. His job was to make Oracle number one. There were plenty of people inclined to think that if that was the case, it might as well be carved on his tombstone now: "Here lies Mr. Second Place."

BILL GATES didn't take the bait in 1995, when Larry Ellison dismissed the PC as a "ridiculous device" whose days of preeminence were numbered. Though Gates followed Ellison to the podium that day in Paris, he didn't even acknowledge the taunt until, after he had delivered his speech, the moderator pressed him for a response. "People who think we're going to have dumb terminals in the world of the Internet . . ." Gates began—but he cut himself off. "I just don't agree with that," he said mildly.

Gates didn't bite, but the Myhrvolds, Nathan and brother Cameron, did. Cameron Myhrvold, a Microsoft executive in Paris for the event, dismissed Ellison's idea as "dorky." That was among the kinder words brother Nathan, the chieftain overseeing next-generation technologies at Microsoft, used when reporters phoned seeking official comment. Depending on the day, the NC was "dumb," "ludicrous," or simply a "crazy" idea. To Myhrvold the whole notion of a diskless computer tied to a network made no sense, and he wasn't shy about saying so. Hard disks are cheap, fast, and reliable; networks are slow and prone to crash under heavy use. Say you wanted to write a letter: First that would mean thumb-twiddling frustration as the NC downloaded a word processing program. Then, did you really want to store something so personal on a public network? "The only thing that grows faster than real computers," Myhrvold liked to say on the lecture circuit when talking about the NC, "are imaginary ones."

Myhrvold seemed in a kind mood the day *Newsweek* called to ask about the NC. "People want *more* from their computers, not *less,*" Myhrvold said. "Sorry, I just don't see it." Certainly he was more polite than the Compaq Computer executive who told *Newsweek,* "It will never happen. They're lying!" But Myhrvold's name followed the Compaq quote, so reading the piece quickly, one might conclude it was Myhrvold who had called Ellison a liar. That, at least, was how Ellison and marketing manager Zach Nelson read the article.

"That quote really sent Larry totally over the edge," Nelson said. "That's when all the rockets left the pad as far as I'm concerned. Every speech Larry gave after that, he'd say, 'Microsoft says I'm lying.' It became one of those blackboard-before-the-big-game quotes that really fires everyone up. The attitude was 'Let's show everyone that Larry's not a liar.' I'm sure he called Farzad and said, 'You got to get the development group going.' "

Farzad is Farzad Dibachi, the division head under whose purview the NC fell and who at the time was a business confidant of Ellison's. Like Nelson, Dibachi believed the NC took on a life of its own because people wanted to defend the boss's pride, but to him the culprit was the flood of media attention paid to this nonexistent product. "If the press hadn't jumped on it, the idea would have died at Oracle," Dibachi told *Upside.*

At Oracle, they called it "dialing for engineers": Ellison's propensity for phoning the programmers working on his pet project of the moment. He would start punching numbers until he connected with a programmer who could satisfy his craving. From the fall of 1995 until Laursen left in the spring of 1996, the engineer Ellison sought out more often than any other was the head of his NC team, Andy Laursen. At times, Laursen said, Ellison phoned as often as three or four times a day.

Laursen doesn't doubt that Ellison genuinely believed in the NC. But the frequency and fervor of his calls also left him thinking that pride was playing a key role in the device's development. "Larry's a very confrontational guy," Laursen said. "He likes to bait his competitors. And if the competition baits him back, he's going to escalate it."

THE FIRST FACE-TO-FACE MEETING between Gates and Ellison had taken place in the late 1980s, at Ellison's Atherton residence. The home was a Japanese-style mansion modeled after a famed villa in Kyoto, Japan, spare and stylish, decorated with museum-quality sculptures and art. The property included three acres of fabulously landscaped Japanese gardens created by trucking in 3.6 million pounds of granite and gravel. There were cherry blossoms, bonsai trees, and imported Japanese maples, a koi pond, a man-made waterfall, and a ceremonial pavilion for taking tea. Supposedly Gates said, "Cool house," then added, "I'm building a bigger one." So maybe it was actually Bill Gates who initiated the ensuing battle of dueling Taj Mahals that served as an entertaining sideshow through the 1990s.

Gates had just started working on his 45,000-square-foot techno-

Utopia that *Esquire* would dub a "palace" and then liken to the mansions built by robber barons such as Cornelius Vanderbilt and John Jacob Astor. In the late 1980s, the reported price tag was $25 million, but by 1996 the estimated cost had reached $30 million. Ellison owned two equally magnificent retreats in the Bay Area: his $15 million home in Atherton and another in San Francisco, thirty miles to the north, a $24 million steel-and-glass pied-à-terre with beautiful views of the bay and hills. The San Francisco home, for those nights Ellison has a date or business in the city, is equipped with a $200,000 home entertainment system complete with THX sound. In one closet is a computer that controls the house's hundreds of lights, dimming them in the midday sun, brightening them when overcast. Yet together these two homes were apparently not enough, for in 1996 Ellison unveiled his plans for a third Bay Area home a few miles from his Atherton abode. This new one would be a replica of a sixteenth-century samurai village, including a 7,000-square-foot main house and three guest homes. The anticipated price tag was $40 million—or $10 million more than the monument Gates was building to himself.

The various buildings that make up the Gates compound have been built with old-growth Douglas fir brought from a mill 100 miles to the south and then remilled 100 miles to the north. Not to be outdone, the many buildings that will make up Ellison's Woodside complex are being built from rare woods that have been carefully cured in kilns, some for more than two years. Every beam is being hand-planed and cut in such a fashion that they interlock in the tongue-and-groove method used to construct wooden Japanese temples still standing hundreds of years after they were built. Supposedly, the entire project will be built without the use of a single nail. When Ellison's neighbors-to-be protested that his plans meant tearing down a Julia Morgan–designed home, he arranged to have it helicoptered to Stanford.

"Everything is inner-focused," Ellison's designer told a *New York Times* reporter while walking her through the twenty-three-acre site for the new home. Ellison is the most un-Zen-like of creatures, needing to own or conquer everyone and everything he comes into contact with. Yet his compound will include a "moon pavilion" for meditation. Every building will be enclosed in a layer of Okabe clay to absorb the home's "physical and spiritual energy." The site plan calls for a "Balance of Elements: Air, Earth, Time, Water, and Wood," but this wasn't a home exactly at one with nature. A carpenter who has worked on the home called it a by-product of the "God complex that so many of these rich guys have." As in "I want my lake here, I want my mountain there."

The Gateses moved plenty of earth to build their palace on the shores of Lake Washington, but except for an underground parking lot, about all they have to show for their rearranging of landscape is a small salmon hatchery. Ellison's plans call for the creation of a three-acre lake filled with purified drinking water and stocked with rare Japanese carp.* The property will also include a pair of manufactured meditative ponds, and the plans call for massive changes in the contours of the land: the creation of a small hillside here, a leveling of bumpy terrain there. Ellison talks about moving into his house by New Year's Day 2000, but the workmen he's hired just snicker behind his back when they hear such claims. "It's amazing how long a project like this can take," the carpenter said, "when your plans include changing the shape of the land."

Had the two been friends, Gates might have counseled Ellison that such a conceit was more trouble than it was worth. Gates wrote in his book, *The Road Ahead,* that his own house "has been under construction for what seems like most of my life"—eleven years would pass from the time Gates started buying property along the large lake that separates Seattle from its eastern suburbs to the time he and his family moved in.

The Gates's house was being built on what had been six individual lots, the first four of which Gates had bought in one fell swoop. But when word got out that the area's richest man was in the market, the adjoining properties suddenly soared in price. Dickering over the final two parcels ate up more than a year. In the end, Gates spent more than $5 million for just under five acres of lakefront real estate. One of those lots included a two-year-old, four-bedroom home that had been appraised at $500,000. That proved another time waster. At first Gates figured he'd just knock the house down, but then his mother and others got on his case about destroying a perfectly good home when so many people were homeless. So then everything sat on hold while he found a buyer willing to move the home. The next challenge, according to the book *Gates,* was to sift through the twenty-three sets of plans submitted by architectural firms around the globe. Gates met three times with

* He has hired a woman whose expertise is the creation of self-containing, self-regulating ecosystems so that it doesn't turn into a giant muck hole.

each of the three finalists. Four years passed between his purchase of those first lots and the laying of the foundation.

The winning plan called for a series of pavilions built into the hillside and connected by underground passageways. That required endless digging and hauling. The architectural plans had been finalized and the house had been partially built when Gates got married, which required a return to the drawing board and some undoing of things already constructed. The new Mrs. Gates, it seemed, had her own ideas about the layout of the home, including larger closets and a room for a nanny in the children's wing.

The delays were one of Gates's enduring irritations, the media's preoccupation with his home another. The first bag of concrete hadn't been poured before *Esquire* declared it "the most talked about residence since William Randolph Hearst's." Hearst's coastal Xanadu seemed everyone's favorite reference point for Gates's home. The local newspapers dubbed the home "San Simeon North," others called it Xanadu 2.0. Tidbits about the house leaked out into the press: the indoor pool featuring piped-in music, a garage large enough for thirty automobiles, a private salmon hatchery.

In *The Road Ahead*, published in 1995, Gates described the home in great detail. A companion CD-ROM even offered a virtual tour. But those close to Gates knew that all the attention paid his home irked him no end. In that wheedling whine of his that made him at times sound like a cross between Julia Child and Barney Fife, he'd accuse the press of invading his privacy. To his mind, his home was nothing like San Simeon, which in *The Road Ahead* he dismissed as a "monument to excess." And his people, ever loyal, pooh-poohed the inordinate attention being paid to something so beside the point. "Bill just wants to spend his time making great software," they would say.

That was one difference between Gates and Ellison: whereas Gates would appear annoyed if someone compared his home in progress to Hearst's, Ellison would say thank-you for the praise. Gates tended to shy away from the media's blinding light, unless someone convinced him it meant an opportunity to sell more software. Ellison, in contrast, was not uneasy in the klieg lights but in fact sought out the glare. Gates would no sooner propose an in-home interview than allow a reporter to paw through his underwear drawer. Ellison pretty much spoke with reporters nowhere *but* in one or another of his homes, as if wanting to demonstrate how tasteful and truly refined a man he was. If you worked on Gates's home, you signed a nondisclosure agreement. If you were the lead designer for Ellison's, you gave a tour to a reporter with the *Times* and shared your site plans with *Newsweek.*

Yet, though Ellison's home would seemingly cost more to build, the fact was that whereas rivers of ink gushed over the interest in Gates's home, Ellison's generated only an intermittent trickle. "I think it genuinely bothered Larry how little people were paying attention to his home," said one former Oracle executive who occasionally has lunch with Ellison. Ellison would cluck over the media's inordinate interest in Gates's mansion in progress, but this friend, like others, figured this view had grown out of jealousy rather than an interest in press criticism. The *Newsweek* feature seemed typical. Ellison's resplendent vision of replicating a five-hundred-year-old Japanese village in the California hills was deemed worthy of a few paragraphs in a sidebar, but the magazine devoted more inches to the Microsoft executive whose home includes an art museum, a video arcade, and a fourth-floor bed that rotates depending on his view preference.

At times Gates and Ellison seemed like the dueling despots in Charlie Chaplin's classic *The Great Dictator,* seated in side-by-side barber chairs, trying to one-up each other by cranking their chairs a few ticks higher, oblivious to the absurdity of their small-minded competition until both came crashing down. In the throes of the NC-PC debate it was their dueling charitable contributions. For years the philanthropic world complained about the stingy high-tech tycoons hoarding their billions, Ellison and Gates included. Then, over a two-day period, first one, then the other, announced that he was creating a big-money nonprofit foundation to help connect the country's youth to the Internet. Gates's announcement came first, but Oracle cried dirty pool, claiming that only hours earlier *it* had sent around a press alert inviting reporters to hear Ellison pledge $100 million at a news conference the next day. Gates pledged $200 million. "Don't Ask Who Was First," advised a headline over a story in *The Wall Street Journal* reporting on this sudden competition to see who was the more generous software mogul.

ARE YOU A LIAR? a writer for *Fortune* magazine once asked Ellison. He answered philosophically, in the fashion of a Zen master inclined to riddles: "Does anyone tell the truth all the time?" The game in the software industry, at least as played by its top two companies, is to tell everyone you've got something and then get busy working on it.

Five months had passed since Ellison had first declared the NC the next great thing, but still no manufacturer had bitten. So Oracle's best deal makers searched the globe for hardware companies willing to mass-produce an NC on the cheap while a small crew of software engineers worked furiously on computer programs that might make it all work. Meanwhile, Zach Nelson's challenge became maintaining the momentum of this device Ellison billed as a "computer for the masses."

Only a few months after Paris, the media interest was already dying down. So at the start of 1996, Nelson leaked preliminary sketches of the NC to the *San Francisco Chronicle*. Actually, these were a few hastily produced line drawings Ellison was carrying to Japan to give manufacturers a sense of what the device *might* look like, but more news stories followed. The next big event was a glitzy San Francisco press conference where executives from Sun, Netscape, IBM, and Apple joined Ellison onstage to endorse Oracle's specs for the network computer. Except that there were no specs to endorse because Oracle was still developing them. So essentially the only thing this Who's Who of anti-Microsoft competitors endorsed was the Internet protocols they all were following anyway.* "We had run out of good ideas," Nelson said with a shrug. "Steam was running out, so we needed something to show market momentum."

Scott McNealy didn't attend the press conference because people at Sun were angry that Oracle, to keep the drumbeat going, had leaked word of the news conference two weeks earlier. Nelson confessed that Oracle was always pulling stunts like that. "The question we asked was 'How could Oracle benefit most from this alliance?' as opposed to 'How can we help the alliance?'," he said. "At Oracle it was always Oracle first and everybody else second." McNealy sent one of his division heads to reveal one of the few scraps of real news: Sun would be developing an NC that might or might not use Oracle software. An executive from IBM said his company would also be testing an NC (but he, too, made

---

* For months reporters pressed Ellison and others at Oracle to explain the term "network computer architecture." Finally confessing that it didn't mean much of anything, Ellison said he had made a "terrible mistake in giving Internet computing our own brand name."

no commitment to buy Oracle software). From the start, Ellison had stressed that the NC would be a consumer device aimed at people such as his mother, a computer novice who would use the device to download video clips of her grandkids. But Sun's and IBM's representatives made it plain that what they would produce would cost far more than $500. Neither Sun nor IBM was thinking of Ellison's mother but rather about bank tellers and airline reservationists using "dumb terminals" hooked to networks, users who didn't need high-powered PCs to do their job.

By that point, the price of PCs was falling. Fully equipped Intel-based PCs were selling for under $1,000, muddying the $500 message. Still, despite this and other disappointments, Ellison seemed unfazed. Sitting on a stool onstage at the press conference, he said of this product still in its infancy, "It will change our economy. It will change our culture. It will change everything." Later that year, in an interview with *Fortune,* he described his NC efforts this way: like "grabbing this Archimedean lever and moving the world."

A SIGNAL TRAIT of Bill Gates's is that he underestimates no one. Larry Ellison was falling on his face, but even so he was threatening Microsoft's crown jewels. The company would increase security even if Ellison was acting no more competent than a two-bit two-story man.

On a chilly Seattle day in January 1997, Gates ambled onstage to address a meeting of his top staff. The collar of Gates's crewneck sweater was off center, bunched up at the shoulder, making him look lopsided. His hair was something to behold, an uncombed mass sticking out every which way, looking like an upside-down bird's nest after a storm or the hair of a housewife who'd fled the beauty parlor midhairdo. He must have known a video team was taping the address for the Microsoft employees, but he must not have cared.

He began with a prepared twenty-minute speech addressing the "threat" posed by the network computer to "core assets" such as Windows and Microsoft Office. Ellison has hit Microsoft where it's vulnerable, he confessed. The PC *is* ridiculously complex. Uninstalling a software product is hard, he said—and other basic tasks he called "beyond opaque." Just the other day, he said, Ballmer's hard drive crashed, yet the company's top support people couldn't rescue many of his files. "It's surprising machines sell as well as they do," he admitted.

The NC "threat" wasn't even a few weeks old when Microsoft assigned a team to study the problem. The company's biggest corporate customers said they liked the idea of computers that could be centrally managed over a network—so Microsoft offered every corporate customer, free of charge, what it called its Zero Administration Kit, software that gave system managers new levels of control over every Windows-based PC in their shop. Microsoft and its usual hardware partners also unveiled what they called a Network PC, or NetPC. The NetPC was a regular Intel-based PC, complete with hard drive and loaded with memory, except that it had no floppy disk drive. The truth was, the NetPC was something of a fraud—"a standard PC with duct tape over the floppy drive," wrote *ComputerWorld* editor Paul Gillin— but what mattered was that Microsoft and Intel had its entry in what was largely a PR battle anyway. The company also announced it was developing a Windows terminal—its offering in the bank teller/airline reservationist market.

Microsoft also invested heavily in a different kind of Internet appliance when it bought WebTV Networks, a small Valley-based start-up that had scooped the market with an easy-to-use, mass-market device that allowed users to navigate the Internet and receive e-mail hooked to a television set. There were more than 100,000 of these devices, which sold for $325 including the keyboard, on the market when Microsoft bought the company, yet several more months would pass before the first consumer product based on the Oracle network computer design hit the store shelves.

Ellison called this phenomenon the "four stages of Microsoft." Dismissing an idea as ill conceived and unworkable is phase one.* Phase two comes when the company allows that there might be some merit to the idea after all (Gates's admission that the PC is an overly complex device); phase three occurs when Microsoft releases a competing product. Phase four? That's when Microsoft claims the product was its idea in the first place.

"The thing I find most contemptible is Bill's lying, this thing about innovating," Ellison said in a speech delivered at Harvard. "It makes me want to puke."

---

* "That's Myhrvold's job," Ellison told *Upside* more than a year after Myhrvold supposedly called him a liar. "To ridicule other people's ideas when Microsoft is about to steal them."

. . .

ELLISON ALWAYS HAD a passion for foot-stomping company meetings, but no one could remember one quite so elaborate or fervid as the one he hosted in November 1996. From around the world the company's management team, six hundred people strong, arrived in the Valley for what could only be described as an old-fashioned pep rally. One slide flashed on a giant screen showed a computer-generated image of Gates giving the crowd the finger; another showed a starving sharecropper, during which Ray Lane, the company's number two, warned, "This is you if Bill Gates has his way."*

Yet it was Ellison who was proving to be his own worst enemy. Without anyone pressing him to do so, he had promised that more than a dozen major manufacturers from around the world would be mass-producing the NC by the summer of 1996. But the autumn came and went without a single NC being sold. To maintain momentum, Oracle set up a series of high-profile demos. In Atlanta, Ellison and Ted Turner took the stage to announce a Web partnership between Oracle and CNN. Ellison's NC machine froze. In Los Angeles, he bathed in applause at an Oracle developers' conference—until the NC again let him down, crashing not once but twice during an event Ellison dubbed a "disaster." More demos and crashes followed, leaving Ellison in the spotlight with egg running down his face. Compounding Oracle's misery, every staged appearance distracted the NC development team, causing it to drop everything to slap together a box to meet the boss's demo deadline.

Initially, Oracle thought it would compete with Netscape by writing a browser tailored to the NC. But then it ditched the project after more than a year of trying. Its engineers spent months on a product code-named "Hat Trick" (essentially Microsoft Office for an NC—a word processor, a spreadsheet, and a low-end database product)—and ended up abandoning that project as well.

---

* Until 1992, Ray Lane lived in Dallas and worked as a top executive with the management consulting firm Booz·Allen & Hamilton. To woo him away, Ellison offered him a 100,000-share option package—but when Lane said he still wasn't interested in the job, Ellison tripled his offer. (In mid-1998, those shares were worth more than $30 million.) Within a few years at Oracle, Lane had divorced his wife, married his secretary, and bought one of Ellison's used Ferraris. He also bought a monster home in Atherton that one guest described for me as "worthy of a fifteenth-century Medici. I mean, *every* inch was totally done up."

Morale was another issue, and not only among the employees working on the NC. Oracle had always been a fractious organization, and the NC only deepened the divisions in his already fractured organizations. "There was a lot of resentment inside Oracle's database group," said Jerry Held, the Oracle executive who headed that group. "They were producing most of the revenues, but with the boss paying all this attention to the NC, they felt ignored." People complained that Andy Laursen was so busy flying around the world hawking the NC, he couldn't do his job properly—then, after he quit to work for an Internet start-up, they complained that the project was leaderless. Farzad Dibachi also left. The man chosen to take over Oracle's NC subsidiary was gone less than a year later.

The more bad news Ellison heard when dialing for engineers, the more he turned up the rhetorical flame. When, in 1997, the Churchill Club, a Valley-based public affairs organization, invited Ellison to give the keynote address at its annual dinner, he opened by predicting Microsoft's demise. At an analysts' meeting that same year, he was asked about a Microsoft product called SQL Server, a database product threatening the low end of Oracle's core business. He wasn't worried, Ellison said, "because everybody hates Microsoft." He sneered at Gates—for his lack of outside interests, for his lack of style, for being the producer of mass-produced middlebrow software.

Ellison's preoccupation was quickly approaching obsession. "Ellison can barely finish a paragraph without some reference to the evil empire in Redmond," wrote *Newsweek*'s David Kaplan. *Fortune*'s Janice Maloney had much the same experience. "In interviews," she wrote, "he quarrels with Bill as if the two were in the same room, even though they barely speak." Addressing a group of reporters at a press conference, he said, "Bill, Bill, Bill—you just don't get it, do you?" He was starting to sound dangerously like a member of Captain Ahab's Club.

NOT ALL THE NEWS WAS BAD. Oprah's people phoned that fall: they wanted Ellison to appear on a segment about "giving back" to the community. So Ellison struck a deal with the principal of a nearby magnet school that a group of Oracle employees (though not Ellison himself) had adopted several years earlier, of donating some Apple computers for the kids to use and then teaching the kids how to use them. Oracle promised to give an NC to every one of the school's 294 students if Ellison could announce the gift on *Oprah Winfrey*. Ellison showed up for the show carrying a gleaming silver NC—an unworkable prototype but real enough to impress Winfrey, who cooed, "That's purty!"

After announcing that Ellison had grown up in one of the roughest neighborhoods on Chicago's South Side, she said, "One of the things I like about you—I mean, you have lots of nice houses and beautiful cars and planes, but you're one of those people who's interested in giving back." That was Ellison's cue to announce his gift. "Every student in the school, every teacher in the school, has a computer," he said, holding up the prototype in his hand. "What a nice guy you are!" Winfrey exclaimed. Actually, his statement wasn't quite true: not a single child or teacher had an NC because it wasn't yet on the market.

The videotape that opened the Ellison segment showed him driving his $350,000 Bentley convertible. Then it showed him sitting in the cockpit of one of his jets. "The man who has it all says he wants to get married again," Winfrey said in a voice-over. And then Ellison: "I'm looking for a woman who is smart and funny and compassionate—and great-looking." Over the next few weeks, scented letters and photos (and also videos, faxes, and of course e-mails) rained down on Oracle headquarters. So then the running joke inside Oracle was that maybe the company should change its automated phone message: "Press one for information about our products, press two for technical support, press three if you want to fill the void in Larry's life."

"He's a total stream-of-consciousness guy," Zach Nelson said. "He'll say whatever's on top of his mind." One time two reporters from *The Wall Street Journal* arrived for an interview on the same day that Ellison had been served with papers in a wrongful termination suit by a young administrative assistant at Oracle named Adelyn Lee. Rather than judiciously keeping quiet, he broke the news to the reporters and dismissed the woman, whom he had dated for eighteen months, as a "total liar."*

---

* Oracle's attorneys settled out of court with Lee for $100,000, but then Ellison met with the county district attorney and his top deputy. He convinced them to prosecute her for fabricating e-mail messages to bolster her case. During the ensuing trial, it came out that Ellison had still dated Lee even though he knew his top people were laying a paper trail to have her fired and that Lee was under the impression he had promised to buy her a $50,000 Acura NSX (under oath he admitted to buying no fewer than four Acura NSXs that year), but ultimately, Lee was convicted of two counts of perjury and one for creating false evidence and ordered to return the money.

They asked, wouldn't it simply be wiser to stop dating subordinates, given the times? And he responded, "I agree, but I can't help myself."

Everyone in the industry seems to have a favorite Ellison story. For one executive, it was the time Ellison had been meeting with him and another dozen or so big customers—and thirty minutes into the meeting, an assistant had brought Ellison a dish of sorbet that he had eaten as his guests watched. For the CEO of a small Valley-based software firm, it was when Ellison had invited him out to lunch to explore the possibility of a deal. "Just my luck, we get a cute waitress wearing this short skirt," he says. "So I'm trying to give my spiel while he's hitting on her. I mean, this guy's over fifty, and he's brushing his hand against her butt, he's flirting shamelessly with her. And I'm feeling like an idiot trying to talk business."

For Jerry Held, a former Oracle executive, it was the time Ellison had been scheduled to address an audience of three thousand in Boston. It was fifteen minutes past the appointed hour, and everyone was still standing outside the locked doors, but Ellison remained onstage with him, chatting about nothing in particular. Held sighed. "A person gets that rich," he said, "I guess he needs to take that extra step to feel a sense of power."

For a time everyone in Silicon Valley talked about the billboard featuring a huge blowup of Ellison's face along Highway 101, where the road passed a pair of gleaming mirrored towers, Oracle's Oz-like headquarters. Then it was all Ellison's talk, on the Agenda stage and in the pages of *Upside*, about his desire to buy (for $20 million) a Russian MiG fighter jet. But the federal authorities put him through so many hoops (and then balked when as an alternative he proposed buying an F-16) that he settled on the smaller Marchetti, used to train fighter pilots. When finally Ellison won a major yachting race, Oracle's PR department actually sent out a press release heralding his victory.

In the Valley people talked about "Good Larry" and "Bad Larry." Good Larry was charming and witty, capable of great acts of kindness. His first wife walked out on him, but when years later her parents fell ill, he bought them a house—and then, when her second husband was recovering from cancer, he gave him a job that paid in the six figures.

Good Larry was remarkably candid. "I was spending a little too much time in Hollywood, enjoying the newness of my celebrity," he once said of his life in the late 1980s. Supposedly, early in his life a woman turned down his proposal of marriage because he wasn't well off enough. He revealed to a writer with *Fortune* that his stepfather had habitually told him, "You'll never amount to anything." His stepfather had saved a clip from the local newspaper about the time Larry had accidentally scored for the wrong team during a basketball game—just so he could pull it out to embarrass him, Ellison said.

Yet this man with a fragile psyche was as capable of stomping on a baby chick as nursing an abandoned one. That was Bad Larry—self-absorbed, cold, maybe even cruel. There was the top employee he fired, out of spite, just before his stock options were to fully vest, costing him millions. When Jenny Overstreet, his personal assistant, decided to quit after thirteen years, she was frightened, she told biographer Mike Wilson. Too many times she had seen Ellison explode when people close to him announced they were leaving. She feared he might call security and bar her from the building; she was scared he would scream mean things at her about how she had never been right for the job anyway. "Larry doesn't take abandonment very well," Overstreet said. When Wilson mentioned the story to Ellison, he said, "I guess that kind of hurts my feelings. Someone who knows me so well, to think that I would just do that to her."

OPRAH WINFREY had its impact on Ellison. By the beginning of 1997, Ellison declared that the NC was about "making a difference." This is what "after the first billion dollars keeps you going," he told *Business Week*. Even if no one else except maybe Oprah was buying the new altruistic Ellison, he was. He traveled to Washington, D.C., to appear at a conference held for some of the country's most promising high schoolers. There he shared a panel with Auschwitz survivor Elie Wiesel and Coretta Scott King. Ellison, however, didn't talk about his newfound notion of giving back to the community (at least once you've earned your first billion) but instead gave them the hard sell on the network computer. Wiesel, King, and the others gave impassioned pleas for racial equality and social activism while Ellison crusaded for Oracle.

"My sister, who's a psychologist, says I have a self-destructive streak," he told a profiler from the *Los Angeles Times*.

The first NCs were shipped in mid-1997, roughly nine months after Ellison's self-imposed deadline. Ellison had vowed to ship 1 million NCs by September 1997, but the company's hardware partners didn't come close to matching that promise. Sun said it would ship its first NC, called the JavaStation, by February 1997 but ended up pushing that date back to March 1998. RCA and IBM were the NCs' two best sellers. IBM shipped roughly 10,000 units in 1997. RCA also shipped about 10,000 NCs—but then recalled every one of them. Relations between the two companies got so bad that RCA dumped Oracle in favor of Microsoft's WebTV. Oracle was stuck with second-string manufacturing, whereas WebTV had Sony, Philips, Mitsubishi, and RCA.

What about his million-unit prediction? "That's a little like asking the Wright brothers, 'If air travel is so good, how many passengers have you flown?' " Ellison snapped in an interview with *ComputerWorld.*

At first Ellison thought the NC would require only a few megabytes of memory. But anyone wanting a machine that can use either the Netscape or Microsoft browser needs at least 16 megabytes of memory, if not 32. That was among the factors driving up the price of a machine IBM sold for roughly $1,000—the same price as some Pentium-based PCs with a modem, a high-speed CD-ROM, and a hard drive.

"Network Computers Fall Short in Contest Against Cheap PCs," blared a page-one headline in *The Wall Street Journal.* The paper quoted a study predicting that three out of every four "dumb" terminals (terminals hooked up to a mainframe) sold by the year 2002 would be Windows-based. "The irony," the *Journal*'s Don Clark and David Bank wrote, "is that the anti-Microsoft alliance correctly identified some trends now sweeping the industry . . . but it is Microsoft, which at first pooh-poohed the problem, that has most effectively used NC advocates' own marketing slogans." When virtually every corporation in America is already using Windows-based machines, and given that employees are already familiar with Windows-compatible solutions, why go with machines that are incompatible with what people already know?

"Three years after Oracle chief Larry Ellison introduced the concept," wrote Julie Pitta in *Forbes* in September 1998, "the NC looks ready for a Smithsonian exhibition on promising technologies that went nowhere."

Unlike Gates, Ellison believes in enjoying himself. He took a three-month vacation on the *Sayonara* in 1997—only to find out, upon his return, that company matters were in disarray. Maybe the company was distracted by Ellison's quixotic quest to beat Microsoft, maybe it was just a bad case of the Asian economic flu in an oversaturated database market, but when the company announced worse-than-expected earnings, Oracle's stock plunged 29 percent in a single Wall Street session. At the start of the day on December 9, 1997, Ellison was worth $7.35 billion. By the end of the day, he was worth $5.2 billion.

Ellison was in a contrite mood when, early in 1998, he addressed an investment bankers' conference in San Francisco. "We certainly screwed up," he said. "We were pitching things we didn't have." The real shocker, though, came later in the year, when the head of Oracle's NC subsidiary told reporters that his programmers were no longer developing software exclusively for the NC. Instead, they were focusing on software that would link television and cable boxes to the Internet. Ellison had ridiculed WebTV as a poor imitation of his NC idea, but now the head of his NC subsidiary was declaring that he would reboot his ailing division by "bringing the Internet experience to the television." That was another Larry story for everyone to tell. He had started this battle, and for two years his rhetoric had fueled it. But he left it to an underling to stand before the press and wave the white flag.

Part 03: Floating Coffins

We asked the captain what course of action he
proposed to take toward a beast so large,
terrifying, and unpredictable. He hesitated to
answer, and then said judiciously: "I think I shall
praise it." – Herman Melville, *Moby-Dick*

CHAPTER 15

RESISTANCE_IS_FUTILE.COM

THE FAITHFUL CHEERED and stomped when computer impresario Steve Jobs took the stage at the Macworld Expo in August 1997. Two months earlier, the Apple board had ousted the company's CEO, Gil Amelio,* and, after a twelve-year exile, Jobs was back in charge, the interim CEO of the company he had cofounded in 1976 in his father's garage. They hooted and hollered when he announced that a new board of directors would be overseeing the company; hearts quickened when Jobs spoke passionately about his plans for reviving a company whose market share lived precariously in the single digits. But then he flashed a slide on the huge projection screen above his head: the Microsoft logo. And, except for a few scattered catcalls, the room fell silent.

Newsweek would report what happened next in a three-article, two-sidebar package that included no fewer than fifteen pictures, as if an armistice had been reached between the Palestinians and Israelis. *Time* ran a more modest, two article/ten photo package, but it put Jobs on its cover, dressed in black, crouched on his knees and—according to a caption—talking on a cell phone to Bill Gates just hours before taking the stage at the Macworld Expo. For his part, Jobs was inclined to view his

---

* Amelio served as Apple CEO for just seventeen months, during which time the company lost nearly $2 billion, but the company paid him $9.2 million in severance and other fees as part of the "golden parachute" he had negotiated prior to taking the job. Filings with the SEC also showed that the company had paid him $471,000 in the previous fiscal year for the fees he had incurred as the owner of his own private jet (landing fees, parking, a pilot and copilot, and fuel) because Amelio had insisted that the company lease his jet as a condition of employment.

decision to strike a blockbuster deal with Gates as inevitable, if not more than a little historic. "Thank you, Bill," he told Gates. "You've made the world a better place." But those sitting in the audience on that summer day in Boston were Apple apostles, those who drove automobiles defiantly sporting a "Windows 95 = Macintosh 89" bumper sticker. Religious in their devotion, rabid in their criticism of Microsoft, they responded about as well as some in the Mideast reacted to Yitzhak Rabin and Yasser Arafat embracing in the name of peace.

They booed and gasped in disbelief as Jobs announced that he had persuaded his former archrival to invest $150 million in much-needed cash in exchange for a 5 percent ownership stake in Apple. They booed some more as he announced that the two companies would share all of their patented technologies and new breakthroughs in the coming years. And then those boos turned to moans and catcalls when Gates appeared via satellite, sitting in his office, a bland, amiable smile across his face, on the screen above Jobs's head. He loomed Big Brother huge, the beneficent dictator, smug in victory, propping up the financially ailing Apple not unlike the victor in a war helping the vanquished rebuild. "We better treat Microsoft with a little gratitude," Jobs chided the noisemakers in the audience.*

A joke passed around Microsoft via the corporation's e-mail system had Gates reprimanding his CFO, "I said *Snapple,* you idiot, not Apple." But from Gates's perspective, this deal worked on so many different levels that it was hard not to shake one's head in amazement. Under the terms of the agreement, Apple agreed to preinstall Microsoft's Internet Explorer on its new machine. That meant that virtually every PC sold in the United States would come with IE preinstalled. Another consideration was the rumors that the Justice Department was again investigating Microsoft. (The two sides had settled the original case when they signed a consent decree approved by a federal judge in 1995.) Propping up Apple meant Microsoft could claim that at least it didn't have a 99

---

* A stricken Mac devotee told fellow members of his on-line Macintosh users' list that he had seen his share of disasters reported on the news, but Apple selling a piece of itself to Microsoft was "a thousand, no a million, billion times worse than the usual string of atrocities! . . . Jobs selling his soul to Lucifer himself for a measly 100 *[sic]* million bucks." Comedian Will Durst joked in an on-air editorial for the public radio show *Marketplace,* "A joint company barbecue between the People for the Ethical Treatment of Animals and the Hog Butchers' Council makes more sense."

percent–plus lock on new personal computer sales.* A feeble Apple was worth more to Microsoft than a dead Apple. The digerati dubbed the deal "antitrust insurance."

A third benefit was that the agreement ended a year-old patent dispute between the two companies; a fourth was the advantage it would give Microsoft over another nettlesome foe, Scott McNealy. For months teams from Apple and Sun had been working to build Java into the Apple operating system. But the deal Gates hammered out with Jobs meant that Apple and Microsoft would develop their own version of Java. McNealy was touting Java as the network's lingua franca—a universal language ideal for a networked world—but like any language developed by two separate cultures, there were differences. Sun's imperative was to ensure that only a "pure" form of Java reached the marketplace. As a consequence, the company pressured every partner to test its software at an independent lab. Microsoft had embraced Java because it had no choice, but since that time its programmers had busied themselves customizing Java so that it worked fastest on Windows machines. It would now presumably do the same for the Macintosh.

One final advantage was the impact the Gates-Jobs bombshell had on Apple's stock. That day, Apple's stock jumped by 33 percent. That meant that in a single trading session, Gates had already earned Microsoft $50 million on his investment. The man seemed to possess the Midas touch.

AROUND THE TIME Gates's emissaries were negotiating the Apple deal, Microsoft hosted its annual briefing for financial analysts. The company's shares had soared 332 percent in the previous two and a half years, meaning that a Microsoft employee holding $100,000 in stock options at the start of 1995 now sat on a portfolio worth more than half a million dollars. The company's stock had doubled, redoubled, and then gone up by another third in just thirty months' time, yet Gates and Company were hardly in a self-congratulatory mood. They were worried—that sales of Windows and Office had plateaued, that the network computer and Java might "Pac-Man up" (Ballmer's term) into their core assets, that they might not be able to maintain their torrid rate of

---

* According to figures provided by Dataquest, Apple's share of personal computer sales fell from 13.2 percent in 1995 to 4.5 percent in 1997.

growth. So they danced the same strange two-step Gates and his lieutenants always performed when addressing this group, dampening people's expectations while simultaneously promising the world.

Executive after executive laid out the various schemes Microsoft had hatched to grab an ever-bigger share of anything tangentially tied to the software market. They were aggressively attacking the high-end corporate market formerly the province of companies such as IBM and Oracle; they were simultaneously moving down into the world of small consumer devices. They demonstrated a host of next-generation on-line computer games and trumpeted the host of Web offerings the company had unveiled in the previous twelve months. An article reporting on the two-day confab, appearing in *The New York Times,* ran under the headline "Jaws, the Return: Microsoft Says It's Still Hungry."

Already Microsoft had built a six-building satellite campus, dubbed Red West (Redmond West) and dedicated to producing what the in crowd called "content." *Slate* editor Michael Kinsley worked at Red West, as did the creators of a wide range of Microsoft-produced Web offerings such as Cinemania Online (movie reviews), Music Central (music and concert reviews plus interviews), and UnderWire, a site geared toward women. Red West was also where a team of writers produced, at least then, the company's on-line travel magazine, *Mungo Park,* and where another team hosted an investment advice site called Microsoft Investor (later renamed MoneyCentral). The company's most audacious "content" investment was MSNBC, the cable news network that Microsoft created in partnership with NBC in 1996. Microsoft's contribution was a Web companion site and at least $570 million cash through the year 2001.

A month before its annual analysts' meeting, Microsoft paid $1 billion for a 12 percent stake in Comcast, the country's fourth largest cable company. Gates said he had no interest in the cable-TV business, but some of the smart guys were predicting that all those thick black cables snaking into people's homes might serve as the perfect conduit for the Internet. Whereas Web pages trickled down to people's computers over the phone company's twisted copper wires, data could theoretically flow like water through a hose via cable. So if nothing else, an ownership stake in Comcast meant Gates would have a place at the bargaining table if and when the various players fought over the common standards for sending data over cable.

And if the Internet's future turned out to be a wireless one, where data were sent via the airwaves as for radio and television, Gates had covered that base as well. He owned a personal ownership stake in Teledesic, a satellite-based wireless communication company. In 1996, Microsoft also bought a piece of Metricom, a company that manufactures wireless modems and a company with designs on a global Internet that operates without wires. Microsoft owned a piece of Navitel, a company working on phone communications via the Internet, and had already bought all or part of no fewer than three companies working on what promised to be the next big thing over the Internet, audio and video played in real time. Gates wasn't a visionary who saw the future so much as a gambler who bet on every horse entered in the race.

"To me, Bill is the great white shark that looks at the minnows with no more consciousness than we look at a plate of food," said Sybase CEO Mitch Kertzman. "The shark has no soul. The shark knows no boundaries. All it has is an appetite. When the shark gets hungry, it thinks, 'I'm hungry,' so it eats."

The big buzzword that summer, when the Wall Street analysts descended on Seattle, was "e-commerce." If 1995 was the year of the Great Internet Land Grab, 1997 marked the start of the Internet Gold Rush, when any enterprising soul with a large enough grubstake could reinvent himself as an on-line car salesman, realtor, or travel agent. That's what Microsoft did. CarPoint was Microsoft's new auto sales Web site. There you could research any make of car, treating yourself to a 360-degree interior view, even hook up with any of the thousands of dealers who each paid Microsoft $1,000 a month to participate. A project codename "Boardwalk" (and later named HomeAdvisor) was a home-buying site, and Expedia was an on-line travel agency that let you search out the best deals and then book plane, hotel, and car rental reservations. The company's most ambitious entry into the world of e-commerce was Sidewalk, a series of on-line city guides providing local arts and entertainment listings. With Sidewalk, according to an internal memo leaked to *The Wall Street Journal,* Microsoft hoped both to capture a slice of the $66 billion local advertising market and to establish a portal for future moneymaking opportunities.*

* Speaking at a newspaper publishers' conference in Chicago in 1997, Gates labeled those who thought that Sidewalk meant Microsoft was getting into the local news and classified business as "overly paranoid." A couple of months later, though, in an interview with the *Journal,* the company vice president overseeing Sidewalk confirmed that Microsoft was indeed looking into the classified business and had hired local reporters.

Gates dubbed it "friction-free capitalism"—capitalism without the middleman—but that wasn't quite right. Microsoft didn't want to eliminate the middleman so much as replace him. Nathan Myhrvold cut close to the truth when he spoke about Microsoft's hope of collecting a "vig" in its role as Web host. The vig, or vigorish, is a gambler's term for a bookmaker's 10 percent cut of the action.

Most publicly traded companies host the Wall Street analysts for one day, not two, but apparently people at Microsoft just have more to talk about. The previous month, the company had struck a deal with First Data Corporation to jointly develop software that would enable people to pay their bills electronically. Microsoft had recently announced that it would be entering the fast-growing network security, or so-called firewall, market. It had bought a stake in E-Stamp, which was working on electronic postage software, and had purchased EShop, which created a product to ease on-line shopping.

"The future of computing," Gates declared in an interview with *Fortune*, "is the computer that talks, listens, sees, and learns." Toward that end, Microsoft paid $45 million to buy speech recognition technology and invested an undisclosed sum in Wildfire Communications, another company specializing in voice recognition. And what Microsoft couldn't buy, it would invent. The company set aside $2.6 billion for research and development for fiscal year 1997, an amount greater than the combined profits announced by Netscape, Oracle, and Sun that year.

For years the pundits had been anticipating the windfall to be earned selling handheld computers. 3Com was the first company to hit a winner, with a product released in 1996 and called the PalmPilot. So now Microsoft was pushing a rival version, called the Palm PC, based on a Windows lite operating system called Windows CE. Microsoft was also working on something it called the Auto PC, a Windows-based device for the car that would serve up maps complete with global positioning and also provide Internet access, allowing you to log on to Sidewalk to find a review of a nearby restaurant. Microsoft's on-line games had once been the subject of ridicule, but since then the company had bought more than a half-dozen gaming companies. Its new offerings were now so strong that the publisher of *Computer Gaming World* declared Microsoft the company most likely to dominate his industry. The company announced a bevy of other consumer products, including an "Interactive Barney" and even a new supercharged, feel-the-G-force joystick called the SideWinder Force Feedback Pro, based on technology developed by a company it had bought in 1996.

With its hand in so many businesses, Microsoft called to mind a computer game it sold called Age of Empires. You start by chopping down the trees needed to build your first village; you win if and when you attain world domination. Your choices include any of a dozen historic empires—ancient Egypt, Rome, Babylonia—but, alas, no modern-day corporations.

MICROSOFT WASN'T INVINCIBLE, of course; the company had its share of failures. In May the company had launched an aggressive push to prove that PCs running Windows NT could handle even the largest computing job. Gates donned an ill-fitting suit and flew to Manhattan for what the company dubbed "Scalability Day." The goal was to demonstrate that forty-five computers yoked together by NT could match the processing power of Unix. But when a Gates aide clicked a mouse to launch a demo, nothing happened. The system had to be rebooted. At Microsoft they "eat their own dog food"—that is, they use NT to handle vital internal chores such as e-mail delivery. So Microsoft employees are always complaining about the company's e-mail system and how sometimes it takes hours to send a supposedly instantaneously delivered message to an office just down the hall.

Walt Mossberg, author of *The Wall Street Journal*'s influential "Personal Technology" column, dismissed version one of the Palm PC as a device with a screen so dim he could barely read it and a keyboard so small his fingers tended to cramp up. MSNBC was a huge money loser, but not as big a loser as Microsoft Network, which some analysts suspected had lost $500 million in two years. Losses at other on-line ventures prompted the company to shut down its Cinemania Online and Music Central sites, fold the *Mungo Park* travel magazine, and lay off some of its Sidewalk staff. *Slate* was proving to be the financial sinkhole that all the big-foot pundits had figured it would be, so the company announced that it would start charging to read the magazine. Then it changed its mind—and when, months later, it did impose a $19.95 annual subscription fee, readership plummeted.

Yet those same articles underscoring NT's many flaws cast it as inevitable. "I can't stand Microsoft," a systems manager would tell a reporter—but then in the next breath she would add that she'd be a fool not to seriously consider NT when she could simplify every user's life by buying, from a single vendor, this product meant to work hand in glove with the PCs sitting on every employee's desk, rather than a hodgepodge of products. Microsoft, the dogged terrier nipping at the heels of Sun and IBM and Oracle, would endure the insults and work slavish hours getting out a new version of NT no matter how much the reviewers ridiculed the early "beta" versions of NT 5 and no matter how long it took. Whereas the company earned roughly $40 in profits per PC, it collected more than $100 per PC loaded with NT.

When reviewing version 2 of Microsoft's Palm PC, Mossberg was kinder. It still wasn't quite the PalmPilot, but it was getting there. The company didn't dump the Sidewalk guides but instead reinvented them as a series of e-commerce sites through which visitors could purchase goods from local retailers willing to pay Microsoft a transaction fee (Myhrvold's "vig") in exchange for a spot on the screen. The new plan called for Sidewalk guides in fifty cities by the end of 1998. Expedia was already handling $6 million a week in sales in two years' time, and Car-Point was hosting more than half a million visitors per month. And even as the company closed down sites, it opened new ones. Yahoo! and AOL stood to make a mint as popular points of entry—so-called Web portals. So Microsoft announced it was launching a "Start" portal, an on-line mall for its own Web services and anyone willing to pay to participate. To draw users, Microsoft offered free e-mail (after buying a free e-mail service that already had 9.5 million subscribers) and announced that Start would be the default setting for the Internet Explorer. Microsoft seemed to be playing in so many games, it couldn't help but win some of them.

By mid-1997, Microsoft was sitting on a $9 billion cash reserve—and so fast was it raking in profits that despite its buying binge, its reserves would surpass $14 billion by the following summer.* What did all that money mean? When Microsoft wanted a small software firm to rewrite its product for NT, it offered the company $100,000 to hire a couple of programmers. Retailers who prominently displayed the company's products were rewarded with generous discounts and rebates, and so that people would recognize how well regarded Microsoft was within

---

* $14 billion was the *combined* annual profits of American Express, 3M, Eastman Kodak, MCI, RJR Nabisco, and Procter & Gamble.

academic circles, the company initiated a "Faculty Speakers' Program": the company would send $200 to any professor mentioning a Microsoft development tool during a conference presentation. Windows CE, facing any number of other miniaturized operating systems on small consumer appliances such as "smart phones," needed to be noticed above the noise. So Microsoft unveiled this new operating system at a press conference featuring a two-hour performance by Cirque du Soleil.

YOU FLY TO SEATTLE on your own, but once you are there everything is taken care of for you. A shuttle van picks you up at the airport, and refreshments are served upon your arrival at Microsoft's campus. There you chum around with fifteen or twenty of your colleagues, fellow reporters whose names constitute some of the best-known bylines in the business—the Sams and Cokies of high-tech reporting. Gates and Ballmer—just "Bill" and "Steve" to the anointed—arrive last, trailed by the PR muffins along to ensure that no one wants for anything. A pair of helicopters fly you to Gates's Hood Canal compound—and you jostle to get on the whirlybird carrying Bill because (or so you tell yourself) that's probably the safer one. And so begins your forty-eight-hour sleepover date at Gates's getaway, a weekend of schmoozing and briefings that Microsoft's PR arm calls an "intimate press briefing" but that you, like every reporter in the know, call "Bill's annual pajama party."

The consensus among pajama party vets is that Ballmer tags along each summer because Gates would rock back and forth and talk about nothing but technology if he didn't have his best friend and number two along to loosen things up. Ballmer, it turns out is a real grizzly in the mornings, but once the coffee and juice start pumping through him his foghorn voice returns and he's again the guy who keeps everyone loose between briefings. Everything is off the record, so Gates and Ballmer are uncharacteristically candid about Microsoft's strategy. But you haven't flown all this way, nor have any of your colleagues, to learn more about Microsoft's "vision" ("Crush Netscape," "Kill Sun"). You're there because Microsoft PR has offered you two uninterrupted days of elbow rubbing with the world's richest man. The wiser among you know there's something a little too cozy about the whole thing, that Microsoft is shamelessly using the Big Boss's celebrity to lure you to what one journalist called "a weird bonding event" (sour grapes—written by a noninvitee) but you're there so you can say, as one PJ party vet did, to those who ask what he's *really* like, "Bill can let his hair down and get relaxed, but he just doesn't have the personality."

You act cool in the morning when Gates shows up in the kitchen, groggy and hair unkempt and you proffer a cheery (but not too cheery!) "Morning, Bill." You lose it slightly on a trip to the bathroom, when you have to walk through his father's room to reach the can and you notice the display of family photos (I'm in his house! I'm in Bill fucking Gates's house!), and then try not to jump out of your skin when, before the big coho salmon cookout that night, it's just you and him, two guys on a beautiful summer night shooting the breeze.

"He's pretty much a regular guy when you get him away from the office," you'll tell people when you relate this story, though the truth is, this brief encounter was an excruciatingly painful ten minutes of staring down at the beer glass sweating in your hand. You end up comparing notes on fatherhood, your generation's new default topic and Gates's favorite (and seemingly only) nonbusiness, nonscience subject since Jennifer Katharine's birth in 1996. But by the time you enter one of the biplanes that will shuttle you back to the airport, you think that you know him a little better, having at least seen his hair sticking up in the morning and even if all you did was trade toddler tales. Which of course is the idea behind the deployment of Microsoft's mightiest weapon, a figure so oversized that for some meeting him is the equivalent of shaking hands with the president. Maybe now that you've had a chance to get to know Bill better, you'll hesitate before describing him as a predator (he's the father of an adorable little girl!) or will react appropriately when reading some of the more excessive comments written by other journalists, such as when Wendy Goldman Rohm, author of *The Microsoft File,* described Gates as a "socially inept, scrawny, insecure, ruthless Lex Luthor . . . Hermes incarnate." After meeting Bill, after talking with Bill, after talking about his *kid* (she'll soon be old enough to read this stuff!), you think, "Pretty random, Wendy." As if you'll ever be invited to Bill's for a sleepover date anyway.

IT WAS AT ITS 1997 annual meeting with analysts that Microsoft first used the term "noise" to publicly describe its most nettlesome foes. It was an acronym, NOIS, that stood for Netscape, Oracle, IBM, and Sun. But as the gay and lesbian world appropriated the term "queer," or as more than a few women started talking about something being a "chick thing," those companies meant to be the target of Microsoft's little joke proudly wore the acronym. That's right they told each other, NOISE— Netscape, Oracle, IBM, Sun . . . and Everyone Else.

Except who was Everyone Else?

Like Apple, Silicon Graphics was a once mighty company that had seen its market shrink and its stock plummet in no small part due to Bill Gates. This once proud star of the Unix world had also cried uncle: it would use Intel's chips to build Windows-based machines to run its 3-D graphics software. "Windows has become the air and water of the computer industry," the company's CEO told analysts.

Stac Electronics was the tiny compression software company that in 1994 won a $120 million jury verdict against Microsoft after accusing the software giant of stealing its technology. "A lot of people make the analogy that competing with Bill Gates is like playing hardball," Stac CEO Gary Clow said at the time. "I'd say it's more like a knife fight." Yet when I sent an e-mail to Clow asking to talk with him about his dealings with Gates, he wrote back, "I really prefer to maintain a low profile." Microsoft had announced it was appealing the jury verdict but simultaneously started negotiations with Clow. Clow, seeking an alliance with the software world's most powerful player, agreed to a $43 million "royalty" payment rather than battling Microsoft through a lengthy appeals process. It also sold Microsoft a 15 percent stake in Stac for another $40 million. A cynic might argue that Microsoft bought Clow's silence, but could you blame Clow, who described the settlement as a matter of "good business sense"?

At AOL, a top employee drove a car with a license plate that read "FG8S" (Fuck Gates), and when Microsoft released MSN, AOL set up a mock war room to track Microsoft's encroachment on its business. But Microsoft then agreed to put the AOL icon on its opening screen, so in May 1997, there was AOL CEO Steve Case, who a few years earlier had joined the chorus of those accusing Gates of violating the country's antitrust laws, feasting on salmon and fiddlehead fern bisque in the dining room of Gates's not-quite-done Xanadu, a prince paying homage to the king. Microsoft was not unlike the U.S. government in the 1960s, imperialists who smiled and bestowed untold riches on those who adopted their ways but sought to crush those who opposed them.

Pete Peterson, the former WordPerfect executive, reemerged on the software scene with a new word processor. Peterson had never been cocky like Ellison or McNealy, but then he was never quite so chastened as he was when promoting his $29.95 Yah Write software package. "We're hoping that we remain small enough so that Microsoft doesn't mind us, where Gates has no reason to kill us because we don't take enough money away from them."

Ray Noorda hadn't given up the ghost. He was well past seventy and reportedly suffering from Alzheimer's disease, but he was the main financial backer behind a company called Caldera. The DR-DOS operating system had been rendered a relic years earlier, but Caldera had bought it from Novell anyway—and that very same day slapped Microsoft with a gazillion-dollar civil suit alleging anticompetitive practices.* But Noorda's old company, once the leader of the anti-Microsoft coalition, now, if not in lockstep with Microsoft, at least recognized that we live in a Microsoft-dominated world. "I like to say we're looking for opportunities orthogonal"—a mathematical term meaning at a ninety-degree angle—"to Microsoft," said Novell CEO Eric Schmidt. Novell's board had hired Schmidt from Sun, where he had played a role he described as "the main Microsoft attack dog."

"When I came here, I thought I'd continue to play that same role," Schmidt said. "But it became clear very quickly that our customers didn't want to hear it. They're using [Novell's] NetWare, but they also have Windows. Our customers want us to work with Microsoft, not bash Microsoft." † Besides, surrounding him in his new place of work was the evidence of what distraction could bring. By 1997, the company's Utah headquarters were so empty that the company's chief counsel pretty much had the top floor to himself. A networking company, Novell had been in a perfect position to cash in on the Internet but everyone had been so busy trying to put together a product to compete with Microsoft Office that no one had noticed.

"I wasn't here, of course, but Ray believed there needed to be an equal and opposite force against Microsoft," Schmidt says. "At the time, there were many people who agreed with Ray. Many people were cheer-

---

* "We could have just purchased a license to DR-DOS, and that's originally what we were talking about with Novell, but by purchasing it outright, we got the right to litigate," Caldera's president told *Forbes*. "I would have been happy with a license."

† Said Schmidt, "I'm so personally tired of getting asked about Microsoft that all I want to say when a reporter asks me about Gates is 'Fuck Bill. Go talk to Bill Gates about Bill Gates. Talk to me about my products and my business.' I mean, I don't really say this, but you know at least half the reporters I have calling me have no clue what Novell actually does or that we're this publicly traded billion-dollar company."

ing as he took on the fight. And had he won, he would have been enormously, enormously famous as a peer of Gates. The man who reined in
Bill Gates. It just didn't turn out that way."

MAYBE THE MOST REMARKABLE turnabout was that of Philippe Kahn,
former head of software maker Borland. People speculated that he was
the off-the-record executive who in 1994 joked that introducing Gates to
a young software entrepreneur was like introducing Mike Tyson to a vir-
gin, but there was no doubting what he said, in an interview with authors Stephen Manes and Paul Andrews, "When you deal with Gates, you
feel raped." But Kahn had not only slipped into bed with Gates, he ended
up defending him as any gentleman protects his concubine. "It's funny
how things change," he said with a half smile born more of pain than
of joy.

There are those who would argue that Kahn suffered a worse case of
Bill Envy than even Noorda did. In less than a decade's time, he had
built a tiny mail-order software firm into a small empire that specialized in the small but profitable niche of programming tools and easy-
to-use software languages. In those fields Borland was besting
Microsoft, but in Noorda fashion, that wasn't enough. Kahn started
buying up smaller companies so he could play with Gates in the big
leagues of office applications, including the $440 million he paid to buy
a rival because he said it would give him the strength to launch a "total
war" on Microsoft. But the strategy failed, and the company's stock fell
from a peak of $86 to $7 a share. Kahn ended up getting the boot from
the company he had founded.

Noorda may have felt only rage at Gates—but if anything, things between Kahn and Gates were more personal. Kahn was solicited by a
Hare Krishna at Sea-Tac Airport. Rather than shoo the guy away, he
gave him Gates's address and $100 to bug the man who answered the
door. The two even duked it out in the field of romance; Gates was the
first man Kahn's ex-wife dated after the two divorced. Maybe it's only a
coincidence that after that, in interviews, Gates was a power-hungry
"little prick."

Gates made the first peace overture. Even before Kahn left Borland,
he had started fiddling with software so slim it could run on computer
devices that fit into a shirt pocket. Out of a job, Kahn rented office space
a highway exit down from Borland and dubbed his new company

Starfish. Gates heard about Kahn's latest and sent him a note via e-mail. He hoped Starfish and Microsoft could enjoy a better relationship this time around, Gates wrote. Kahn said he was touched, even if he was still dubious.

Kahn was chastened. Prospective employees started throwing his anti-Gates crusade in his face, so he started promising people, cross his heart and hope to die, that he would say no more nasty things about Gates. "We're in a very different business now," he would tell them. "We're a long way from anything Microsoft's interested in doing." He would crack a joke about how Microsoft was in the bloatware business while Starfish was residing safely in the world of slimmed-down software, but that was just his way. He had gotten into what he called the "wearable device" business as an admission of defeat. "I was purposely looking for a safe harbor out of Bill's sights," he said.

By 1997, the Starfish Web site would prominently feature the Microsoft logo. "Microsoft," Kahn explained, "is one of our key partners." And in the coming months, when Gates would increasingly come under attack from everyone from Ralph Nader to the government to a pie-throwing band of pranksters, Gates would turn to his newfound friend to defend him. And there was Kahn in the papers offering his sympathies.

"Bill's won, I lost," he said. "I accept that now." And then, "You shouldn't fight battles you can't win. You get yourself in trouble." He sounded more like a twelve-stepper who had long before made his peace with his foibles, surrendering to his Higher Power, rather than like a bitter man. He probably wasn't ready to hang out at the Bill_Is_Lord.Com Web site that some trickster had registered in Microsoft's name, but he seemed a de facto charter member in the one called "Resistance_Is_Futile.Com."

AND WHAT ABOUT the named members of NOISE? At Netscape, people were no longer spewing venom but instead talking respectfully about Microsoft, like a Democratic senator who takes the floor to talk about his esteemed colleague from across the aisle. Word had come down from the top that everyone was to cool it on the Microsoft bashing. The spin was that it was a matter of respecting Netscape's customers, the vast majority of whom also used Windows, but of course the mauling Netscape had suffered after poking the beast might also help explain things. Microsoft's goal was to cut Netscape's market cap by a factor of three, but when Netscape's stock hit an all-time low that meant it had cut it by more than four. After another bad quarter, Netscape initiated layoffs. Marc Andreessen was still good for the occasional anti-Microsoft crack, but even he had cleaned up his act, like a comedian hoping to break into the big time. Besides, that was Andreessen, the Boy Wonder who reported to no one and to whom no one reported.

Larry Ellison wasn't about to edit himself for anyone, but he also wasn't going to walk away from a potentially lucrative market. His programmers would rewrite Oracle 8, Oracle's flagship database product, so that it would run on Windows NT. Not for a minute did Ellison believe that Microsoft could ever match the power and performance of the Unix vendors, but not porting to Windows NT meant conceding the market to Gates, and Ellison would concede nothing to anybody, especially Bill Gates. So he'd warn that unless the world stopped Gates, we'd have an "Age of Bill" just as surely as we had an "Age of Napoleon." But he'd also make sure that his company's range of weaponry worked with the armaments manufactured by Napoleon's army, just in case.

At IBM, people hated Microsoft with a passion that didn't seem possible at such a place. So when Java came along, they jumped on it. Post-Java, one veteran industry watcher said, "I saw IBM guys smile during their presentations for the first time in years." IBM assigned no fewer than 3,000 programmers to its Java team—more than even Sun had done—and its top people would crisscross the country stumping for the Java cause. Yet though IBM still had six times as many employees as Microsoft, it stepped cautiously. NT threatened to take a big bite out of IBM's revenues, but IBM bundled NT for any corporation wanting it and made sure its products supported the operating system.

That left only Sun. McNealy made his company's position clear in a series of interviews in which he announced that only over his dead body would Sun become a mere "distributor" or "dealer" for Microsoft products. He wouldn't sell Sun machines with Windows NT preinstalled. He wouldn't sell *any* Microsoft technology, he told a reporter for *Forbes.* And in case she missed the point, the company's number two screamed out as she passed his office, "I will not sell NT!" So intent was Sun on beating Microsoft that McNealy cut a deal with another bitter rival, Intel, to run Sun's operating system on Intel's new chip, even though Sun was also in the microprocessor business.

McNealy, always ready with a quip, the funniest CEO around even if not always the canniest, said, "We're the only ones who haven't joined the Dark Side or caved in or vaporized." So maybe it wasn't NOISE after all but SOS—Sun and Only Sun.

ACTUALLY, SUN WASN'T ENTIRELY ALONE. There was tiny Corel, which bought WordPerfect at a remainder-sale price and then came out with what it called the Corel Perfect Office to compete with Microsoft Office. Corel was feisty, there was no denying that, and its price (the entire suite for $99, versus $499 for Office) was hard to beat, but its problem was a lack of profits. "We have clearly established ourselves as the alternative to Microsoft," Corel's CEO declared boldly at the end of 1996, perhaps not noticing that his company had recorded losses in three of the four previous quarters.

There would be the occasional small company that, seeking a headline, would call a press conference together so its CEO could announce, Evel Knievel style, that his eleven-person start-up was taking it to Microsoft with a new such and such that promised to bring Microsoft to its knees. Farzad Dibachi proudly turned Microsoft away when it knocked on the door of Diba, the start-up he created after leaving Oracle. He wouldn't entertain its offer of a buyout, not because he was set on succeeding on his own but out of principle. He wasn't about to be a cog in the Gates machinery. Sun bought Diba for less than $100 million—five months after Microsoft paid $425 million for Diba rival WebTV.

But most companies, even those run by peach-fuzzed CEOs, understood. You want venture money? You want the people who count most to take you seriously? Then figure out a way to work with Microsoft rather than against it. "I won't invest in any company standing in the way of Microsoft," said venture capitalist Kathryn Gould, echoing a sentiment voiced by a great many of her colleagues. "I'm not stupid," said Gould, whose investments rank her among the Valley's top-twenty venture capitalists. "Why hit my head against the wall?"

Venerable Hewlett-Packard, which for so many years had self-consciously portrayed itself as a neutral Switzerland, sided with Microsoft on several high-profile issues. H-P, another top Unix shop, has tied itself closely to NT. Even top executives at mighty Intel, the other half of the Wintel cartel, seem like mere mortals, muttering out of Microsoft's earshot about the latest dose of crow their partner in Redmond has fed them.

"Look around the Valley," said industry veteran Sheldon Laube from the top floor of an office park just off Highway 101. There was a time when Laube had been one of computerdom's best-known anti-Microsoft poster children. As the chief technology officer at Price Waterhouse, he had driven Gates crazy by recommending non-Microsoft products to the firm's corporate customers. But now, as the chief technologist for a company hoping to strike it rich managing corporate Web sites, he has staked his company's future on the Internet Explorer. "Just about every company out there is making money based on Microsoft technology," Laube said. "They're writing for Windows. They're working with Microsoft's IE team. They're using Microsoft tools."

Jean-Louis Gassée is a former Apple executive so mistrusting of Microsoft that he refused Microsoft board member and venture capitalist David Marquardt entry into his office even though Marquardt was interested in putting up seed money for Gassée's latest venture.* Gassée sometimes refers to Microsoft as "Megasoft," and he's joked that Gates lives by the Foreign Legion credo that you shoot the dead. (You never know when a body lying in a field might be an enemy soldier feigning death, so you pump a bullet into each corpse, to be sure.) But he also thinks that a CEO that would refuse to sell to Microsoft out of principle is an "idiot."

"They'll pay a fair price," Gassée said, "and your technology has a bigger chance of succeeding with Microsoft's marketing behind your products."

Maybe there was a time when more Valley entrepreneurs turned away if Microsoft arrived to talk a deal. But if so, that was before Microsoft paid $425 million for WebTV. The WebTV deal changed everything. Suddenly all these young entrepreneurs hoping to make their first billion before age thirty dropped their *mano a mano* anti-Microsoft macho, replacing it with dreams of a tender offer from Redmond. A Microsoft buyout rose to the top of the hierarchy of rosy scenarios, not quite as thrilling as a public offering but one that offered instant gratification without the turmoil of a roller-coaster ride. Microsoft paid in a currency more valuable than gold: Microsoft stock. $425 million was

---

* They instead met at a restaurant—and Gassée would end up striking a deal with Marquardt.

a staggering sum for a company that had been created just two years earlier, but consider the worth of that portfolio twelve months later, assuming WebTV's three cofounders didn't sell many of their shares—well over $1 billion.

To read the press accounts, and to breathe the fumes of those working there, Silicon Valley was a boomtown smack in the middle of the universe. Yet how could that be when everyone—from the shiny-shoe money set to club-clothes-cool entrepreneurs to crusaders like Scott McNealy—was turning their attention northward toward Redmond? There were success stories aplenty in Silicon Valley, but the magnetic center had shifted north. Some of the Valley's best-known venture firms were establishing outposts in the Seattle area. The Silicon Valley Bank opened a branch there, as did the area's best-known high-tech law firm. Many of the Valley's best and brightest had already moved to what some actually referred to as "Bill-ville" (the Seattle area), and more were moving all the time. They were going to work for Microsoft or for the "Baby Bills," companies started by Microsoft multimillionaires not quite ready for the golf links.

And there were the vanquished tones in the voices of most everyone in the Valley except McNealy. No longer were people buzzing with giddy delight about the Internet hobbling Microsoft as the PC had done to IBM. Now the question was whether anyone or anything could stop Microsoft from dominating the Internet, a technology that had been part of the popular culture for all of two years.

CHAPTER 16

THE ANTI-BILL

Two MONTHS AFTER my sit-down with Microsoft's Nathan Myhrvold, the cable television station TNT premiered a new adaptation of *Moby-Dick,* starring the actor Patrick Stewart as Ahab. The day after the final episode aired, Myhrvold sent me an e-mail that expanded on his Ahab theme. "Competing with Microsoft is a perfectly fair and honorable thing to do," he wrote. "But there are people who take it so personally, and make it so personal an ego clash, that they're destroying their companies just like Ahab destroyed his ship."

Was Scott McNealy's preoccupation with Gates taking on Ahab-esque proportions? If McNealy had simply defended his decision to spurn NT as a strategy for dominating the still lucrative Unix market, the answer might have been no. But quietly going about one's work was neither McNealy's nor Sun's style. "Friends Don't Let Friends Load Windows NT" reads a banner posted on Sun's corporate Web site. The company ran an ad in *The Wall Street Journal* claiming that while Sun loved Windows NT machines, "we're always careful not to swallow 'em after they come out of the cereal box." But even that might have fallen into Myhrvold's category of legitimate, un-Ahab-like fair play had McNealy not cast the competition as an ego clash with Gates.

McNealy was in Cambridge to address Harvard's annual conference on the Internet. He was the keynote speaker on day one, Gates on day two. Onstage he peered up at an ancient wooden balcony groaning with people and remarked, "I almost filled the place." Then, after pausing for roughly the length of a George Burns cigar draw, he said, "I'll be bummed if Gates fills it tomorrow." In Australia, he walked into the boardroom of that country's National Press Club just before he was to deliver a speech to its membership. He stopped dead in his tracks. A framed photo of Gates, a past speaker, hung on the wall. The first words out of his mouth, after thanks-it's-great-to-be-here, were, "I was kind of surprised when I saw the picture of Darth Vader in there." So caustically did McNealy taunt Microsoft and Gates over the next hour that the moderator said, "After that speech, I'm a little frightened to invite questions."

"I cringe every time I'm sitting on an airplane and looking through *Business Week,* and there's my picture," McNealy once confessed. "I think, 'Oh, God, what did I say now?' "

On one level, McNealy's anti-Gates shtick was working. Whereas once McNealy had toiled in relative obscurity, he was now a crowd-drawing, center-court celebrity despite running a company that sold its products exclusively to corporations, not consumers. He was one of the industry's budding stars. A large color photo of McNealy appeared on the front page of *USA Today* ("CEO McNealy Sets Sights on Microsoft"). He was glowingly profiled in the pages of *The New Yorker,* and though he turned in a lousy performance—stiff in his delivery, and too much client-server, "mission critical applications for the enterprise" geek talk—he won a one-on-one with Charlie Rose. McNealy would even make the cover of *Newsweek* in 1997, when he was one of two dozen people included in a gallery of faces in a special issue about "The New Rich." With a net worth of a mere $320 million, though, he was a relative pauper among this group.

Yet as Ahab learned only once it was too late, a preoccupation with so large and nasty a beast could prove fatal. Back in those brief but glorious days when Netscape was running around the Valley declaring Windows a bloated, aging relic plump for the taking, people in Redmond had remained quiet, preferring action to words. And when Ellison declared that the PC's days were numbered, only Nathan Myhrvold took the bait. But McNealy touched a nerve. In one interview, Ballmer referred to the "sub-fifty-I.Q. people at Sun"; in another he dismissed McNealy's speechifying as just a bunch of "yap yap yap yap yap." Even Gates got into the act when he dismissed McNealy as a desperate figure fighting a doomed battle. "The tide of the revolution is rising around them," Gates told *Business Week,* "and they can move up the tree for only so long."

At the end of that summer, McNealy flew to Palm Springs to address an annual industry conference sponsored by the pundit George Gilder. Over drinks and dinner, Patrick Naughton, his former hockey buddy, lobbied McNealy to cool his rhetoric. "But the next day he basically did his usual trash-on-Bill thing," Naughton said. "And when he got asked tough questions, it would be more trash-on-Bill and more of his trash-on-the-PC thing." McNealy made jokes about Gates's house and the obscene size of his bank account, and supposedly he cracked a few tawdry jokes about Gates and his wife later in the bar. That, at least, is how they heard it up at Microsoft, where they were monitoring McNealy with the intensity of a Soviet spy eavesdropping on his American counterparts. At Microsoft, people were not pleased. (Bill's house! Melinda!) Stewart Alsop, who considered Gates something of a friend, was also in Palm Springs. In a column for *Fortune,* Alsop chided McNealy for his bad manners and then tried to give him a friendly heads up. "The ogre is teed off," he warned. "The ogre is hell-bent on destroying Java. And this is a very nasty ogre."

IN THE LATE 1980s, when Borland's Philippe Kahn was giving Microsoft fits, a company executive named Tod Nielsen created what he described as a "Philippe Kahn war room." Nielsen ripped a picture of Kahn out of a magazine and photocopied it more than a hundred times. He then plastered the photocopies to the walls of his office—"to give a face to the enemy," he explained. There he and his cohorts would hold what came to be known as "Borland War Councils." They'd meet for hours at a time, examining every last detail of Borland's competing product line, dissecting its strengths and weaknesses, devising a counterstrategy. Sometimes Gates took part in these war councils. The way the story is told, Gates once tossed a photo of Kahn on the table and said, "How can I get rid of this guy?" So that became the joke at Microsoft: the boss says to delete Philippe. They printed up "Delete Philippe" T-shirts, cracked "delete Philippe" jokes, and code-named the product they were working on "PK," for "Philippe Killer."

Java threatens Microsoft in ways that Kahn only dreamed about. If McNealy has his way—if Java matures as he expects it will, and if it gives rise to a cottage industry of easy-to-use tools and off-the-rack software solutions for communicating with modems, printers, and such—he'll have attained computer Nirvana, a platform to which the rest of the world's programmers will write. Imagine a new layer of software above the operating system; just as Windows rendered it irrelevant whether one bought a box from Dell or Gateway or IBM, Java could do the same if and when it attains platform status. McNealy's familiar refrain was "Write once, run anywhere." Why bother writing a program countless times (for the many versions of Windows, the Mac OS, and Unix on the market) when you can write it once? In that scenario, Microsoft would lose its stranglehold over the wider world of programmers, which is why, in 1997, Nielsen returned to the photocopy machine, this time with a picture of McNealy in his hand. Papering his office with a competitor's picture had served him well in the past, so this time he taped to his walls no fewer than 241 pictures of McNealy's mug, along with 241 copies of Java's steaming-coffee-cup logo. Every time he felt a member of his team had accomplished something to knock McNealy down a peg, he would draw a black check mark across a McNealy face.

By that time Nielsen was responsible for Microsoft's relationship with the tens of thousands of programmers writing products for the Windows platforms. He countered McNealy's message by proselytizing a write-once message of his own, though with this twist: write for Windows, because writing for Windows means that you will reach virtually every computer user on the planet. At his disposal Nielsen had whatever it took to please the wider world of programmers, including deep discounts on Microsoft products, assorted freebies, and, most important, entire buildings of people whose sole job was the support of outside programmers. For Sun's Java evangelists, winning over the hearts and minds of programmers meant dueling with the likes of Nielsen, who, one competitor begrudgingly admitted, "does a better job of developer relations than anyone on this planet."

Tod Nielsen is the friendly face of Microsoft. He's intense, sure, but his job is to win programmers over through kindness. Charles Fitzgerald's job, on the other hand, is to throw mud. If Microsoft's assault on Java can be likened to a political campaign, Nielsen is the press secretary who smiles for the cameras while Fitzgerald is the shadowy behind-the-scenes political consultant feeding dirt to reporters and responsible for all those name-smearing negative commercials. Whereas even competitors describe Nielsen as the nicest guy you would ever want to meet, what they say about Fitzgerald is unprintable.

Java had just recently turned two years old when, in mid-1997, Fitzgerald visited the country's most influential business publications to launch his Java offensive. "Set aside two hours," he would write in an e-mail in advance of his arrival. "This is going to take a while." He was a lean, terminally intense man, flitty and unable to sit still, armed with a slide show that cast every Java shortcoming and every McNealy promise so far unfulfilled in the worst possible light. Have you by any chance, he asked, read the *PC Magazine* article showing that only 48 percent of the Java programs the magazine tested ran glitch-free? Or did you notice where analyst so-and-so, in an interview with *Computer Reseller,* backed away from his earlier endorsement of Java? He was sarcastic ("I'm convinced Sun's marketers and its engineers have never met"), he was deceptive (like the performance figures he later admitted were "cooked"), he even expressed mock sympathy. "I was part of an equally ambitious project at Microsoft," he would say. "I know what it's like to start on a project that turns out to be infinitely more difficult than you ever imagined." He even offered reporters lists of questions. He would ask them, "Which do you prefer, the 'nice' version or the 'nasty' one?"

You could see Fitzgerald's fingerprints all over the articles that appeared during the next few months, even if his name rarely appeared. Ironically, the story that industry insiders would cast as his biggest coup—an article appearing in *The Wall Street Journal* under the byline of two of technology's more highly regarded journalists, staff reporters Don Clark and Lee Gomes—was actually one that had been in the works before Fitzgerald took to the skies to launch his Java offensive. Still, at Microsoft the piece must have been received as if a gift from the gods. There, on page one of the business world's most important periodical, was this unequivocal statement: "There is widespread evidence that the dream of using Java as an alternative to Microsoft's dominant Windows operating system is faltering—or at least, that the hype over it, like much of the hype over the Web itself, is premature."

From Fitzgerald's perspective, the timing of the *Journal* piece couldn't have been better. Like Sun's top people, Fitzgerald was in New York for a Sun-sponsored convention held to promote "the unstoppable Java phenomenon." Fitzgerald was like a guest who wiles away his time at a party complaining about the food and cheap drink; he lurked in corners, whispering into the ears of the reporters who counted most, delivering his usual battery of kidney punches. Yet Fitzgerald wasn't the only one. Sun's partners grumbled that the early releases of Java were still exceedingly slow and that Sun was running in so many different directions at once (the JavaStation NC, a Java operating system for small devices, Java chips, to name but a few) that its programmers were shirking basic foundation work. Two years after its launch, you still couldn't print in Java.* By the time the *Journal* piece hit, Sun executives could be forgiven for thinking it was part of a giant plot to ruin their convention. To prove it was a Big Boy company, Sun had hired a couple of dozen freshly scrubbed, cheery muffins to hand out free copies of the *Journal* each morning. But as it turned out, that only guaranteed that the convention floor would buzz all day about this article appearing three columns over from the "It's Everywhere" Java sticker affixed to every paper.

THAT SUMMER, *Wired* put Silicon Valley lawyer Gary Reback on its cover and declared him "Bill Gates's Worst Nightmare." Up in Redmond people looked at that issue and scoffed. "The general sentiment here was that it should have been John Doerr's face on that cover," said a top Microsoft executive. "Doerr's about the only guy we see who's got the money and the connections and the wherewithal to launch a serious attack."

Reback is a partner specializing in antitrust and intellectual property law with the Silicon Valley behemoth Wilson, Sonsini, Goodrich & Rosati. Over the years he has represented a veritable Who's Who of anti-Microsoft competitors, including Sun, Novell, Borland, and, most recently, Netscape. But to borrow *Wired*'s nomenclature, Reback was "tired" whereas Doerr was "wired." Reback was legal briefs, endless continuances, and dark business suits—what the magazine likes to call "old economy." Doerr, by contrast, was strictly "new economy"—a financier, a fixer, a daredevil living at technology's edge, rich. His was the first venture money invested in Sun and Netscape; his other hits included @Home (a Microsoft rival on the frontier of cable Internet access), Intuit (another Microsoft competitor),† and Amazon.com, which wasn't exactly competing with Microsoft except in the sense that it was draw-

---

* "It's like they made this great new car—except the doors wouldn't close," said one seasoned CEO running a company working on a line of Java-based products.

† Microsoft announced in 1994 that it was purchasing Intuit for $2 billion, but the Department of Justice would block the deal, in no small part because of the impassioned white paper Reback filed on behalf of several unnamed clients who argued that a Microsoft-Intuit merger would smother innovation in the personal financial software field. Intuit is the market leader in that field, Microsoft Money—at least as of this writing—a distant second.

Gates's famous response when asked what impact the Justice Department ruling

ing in so much in revenues (by mid-1998, its stock value exceeded that of Barnes & Noble and Borders combined) that it no doubt stimulated some Pavlovian salivating among Microsoft executives.

George Paolini, Java's top media strategist, doesn't often find himself agreeing with his counterparts in Redmond, but he, too, noticed the *Wired* cover, and he, too, thought that if Bill Gates feared anyone, it would be John Doerr. "Gary's a smart guy, but John's the guy who gets everyone together," Paolini said. "If anyone can make something happen, it's John." Paolini had witnessed Doerr's magic firsthand in the spring of 1995, when people at both Sun and Netscape had adamantly opposed a Java deal with Netscape. "It was vintage John," said Sun's Bill Joy. "He calls me and a couple of other people, and the next thing everyone knew it was a matter of agreeing on the contract language and a price." If anyone in the Valley wore a Superman cape, it was Doerr.

"We're all part of the same family," Paolini said. "We're all members of John Doerr's extended family."

Comments like Paolini's fuel talk that Doerr is the padrone of a loose collection of families belonging to the ABM* confederation. "There's no doubt in my mind John's the ringleader of the anti-Microsoft cause," said publisher David Bunnell. "John's the catalyst for all these guys: for Scott, for Barksdale, even for the Ellisons of the world. He's the one who's making sure they all talk, they all know what everyone else is up to. They all look to John as the guy who can make things happen. This is a guy whose job it is to talk to people and make connections all day, so he has the time. They have to go to work in the morning."

Doerr vociferously denies that he heads a secret society of anti-Microsoft caballeros, but even the fervor with which he makes such denials ("Absolutely positively less than zero truth to it," he told me) encourages speculation that he's the behind-the-scenes don bringing together the families. Of course he denies it. Doesn't Cosa Nostra deny its existence? "There's no doubting that Doerr is the anti-Bill," said the same Softie who thought Doerr merited Reback's place on *Wired*'s cover. "He can deny it all he wants, but he's still at the meetings where our foes pick the color of the spray paint used to graffiti us up."

The truth, of course, is more complicated. John Doerr doesn't wake

---

might have on his company: "We'll probably wait at least a week or two before doing anything like this again."

* Anyone But Microsoft.

up each day and ask himself what he can do to take down Microsoft. He thinks about making money, as much of it as he possibly can within the bounds of the law on behalf of those who invest money with Kleiner Perkins (mainly university endowments) and his partners, who rake off a 30 percent cut before distributing the profits. Even Bunnell allowed that "for John it's a tug of war between money and beating Microsoft, except, at the end of the day, the money will be slightly more important." But people at Kleiner dream Microsoft-scale dreams. And building billion-dollar software companies inevitably means taking on Microsoft.

Doerr, like many of the Valley's more successful venture capitalists, might be compared to a baseball slugger who ranks as one of the game's biggest stars despite a low batting average and high ratio of strikeouts. Doerr is the Mickey Mantle of venture capitalists, ranking among the leaders in both homers and strikeouts. His tape-measure jobs are something to be admired, but his whiffs are nearly as spectacular, like the $75 million he saw go down the drain (including $4 million of Harvard's money) when he backed a company that bet its future on pen-based computers. That was a knock against Doerr: an exaggerated self-confidence that led him to believe that a few smart people in a room, if they worked hard enough, could build a new industry. Another criticism was that he was a pie-in-the-sky optimist inclined toward pronouncements so giddy with expectations ("I think it's possible the Internet has been *under*hyped!") they defied not only conventional wisdom but arguably all common sense.

It's no wonder, then, that when McNealy went looking for a secret weapon in his fight with Microsoft—when he needed to prove that Java was not just a language but a platform with a group of companies banking their future on it—he turned to Doerr. Who else had not only the reputation but the faith and temerity to think he could kick start a veritable cottage industry of programmers? Doerr's answer was the Java Fund, a $100 million pool of available cash for entrepreneurs working on products that would advance the Java cause. Doerr chased down the financing and wrangled the support of a bunch of big-name companies. He helped recruit a high-energy thirty-two-year-old dynamo to run the fund and even established it in Kleiner's offices to lend it credibility. Tens of thousands of software developers were using Java to enliven Web pages, but a whimsical plaything for the globe's hackers wasn't exactly going to help McNealy win his war with Microsoft. So the fund targeted entrepreneurs working on what people in the Valley call "mission-critical apps," the dull but essential moneymaking software packages that only a plant manager or chief information officer could love. Among those throwing at least a few million dollars into the Java Fund kitty were Netscape, Oracle, IBM, and Sun, as well as less conspicuous anti-Microsoft companies such as cable giant TCI (a partner in the @Home deal). That, of course, only fueled the talk that Doerr was the unofficial godfather of the ABM movement.

Doerr unveiled the Java Fund in August 1996. The timing of this announcement only added to the Doerr legend, coming the day after his face was all over the news as the prime organizer behind a Bill Clinton endorsement session that brought out some of the Valley's biggest names. The local Bay Area papers, *The New York Times, The Wall Street Journal,* assorted trade publications, all ran articles announcing the fund. Industry pundit Dick Shaffer, who specializes in the world of venture capitalists and start-ups, was impressed, even if all the press attention paid the Java Fund rubbed him the wrong way. "There must've been twenty funds at least as big [$100 million] or bigger raised within three months of that, but that's the draw of John Doerr," Shaffer huffed.

Hundreds of pitches flowed into Kleiner headquarters over the coming months. But Ted Schlein, head of the Java Fund, had two problems. One was the problem of all venture capitalists, mining for the rare golden nugget amid the silt and waste coming down the sluice. The other problem was unique to this effort aimed not only at making money but advancing a cause: keeping the peace among the Java Fund investors. With a roll of his eyes and a rare display of irritation, Schlein confessed that that was probably the hardest part of his job. At the end of one particularly exasperating morning contending with dueling parties, he told me, "Sometimes I feel like I spend half my days dealing with family feuds."* The idea was that everyone would collaborate on every one else's technology, but though this group shared an aversion to Microsoft, that didn't mean they necessarily liked one another. Each dreamed of knocking Gates down to number two—so long as that meant that his own company was the new number one.

---

* From McNealy's point of view, Schlein may have seemed a strange choice to head the Java Fund. "I've never understood this anti-Microsoft hostility," Schlein says. "How can you not admire Microsoft? Look at all they've accomplished. They've earned everything they've gotten. No one ever handed Bill anything on a platter."

Sun, of course, thought that Java was the ABM confederation's unifying force. Those at Netscape were inclined to think the linchpin was the browser, at Oracle the network computer. IBM's representatives, who were bound to think the real battle was over the metal running corporate America, were always complaining that they felt like grown-ups constantly interceding in playground fights as the children fought over whose turn it was on the slide.

"Our relationship with Netscape is more like a sibling rivalry," said George Paolini with a sigh. "The volume of the disputes is much higher. As opposed to our dealings with Microsoft, who are our enemies, but our discussions are far more civil."

From the outside the group might have seemed as tight as the College of Cardinals. The four companies, or some combination of the four, were forever calling press conferences to announce that they were collaborating on something: so-called smart cards, mix-and-match software for corporate customers, this standard or that. Oracle promised to develop Java development tools for a range of its products. Netscape would rewrite its browser in Java. Everyone endorsed Oracle's network computer.

Yet behind the curtain the key players were often smiling through gritted teeth. One month before Netscape's Marc Andreessen took the stage with Larry Ellison and other NOISE executives, Ellison had said of Netscape's browser, in an interview with *Forbes ASAP*, "I think their stuff is very thin." His advice to Barksdale: Invest your cash on hand in real estate and oil tankers. Andreessen, for his part, in an interview with the magazine *Red Herring*, said of Ellison, "I can't believe people still listen to him. . . . As Tevye said in *Fiddler on the Roof*, 'When you're rich, they think you know.'"

Those at Netscape never grew tired of talking about Sun's "betrayal" when it licensed Java to Microsoft, picking apart the deal in an "oh-why, oh-why?" way. (Handing Microsoft the keys to the kingdom only eight months after licensing Java to us!) Executives from Netscape and IBM, which had bought Lotus, would share the podium for a morning press conference and maybe break bread over lunch, but the rest of the time the two companies were engaged in a fierce battle over a market that let groups of users share files and manage their e-mail (Microsoft was also a competitor in this field). Netscape announced that it was suspending its plans to rewrite its browser in Java, a project code-named "Javagator," in part because Java was proving too slow.* So then someone taped a sign to one door of a particularly slow elevator at Netscape headquarters: "The Javalator." It seemed that keeping the peace would strain even the capabilities of Superman and his high-energy sidekick. Kleiner couldn't make Java go any faster, and it couldn't fix the many glitches in this young technology.

Schlein insisted that evaluating the Java Fund's success anytime prior to the year 2001 would be premature, because at least five years must pass before one can judge such a long-term investment. But the Java Fund wasn't just another venture fund but one created to prove a point. A year after it was established, the Java Fund had invested in ten start-ups, two of which were not using Java at all. Of the remaining eight, most sold products that were in part written using non-Java computer languages. Even the Java Fund's highest-profile investment, Marimba, founded by four former members of Sun's Java team, was using a hodgepodge of languages.

"Exhibit A of Java's problems trying to live up to its billing is the $100 million Java Fund," wrote Don Clark and Lee Gomes in their *Wall Street Journal* piece. Doerr, whom entrepreneur Michael Wolff once described as a "combination of [Michael] Milken and agent extraordinaire Michael Ovitz," had tried and failed to pull off the miracle, only adding to its significance. Said the defiant CEO of one Java Fund start-up who was writing the majority of its software in languages other than Java, "We're not going to die on some religious sword."

AT TIMES McNealy could be inspiring. He would rhapsodize about what lay beyond the mountaintop if only the world would embrace Java, a programmer's Esperanto, computerdom's solution to the Tower of Babel of dueling operating systems and incompatible hardware.

But in McNealy's mouth, Java wasn't just a new portable programming language perfect for a networked world connecting a variety of computers. It was computerdom's equivalent of the Berlin Wall falling

---

* Because Java is what is called an "interpreted language," not written for any particular operating system, it must be interpreted one line at a time. Just as an interpreter can't possibly translate a speech as fast as someone speaking his or her native language, a program written in Java can't possibly execute as fast as a program tailored to a specific machine.

and flowers being placed in the gun nozzles of the tanks in Tiananmen Square. And by extension Gates was the Communist Party boss ("They don't call it *Red*-mond for nothing," McNealy has said) and Microsoft's product line the root cause of much that was wrong with the world. He imagined future archaeologists spotting a "massive reduction in productivity" in the late twentieth century. "They're going to blame it entirely on Microsoft Office," McNealy would crack—a feature-laden hairball bloated by fifty font choices and hundreds of time-wasting bells and whistles. He would describe Microsoft's rejection of pure Java this way: "If you're Kleenex, you don't want a cure for the cold, right? But at some point, don't you want to make the world a better place to live?"

Hard-core programmers were inclined to agree with McNealy's analysis of Microsoft. Yet embracing McNealy and Sun as the world's saviors was another matter entirely. To many, a new operating system called Linux, not Java, was the Holy Grail that would deliver them from Windows.

Linux's progenitor is Linus Torvalds. Just as Gary Kildall invented CP/M to save himself an hour's commute from Monterey to Intel headquarters, Torvalds created the skeleton of Linux because he was tired of waiting in line for the Unix machines at the University of Helsinki computer center. As a twenty-one-year-old undergraduate, he hacked a quickie way to work on Unix files on his home machine. Torvalds made this "kernel" of an operating system available over the Internet, and Linux was born, a labor of love among a loose confederation of programmers who built upon his work, sending in bug fixes and hacking new features.

Linux is a free operating system that can run on a variety of machines, including Intel-based PCs and workstations. Its starring role in driving many of the special effects in the movie *Titanic* is one claim to fame, its heroic performance at Los Alamos National Laboratory another. There, in April 1998, scientists used Linux to link together sixty-eight PCs (Windows NT could connect four or maybe eight reliably) to run an experiment simulating atomic shock waves. Linux pulled off what Microsoft can only hope NT will eventually be able to do. These yoked-together PCs performed like a multimillion-dollar supercomputer but at a fraction of the cost and without crashing.

By the start of 1999, Linux would have anywhere between 7 million and 10 million users, depending on whose estimates one believed. (That's a problem with a free software system: the research firms track usage based primarily on reported sales.) Yet, except for a feature article in *Wired* ("The Greatest OS That (N)ever Was"), Linux remained largely an untold story through much of 1998. The problem was that its advocates tended to be die-hard programmers who stressed its technical prowess rather than its Gates-beating potential. Sure, they saw it as being far superior to Windows; as a Linux devotee put it in a posting when *Forbes* asked its on-line readers to name their top Internet icons (Torvalds won the top ranking), "A free operating system 10,000 times better than anything Microsoft has ever made. Need I say more?" That might be the ultimate irony of the Microsoft story if the popularity of the Linux operating system spreads. It might not be Ellison, McNealy, or any member of Captain Ahab's Club who finally manages to check Gates, but a band of rebels who don't stand to make a dime off their efforts.

"The Linux people haven't come out and waved the flag, saying 'Microsoft sucks, Microsoft sucks,' " said a seasoned Silicon Valley CEO who has been watching the Linux story with great delight. "They didn't make a big show of offering this alternative to Windows. You see, they don't suffer this same testosterone poisoning à la Mr. McNealy, Mr. Ellison, and Mr. Doerr. They don't have Bill Gates envy. They just believe they have a superior product, and they're doing what they need to do to convince the world that they're right."

EVEN AS HIS PARTNERS and some within Sun were pleading with McNealy to throttle his expectations, he built them up ever higher. He was like a parent so convinced his son will grow up to achieve greatness that he doesn't notice—despite the gentle urgings of even a concerned set of aunts and uncles—that the toddler is in the midst of a particularly bad case of the terrible twos. Was he disappointed that Java hadn't taken off at quite the pace he had hoped? "By any comparison—fire, electricity, the wheel," the rollout of Java had happened at unprecedented speed, he told the *Journal.* And why weren't people dumping the Microsoft "hairball" in favor of stripped-down office applications? "People still do drugs," he said. "Some people just don't know how to change."

"I cringe sometimes with the way he says things," Bill Raduchel, a top Sun executive, confessed in the fall of 1997. "Now he's trapped. If he makes a moderate statement, people expect more." In a speech in New

York before an auditorium of corporate customers, McNealy listed face-tious "top ten" new shows on MSNBC, including one called "Ballmer and Butt-head." In Berlin to address a Java developer's conference, McNealy gave out Gates's e-mail address and urged his audience to "flood his mailbox" with demands that Microsoft leave Java alone.

Occasionally, McNealy couldn't help but give the occasional nudge and wink, offering a glimpse of his true face without the greasepaint and rubber nose. On the Agenda stage (with Gates sitting in the audi-ence) he explained that "outrageousness" was his only option, given that he was up against "the most written-about subject in business today." In our era of information overload, how else could he get above the noise? "If I want press and if I'm competing against the biggest bully pulpit on the planet, I gotta be quotable," he told USA Today.

In October, Sun sued Microsoft for $35 million, alleging that the software giant had violated its 1996 Java licensing agreement.* (Sun ac-cused Microsoft of releasing an incompatible version of Java, in viola-tion of its contract; two weeks later, Microsoft countersued, also alleging a breach of contract.) McNealy broke the news during a speech to those in the business called "IT managers"—people responsible for managing the complex computer systems that run the country's largest companies. McNealy mimicked Gates by rocking back and forth and re-peating in a high, whistly voice, "Java is just a programming language, Java is just a programming language."

---

* In November 1998, a federal judge ordered Microsoft to rewrite parts of Windows 98 and Internet Explorer so that they complied with Sun's version of Java. The ruling was far-reaching for a preliminary injunction, but one the judge imposed because of the "strong likelihood" that Sun would prevail in a full trial. In December, the judge ordered the two sides to begin settlement talks aimed at avoiding a trial.

CHAPTER 17

THE LOVE SONG OF
RALPH NADER

BILL GATES FINALLY MOVED into his new house just after Labor Day 1997. He might have figured that that meant the end of the preoccupation with his accommodations, but there was at least one more round to endure as the media granted this entirely pedestrian event—a couple and their toddler moving into a new home—roughly the same attention as it gives, say, a plane that crashes but with no Americans on board. The major wire services filed dispatches that were picked up by newspapers around the country. The blessed event even generated a four-page spread that *U.S. News & World Report* promoted on its cover. The public radio show *Marketplace* invited listeners to suggest an appropriate housewarming gift (among the suggestions: a case of Lemon Pledge to clean all those wood surfaces) after opening with a quote from George Bernard Shaw, who had said of the Hearst castle, "It's what God would have built if God had the money."

Gates's mansion came in so horrifically over budget as to defy comprehension. In 1991, Gates estimated that his estate would cost roughly $10 million. That figure jumped to $25 million by the time the first concrete was poured. The wires reported a final price tag of $50 million, but the figure was $60 million in *Vanity Fair. U.S. News,* which had obviously invested the most in the story, placed the number at $100 million. The magazine's best tidbit was its revelation that Gates had had inscribed this quote from F. Scott Fitzgerald's *The Great Gatsby* around the dome of the compound's library: "He had come a long way to this blue lawn and his dream must have seemed so close he could hardly fail to grasp it."

Officially, the home was worth $53 million, according to the county assessor's office. But Gates disagreed, filing papers to have the assessed value lowered, protesting the annual $620,000 in property taxes owed on a $53 million home. How big a property tax bill was that to the likes of a Bill Gates? To borrow Brad Templeton's notion of "Gates dollars," that's an annual tax bill roughly equivalent to $1.50 to a family home worth $100,000. That fall, Gates's net worth had jumped by $2 billion on a single morning.

In *The Road Ahead,* when writing about his home, Gates told the reader that he sought "craftsmanship but nothing ostentatious." Apparently other, stronger forces prevailed. He was never an ascetic like John D. Rockefeller, but he was also never the billionaire equivalent of the boomer who has no room for a fresh-pasta machine because the bread maker and sushi-rice roller occupy too much counter space. He ate tuna fish sandwiches for lunch at his desk, and he used the discount coupons his friend Warren Buffett, a major stockholder in McDonald's, periodically sent over. Still, he was someone who had once told *USA Today,* "I have an infinite amount of money"—and he seemed intent on spending it on this one project.

The new home had twenty-four bathrooms, six kitchens, and a garage so large—6,300 square feet—that it was nearly four times the size of the average U.S. home, according to the National Association of Realtors. The exercise facility, *U.S. News* reported, was "better appointed than many health clubs." There were a helipad, a twenty-seat Art Deco movie theater, and two dining rooms: a more intimate room that sat twenty-four guests and a larger one that doubled as a reception hall that could seat 150. There were the innumerable technogadgets Gates had had built for the house: a sound system that could sense who was in the room and play that person's programmed preferences; video monitors that displayed a menu of art masterpieces depending on one's mood; and a light system that changed depending on the ambient light. Some saw the home as the perfect metaphor for the Microsoft product line: a feature-laden, excessive, bigger-is-better behemoth delivered over budget and years overdue.*

Those defending Gates's homage to himself (the one indulgence of a

---

* Shortly after the Gateses moved in, a spoof making its way around the Internet imagined a conversation between Gates and the contractor. Gates complains that the light sockets are the wrong size. "Oh, those bulbs aren't plug and play," says the contractor. "You'll have to upgrade to the new bulbs." He tells Gates that the only solution to the toilet that won't stop flushing is to completely shut down the water system and then reboot.

man who works so hard for his money!) argue that his home doubles as a venue for business functions. It's a point Gates himself raised when years earlier he proposed to Microsoft's board of directors that the company defray some of the cost of building this technopalace. "Ours is a board that doesn't find itself disagreeing much with Bill," David Marquardt said. "That, however, was one of those times."

The timing of the move couldn't have been more perfect. The asterisk had been dropped from Gates's name that fall when his net worth surpassed that of the sultan of Brunei. Gates was now officially the world's richest man, royalty included. Arguably, he was the richest man to ever walk the planet, even factoring in inflation. *The New York Times* calculated that if Microsoft stock grew at its then-current rate, Gates would become the world's first trillionaire by age forty-eight. At that same pace, he'd own *everything* by the year 2020—all the world's real estate, every share of stock, the assets of every bank. But true pleasure, if you were Bill Gates, wasn't in making more money but in seeing your competition falter. It was seeing the guys on his Internet team working hard, knowing that their hard work was paying off.

The deals the Internet Explorer group had muscled their way into were succeeding. The browser's market share was nearing 40 percent, increasing fourfold in twelve month's time. Netscape's big-mouthed Boy Wonder, the $100 million man whom the media had touted as the next Bill Gates, was now a guy who had lost more than $75 million in twelve months' time. And there was Sun: the even bigger-mouthed McNealy blared on, but his company showed it was feeling the NT pinch when it released a cheaper line of workstations. Wall Street understood—after peaking at $50 that summer, Sun's stock was nosediving, hovering in the low 40s that October and heading lower still.*

Then there was Larry Ellison, Mr. You-Ain't-Nobody-Till-You're-Number-One. He would distinguish himself in ways Gates hadn't, all right. When, that autumn, Oracle's stock fell by nearly a third in a single six-hour session, the tumble set off a NASDAQ record for the most shares traded in a single session—except that technically it wasn't a

---

Other problems won't be fixed until the next release, which may or may not be out next year.

    * Sun's nosedive was temporary. By the start of 1999, the company's stock would be trading at more than $90 a share. Sun's raised profile, not to mention its white-hot Web server sales, were fueling Sun's Microsoft-like growth.

record because that had been set by some penny stock years back, so he took second place even on that dubious distinction list. When Ellison dropped from number four on the Forbes 400 list, the cherry atop the Bill Gates parfait was that Ballmer moved into the spot Ellison vacated.

Gates was feeling so swell in October 1997 he even decided to buy himself a jet for his forty-second birthday—clicking up that barber's chair another notch higher than that of software's other Great Dictator. The price tag was $21 million—or $1 million more than the $20 million Ellison was looking to pay for a MiG. Gates gave a speech at the World-wide Economic Forum in Davos, Switzerland—and though he had gone head-to-head with then-German Chancellor, Helmut Kohl, his people assured him that he had drawn more than twice the crowd. And there was Agenda shining like a beacon on his calendar—Agenda, where he could enter a room and watch the crowd split as if he were Moses parting the Red Sea.

At first the rain on his parade was nothing but a light sprinkle: a couple of consumer groups and a single U.S. senator on an anti-Microsoft jihad. Gates was alarmed, but his people assured him that a few stone throwers came with the territory—it was part of life as a Wall Street Big Boy. But a downpour began when Janet Reno entered the fray, charging Microsoft with violating the 1995 consent decree it had signed with her department. From there things grew stormier still. Word leaked to the press that Justice's Antitrust Division was putting together an entirely new case against Microsoft and that it was only a question of time before the company would face an entirely new set of charges. These same dispatches reported on the half-dozen state attorneys general looking into Microsoft's affairs. The numbers kept swelling—from nine to eleven to twenty. Then investigators from Japan and the European Union stepped in. It got so the hallways in some corridors of Microsoft were full of so many boxes of subpoenaed evidence that you had to turn sideways and walk like a crab just to get by.

According to people close to Gates, the boss cried when he heard the news that the government was again nosing into Microsoft's business. And he would shed more tears over the coming months as the ranks of officials aligned against him swelled. *I just want to make great software,* he'd say. *I only want to come to work every day and do the best job I can. But now this—and it doesn't stop.* His eyes watery and red, his reedy voice heavy and full, he'd ask pleadingly, "Why does everybody hate me?"

. . .

A BILLION DOLLARS is a million dollars times a thousand. According to that October's Forbes 400 list, Gates was worth $40 billion. From a set of products that didn't really exist except as magnetic impulses—nothing but a series of zeros and ones the company sells on CD-ROMs stamped out for pennies—this one man had the net worth of forty thousand millionaires rolled into one.

The upsides of being a billionaire are obvious. You don't sweat the mortgage payment each month, you buy that special vintner's reserve if it strikes your fancy while perusing the wine list. To inaugurate your cool new dining room—the one that comfortably seats 150—you announce what you call a "CEO summit," and Vice President Al Gore, presidential hopeful Steve Forbes, and Washington's governor are among those RSVPing in the affirmative. You find yourself taking a few days of R and R at Martha's Vineyard, visiting with Katharine Graham—in your circles just "Kay"—at her summer home, when you hear from Bill Clinton's people: Maybe you'd like to shoot a round of golf with the president? You and Bill and Hillary sup that night at Kay's—you have a nice time and the president is a nice enough guy, but you complain to more than one associate that the truth is, he doesn't know the first thing about technology.

The downside—well, it's as Christopher Marlowe wrote four hundred years earlier, in *Edward II,* "Libels are set against thee in the street; ballads and rhymes made of thy overthrow." One of the trash weeklies reports that you grilled your wife, *Diner*-style, agreeing to marry her only after she passed your test. Another has you hoarding gold in the bowels of your house, a miserly, fanged Scrooge. Book writers publish unattributed accounts of wild skinny-dipping parties and randy sessions with high-priced hookers. An episode of *The Simpsons* shows you threatening Homer about his Internet start-up. The cartoonist Berkeley Breathed, syndicated in around 400 newspapers, spoofs a nerdy gnat of a man named Tycoon, founder of a company called Micro-Squish, who can't get a date with his dream girl until he promises to buy her Norway.

Then there's the question of a prenuptial agreement. For a time that was *the* topic of conversation in the money-obsessed software industry. Gates had already declared himself firmly against a prenup, deeming it "unnecessary," but that was long before he proposed marriage. The Microsoft board, throwing around unromantic terms such as "fiduciary responsibility," no doubt pushed Gates to obtain one—a fight over a quarter of the company's assets in the event of a messy divorce had to be a consideration.* The smart money, though, figured Gates was too much of a romantic or too spineless to ask the future Mrs. Gates to sign on the dotted line, despite his Hun-like determination on the business battlefield. An *Upside* writer quenched everyone's thirst with a lengthy and intimate account of a procrastinating Gates sending Ballmer to do the deed. This writer later confessed that, upon reflection, the story was probably not true, but he nonetheless stood firmly by this flight of fiction just the same: when writing about a character like Gates, larger than life and therefore terribly overexposed, reaching a higher truth sometimes means fudging the facts. "You can't be interesting about Bill Gates," he said, "unless you leap from the literal and move into something more symbolic."

Possessing the net worth of forty thousand millionaires meant that profile writers and armchair shrinks dissect you as though you were a formaldehyde-soaked frog, asking how it *feels* to have enough money to buy Nigeria if the whim hits you. It means that your every idiosyncrasy and foible see print: the shower you didn't take before a big meeting, your dandruff, the way you walk. Every blooper is fodder for entertainment.

A $40 billion nest egg also means that we as a society need to knock you off the pedestal that we put you on, to tame you, to fit you into an oddly shaped box. Consider Albert Einstein. There's the theory of relativity, of course, but when I was a teen the thing that really stuck in my head about Einstein was that once he was supposedly so distracted by some Big Thought that he walked away from his car, motor running, parked at a traffic light. The story is a great one, but who knows if it's true or merely urban legend? We want to understand a man who in his twenties can scribble a mathematical formula on a chalkboard and give rise to the nuclear age, so we writ him smaller than life or larger than life—just as long as we render him different from the rest of us. Sure, this mass of brain matter can figure out that $E = mc^2$, but can he drive to the store? He's a genius, but can he remember to zip his fly after flushing?

Gates is no Einstein; in that realm, he's a bit player compared to

* Microsoft's Pam Edstrom vehemently denied that the Gateses signed a prenup, but one Microsoft executive laughed when he heard that denial and said, "Right, and violins play whenever Bill and Melinda kiss."

those who did the truly groundbreaking work on the computer. But his wealth places him in that same man-for-the-ages stratosphere—and so, not surprisingly, many people's all-time favorite, and probably the best-traveled, Gates story is a tale of utter cheapness. It has its roots in Robert X. Cringely's book *Accidental Empires*. As Cringely tells it, Gates—"William H. Gates III—was at an all-night convenience store at around midnight holding a container of butter pecan ice cream. It was supposedly 1990, so he would have been worth roughly $3 billion. For some reason, the store was crowded and there was a line of people waiting, but when Gates finally reached the checkout clerk, he remembered a 50-cents-off coupon for which he searched in vain. Meanwhile, according to Cringely, "the clerk waited, the ice cream melted, the other customers, standing in line with their root beer Slurpies and six-packs of beer, fumed." Finally, the guy standing behind him tossed two quarters onto the counter, Gates scooped up the money, and the transaction was completed.

"He *took* the money," Cringely wrote incredulously. "What kind of person is this? What kind of person wouldn't dig out his own 50 cents and pay for the ice cream? . . . Some paranoid schizophrenics would have taken the money (some wouldn't, too) but I've heard no claims that Bill Gates is mentally ill. And a kid might take the money—some bright but poorly socialized kid under, say, the age of 9.

"Bingo!"

It's a good story with a perfect punch line, nicely delivered, but not for a moment do I believe it. It's possible I'll get some angry call from a Seattle resident saying he has a friend who *swears* he was the angry man tossing down the 50 cents (or from a motorist in Princeton, New Jersey, who was behind Einstein that day). But first consider the source. Cringely is actually Mark Stephens, a former Stanford grad student studying in the engineering department who adopted a pen name when reinventing himself as a popular gossip columnist for one of the big computer trade magazines. His book is funny and entertaining, an early history of the PC full of broad-brush insights—but let's just say that some of the technology world's better-regarded reporters wonder whether the book is actually nonfiction or one of the new breed of "nonfiction novels" that distort and invent in the name of higher truth.

The two-part documentary Cringely went on to produce and narrate for PBS, *Revenge of the Nerds,* stands as maybe the single best introduction to the personal computer ever presented for a lay audience. But it's telling that he didn't include the convenience-store tale in this three-hour documentary—and it's also telling that when Randall Stross, author of the 1996 book *The Microsoft Way*, tried checking the tale's veracity, Cringely ignored his repeated messages.* Gates's reaction to the tale is also instructive. Though Cringely portrays him as someone who views the PC as nothing but "a tool for transferring every stray dollar, deutsche mark, and kopeck in the world into his pocket," and though the book is crammed with unflattering Gates tales, this is the one anecdote that made Gates sputtering mad.

Who knows, maybe Gates didn't want to break a hundred-dollar bill. Or maybe—as he's done plenty of times—he walked out of his home without his wallet and found himself short. Or maybe it's strictly urban legend. But the story lives on. It's one of the anecdotes reviewers of *Accidental Empires* zeroed in on, simple and punchy; it's a story that those who felt like Microsoft roadkill would repeat with zeal: He takes the money! Do you see my point, honey? What kind of freak takes the money?

THE MAN WHO STARTED sending Gates letters in March 1997, marked "private and confidential," may not have chosen Edwardian ballad or rhyme for expressing himself, but certainly he had something like overthrowing Gates in mind. "What I'm offering you is simple," he wrote. "Your life for $5 million." He identified himself as a thirty-four-year-old former army Ranger, an assassin for hire with a 100 percent 38-for-38 kill rate. At first he threatened Gates and his wife, but in subsequent notes he upped the demand by $200,000 and also threatened to take out daughter Jennifer and Steve Ballmer.

This "trained assassin," it turns out, was a twenty-two-year-old who didn't prove himself much of an extortionist, let alone a bona fide hit man. Adam Pletcher was wily enough to send four notes without leaving fingerprints, but the FBI learned his identity when he left his parents' name on the diskette he sent with his final note. Pletcher, an office assistant in his father's chiropractic office, dreamed of opening a nonalcoholic nightclub for the younger set. He had even chosen a name, Club

* Several years earlier, Cringely had told *The Seattle Times* that he stuck by this story, which "fit Gates's known behavior." Cringely, however, ignored my messages as he had ignored Stross's.

Haven, but where would he get the money? On the witness stand, Pletcher claimed the whole thing had been a ruse to gather material for a novel he was writing, but the jury didn't buy his story. It found him guilty on four counts of extortion, and a judge sentenced him to 70 months in prison.

You're Bill Gates, and you read a novel written by Pat Dillon, a former business writer for the *San Jose Mercury News.* The first time you're mentioned in *The Last Best Thing,* a computer-world spoof set in the Valley, you're suspect number one when laptops start spontaneously combusting. Later, the book's protagonist cracks that Gates and Intel's Andy Grove are "the only remaining dictators besides Castro in the entire Western Hemisphere." Or you pick up *Ulterior Motive,* a novel by an ex-employee, Daniel Oran, who has set his first novel at a Seattle software giant called "Megasoft." One employee murders another, security covers it up—but this technothriller casts you as too busy running for president to get involved. Even Arianna Huffington jumps on board with *her* first novel. In *Greetings from the Lincoln Bedroom,* you've worked it out so that your face automatically pops up when people turn on a television. You've also licensed the name Bill.

You're spoofed in *Doonesbury* by Garry Trudeau and on HBO by Dennis Miller, who says of you, "Bill Gates is only a white Persian cat and a monocle away from being the villain in a James Bond movie." A comedian playing you on *Saturday Night Live* makes you sound like Truman Capote. Even Howard Stern gets into the act: "I don't want that guy Bill Gates to rule the world." *ComputerWorld* commemorates the Yuletide season with "A Microsoft Christmas Carol" that has letters to Santa "rerouted to Washington State/Because Santa's workshop had been bought by Bill Gates."

You're the CEO of America's most successful company but also one of its most hated; that makes you a mighty fat target. Every wannabe governor (because what, after all, is a state attorney general?); every politician, whether or not he knows a C prompt from an A drive; every once mighty consumer activist looking for a new cause; and every foe looking for a new platform shoots a quiverful at the bull's-eye painted on your back. And if it draws blood, all the better.

THAT SUMMER a group calling itself NetAction had posted on the Internet a notice calling on people to join them in Washington, D.C., for a

THE PLOT TO GET BILL GATES

"Don't Be Soft on Microsoft!" day. The group's executive director, Audrie Krause, ran the organization from her San Francisco apartment while juggling her paying gigs as a full-time activist, but NetAction was starting to gain a reputation among Microsoft's more devoted opponents. It published a well-traveled, semiregular publication called *The Micro$oft Monitor,* and its Web site served as a learning center for those possessing the patience to read "From Microsoft Word to Microsoft World," a chapter-and-verse thirty-four-page research paper that documented Gates's insatiable appetite. It was written by NetAction's other principal member, Nathan Newman.

The plan for "Don't Be Soft on Microsoft!" day called for Web-savvy activists from around the country to descend on the Capitol for an intensive all-day lobbying effort. Krause and Newman pointed out that few members of Congress understood the Internet and fewer still understood Microsoft's various schemes to dominate it. There was no disputing that. One example was Wyoming Senator Alan Simpson's reference to Microsoft as a "chip" company. But attendance was sparse (only around a dozen people showed up) and media attention virtually nonexistent. Microsoft shrugged the whole thing off, but only after maligning Krause and her organization. Microsoft's PR minions dismissed NetAction, a tiny volunteer-driven group that survives on donations, as a pawn of the company's corporate rivals because, in an interview with a Seattle paper, Krause admitted having received a contribution from Sun. Apparently, Krause has also accepted free legal advice from a lawyer who does work for Netscape and Oracle—that at least according to materials Microsoft has handed out to discredit her.

The next critic to step into the spotlight was Senator Orrin Hatch of Utah, when he announced the first in a series of hearings that would delve into Microsoft's business practices. Though he chaired the Senate Judiciary Committee, and though this committee had oversight authority over the Justice Department's antitrust division, Hatch was another critic Microsoft's minions were inclined to dismiss with a wave of the hand. At Microsoft they dismissed Hatch with a one-liner: the "Good Senator from Novell."* Maybe Microsoft was right to respond with a

---

* If Novell has been attempting to purchase the goodwill of Hatch, the Orem, Utah–based company has taken an odd approach, according to records provided by the Washington, D.C.–based Center for Responsive Politics. During the 1997–98 election cycle, Novell contributed $35,000—all of it soft money to the Democrats. During that same period, Novell officers contributed a grand total of $3,500 to various politicians—

big yawn. On the eve of that first hearing, Hatch had said, "Microsoft now has the ability to virtually annihilate any competitive product it wants by bringing it into the next version of Windows." He dubbed the company an "entrenched monopoly" that entered into "restrictive" contracts that, to his mind at least, were clearly in violation of the country's antitrust laws. But the Hatch hearing featured no big-name witnesses, so, despite his harsh words, the press coverage was sparse.

Then Ralph Nader jumped into the fray with a love note he sent to Bill Gates at the beginning of October: "People in many different kinds of businesses have been expressing fear and criticism . . . you are moving to position yourself as the 'new middleman' on every possible lane of the information highway . . . a 'partner then a competitor' approach . . . monopolistically garnered profits." Then, having buttered Gates up, Nader asked him if he would fly to D.C. to address a two-day confab he was hosting. People at Microsoft debated whether they would send anyone to address the crowd at the Nader conference, and it wasn't until a few days before it was to begin that they finally decided against it. But not for a moment did Microsoft consider sending its most precious commodity. Gates's celebrity would have guaranteed a full press gallery and lent credibility to Nader and his rabble.

Nader's people set a press conference for the following Monday but then leaked the story early to select reporters, yielding front-page coverage in *The New York Times*' business section. Well schooled in the art of playing the media, even this new medium, Nader's group posted his letter to Gates on his organization's Web page—and other Web masters immediately linked it to their own.

The Hatch hearing featured the testimony of a former government bureaucrat, the head of a computer trade association, a lobbyist representing travel agents, and a Microsoft hired gun. Before announcing their event Nader's people had already signed up a cavalcade of big names sure to draw media attention: Scott McNealy, Gary Reback, a former FTC commissioner—and of course Nader himself, a bona fide household name synonymous with public-interest activism. Just after graduating from law school, Nader had taken on and beaten General Motors when the auto giant was still a worldwide symbol of America's might. Thirty years later, his hair graying and his back slightly stooped,

---

but not to Hatch. A long list of Novell employees contributed to political candidates during the 1990s, but not a single one wrote a check to Hatch.

the sixty-three-year-old Nader was now challenging this man symboliz-
ing U.S. dominance into the twenty-first century. So though the actual
event would be dominated by lawyers and economists offering mini-
tutorials on the nature of monopolies, the story's broad outlines were
tailor-made, guaranteeing an avalanche of media coverage in the coming weeks. There was also Nader's gift for hard-hitting soundbites. "In
the Middle Ages there was competition among the peasants, but they all
knew who the lord of the manor was," Nader said in an interview with
the *San Jose Mercury News*. "Unless something changes, there will be
less and less competition and Silicon Valley will become a very major
colony of Microsoft." Hatch's hearing was the filler editors ran on page
A8, while Nader's charges made national television even before the first
"Appraising Microsoft" speech.

Nader's people didn't need any help on the media front, but that's
what they got two weeks after their announcement and three weeks before the actual conference was to begin. A year earlier, one of Nader's
featured speakers, Gary Reback, had charged in a letter he sent to the
Justice Department that the standard marketing methods Microsoft
employed in the browser war—for instance, forcing computer manufacturers to include Internet Explorer with Windows 95—violated the
consent decree it had signed with the government in 1995. Unattributed
sources indicated that the Justice Department had taken the bait, but
only when Janet Reno took the podium on a Monday morning in late
October were those rumors confirmed. Reno announced that, after a
fourteen-month investigation, her department was suing Microsoft.
She accused the software giant of violating its consent decree and imposed a million-dollar-a-day fine for contempt of court.

The suit itself was a matter of semantics. If Internet Explorer was an
entirely separate product, the success of which Microsoft was "tying" to
Windows, that was a clear violation of the decree. If it was a single bundled product (akin to an auto dealer "bundling" a car radio with the car
he sells you that you're then free to use or replace as you see fit), that
would be legal. The consent decree allowed Microsoft to "integrate"
technical advances into Windows. But the narrowness of the core issues
aside, the government's broadside—to quote *Newsweek*'s Steven Levy—
"is being followed with O.J.-like intensity." It was a "nationwide blockbuster," a reporter with the *Merc* wrote, a "cyber-era David vs. Goliath,
Ali vs. Frazier." Reporters were inclined to use words such as "earth-
shattering," "landmark," and even "Armageddon" to describe its impact.

And given that the first court date was still a month off and that the media abhors a vacuum, Washington, D.C.'s Omni Shoreham Hotel stood as the center of the known software universe in mid-November 1997. A reported 500 people signed up for the "Appraising Microsoft" conference, 125 of them credentialed reporters.

THE SHOREHAM proved to be the perfect setting for Nader's conference, a once glorious hotel now slightly threadbare, trying hard to remake itself with an ambitious restoration plan. Nader's point man, Jamie Love, director of Nader's Consumer Project on Technology, told me that Nader had been working around the clock in a crash-course attempt to learn about the business; until recently, he confessed, his boss had been a bit of a dolt on the bits and bytes front.

There was something strange about seeing Nader sharing the stage with some of the paid lobbyists who had been invited to address the crowd, including a woman representing the nation's largest banks, which felt threatened by Microsoft's development of bill-paying Internet software. Nader himself addressed this issue at the conference when he said, "We very rarely have to pick up the cudgels for an intimidated industry. That's fairly new. But someone has to be a catalyst to put all the pieces of the puzzle together." Still, at times Nader laid it on more than a bit thick, as in his fawning introduction of Scott McNealy, who one month earlier had told the Agenda crowd that he only *wished* he could be accused of having a monopoly. Nader hailed McNealy as a man who embodied free speech in America because he had the temerity to speak out when he saw wrongdoing.

McNealy, a rock-ribbed Republican whose inclinations run toward libertarian, doesn't believe in lawyers and doesn't believe in government sticking its nose into the affairs of business—and he certainly doesn't believe in Ralph Nader's brand of activism. But he showed up in Washington because Nader now represented the newest, best hope against Microsoft. "I'm certainly not here because I grew up in Detroit idolizing Ralph Nader," McNealy cracked. With that, Nader leaned back and roared with laughter—the only time he so much as cracked a smile in the two days he sat on the dais. The rest of the time, he wore a perpetual frown, as if shouldering the world's woes.

Microsoft decided against playing any formal role at Nader's coming-out party, but the company certainly made its presence felt. Before

Nader could even introduce his first speaker, Microsoft lit a stink bomb, seeking out anyone wearing a reporter's badge to hand him or her a five-page statement written by the company's chief operating officer, Robert Herbold. Herbold had addressed his missive to Nader, but it was obvious that it had been written with both eyes on the 125 reporters in the audience. Herbold first expressed his admiration for Nader but then proceeded to throw mud at this so-called consumer activist who was charging $1,000 a head admission to what amounted to a "kangaroo court." He then spent the next three pages throwing any available trash at the upcoming rostrum of speakers.

Microsoft's representatives were hardly the only ones taking pot-shots. There was McNealy, of course, who offered his usual array of Microsoft jokes ("Microsoft is the most admired company in America." Pause. "Dennis Rodman is a hero in America."), as well as a lawyer named Steve Susman, a Texas-based trial attorney representing Caldera, a company that had been funded by Ray Noorda, in an antitrust suit against Microsoft. With a twang and a folksy all-smiles manner, he read aloud from a letter a Microsoft lawyer had sent him after the company had learned he would be speaking at Nader's conference. The lawyer had warned Susman against sharing any evidence obtained through discovery, especially the Gates deposition he had videotaped several weeks earlier. So of course Susman defiantly showed a short bit from that video, of Gates sipping a Sprite while someone else was saying he didn't want to see the deposition used at the Nader conference. Then Susman offered the kind of statement any trial attorney worth his sub-stantial retainer utters at least every few years: In all my years of lawyer-ing, he said, Gates is the single most slippery witness I have ever deposed. "He couldn't give a straight answer," Susman said. "He was ar-rogant, he was nonresponsive, he was argumentative."

Yet Susman and McNealy were nothing compared to a pair of Brits whose comments were so over-the-top that even Jamie Love would say that he was "appalled listening to their speeches." First up was Graham Lea, a large and ruddy man with a disheveled air that was exacerbated by a dangling shirttail and the bent oversized tortoiseshell glasses that kept slipping down his nose. Lea had contacted Nader's people about speaking—and, given his résumé, it's easy to see how they would have been seduced. He had described himself as a man with a science and computing background now working as an analyst with a London-based firm called Heterodox and offered an impressive list of honors in the field and an equally long list of the monographs to which he had contributed. For a time, he had written the weekly "Bill Watch" column for a publication called *Computing.* More recently, he had been editing a monthly newsletter called *Microsoft Monitor.*

Lea had offered as his area of expertise the European Union's investigation of the software giant on antitrust charges, but his preferred topic was his pet theory that, unbeknownst to those of us living in the United States, Gates actually suffers from a rare form of autism called Asperger's syndrome. The symptoms include uncontrollable rocking, a general lack of human empathy, a tendency toward angry outbursts, and an exceptional memory but an intelligence limited in its domain. As Lea saw it, Asperger's syndrome explains Gates's voracious appetite for gobbling up markets. He boasted that he had written "the definitive paper on Gates and Asperger's syndrome," and I don't imagine that many people in the audience that day doubted him.*

For months I tried to persuade Lea to send me that paper. He'd write back encouraging messages ("All strength to your arm"), discuss a Microsoft book project he had in the works, and share intelligence about other journalists working the Microsoft vineyard. But whenever I'd press him about his paper or ask for a couple of back issues of *Microsoft Monitor,* our e-mail correspondence would break off. He always seemed to be on his way to or from somewhere—Provence for a ten-day rest, two weeks in Amsterdam on business, Hannover, Germany, for Europe's version of COMDEX. He was happy to share, he would write, but he was always in the middle of reorganizing his materials, or rethinking his thesis—in the middle of *something.*

The other Brit is a colleague of Lea named Ray Hammond. Hammond is a British-based futurist whose book *Why Bill Gates Must Be Stopped* has been rejected by a veritable Who's Who of New York publishers, which of course he offered as evidence that Gates's power ex-

---

* Lea might have written the definitive paper on the topic, but he wasn't the only one to make the connection. *Time* magazine, in 1994, compared, side by side, quotes from John Seabrook's *New Yorker* profile of Gates ("E-Mail from Bill") with a lengthy piece about autism ("An Anthropologist on Mars") published in the previous issue. "An Anthropologist on Mars": "The home of one autistic family had a 'well-used trampoline.'" "E-Mail from Bill": "[Gates] has planned a full-size trampoline [room]" in his new house. Autistics suffer "impairments of social interaction with others"; Seabrook quotes an ex-girlfriend: "you have to bring him into a group . . . because he doesn't have the social skills to do it on his own."

tends even into the book-publishing world. Hammond is a pursed and angry white-haired man who talked to the audience with his chin pushed defiantly forward. His bugaboo was one of the few big charitable contributions Gates has actually made, the $12 million he donated to establish the Human Genome Project at the University of Washington, thereby luring to Seattle one of the country's preeminent geneticists. Hammond hinted darkly about what Gates might do if he controlled the "human source code," and closed his talk with this warning: "The future of mankind is at stake. Bill Gates must be stopped."

NADER'S CONFERENCE was more than a cavalcade of showboating lawyers, peevish CEOs, and cranks. There were the Graham Leas and the Ray Hammonds, but the conference also included the likes of Brian Arthur, a soft-spoken economics professor formerly of Stanford University and now with the Santa Fe Institute. Arthur argued that the real issue wasn't whether Microsoft was a monopoly—after all, monopolies are inevitable in the sphere of high tech, where standards are crucial and a "winner-takes-most" dynamic rules—but whether Microsoft played fair. He drew an analogy to the Great Land Rush. Microsoft has staked out a rather vast terrain with its operating system, but that's its reward for winning the race. The question boils down to the methods the company employed to get there (did they hobble a competitor's horses under cover of darkness?) and the methods it continues to use in each subsequent land rush (do they forbid people to cross their land and thereby make it impossible for anyone else to win?).

The significance of Nader's conference shouldn't be diminished. It was, as *The Village Voice*'s James Ridgeway had declared, "the first stirring of a revolt." Microsoft's PR arm has gone to great lengths to portray Gates as a lovable nerd, yet here was no less a figure than Ralph Nader declaring him a bully and a dangerous monopolist. Celebrity is a fragile commodity, and Nader no doubt prompted a great many people to at least take a harder look at Gates. Also, the central question addressed—whether Microsoft's very success selling Windows rendered it what antitrust lawyers call an essential facility—*is* an important question. Earlier this century, the Supreme Court ruled that the railroad company that built the first bridge across the Mississippi, connecting St. Louis to the West, didn't have the right to bar competitors from crossing it because it was essential to the community's commercial viability. So, too, did Ma Bell lose its right to bar a feisty start-up called MCI from using an essential facility we call the dial tone.

Nor should the significance of Nader and Love's involvement in the anti-Microsoft cause over the coming months be diminished. An intern working for Jamie Love's Consumer Project phoned fourteen computer manufacturers, searching in vain for a company that would sell him a PC loaded with a rival operating system—IBM's OS/2, Linux, or one tailored for audiovisual users called the BeOS. Failing that, he asked for a PC with no OS at all. He went 0 for 14: Windows came preinstalled on every machine, even those sold by IBM. IBM did permit purchasers to buy OS/2 for another $199, but, like every other vendor, it refused to make any kind of refund to those preferring to buy a Windows-less machine. Nader also had the stature to cast the media spotlight on an astonishing statistic arrived at by Edward Wolff, an economics professor at New York University. Wolff added up the net worth of all the pension funds, 401(k)s, and equity holdings (including home ownership, stocks, and bonds) held by the poorest 40 percent of the country. At $40 billion, Bill Gates's net worth was greater than the collected net worth of those 106 million people whose income places them in the country's bottom two fifths.

Yet measuring it against the standard Nader himself set, the conference was a failure. In preconference interviews, Nader argued that he was offering a forum for those who were feeling Microsoft's boot on their necks. He was the tree shaker who would loose the evidence that would benefit the government's antitrust investigators—and indeed, several Department of Justice employees attended the conference.* Yet in the end, the conference's leitmotif became not concrete examples of foul play but pleas for those with a tale to tell to please come forward. The conference was frustratingly thin on chapter and verse. Nader himself addressed this point in his closing remarks, when he suggested that an understaffed Justice Department needed brave souls not cowed by "Microsoft's intimidation tactics." It was McNealy, not Marc Andreessen, who delivered a keynote address, but it seemed as if a little of the Boy Wonder had rubbed off on Nader when he said, "People in gov-

* I spent part of an afternoon session sharing a table with two of them. They sat with fresh legal pads in front of them, pens poised, dutifully scribbling down the name of each speaker, but then ended up writing nothing else. "A general lack of content," lawyer Jeremy Eisenberg complained. Sitting beside him was a Justice Department economist named David Reitman, who looked toward the heavens and said, "Too many cranks."

ernment say, only half jokingly, that they may need a witness protection program to get people to come forward."

ONE PERSON who needed no prodding from Nader, or anyone else for that matter, was Gary Reback, who reigned as the conference's shining star. Reback's opening presentation featured a set of slides crammed with statistics, lists of markets on Microsoft's wish list, and excerpts from Microsoft contracts that he had obtained through public records or third parties sympathetic to his cause. He may not be Bill Gates's worst nightmare, but he has no doubt caused Gates to lose some sleep. And no one can accuse him of arriving short on specifics when the topic at hand is Microsoft. As a former coworker told James Daly, author of the *Wired* article about Reback, "I could be talking about something that happened in Indonesia—he'd relate it to Microsoft."

At first Reback didn't see much significance in Nader's conference. He was largely apolitical, if anything a moderate Democrat who got the heebie-jeebies if he spent too much time around the party's left-wingers. He even argued with Nader when Nader first phoned him about giving a speech. I'm a corporate attorney representing corporate clients, he argued, not a crusading consumer lawyer. But Nader convinced him that this was one of those times that they were both on the same side. Besides, this offered a high-profile chance for Reback to give the Microsoft-as-dangerous-predator speech he had been delivering to corporate America for years. "As far as I was concerned, my audience that day was the media," Reback later told me.

At Nader's conference, Reback focused on the Internet. Time Warner has big plans for cashing in on the Internet. So, too, do other oppressively large corporations such as AT&T, The Walt Disney Company, General Electric, and Rupert Murdoch's News Media. The difference in the case of Microsoft, Reback said, wasn't just that Microsoft had produced the underlying software, it was also the unsavory tactics the company was employing to conquer the Internet. "They used the same old dirty tricks that have served them well so many times before," he said. Microsoft, he charged, wasn't as interested in promoting Internet Explorer as it was preoccupied with destroying Netscape Navigator, an arguably illegal act of a monopoly.

It is perfectly legal in this country to own a monopoly, assuming you obtain that monopoly through legal means. You can even act like a monopolist if you can show legitimate business reasons for doing so. What's illegal under this country's twin pillars of antitrust law, the Sherman and Clayton Acts, is to *act* in the fashion of a monopolist for no other reason than to maintain your monopoly. One blatant example is the St. Louis railroad company that, earlier in the century, wouldn't rent its tracks to rival shippers so that it would remain the only game in town. Another less obvious example might be a company that forces on a partner a contract so restrictive that a company signing it is forbidden even to mention the competition.

Microsoft, for its part, denies it is a monopoly, despite having a 90 percent share in the operating systems and office applications markets, and technically no court has ever declared it such—so how can it act like a monopolist? To Reback, though, Windows is not only a monopoly but "the most valuable monopoly in the world today." He doesn't doubt that Microsoft's business practices in pursuit of the browser market have been predatory and exclusionary and thus in violation of this country's antitrust laws. To defeat Netscape, it coerced computer manufacturers such as Compaq into carrying Internet Explorer by threatening to cut off access to Windows. It practically bribed companies such as AOL to adopt IE. And then, as if that weren't enough, it imposed on them onerous conditions, examples of which he offered on several slides. An Internet access company that wanted its software included in Microsoft's registration wizard was forbidden from mentioning Netscape in any of its promotional materials ("The Internet Service Provider must agree not to advertise or promote any non-Microsoft Web browser," according to one Reback slide). Under the contract, its help desk couldn't even mention the existence of an alternative browser ("The company, meaning the Service Provider, shall not express or imply that an alternative browser is available," according to another slide).

What might it mean if Microsoft controlled both the content and the platform delivering information to people's PCs? To the delight of the crowd, Reback closed his talk by flashing two side-by-side descriptions of Gates. The first was Gates's biography in the *Funk & Wagnalls Encyclopedia before* Microsoft purchased it to kick start its CD-ROM encyclopedia called Encarta. The original was a generally flattering description that nonetheless described Gates as "a tough competitor who seems to value winning in a competitive environment over money." The second was Gates's new Encarta biography; that segment had been dropped in favor of these words: Gates was "known for his personal and corporate contributions to charity and educational organizations." People were laughing, but not Reback, who asked his audience to imagine all those grade-schoolers writing papers on the famous Mr. Gates and turning to Encarta, today the world's most popular encyclopedia, for guidance.

SHORTLY AFTER NADER'S CONFERENCE, *The New Yorker*'s lead item in "The Talk of the Town" was a profile of Reback running under the headline "A Lawyer Who Thrives on Making Mischief for Bill Gates." Reback, staffer John Heilemann explained, is "a man who gets paid to complain about Bill Gates—the rough Silicon Valley equivalent of drawing a salary for breathing." He was also a tough man to please. He was happy that the Justice Department had finally moved against Microsoft, he said, but he described its action as a "wonderful start, but only the first shoe to drop." The government's contempt-of-court suit addressed Microsoft's practice of tying IE to Windows but not the myriad of deals it had signed with Internet service providers and content providers, nor other efforts to control Internet standards such as video and audio.

By the time I caught up with Reback, the other shoe had seemingly dropped. Since the beginning of 1998, the country's business pages, citing "unnamed lawyers familiar with the investigation" or something along those lines, were reporting that the government was preparing a second, more sweeping antitrust case against Microsoft. That February there was word of a two-day meeting in San Francisco between Justice officials and ten state attorneys general; then, in April, there was a meeting between Justice's trustbusters and Microsoft lawyers. The state attorneys general generally made no secret of their probe, which got everyone speculating that the feds, loath to see the states take action while they sat on the sidelines, would have no choice but to file suit against Microsoft. By mid-May, the big news was a face-to-face meeting between Gates and antitrust chief Joel Klein that apparently didn't get very far: according to published reports, Gates was still insisting that Windows wasn't a monopoly, citing Apple, OS/2, and Unix's potential to trickle down to the PC. There was a flurry of last-minute negotiations between Justice and Microsoft's lawyers, but then, in mid-May, the federal government and twenty state attorneys general filed separate antitrust suits against Microsoft, claiming Microsoft had used Windows to block competition over the Internet.

The New York Times dubbed the twin suits "the most concerted government attack on a single company in a generation." Other periodicals used terms such as "epic," "extraordinary," "landmark." A small fraternity of antitrust attorneys whose names were always popping up in Microsoft antitrust articles were inclined to compare the suit to the AT&T case in the 1980s and IBM in the 1970s, if not to the four cases the government had filed before finally breaking up Standard Oil at the start of the century.

Reback, however, was one of the few skeptics whose voice was heard in the vast acreage of paper devoted to this new Microsoft suit. The government was asking the court to bar Microsoft from engaging in what it deemed to be predatory practices, such as its exclusionary contracts, but was not asking for anything remotely like the court-ordered breakup of Microsoft that Reback sought. Like anyone following the Microsoft antitrust story, I knew Reback's general perspective before I phoned, but he left this sound bite on my voice mail: "I think the Department of Justice has asked for the wrong things. Even if they won, it wouldn't make a difference to anybody. Microsoft has already acquired this huge installed base in browsers, but nobody's requiring them to give back the money they've stolen from the bank. They've accumulated tons of evidence, they've conjured up the Devil—and propose to shoot him with a popgun. And by the way, I prefer the phone over e-mail. It's widely rumored that my e-mail is bugged."

In person, Reback was a trim forty-nine-year-old with short-cropped hair showing wisps of gray. He was cadgy about who was paying his bills—he plainly represented Netscape, or at least did through early 1998,* but it was unconfirmed speculation that Sun was also footing his bill. His life, as he described it, was as frantic as that of any client he might or might not have. His days were filled with a jumble of speeches, press interviews, phone calls with Justice, visits with Justice, and the constant stream of e-mails and phone calls he received from those viewing him as a central repository of Microsoft horror tales—and Microsoft, he claimed, accounted for only 25 percent of his practice. As James Daly wrote in *Wired*, "It's like he grabbed a downed power line and can't let go." He had a demeanor that can best be described as manic.

* That's when Netscape hired Robert Bork to shape its antitrust strategy.

Like his cohorts in the Fraternal Order of Antitrust Attorneys, Reback evoked memories of Standard Oil, though for him that case was nothing but a bright shining possibility that bears no relation to the current case against Microsoft. Some have spoken of splitting Microsoft into two pieces. Its Windows franchise would be the pillar of one company, office applications a pillar of another. Others have proposed breaking it into three, creating a separate Internet/multimedia company. Reback, however, rejected these proposals in favor of the solution the judge applied in the Standard Oil case. Reback argued that Microsoft should be broken into a series of separate companies, each of which would retain the rights to Windows and Office. These fractured Microsofts would compete against one another, just as Standard Oil of New York (Mobil) competed against Standard Oil of Indiana (Amoco). "The government's approach is to impose some rules," Reback said. "My approach says that the only way you'll get Microsoft to behave is if they actually face competition.

"If you go around the Valley and talk to people, I think almost uniformly they believe that the only remedy that will have any effect on Microsoft is a structural remedy," he continued. "The only debate is how we ought to do it. Five companies as opposed to seven. Auctioning off this. Drawing the line there." Reback chose seven and even offered his nominations for company CEOs: "Gates heads up one, Ballmer another, Myhrvold another, [group vice president Paul] Maritz another."

Reback was confident that the government, if its top trustbusters had the temerity to do so, could have made and won so sweeping a case. He pointed to what he called the "smoking gun" e-mails the Justice Department and state attorneys general released when it filed its May 1998 suit against Microsoft. "It would be very hard to increase browser share on the merits of IE 4 alone," a Microsoft executive had written in February 1997. "It will be more important to leverage the OS asset to make people use it instead of Navigator." In a note addressed to Maritz, a Microsoft vice president wrote, "I do not feel we are going to win on our current path. . . . I am convinced we have to use Windows—this is the one thing they don't have." Long-time Microsoft executive Jeff Raikes put it more simply, "Netscape pollution must be eradicated." Another employee had written, "Screw Sun. Cross-platform will never work. Let's move on and steal the Java language."

In the estimation of many in the Fraternal Order of Antitrust Attorneys, these e-mails are no doubt embarrassing in the court of public opinion, but they're not going to do much to persuade an experienced judge accustomed to what in the business are called "smoosh 'em like a bug" internal documents. But that perspective prompted Reback to react with a near-apoplectic fit.

"Do we ignore what they've put in the e-mails?" Reback asked, his eyes blazing. "Have you lost your mind? Have all these lawyers lost their minds? What's unique about this case is, they've made absolutely no pretense of what they intend to do. They stated their intent, and we've witnessed the fulfillment of that intent through conduct." Then, with a loud cry, he asked, "Should we ignore the fact they said what they did and then did it? Come on!"

In the months before our interview, the rumor mill had Netscape on the auction block. But even at a price of $2 billion—a quarter of what the company had been worth 18 months earlier—the Street's smart guys were declaring it overpriced. "How many dead bodies will there be before they intend to do something that makes a difference?" Reback asked, his voice jumping an octave. "How many more companies must we see crushed in the Valley before the government says, 'Enough is enough'?"*

When Reback talks about "the Valley," he's not merely talking about a two-county area lying south of San Francisco once covered by peach

---

* Two days before Thanksgiving 1998, AOL pulled the trigger on what *Time* dubbed "the most momentous merger in Internet history": the purchase of Netscape for $4.2 billion in stock. By that point, the analysts weren't focused on the Netscape browser but the company's value as both a popular Web portal and as a purveyor of a full suite of e-commerce software. With more than 14 million subscribers, AOL was already a popular Web on-ramp; adding Netscape's traffic to the mix, the smart guys declared the new AOL the Web's most popular portal (and therefore potentially the most lucrative one). The browser wars were a thing of the past, and the Sun-Microsoft Java wars old hat: the future of the Internet was cast as a battle of popular portals, with AOL and Microsoft the consensus top combatants.

Sun was also part of the deal: AOL committed to buying at least $500 million in Sun equipment and services; in return, Sun agreed to pay AOL $350 million over three years to license and sell Netscape's Internet software to its corporate customers. That provides Sun with another weapon in its fight against Microsoft's Windows NT. Sun (like IBM) can now offer corporate customers not only the machines and core software to set up centralized host computers but the critical components needed to facilitate electronic commerce and other business over the Web.

Shortly after the merger was announced, McNealy met with Netscape's employees. He began his talk with a top ten list laying out the reasons why Netscape should have purchased AOL rather than vice versa. Among his reasons? "The first three are Microsoft bashing, and I was told I can't tell those."

and plum orchards and now home to millions of driven souls working in an endless string of office parks. No, as he sees it, he's protecting the "Tigris and Euphrates Valley of the new society." All around him he sees entrepreneurs and venture capitalists cowed by Microsoft, viewing vast tracts of the Internet as being strictly off-limits because Microsoft has claimed it as its own—so to him a Microsoft victory would be nothing short of the fall of Mesopotamia. As he tells it, his goals are far loftier than representing the narrow interest of several unspecified companies: "Fundamentally, I'm trying to restore the investment milieu, if you will—or the investment outlook that has occurred since time immemorial in Silicon Valley up until a few years ago, when, if you had a great idea, people would invest it in it notwithstanding the fact that you would be competing against an entrenched monopolist."

But is Reback right? Is Microsoft an anomaly of the business world, a mutation run by a superannuated nine-year-old? Is he the defensive player who aims to hurt opponents or just a guy playing a very competitive sport who rattles foes because he's Mean-Joe-Green good?

I keep a file folder I've labeled "Death to the Competition." By now it's crammed with articles clipped from publications such as *Business Week* and *The Wall Street Journal* over an eighteen-month period. Anheuser-Busch, with a commanding 44 percent of the U.S. beer market, felt threatened by the microbreweries, so it launched a campaign to discourage distributors from carrying the beers produced by its pint-sized rivals. Anheuser-Busch offered monetary incentives to those who complied, sweetening the pot with subsidized advertising. Philip Morris, which enjoys more than a 50 percent share of the domestic cigarette market, for years has promoted its "Retail Masters" program among independent retailers: the more Philip Morris cigarettes you sell, the more "FlexFund" dollars you're paid. "Philip Morris backs it up with an army of salespeople who press retailers to take down rivals' signs and even redesign store layouts to put Marlboro in the choicest position," *The Wall Street Journal*'s Yumiko Ono wrote. Ono spoke to one retailer who told her that to earn extra FlexFund dollars, he and his staff offer free Marlboros to those who smoke rival brands and suggest they switch.

Seeking to control a market is nothing new. The Department of Transportation has felt pressured to propose new guidelines to define new anticompetitive activities in the airline industry because larger airlines are forcing smaller carriers out of their "fortress hubs" via predatory pricing strategies. Small banks are being gobbled up by bigger banks, which in turn are being gobbled up by larger financial institutions. The Walt Disney Company is renowned for the cutthroat game it plays—but then, according to the authors of *The Gorilla Game,* so is virtually every market leader in America. By the time the United States and those twenty attorneys general sued Microsoft, the FTC or Justice Department was investigating, or said to be investigating, the alleged antitrust activities of Philip Morris, Anheuser-Busch, Visa, MasterCard, United Airlines, and McCormick/Schilling, the spice packager. The *Journal* even ran a front-page story on the cutthroat nature of the high school yearbook-publishing market. It seems that one player has locked up half the market and is using every device it can think of to lock up the other half—or so the $36 million antitrust verdict a jury slapped on market leader Jostens Inc. would suggest. "The $500 million-a-year yearbook-publishing industry, for all the warm, fuzzy feelings its products engender, is a down-and-dirty business," wrote the *Journal*'s Brandon Copple.

And consider some of Microsoft's fellow travelers in the computer industry. In 1996, *Upside* launched a three-part series it called "Software Predators." None of the three was Microsoft. The next year the magazine ran a feature story about Cabletron, a company that manufactures networking equipment. The magazine reported that its CEO was renowned for dressing up like Rambo and thrusting combat knives through basketballs to psych up his company's sales force. For a while Cabletron and Cisco were partners, but then they weren't, so the company hired two boxers to fight at a trade show, where people got to watch a mass of muscle named Cabletron beat the shit out of an overweight shlub named Cisco. And of course there's Silicon Valley giant Oracle.

"The advantages Microsoft has taken, I don't know very many in the industry who wouldn't do the same," said former WordPerfect executive Pete Peterson. His old WordPerfect colleague Duff Thompson said, "You can talk yourself into an awful lot of stuff given enough time."

What's the nastiest fight in all of software? I asked one source. One way or another I figured that of course the answer would involve Microsoft, but he didn't hesitate: Network Associates and Symantec, two companies duking it out selling programs that safeguard computers from viruses. A few months later, *The Wall Street Journal* ran a feature about these two companies. Said one CEO about the other, "Bill [Larsen] is the type of guy who could sit on your chest, cut out your heart and smile. And I don't mean that with any negative connotation."

That's business nowadays, a world in which "stomping" or "destroying" a rival is a garden-variety way of expressing one's aim. It's Starbucks, it's Blockbuster Video, it's a long list of companies growing by conquering small foes in a competition that won't end until one company dominates the market. Polling shows that among business leaders, Gates ranks one or two in terms of respect. His only challenger is Jack Welch, who heads General Electric, the one U.S. company that by mid-1998 could boast of a higher market cap than Microsoft. The motto for which Welch is renowned? "I don't want our fair share of the market. I want our unfair share."

But of course people in Silicon Valley see themselves as standing in the center of the universe, and in that universe they see only one looming giant that will do anything to win. They are like the baby boomers who treat child rearing, concerns about retirement, and menopause as if they were new phenomena. "You know, people are always talking about how competitive the software industry is today," said Mitch Kertzman.* "But if they think this is tense, they should've been around when the mainframe companies were really going at it. Back then, you basically had two companies, and only two companies, selling applications for mainframes. The two companies knew each other's products inside out, they knew each other's salesmen and who they were pitching and when. So they'd call up airlines and cancel plane reservations. They'd cancel wake-up calls. There's even one story, perhaps apocryphal, that one salesman was in a messy divorce, so the competitor arranged it with the guy's wife so he was served with papers in the middle of a big sales call."

It's a funny business, Kertzman said of the software world. Until recently he was the CEO of a publicly traded software company, but he's also a jovial, well-liked man with a propensity for smiling. He knows that that's his biggest drawback as CEO. "Basically, all the big companies, all the companies that have won, are run by bloodthirsty killers," he said. "Look at Microsoft, look at Oracle. In fact, the question I have about Scott [McNealy] is, Does he have the killer instinct?" He then interrupted himself to apologize—he admired McNealy, he said. He con-

* In late 1998, Kertzman stepped down as CEO of Sybase to take a top post at Oracle.

sidered him a friend and didn't want to malign him. And then we both laughed. It *is* a funny world when you find yourself apologizing for implying that someone may *not* be a bloodthirsty killer. Because how would the Wall Street analysts react if they didn't think he had the killer instinct?

Most of us play a supporting role, albeit a small one, as customers of Microsoft or Budweiser or Visa. Or we benignly say that we want to invest our small retirement stakes in blue chips. But what are blue chips but GE, Microsoft, Disney, and Philip Morris? Even those who can't stand Microsoft's business practices and find its gluttonous eating habits revolting might wish they had invested $10,000 in Microsoft stock in 1986. Say no if that's not true for you, but say so knowing that had you done so, that investment would have been worth $3.1 million in April 1998, and worth more than $4.5 million shortly into 1999.

CHAPTER 18

BILL GATES 3.1

IT WAS ONE OF THOSE late-night bull sessions the two regularly had when Gates was in town. They were sitting in Gates's office past midnight, Gates lying on the couch like a pile of dirty laundry. The year was 1995, and they were talking about Gates's recent victory in a federal courtroom. They were talking about Judge Stanley Sporkin.

For five years, Microsoft had been battling federal antitrust regulators. First it was the Federal Trade Commission and then the Justice Department, which picked up the case in 1993, after the FTC deadlocked two–two (the fifth commissioner recused himself because of his investments in companies connected to the case). The woman whom Bill Clinton had just named to head Justice's antitrust division, Anne Bingaman, no doubt frightened Gates, who, after all, spoke about how "scary" it was to go up against even mouse-sized competitors. Bingaman was a well-connected Beltway antitrust attorney, a bulldog of a litigator who had once won a billion-dollar verdict against a uranium cartel. Just outside her office hung a drawing of Teddy Roosevelt, the Great Trustbuster, dressed in hunting gear, stalking Rockefeller and the other robber barons, rifle in hand.

But Bingaman was also a political animal, a popular D.C. hostess married to a U.S. senator (Jeff Bingaman of New Mexico). She was a friend of Hillary Clinton's. The many accounts documenting this first case against Microsoft hint at the pressures Bingaman felt from above, from a new administration not anxious to take on software's golden boy. To the disappointment of Microsoft's critics and competitors, the case was settled like so many others of this sort, in cozy lawyer-to-lawyer sessions held in paneled boardrooms and then chief executive to chief executive, when Gates and Bingaman spoke by phone to hammer out the final sticking points.* All that remained was the rubber stamp of a federal judge.

Judge Sporkin was a crusty, independent-minded federal judge, sixty-three years old when he was assigned to the Microsoft case, a D.C. legend who had once taken over the government's cross-examination of Charles Keating Jr., grilling the savings and loan mogul for five hours and then accusing him of "looting" his bank's funds. He had served as the head of enforcement at the Securities and Exchange Commission (SEC) and as general counsel for the CIA. He was a man who had been around the block and not the sort to rubber-stamp anything. During one hearing, he described Microsoft's attorneys as "LLFLs"—lawyers looking for loopholes. Another time he said, addressing Microsoft's lead counsel, "You can stand on your head" if you want, but "I cannot accept your word anymore." Before rejecting the government's settlement agreement for not going far enough in addressing Microsoft's "monopolistic practices," he described Microsoft as "a rather new corporation [that] may not have matured to the position where it understands how it should act with respect to the public interest and the ethics of the marketplace." He then dressed Bingaman down when he said, "The U.S. government is either incapable or unwilling to deal effectively with a potential threat to this nation's economic well-being." To Microsoft's more vociferous critics, this was their Declaration of Independence. Quite literally, some started wearing T-shirts bearing Judge Sporkin's image, caricatured in a line drawing as if he were Sartre or Einstein.

For Gates, the celebrating came after Sporkin was reversed on appeal. The case was assigned to Judge Thomas Penfield Jackson, who approved the consent decree at a hearing that lasted less than thirty minutes. Flush with victory, talking late one night with a Microsoft vice president who prefers to remain anonymous, Gates gloated about beating a federal judge. "Think about it from Bill's point of view," this executive said. "This was a wonderful moment. Sporkin's very smart, he has this reputation as a good judge, for being politically well connected. Yet

---

* Microsoft agreed to end two onerous licensing practices. One was its infamous "per processor" licensing fee, which gave computer manufacturers a price discount if, rather than paying for each copy of Windows shipped, they agreed to pay the royalty on every PC shipped, period. The other was the agreement the company had coerced some outside developers into signing: you can have early access to changes in Windows, but only if you agree to certain restrictions on your work with other operating system vendors.

Bill beats him. He not only beats him, but the guy [Sporkin] takes a spanking from the appeals court, saying he had obviously shown himself to be biased. That's a dangerous lesson to learn: if you stick by your guns, you can be vindicated."

That night, though, it wasn't a well-formulated thought going through this executive's head, only an ominous feeling as he listened to Gates talk about his victory. It was small things, such as the small, satisfied grin on his boss's face and the way his eyebrows danced up a couple of times, as if he were Groucho Marx on *You Bet Your Life,* master of his own destiny, invincible. And he thought:

Doomed.

BILL GATES must have felt as if he had hit the jackpot when the contempt suit the government filed while he was at Agenda was assigned to Judge Jackson. "This hearing will be short and sweet, ladies and gentlemen," Jackson had said after taking over the case after Sporkin. On the Agenda stage Gates dismissed the contempt suit as "a very strange case," but he left it to his lieutenants and lawyers to beat up on the government for accusing Microsoft of violating its consent decree. (By this point, Joel Klein had replaced Bingaman.) Gates could afford to remain above the fray. On the same day the Justice Department announced its suit, Microsoft's stock had actually gone *up* as the company announced better-than-expected earnings for the quarter. That meant that on a day one aide described as "maybe the worst day of Bill's life," Gates made another $152 million on the stock market.

Microsoft's lawyers responded to the government's lawyers by insulting them. Papers they filed with the court dismissed the case as "perverse" and proof that "poorly informed lawyers have no vocation for software design." As they read it, the original consent decree gave them the right to package whatever they wanted in Windows, "even a ham sandwich." At Microsoft, there were jokes about the Federal Bureau of Operating Systems—and how if the government took over Microsoft, the bathrooms would be outfitted with $800 toilet seats. It was Ballmer, though, with typical bombast, who gave the most unadulterated version of the Microsoft perspective when he boomed in a public speech, "To heck with Janet Reno!"

Maybe Judge Jackson was feeling the sting of rubber-stamping a consent decree that Microsoft believed permitted it to bundle a ham sandwich. Because though the government hadn't asked him to do so, Judge Jackson slapped Microsoft with an injunction—until I make up my mind in this case, he said, I order you to offer PC manufacturers a browserless version of Windows 95.* Instead, Microsoft gave computer manufacturers a choice between a two-year-old version of Windows, without the many bug fixes that had gone into the current version, or a crippled version of Windows 95 with IE ripped out—the software equivalent of a prison doctor who has been ordered to remove someone's appendix but then leaves the guy lying there on the operating table with his guts dangling. From the start, one sensed that Jackson was peeved, but his attitude quickly blossomed into open hostility when Microsoft responded to his injunction like a wiseass teenager who, when asked if he knows the time, simply answers, "Yes."

The transitional moment in these hearings—the O.J.-struggling-to-slip-on-the-bloody-glove moment—came the Friday before Christmas 1997, when Jackson, a layman, said that he had deleted Internet Explorer from his copy of Windows, accomplishing in minutes what Microsoft said could not be done. Anyone with a modicum of technical expertise knew that the judge had only removed the IE icon, not the actual program, but that was the point. If its browser was inextricably mingled with the rest of Windows, as Microsoft claimed, the rational solution would have been to allow computer manufacturers the option of removing the icon and replacing it with Netscape's Navigator button. In addition, *Computer Reseller News* did a test and found that disabling IE was as simple as removing a single "exe" (executable) file that had no impact on the rest of Windows.

Following Jackson's demo, *The New York Times*'s Steve Lohr wrote of Microsoft's "uncompromising stance" and its "stubborn position," and quoted the editor of a Microsoft-friendly monthly called *Windows,* who dubbed the whole thing "a public-relations disaster"—and that was just in the first four paragraphs. That was the spin everywhere, whether in the general press or the pages of the trades: "Microsoft is making a mockery of the court. . . . They came across as a petulant, arrogant child. . . . Microsoft must take off the brass knuckles." Rich Gray, a member in good standing of the Fraternal Order of Antitrust Lawyers, summed it up well when he said, "It's one thing to play hardball with

---

* The appellate court set aside Jackson's injunction, ruling that he had overstepped his bounds and denied Microsoft due process.

competitors . . . but it's quite different to play hardball with a court injunction." The pundits questioned how smart the people up in Redmond really were, considering that, despite all the years of intense government scrutiny, people still openly spoke of "cutting off Netscape's air" and "leveraging" their Windows advantage. And of course much of the criticism centered on Gates. "He still has that 'I'm-smarter-than-you, we-don't-need-no-stinking-standards' attitude," one industry exec told the *Computer Reseller*. "He's absolutely stubborn to a fault."

Microsoft claimed that it was fighting hard as a matter of principle. "Sometimes you have to take positions in legal cases for a larger purpose, even if it does give you public relations problems," said William Neukom, the company's chief counsel. Yet the upshot was that journalists who had never paid much attention to Microsoft before were now taking notice, and what they saw and heard was hardly flattering. Typical was the *Times*' influential political columnist Maureen Dowd, who wrote that the Justice Department had "properly pegged Microsoft as an egomaniacal, dangerous giant that has cut off the air supply of competitors . . . more brilliant at marketing and purloining and crushing than it has been at innovating." Even a Microsoft employee named Jacob Weisberg, a political writer who had gone to work for *Slate*, lamented in an article written in the form of a memo to upper management, "A few months ago, everyone I met seemed to think that working for Microsoft was pretty cool. Now strangers treat us like we work for Philip Morris."

Ballmer admitted that the press pummeling was hurting morale. Business customers were calling to complain, and the company's many partners griped that they felt caught in the middle. The on-line world deluged Microsoft's Web site with uncomplimentary e-mail messages, some that began, "I've never been one to bash Microsoft but . . ." A Merrill Lynch survey of chief information officers showed that just under 60 percent believed that Microsoft was abusing its power.

It was inevitable, then, that the company would soften its stance. Sometimes one fights because of a principle, but sometimes one pragmatically relents. At the end of January, Microsoft capitulated, agreeing to offer computer manufacturers a version of Windows that eliminated the browser icon. Then its PR arm went about the tough job of repairing the damage done to the company's image. That meant projecting a warmer version of the company, which meant a new release of the marketing department's single most important product, Bill Gates.

. . .

"ONE MADDENING Microsoft maneuver well-known to average PC users," *The Wall Street Journal*'s Walt Mossberg once wrote, is the "Version 1.0 Problem." The Version 1.0 Problem is Microsoft's tendency to release a new product long before it is ready to be shipped. "Too often, this version 1.0 has serious design flaws, missing features, and outright defects," Mossberg wrote. But what Microsoft does so well is to improve its product based on the feedback it aggressively solicits. "The fix begins with version 2.0," according to Mossberg, "and usually culminates in a version 3.0 that works pretty well, or even very well."

Bill Gates 1.0 spoke openly of monopolies. It's inevitable if one is to create standards, he said at an industry event held at the Playboy Resort in Lake Geneva, Wisconsin, in 1981. There he predicted that one company would gain an overly strong position—"through momentum, user loyalty, reputation, sales force, and price." When that happens, well—here's what Gates said as a twenty-five-year-old CEO that day in Lake Geneva: "I really shouldn't say this, but in some ways it leads, in an individual product category, to a natural monopoly."

Gates 1.0 spoke casually about "owning markets" and of "domination." That version also dreamed openly of running *all* the world's software. The motto a young Bill Gates coined for his fledgling company was "A computer on every desk and in every home—all running Microsoft software." That's still a Microsoft motto today, except it has been shorn of the overgrasping ambition of its second half.

Version 1.0 harangued important customers, like the time he ran into Sheldon Laube, the chief technologist of PriceWaterhouse, a consulting outfit that evaluated software on behalf of some of the country's largest corporations. "I'm sitting there at some conference, and it's not, 'Hello, Sheldon, how are you, can we talk?,' it's Bill immediately all over me about never buying Windows applications and how I must not understand this or that. . . . It was really quite humorous," Laube said. Stewart Alsop, when he was editor of *InfoWorld,* was driving on a freeway in Dallas when his cell phone rang. It was Gates, irate that *InfoWorld* had just given the latest version of DOS a poor write-up. He accused Alsop of incompetence and of intentionally sabotaging the test because of an anti-Microsoft bias. "It's like Bill back then could operate at one and only one speed," said longtime Microsoft board member David Marquardt. "That was the hard sell. He wasn't much at working a big customer over drinks or out on the golf course."

Version 1.0 may have been lacking certain core features, such as personality and grace, but there was a certain charm in its unfinished, unpolished nature. Maybe it's because no one had yet added a user-friendly interface—it wasn't "Click on this icon and hear the tape." Over the years his handlers have deleted the message lines that indicate any political leanings, but before those fixes Gates had revealed himself to be something of a liberal.* He derided the "out-of-control" Japan bashing in vogue earlier in this decade as "almost racist" and in 1993 contributed $80,000 to fight a ballot initiative aimed at rolling back state taxes. He admitted to one set of biographers, "I'd probably be a Democrat." Once a political novice running for state representative in Gates's district sent him an e-mail. The candidate laid out his positions, contrasting them with his opponent's: more funding for schools, stricter gun control, and pro-choice. Gates wrote back that he liked the positions laid out in the message and would be happy to support him. Within days, the endorsement was page-one news in the local papers. Microsoft PR was apoplectic: their boss had endorsed a relative nobody over a well-financed incumbent.

This version sat in airport snack bars munching hot dogs. He'd be spotted walking casually through airports, splayfooted, lapping at an ice-cream cone, not a care in the world. Later, it would be a swell woman with a swell personality who would gosh darn make a swell wife and mother, but in 1991, when he was featured on ABC's *20/20*, he'd say, "I like to go out with smart women so they're smart enough to know they're not going to get my money."

This version would only smile like a Cheshire cat when a *Playboy* interviewer asked him about drug use ("Ah, a look of recognition?" the interviewer asked—and Gates kept smiling) and react playfully when asked about all his billions. "I have it buried in the lawn," Gates said. "It's bulging a little." How do you use the money to have fun? "I swallow quarters, burn dollar bills, that kind of thing."

Yet the higher the stress on a Version 1.0 release, the more noticeable the bugs are; the greater demand placed on its limited capacities, the

---

* One notable exception is his, or perhaps Melinda Gates's, philanthropic choices. The lion's share of the money they've contributed has gone to universities and to their Internet-in-the-libraries program, but their list of charitable recipients include: a Bellevue, Washington, social service center ($1.2 million), a New York–based birth control organization ($1.8 million), and the Friends of Mandela Children's Fund ($1.1 million). He also contributed $35,000 to support a 1997 state ballot initiative in favor of gun control.

more likely there is to be a major crash. *The New Yorker*'s John Seabrook wrote a generally flattering profile of Gates in early 1994, but he also wondered about this man fluent in the language of software functionality who at best spoke a pidgin language when talking about the world of the personal. "Did we really want someone who sometimes sounded like a 10-year-old boy to be the principal architect of the way people will communicate with each other in the future?" Seabrook asked.

The highest-profile crash occurred later that year, when Gates agreed to sit for a long interview with CBS's Connie Chung. One problem that any developer faces is the fact that no piece of software operates in isolation—it must run on a wide assortment of platforms, interacting with other products that have glitches of their own. Chung contacted Gates via e-mail (Seabrook had printed Gates's e-mail address, so that was easy enough), leading him to believe that she might know something about technology. As Microsoft PR maven Pam Edstrom told it, Chung pitched the story as a history of the company, with Interactive TV and the company's new line of consumer products as her hook. "You know how much she knows about computers?" Edstrom asked. "Nothing. Nada. Zero. Less than zero. I mean, she couldn't even pronounce DOS right. She says 'doze.' I mean, come on."

Chung instead asked Gates about falling in love with Melinda. She asked him, "Do you think you're successful?" In other words, she posed precisely the same kinds of vacuous questions that Barbara Walters would ask Gates in 1998, in an equally content-free interview. But whereas the later version of Gates would answer with a smile when Walters brought up the government's antitrust investigation, version 1 reacted to Chung's quoting of an adversary who compared competing with Gates to a knife fight by storming out of the interview. With the tape rolling—and as the millions of viewers who watched that week's *Eye to Eye with Connie Chung* would later see—he abruptly declared the interview over and stormed out of his own office. There had been some minor revisions over the years, but it was time for a major reworking back in the lab.

THE THING ABOUT 2.0 releases is that they invariably disappoint. Obvious bugs have been worked out—in this case, for instance, the product didn't simply stop working if asked a prickly question—but the fixes never quite justify all the hoopla that accompanies a new release.

Microsoft hired a seasoned PR flak from Hollywood to head up corporate communications, but there were still plenty of malfunctions. He arranged it so the boss was invited to speak before a group of media executives at the Radio and Television Society. Yet when Gates was asked to name his favorite program, he told the assembled audience of 1,200 that he doesn't like TV—and, moreover, after watching a couple of episodes of *Late Show with David Letterman* in preparation for an appearance, the experience only confirmed his view that television is "stupid." To stoke the Windows 95 publicity engine, a *USA Today* reporter was invited to tag along at a dress rehearsal—and the headline over the resulting piece read, "Glitches at the Rehearsal Turn CEO's Mood."

Techies call it the "kernel"—the central attributes of any piece of software. The kernel controls access to memory and other key functions. Think of it as a software's core personality: the kernel can be modified, but programmers are loath to do so because even simple changes cause unintended problems. When Microsoft launched its annual pajama party in 1996, one aim was to humanize Gates among the country's most influential business reporters. Yet they ran up against the restraints of the kernel's capabilities. "He's a charisma black hole, said one. Said another, "The guy doesn't have a gracious bone in his body."

In 1995—early in the life of version 2.0—*Time* put Gates on the cover and dubbed him "Master of the Universe." The inside story, however, was hardly flattering: "Mine, All Mine" read the inside headline. The accompanying picture showed a smiling Gates with his hands clasped together. The picture caught Gates in midclap, but it looked as if he were rubbing his hands together like Simon Legree over a stack of gold coins, especially given the headline. But people at Microsoft PR don't believe in revenge so much as in justice. As Mossberg wrote, Microsoft improves based on the feedback it aggressively solicits. So in Microsoft PR they asked themselves, How can we better facilitate *Time*'s next experience with Bill so that it understands more fully?

Eighteen months later, Gates again appeared on the cover of *Time*. This time it was a much softer shot—not smug as in 1995 but friendly, almost nebbishy, like a WASPy Woody Allen. "The Private World of Bill Gates" read the cover line of this story written by the magazine's managing editor, Walter Isaacson. The spread included a full-page black and white of a young, crew-cutted Bill next to his mother. There was a shot of Gates looking lovingly at Melinda and a photo of him with baby Jennifer on his lap. Gates's father, Bill Gates II, spun stories from "Trey's"

(Bill Gates III's) childhood ("I remember him fretting for over two weeks before asking a girl to the prom"), and readers learned several improbable facts about Gates. He's a man for whom a well-written feature article in *The Economist* is high literature, but we're supposed to believe that Philip Roth, Ernest Gaines, and John Irving are among his favorite writers.

Yet again there were problems with the kernel. Isaacson asked Gates about integrating the browser into Windows, and he answered, "Any operating system without a browser is going to be fucking out of business." Does he have any regrets? Sure, Gates answers—not getting a Microsoft e-mail program quickly enough to market. "Broad discussions bore him," Isaacson wrote. "He shows little curiosity about other people, and he becomes disengaged when people use small talk to try to establish a personal rapport." The two spent days together, including time in Palm Springs, dinners out, and a late-night drive to the lake so the two could tromp around Gates's unfinished home. But Isaacson noted that his companion never asked him where he lived or if he had a family. When Gates was in his office and grabbed himself a soda, he didn't think to offer one to his guest.

The trained eye could pick out differences between versions 1 and 2. For years Jesse Berst was the editorial director of a publication called *Windows Watcher* before taking a job as a columnist for the Ziff-Davis Publishing Company. He noticed that sometime in the early 1990s— maybe it was a late 1.0 release or a 2.0 beta—Gates picked up the habit of using the word "great" every time he spoke about Microsoft's product line. "Leadership" was another word you began hearing a lot in version 2.0. One rationale for this change was that Microsoft PR was seeking to repackage Gates. No longer would it sell him as Young Overachiever, he was now Computer Visionary. Another reason came from the legal department, which purged words such as "dominate" and "own" from Gates's vocabulary—Microsoft's goal was now a "leadership" position in a given sector.

Gates 2.0 also saw the stripping of extraneous features. *The Road Ahead* provided one good example. If the book were an e-mail message, he'd have stamped the smiley emoticom after every third sentence. The cover showed a relaxed Gates standing on a deserted highway, hands in pockets, wearing a crewneck sweater and loafers, unthreatening and benign, someone to be trusted. Though the book was released in 1995, Gates managed to write 286 pages without once mentioning government antitrust probes or addressing a single competitor's complaint. He's a fascinating figure because—as one sometime partner told me— "he's a masterful and extraordinary businessman with this absolutely remarkable ability to calibrate his every word and action with both eyes on the bottom line." But here he is, Mr. Rogers for adults. "Gates's presentation of himself in the book is consistent with the blandness of his formal speeches," James Fallows wrote of *The Road Ahead* in *The New York Review of Books*. "The intense intuitive man who ridicules sloppy thinking is missing from the book, replaced by someone determined to sound respectable in front of the grown-ups." Reading the book is like eating from a bag of refined sugar—much like the biweekly column that appears under his byline, carried by the New York Times Syndicate. He doesn't actually write these columns, of course—as *Brill's Content* revealed, he talks his points into a recorder, and someone in corporate relations turns them into columns. Topics have included "Ten Attributes of a Good Employee" and "A COMDEX Treasure Hunt."

Every software product protects itself from outside actions that might corrupt the program and cause it to crash. For Gates, celebrity and the accoutrements of limitless money could be "very corrupting," and thus he disavowed limousines, corporate jets, and squadrons of handlers even late into the cycle of Gates 2.0. Mitch Kertzman and Gates were both in Florida in the fall of 1997 to speak before a group of IT executives. This was the annual extravaganza put on by the Gartner Group, a big consulting house specializing in technology—so big a fete, in fact, that a makeup artist is on hand to prep speakers for an event that is memorialized on video. The previous year, IBM's CEO, Lou Gerstner, had given the big keynote. As one Gartner-ite told it to Kertzman, Gerstner had showed up surrounded by an entourage of IBM security people, linebacker-sized men in dark suits with microphones hidden in their sleeves. They had the Gartner people clear a hallway "for security reasons" before they allowed the chief to pass. Supposedly, Gerstner even brought his own makeup person.

Gates was the big keynote speaker the next year, yet Kertzman remembered Gates showing up with a single assistant. "It's just Gates walking that slightly pigeon-toed walk of his," Kertzman said. Afterward, he mentioned Gates's casual attitude toward security to a couple of Gartner-ites. "They tell me when Gates came by their Manhattan offices for a meeting, he again showed up with a single Microsoft staffer, this really slight guy who couldn't possibly be a security guy," Kertzman said. After the meeting, the two hailed a cab.

GATES 3.0 was launched at COMDEX 1997, in a speech he gave at the Aladdin Casino and Hotel. There, he poked fun at himself and his Microsoft technology; even his company's myriad of woes was part of his stand-up routine. He began with a "Top 10 Reasons I Love My PC" list. Reason five: "I can sit at my PC, collaborate with attorneys all over the world, comment on a forty-eight-page legal brief, and e-mail it to the Department of Justice." Reason one: "I can use Microsoft CarPoint to show Ralph Nader my Corvair collection." He joked that he was maybe the only person in America who got an NT error message when he tried turning on a light in his new house. He ran a self-mocking tape clip of himself repeating the same phrases over and over again—"supergreat," "very, very," "and so we see." He talked about how much he loved to sit with his daughter and play with his company's Barney software: "Now I constantly find myself humming Barney's song." He even sang a lullaby during his sit-down with Barbara Walters. He started appearing in ads for Callaway golf clubs, which portrayed him as just another weekend duffer.

There were superficial changes: improvements in his wardrobe, a CEO's haircut, new glasses. And there were more substantive changes, such as a friendlier interface with reporters. *The Wall Street Journal's* Jim Carlton came out with a book on Apple, prompting Gates to send him a friendly e-mail saying he had enjoyed the book but felt he was "treated unfairly on pages 27 and 326." Those are the pages on which he is described as the "Great Satan," "gangly," and a "cold-blooded killer."

There were glitches, as inevitably there are with new releases. This version now included an entourage of armed bodyguards and a limousine. Indeed, while in England, he showed up in Cambridge to gladhand with British Prime Minister Tony Blair but ended up a laughingstock for hiring the city's only limousine to drive the two hundred meters from his helicopter landing pad to the scene of the photo op. Ballmer arrived in Silicon Valley in early January 1998 to offer his mea culpas (he said his "To heck with Janet Reno" comment had been "a horrible utterance . . . I'll regret it for the rest of my days"). Presumably that's what Gates was programmed to do in a day's worth of speeches and campaign-style appearances in Silicon Valley later that month, but instead he turned belligerent, blaming the press and the political shenanigans of his foes for his company's woes and repeatedly arguing that he'd accept no restrictions on what he could add to Windows. And though his lawyers had already yielded on the point, he stuck by Microsoft's decision to respond to Judge Jackson with a non-working version of Windows. "We didn't know we were supposed to cripple our products," he said sarcastically. A pack of reporters the size of a presidential candidate's followed him around the Valley that day, including no fewer than eight camera crews. But as one beat reporter trailing Gates that day said, "Microsoft PR was working so hard to soften his image, but their mistake was to let him out of his cage."

SHORTLY THEREAFTER, Gates became the twenty-fifth victim of a man renowned in Europe as *"Le Gloupier."* The incident was at once a PR disaster and a PR triumph. The disaster was the film clip the world saw of an obviously agitated Gates, his hand shaking, wiping creamy goo from his glasses and face outside a government building in Brussels. This one picture was worth a thousand Web sites dedicated to hating Gates. The triumph was the line his handlers put into his mouth as news outlets from around the world phoned Redmond for a comment: "Bill said he wouldn't have minded so much if they'd used a better-tasting pie." As Charlie Chaplin said, tripping a hobo who's down on his luck is cruel, but doing the same to a man in a top hat is slapstick. At least this version of Gates had the good sense to say nothing, letting his handlers put their best spin on it.

The prank was the handiwork of pie-thrusting mastermind Noël Godin, a paunchy fifty-two-year-old part-time actor living in Brussels. This man, who has written an autobiography called *Cream and Punishment,* was aided, if not inspired, by a traitor working for Microsoft in Belgium. According to an interview Godin did with the *Netly News,* the Softie gave Godin and his group a precise schedule of Gates's activities in Brussels that day.

"This man told us he really loved Bill Gates in the past, saying that he was very cool and passionate," Godin said. "But little by little he considered that his power had tainted him and that he was becoming more and more haughty." Through some Parisian "accomplices" who had tracked Gates, Godin learned that Gates "was always escorted by five armed bodyguards." That made Godin and his fellow conspirators nervous—"we didn't sleep very well the night before"—but he plied his troops with beer and encouraged them to smile, so as not to appear threatening. He broke his pie-throwing soldiers into three "fighting units" of ten, who converged on Gates as he was climbing a set of stairs. Godin claimed that four of their twenty-five pies hit their target.

"The bodyguards were completely distraught," Godin said. "None of them even took out his gun. They were as dazed as Bill was." He said of Gates's reaction, "He had a kind of promotional smile that became a kind of smile made of sand."*

"He really was the idyllic victim, more than I thought," he said. "Bill Clinton, [Britain's] Tony Blair, [France's] Jacques Chirac: they are puppets; only Gates is pulling the strings." Godin doesn't own a PC, and he wouldn't know from a Web browser, but except for the pope, he couldn't imagine a better target than Gates. "In a way he is the master of the world," Godin said.

SOMETIMES A SOFTWARE COMPANY has to publish an intermediate update—a .1 release meant to fix a particularly gnarly bug. In March 1998, Gates traveled to Washington, D.C., to testify before Hatch's committee. Also there were Scott McNealy and Netscape's James Barksdale. Gates smiled broadly when McNealy extended his hand, and the two chatted amiably while awaiting the bang of the gavel. McNealy called Gates "the most dangerous and powerful industrialist of our age"—and Gates, immediately to McNealy's right, sat with a bland, noncommittal look on his face. The hearing lasted four and a half hours, during which time several senators peppered Gates with sometimes hostile questions, but he answered them calmly. After it was over, Hatch said, "I would have liked stronger and more forthright answers," but the point wasn't to change Hatch's mind. This was the launch party for Gates 3.1.

The group of schoolgirls who passed Gates in the corridor and jumped up and down and squealed in delight was spontaneous, as was Senator Patrick Leahy of Vermont standing by to snap a picture, but little else was. A couple of weeks before the hearing Gates made a speech

---

* Shortly after the incident, *ComputerWorld* ran a cartoon showing Larry Ellison, his face splattered with pie remains, claiming at a press conference that he, too, had been hit by a pie, though one bigger than the one that had struck Gates.

on the importance of software for people with disabilities. That week-end, Microsoft announced that it would no longer forbid its Internet partners to promote a rival browser, as long as they gave at least equal billing to its own.

That evening, after the hearing, Gates flew to New York. The next day, he visited a Harlem elementary school, where he answered questions put to him by a classroom of sixth-graders. He then appeared at the New York Public Library to talk about the money his philanthropic founda-tion had given the institution to help with better access to the Internet. "Kind of fun" is how he described the experience of testifying before Congress in a sit-down with Charlie Rose. *Slate* published a daily diary of the week that *Time* later ran in its entirety. He and Melinda shared a pizza the night before the hearing; that morning he ate a donut in Sena-tor Patty Murray's office. Of Scott McNealy he wrote, "Even though he doesn't like PCs and wants to put them out of business, he's a very charming guy."

THAT GATES WOULD WRITE something that inane is one thing. That *Time* would publish it is something else entirely. But that is Gates's celebrity. That week any number of media outlets were phoning Mi-crosoft headquarters for any spare tidbit about the World's Richest Man. A reporter from *USA Today* asked what brand of eyeglasses Gates wears. A business weekly called to ask if Gates had done any sight-seeing while in D.C.

No detail is too minute if it is about Gates—or his wife, Melinda. From reading the innumerable articles and books that have been writ-ten about the man, I know that the future Mrs. Gates and her brides-maids wore gowns custom-designed by Victoria's Bridal of Seattle and that her favorite subject while attending the St. Monica grade school was mathematics. At the Ursuline Academy, an upper-crust private school in the Dallas area, the former Melinda French belonged to the school drill team; at Duke, she was a Theta girl who gave guided tours to prospective students. I also know Gates's golf handicap (23.9) and that once he spent a day and a night in Moscow and ate all his meals at the McDonald's near his hotel.

The pundits compare Gates to Carnegie, to Rockefeller, to Ford, to the robber barons, but of course this pantheon of the country's most craven capitalists lived before our supersaturated, overload-the-brain media age. Gates is Jackie O., Gates is The Donald, Gates is Michael Jackson—the first figure to sell out an appearance before the National Press Club since Sharon Stone. A cabdriver quoted in one book says he's driven Gates on two separate occasions. One time Gates slept, but the other time he struck the cabbie as a very nice man. He doesn't indicate, however, what kind of tip Gates gave on either occasion. In 1997, *Worth* magazine tracked down 100 people from the Harvard Class of 1977 to ask them a range of questions: "If you found Gates's wallet, what would you do? . . . If you met him in an elevator, what would you say? . . . What graffiti would you write on the building he and classmate Steve Ballmer have given Harvard $20 million to build?"

"We live in a culture that routinely eroticizes and glamorizes consumer technology," Salman Rushdie wrote in *The New Yorker*. What, then, of a man who might be the richest human *ever* to walk the planet, who made his fortune entirely on a glamorized piece of consumer technology like the PC—in a culture so perverse a letter Eleanor Roosevelt wrote to *Women's Wear News* is auctioned off for $230 but one from Madonna to Dennis Rodman fetches $5,175? *Fortune* covers Gates like a fanzine. In one issue, there's a cover story about "America's Billionaire Buddies" Gates and Buffett, in another a story about billionaires Gates and Allen, "the ultimate buddy act in business history." In that piece, the writer (who described Gates as "the skinny one") can't help but pinch himself through the first two paragraphs because he's actually sitting on a deck overlooking Lake Washington, sipping Cokes with two people so wealthy: "Hard to believe," Brent Schlender wrote, "they're so nonchalant . . . [these] undisputed masters of the digital universe." On April 19, 1998, one share of Microsoft stock hit $93.32. A front-page headline above the fold in *The Seattle Times* blared, "Gates Worth $50 Billion." That headline would appear in newspapers around the country as Gates, at forty-two years old, became the world's first fifty-billionaire. In October 1998, when his net worth briefly crossed $60 billion, *Vanity Fair* figured he could pay for a four-year college education for every eighteen-year-old in the country or pay Habitat for Humanity to build a three-bedroom house for every homeless person living in the United States. Shortly into the new year, Gates crossed the $70 billion mark, generating yet more news articles.

But, in the end, we study the bug from so many different angles that it's we who become the interesting specimen. Gates's father travels to Taiwan, and his picture lands in a Taiwanese business paper. Why?

"People want to know what Bill Gates will look like when he gets old," You Mei-yueh, director of Taiwan's *Economic Daily News*, told *The Wall Street Journal* (portly and bald). *Slate* at least cleared up one fact when it reported, at the end of 1997, that a *Time* Web search had revealed 410,000 references to God but only 25,000 to Gates.

APPENDIX:
A COMPENDIUM OF BILL GATES
AND MICROSOFT JOKES

A press release posted by the Bogus News Network:

Redmond (BNN)—World leaders reacted with stunned silence as the Microsoft Corp. conducted an underground nuclear test at a secret facility in eastern Washington state. The device exploded at 9:22 A.M. PDT and was aimed to coincide with talks between Microsoft and the U.S. Department of Justice.

"Microsoft is going to defend its right to market its products by any and all necessary means," said Microsoft CEO Bill Gates. "Not that I'm anti-government, but there would be few tears shed in the computer industry if Washington were engulfed in a bath of nuclear fire."

In Washington, President Clinton announced that the U.S. government would boycott all Microsoft products indefinitely. Minutes later, the president reversed his decision. "We've tried sanctions since lunchtime and they don't work," said the president.

Rumors suggest a second weapons development project is underway in California, headed by Microsoft rival Sun Microsystems. "They're doing all of the development work in Java," said one source close to the project. The development of a delivery system is said to be holding up progress. "Write-once, bomb anywhere is still a dream at the moment."

A post to an anti-Microsoft mailing list called anti-ms@enemy.org, from a woman calling herself Ladydeath:

"I am facing a very serious problem. You see, I am a Vietnam-era deserter from the U.S. Marines. My mother peddles Nazi literature to Girl Scouts and my father, a former dentist, is in jail for thirty years for raping most of his patients while they were under anesthesia . . .

"My problem is this: I have just gotten engaged to the most beautiful, sweetest girl in the world . . . But I am worried my family will not make a good impression on hers. In your opinion, should I or shouldn't I tell her about my cousin who works for Microsoft?"

Al Gore, Bill Clinton, and Bill Gates find themselves in Heaven standing before God, who is sitting in a beautiful white throne. And God asks Gore, "What do you believe in?"

"I believe that CFCs are killing the Earth, and that until this is corrected, the ozone layer depletion and greenhouse effect imperils all of humanity."

And God says, "Okay, you can sit at my feet."

God then asks Clinton, "What do you believe in?"

"I believe that all people are equal and everyone should be able to live their lives as they see fit. I believe in empowerment to the people and freedom for all."

And God says, "Okay, you can also sit at my feet."

God then asks Bill Gates, "And what do *you* believe in?"

Bill Gates replies, "I believe you're sitting in my chair."

Someone imagines the Microsoft God package. It includes a feature called Microsoft Missionary, which can be used to convert God "from competing products like Buddha or Allah." Said the director of Microsoft's newly formed Religions division, "Microsoft God will make Our Lord more accessible, and will add an easy, intuitive user interface to Him, making Him not only easier to find, but easier to communicate with."

A post to another electronic mailing list (am-info@essential.org), home to more than its share of Microsoft critics:

"If Bill Gates had a dime for every time a Windows box crashed . . . Oh, wait a minute, he already does."

Contraceptive98

Microsoft Corporation has taken another step toward dominating every aspect of American life with the introduction of Contraceptive98, a suite of applications designed for users who engage in sex.

Microsoft has been a pioneer in peer-to-peer connectivity and plug and play. It believes these technologies will give it substantial lever in penetrating the copulation enhancement market.

The product addresses two important user concerns: the need for virus protection and the need for a firewall to ensure the non-propagation of human beings . . .

While Contraceptive98 does not address non-traditional copulatory channels, future plug-ins are planned for next year. They will be known as BackDoor, AuraLee, TitElation, and JerkOff.

Bill Gates dies and finds himself being sized up by God.

"Well, Bill, I'm really confused on this call," God says. "I'm not sure whether to send you to Heaven or Hell. After all, you've enormously helped society by putting a computer in almost every home, yet you also created that ghastly Windows 95. I'm going to let you decide where you want to go."

"Well, what's the difference between the two?"

"I'm willing to let you visit both places."

"Fine. Let's try Hell first," Bill said.

So Bill went to Hell. It was a beautiful, clean, sandy beach with clear waters and lots of beautiful women running around, playing in the water, laughing, and frolicking about. The sun was shining, the temperature perfect. Bill was very pleased. "This is great. If this is Hell, I really want to see Heaven."

"Fine," said God, and off they went. Heaven was a place high in the clouds, with angels drifting about, playing harps and singing. It was nice, but not as enticing as Hell. "I think I'd prefer Hell," he told God.

"Fine," replied God, "as you desire."

So Bill Gates went to Hell.

Two weeks later, God decided to check on the late billionaire to see how he was doing in Hell. When he got there, he found Bill shackled to a wall screaming amongst hot flames in dark caves, being burned and tortured by demons, with no one to help him out of his dilemma no matter how loud he screamed.

"How's everything going?" He asked Bill. Bill responded, his voice filled with anguish. "This is awful. This is nothing like the Hell I visited two weeks ago. I can't believe this is happening. What happened to that other place, with the beaches and the beautiful women playing in the water?"

"Oh," God said, "that was Hell 3.1. This is Hell 95."

Q: How many Microsoft engineers does it take to change a lightbulb?

A: None. Bill Gates will just redefine Darkness™ as the new industry standard.

ACKNOWLEDGMENTS

First, my thanks to all those who generously took the time to talk with me despite the invariable crush of other obligations weighing upon them. My thanks, too, to those journalists who came before me, for their hard work and sweat. This book was based on interviews with more than two hundred people, but also on the discoveries and insights of previously published works.

I've tried to give credit where credit is due in the body of this work, but I want to call special attention to a number of works because they proved especially helpful, if not inspiring. First and foremost there is G. Pascal Zachary's *Upside* article about Gary Kildall, "Fatal Flaw," published shortly after Kildall's death in 1994. That piece stands not only as a fine piece of journalism but also as the article that planted the seed that eventually gave rise to this book.

The disadvantage of reporting on so overexposed a figure as Gates is also an advantage: there are no lack of secondary sources to mine for the nuggets and telling details that help bring the narrative alive. There have been several good biographies written about Gates, most notably the meticulously researched *Gates: How Microsoft's Mogul Reinvented an Industry—and Made Himself the Richest Man in America* by Stephen Manes and Paul Andrews, and the livelier and juicier account of Gates's life, *Hard Drive: Bill Gates and the Making of the Microsoft Empire* by James Wallace and Jim Erickson. Both were published earlier this decade; both proved particularly useful, especially in writing this book's earliest chapters. Wallace followed up *Hard Drive* with the equally entertaining *Overdrive: Bill Gates and the Race to Control Cyberspace*, which offered a good snapshot of Gates and Microsoft through the first half of this decade (and also a wonderful re-creation of the Windows 95 launch). Also notable is Randall Stross's *The Microsoft Way,* which for my money stands as the most well-reasoned, dispassionate assessment of Microsoft to be found anywhere on the open market.

There were no lack of magazine articles to mine. *Time* alone revealed at the start of 1997 that it had mentioned Gates's name in no less than 114 issues of the magazine up until that point. Of special note: John Seabrook's "E-Mail from Bill" in *The New Yorker;* Fred Moody's "Mr. Software" and James Gleick's "Making Microsoft Safe for Capitalism," both of which appeared in *The New York Times Magazine;* in *Business Week,* Kathy Rebello's inside account of Microsoft's awakening to the Internet; and G. Pascal Zachary's coverage of Gates for *The Wall Street Journal.* Also, while I may chide *Fortune* magazine in these pages for covering Gates as if he was a rock star, such attention gave rise to plenty of interesting facts and quotes I was able to use in this book. Many of those articles had been written by *Fortune* staffer Brent Schlender, who writes like an angel even if—as another big-name technology reporter put it—"he's never met a billionaire he doesn't like."

Not nearly as much has been written about Scott McNealy and Larry Ellison, at least in the national press or the big business magazines— much to the chagrin of both men. Particularly useful in the writing of the Ellison/Oracle chapters were Mike Wilson's well-researched *The Difference Between God and Larry Ellison* (*God Doesn't Think He's Larry Ellison*); Bryan Burrough's "The Man Who Would Be Gates," in *Vanity Fair*; and Richard Brandt's coverage of Ellison while at *Business Week* and later at *Upside.*

Helpful in the construction of the Scott McNealy/Sun chapters were: the Sun chapter in Randall Stross's book, *Steve Jobs and the NeXT Big Thing,* Tom Abate's terrific profile of James Gosling in the *San Francisco Examiner Magazine* ("Code Warrior"); Schlender's profile of McNealy in *Fortune* ("Javaman: The Adventures of Scott McNealy"); and Kevin Maney's front-page profile of McNealy in *USA Today* ("CEO McNealy Sets Sights on Microsoft").

I'd also like to thank the *San Francisco Chronicle* for its terrific series, "The Digital Divide"; George Gilder for the many well-researched pieces he wrote for *Forbes ASAP*; Robert Samuelson for his piece, "Bill Gates Isn't God (or Even Henry Ford)," appearing in *The Washington Post;* Steve Hamm and Robert Hof for their *Business Week* article "Operation Sunblock: Microsoft Goes to War"; Julie Pitta, for her "Bill Gates and the Billophobes" article in *Forbes;* Mike Romano for his Windows NT piece for *Upside*; and Jack Fischer, for his piece on Ralph Nader in the *San Jose Mercury News*. The Netscape portions of the book were rounded out by *Speeding the Net: The Inside Story of Netscape and How It Challenged Microsoft*, by Joshua Quittner and Michelle Slatalla; Kara Swisher's *aol.com: How Steve Case Beat Bill Gates, Nailed the Netheads, and Made Millions in the War for the Web* also proved helpful, as did *Computer Wars: The Fall of IBM and the Future of Global Technology*, by Charles Ferguson and Charles Morris. My thanks, too, to Pam Edstrom and her PR minions, for opening doors for me while on Microsoft's campus (though never unescorted!); Pete Peterson, for sending me a copy of his book, *AlmostPerfect*, an account of his years at Word-Perfect; to Stewart Alsop and the people at IDG for providing the Agenda conference proceedings; and to Gregg Zachary, for allowing me to root around in his old notes.

A special note about *The Wall Street Journal*, which I faithfully read during the 1,000 (or so) days the computer world was the center of my work universe. I was constantly impressed by (and also aided by) the quality of its coverage of the software world. The same bylines kept coming up over and again, both when I read that day's paper and when I searched back through the archives for past pieces: David Bank, Don Clark, Lee Gomes, and G. Pascal Zachary. Also, a piece by *Journal* reporter Jim Carlton served as my source for the footnote about Gil Amelio's astonishingly generous golden parachute. Among my other regular companions, retrieved when looking for a daily dose of technology news via the Internet: the *San Jose Mercury News*'s "Good Morning Silicon Valley," ZDNet, Upside.com, and CNET.

Thanks also to Jessie Deeter, Gina Kim, and Lisa Nishimoto for their research assistance. For reading all or parts of the manuscript: my thanks to Randy Stross, Don Clark, Lee Gomes, Mike Loftin, John Raeside, Mike Buchman, and my all-time favorite computer programmer, who here shall remain anonymous. My gratitude, too, to Sue Matteucci for her well-timed, passionate rant about sacrifices to the Gods of Wall Street; to the gang at the Linden Street Studio; and to Tiffany Martin and Lisa Borromeo for all their wonderful support. As always, thanks to the world's greatest proofreader (and also my mother), Naomi Rivlin. It's amazing what she's caught in previous books even after it has been worked over by a team of copy editors and proofers.

I've been blessed since the start of my book-writing career with a supportive and effective agent, Elizabeth Kaplan. I can't begin to thank

Jon Karp, my editor at Random House, tireless and talented, a partner in this project who offered encouragement and valuable advice every step of the way. At times I cursed his name, but that's only because from the start he saw this book more clearly than did I. Thanks, too, to Lynn Anderson, for her care while reading this manuscript, and for several times saving my bacon. And Heidi North for her stylish and smart jacket design. Peter Bernstein and Carie Freimuth of Times Books have been especially attentive to this book, for which I am grateful.

I'd also like to give heartfelt thanks to the Suches and the Romascos for their hospitality while I was up in Redmond, and extra special thanks to Betsy and Michael for the refuge of Humbug, generously offered during the bad maximum incoming days as my deadline for this project loomed.

And, finally, my gratitude to Denny Martin, no fan of the technology world, or business books for that matter, who endured a lot during the writing of this book, especially near the end, when my seven-day-a-week work schedule prompted her to recast that popular Redmond-area term, the "Microsoft widow."

INDEX

Index

Index